Anne Marie Doherty

Human resource management

This important volume of studies provides a definitive view of where human resource management has come from and where it is going. A sequel to the immensely successful *New Perspectives on Human Resource Management*, this new student reader crystallizes the key arguments that have emerged since the human resource management debate took off in the 1980s.

Written in an accessible style, the volume has been designed to provide comprehensive coverage for students of all the key topics taught in current professional and undergraduate HRM courses.

All of the chapters have been authorized by leading experts in the field. The material is arranged in four parts. The first of these contains chapters which make authoritative and up-to-date assessments of HRM; the second attends to strategic issues; the third covers the key practice areas of HRM, from planning and selection to reward and participation; the fourth contains important chapters on international themes.

This book is written primarily to meet the needs of advanced students of management who require in-depth, authoritative, critical and original material. Each chapter blends a review of the current state of knowledge in that area with a summary of the latest research findings.

John Storey is Professor at the University of Loughborough and Director of the Human Resource and Change Management Research Unit. His previous books include *Developments in the Management of Human Resources*; *New Wave Manufacturing Strategies*; *Managing Human Resources and Industrial Relations* (with Keith Sisson) and *New Perspectives on Human Resource Management*. He is Editor of the *Human Resource Management Journal*.

Human resource management

A critical text

Edited by John Storey

London and New York

First published 1995
by Routledge
11 New Fetter Lane, London EC4P 4EE

Simultaneously published in the USA and Canada
by Routledge
29 West 35th Street, New York, NY 10001

Reprinted 1995

Typeset in Times by
Pat and Anne Murphy, Highcliffe-on-Sea, Dorset
Printed and bound in Great Britain by
TJ Press (Padstow) Ltd, Padstow, Cornwall

British Library Cataloguing in Publication Data
A catalogue record for this book is available from the British Library

Library of Congress Cataloguing in Publication Data
A catalogue record for this book is available from the Library of Congress

ISBN 0-415-09149-7 (hbk)
ISBN 0-415-09150-0 (pbk)

Contents

Illustrations

FIGURES

TABLES

Contributors

Peter Armstrong, Lecturer, University of Sheffield.

David Ashton, Professor and Co-Director of the Centre for Labour Market Studies, University of Leicester.

Chris Brewster, Professor of European Human Resource Management, Cranfield University School of Management.

Lee Dyer, Professor, Center for Advanced Studies, Cornell University.

Alan Felstead, Research Fellow, Centre for Labour Market Studies, University of Leicester.

David E. Guest, Professor of Occupational Psychology, Birkbeck College, London University.

Paul Iles, Professor, Liverpool John Moores University.

Ian Kessler, Research Fellow, Templeton College, Oxford University.

Thomas Kochan, Professor, Sloan School of Management, Massachusetts Institute of Technology.

Karen Legge, Professor of Organizational Behaviour, University of Lancaster.

Mick Marchington, Senior Lecturer, School of Management, University of Manchester Institute of Science and Technology.

John Purcell, Fellow, Templeton College, Oxford University.

Sheila Rothwell, Director, Centre for Employment Policy Studies, Henley Management College.

Graeme Salaman, Reader, Faculty of Social Sciences, The Open University.

Hugh Scullion, Senior Lecturer in Human Resource Management, University of Newcastle.

Keith Sisson, Professor of Industrial Relations and Director of the Industrial Relations Research Unit, University of Warwick.

John Storey, Professor of Strategic Human Resource Management and Director of the Human Resource Change Management Research Unit, Loughborough University Business School.

Preface

This book is a sequel to the highly successful *New Perspectives on Human Resource Management*, which was published by Routledge in 1989. That book helped to spark extensive debate about new employment practices, not only in the United Kingdom, but in many other countries. Many of the seminal contributions to that volume remain as valid today as they were when first published. Consequently, *New Perspectives* remains in print; this new volume is *not* a second edition but an entirely new book.

Human Resource Management: A Critical Text covers all the key subject areas of HRM and is designed to serve as a main course text. It takes in everything from the debate about the meaning of human resource management as a distinctive approach; the link with corporate strategy; implications for the personnel function; human resource planning; recruitment and selection; training and development; involvement and participation; and implications for trade unions and industrial relations. In addition, there are three chapters on various aspects of international HRM. Unique to this collection there is, additionally, a chapter dealing with accountancy as a set of logics which pervades managerial thinking and practice and which therefore sets the parameters for much of the decision-making on people management.

This collection is distinctive for its coherence across a wide range of topics and because, given the standing of all of the contributors, it is by far the most authoritative source available. Each chapter was specially commissioned from the leading authority in that field. The collective result is a mature analysis which blends the latest literature with up-to-date findings from research. Perhaps because of the strong research base which each contributor brings to this book, there is a highly realistic quality to the analysis. This is not a textbook which peddles abstract models and techniques which find no reflection in the real world. Indeed, the general stance is critical of the rhetoric of so many of the utterances on HRM which simply fly in the face of everyday employment practice.

Why is this book sub-titled 'a critical text'? For three reasons. First, because all the chapters in this book eschew the evangelical, simplistic, proselytizing of the 'excellence through people' school. The phenomenon of HRM is scrutinized very closely and its (various) meanings, implications, origins and stakeholders are subjected to close and detailed analysis. Second, the text is 'critical' in the positive sense. The contributors are experts in their respective fields and their chapters are vital and noteworthy. Third, there is also an element of stricture and critique. This centres on the gap between the rhetoric of humanistic values and the practices which disavow and even mock those values.

The main audiences for this book are likely to be advanced students on master's level courses and senior undergraduates. The critical evaluations entered into assume that the reader has some prior familiarity with the basics of the subject.

John Storey

Part I

Introduction

Chapter 1

Human resource management: still marching on, or marching out?

John Storey

When a group of academics came together in the late 1980s to produce the first British book on human resource management – *New Perspectives on Human Resource Management* (Storey 1989), the standing of and prospects for this concept or approach were very uncertain. Arguably, they still are.

But a great deal has happened since 1989. At that time the majority of academics and other observers of the employment scene were very chary indeed about using the term 'human resource management'. The fragile plant was beginning to poke its head through the soil and there seemed every likelihood that it would wither, along with many other fads. There was great scepticism about its intellectual credentials and also about the degree to which change in any fundamental sense could be said to be occurring in British industrial relations and personnel management.

Since that time there have been many signs that HRM has taken a rather more secure hold. There has been a mushrooming of books on the subject (Blyton and Turnbull 1992; Beardwell and Holden 1994; Bratton and Gold 1994; Towers 1992; Legge forthcoming; Goss 1994; Beaumont 1993; Harrison 1993; Clark 1993) – and that is just to cite books published in, and about, Britain. The contribution which these books have made to the stock of knowledge on HRM we will consider below.

In addition, and perhaps even more noteworthy, the intervening period has seen the successful launch of two significant journals – the *Human Resource Management Journal*, edited by Keith Sisson at Warwick University, and the *International Journal of Human Resource Management*, edited by Michael Poole at Cardiff. Both journals have continued to grow in strength since their launch in 1990. Since the turn of the decade the number of new courses and modules in HRM in universities and colleges have simply become too numerous to count. At the same time, university chairs in human resource management have now become a normal part of the scene.

What has also happened since 1989 has been a fillip to the idea of HRM offered by significant (although sometimes distantly related) theoretical developments from the areas of industrial economics, business strategy and organizational change. Perhaps the most important of these has been the resource-based theory of the firm elaborated in the corporate strategy literature (see e.g. Barney 1991; Hall 1992; Mahoney and Pandian 1992). The argument at the heart of this flurry of activity suggests that sustained competitive advantage derives from a firm's internal resources. For these to offer ongoing advantage these resources must have four qualities: they must add value, be unique or rare, be difficult for competitors to imitate and be non-substitutable (e.g. by technology). As is increasingly being noted, human capital resources can fit this demanding list of criteria rather well. This type of resource can embody intangible assets such as unique configurations of complementary skills, and tacit knowledge, painstakingly accumulated, of customer wants and internal processes. Notably, these sorts of criteria obviously mark a departure from the traditional Tayloristic and Fordist formulae.

Associated theoretical developments (in many ways predicated on the resource-based theory of the firm) are the important works on 'intelligent enterprises' (Quinn 1992), and 'core competencies' (Prahalad and Hamel 1990) and 'competing on capabilities' (Stalk *et al.* 1993).

Nor is this all. Slowly, but surely, sets of empirical data have begun to be published which, while far from 'proving' the onward march of HRM, at least provide sufficient evidence of change in order to give the debate some sustenance on which to work. But work on what? What is this thing called HRM? It is necessary to start with the basics.

In response to new and qualitatively different competitive conditions, it is argued that companies need to alter fundamentally the way in which they manage employees. It is further sometimes said that certain companies have already actually done so. In what precise ways, and to what extent, and with what consequences? These are the questions which run throughout this book.

The term which has been most commonly attached to the idea of 'the new way' is human resource management (HRM). It seems to promise the set of guidelines which so many managers have been so desperately seeking. It is necessary, however, to understand at the outset that this term is used in Britain, and in many other countries, to convey two different meanings. Some people use it simply as a catch-all to encompass the whole field of 'people-management'. Thus, courses on the management of human resources frequently include sessions on interpersonal skills, organizational behaviour and personnel management. Used in this sense, no particular approach to people management is signalled as preferable. Under the second usage, however, HRM stands for a rather distinctive approach, among many possible others.

It is, of course, this second version which has rightly attracted all the attention. But even with regard to this, the concept has been, and remains, highly controversial. There are three main reasons for this. These reasons stem from questions of:

- meaning
- fact
- values.

These three aspects of the HRM debate constitute the subject of the first three sections of this chapter. In the fourth and final section, an introduction is made to the additional key themes addressed in the body of this book.

MEANING

Controversy in the area of meaning turns on the imprecision, variability, ambiguity, and even contradictions which have been seen to imbue the construct. Noon (1992) asks whether HRM is 'a map, a model or a theory?' Keenoy (1990) refers to its ambiguity. Legge (1989) exposes its contradictions – as do Blyton and Turnbull (1992). For Keenoy and Anthony (1992), the whole point of HRM is that it is designed to inspire – 'to explain it is to destroy it' (ibid.: 238). That may be going a bit too far. But there is much truth in the point that there is often a certain evangelicalism about HRM and associated managerial movements. The big ideas can lose something when translated into detail. Nonetheless, if any progress is to be made, it is necessary to attempt a description and analysis of the phenomenon. I even propose to start with a definition:

> Human resource management is a distinctive approach to employment management which seeks to achieve competitive advantage through the strategic deployment of a highly committed and capable workforce, using an integrated array of cultural, structural and personnel techniques.

The key elements are summarized in Figure 1.1. As can be seen from this figure, HRM is an amalgam of description, prescription, and logical deduction. It describes the beliefs and assumptions of certain leading-edge practitioners. It prescribes certain priorities. And it deduces certain consequent actions which seem to follow from the series of propositions. The first element shown in the figure concerns beliefs and assumptions. The most fundamental of these is the idea that, at bottom, it is the human resource among all the factors of production which really makes the difference. It is human capability and commitment which in the final analysis distinguishes successful organizations from the rest. It follows logically from this premise that the human resource ought to be treated with great care. It is a special resource requiring and deserving managerial time and attention. Moreover, the human resource ought to be nurtured as a valued asset, and not be regarded as an incidental cost. A further underlying belief is that the aim is not merely to seek compliance with rules and regulations from employees, but to strive for the much more ambitious objective of commitment. This last is so crucial that some commentators (e.g. Wood 1993) have even preferred to talk in terms of 'high commitment' policies as a working substitute for HRM.

1. *Beliefs and assumptions*

- That it is the human resource which gives competitive edge.
- That the aim should be not mere compliance with rules, but employee commitment.
- That therefore employees should be very carefully selected and developed.

2. *Strategic qualities*

- Because of the above factors, HR decisions are of strategic importance.
- Top management involvement is necessary.
- HR policies should be integrated into the business strategy – stemming from it and even contributing to it.

3. *Critical role of managers*

- Because HR practice is critical to the core activities of the business, it is too important to be left to personnel specialists alone.
- Line managers need to be closely involved both as deliverers and drivers of the HR policies.
- Much greater attention is paid to the management of managers themselves.

4. *Key levers*

- Managing culture is more important than managing procedures and systems.
- Integrated action on selection, communication, training, reward and development.
- Restructuring and job redesign to allow devolved responsibility and empowerment.

Figure 1.1 The HRM model

The second main element in Figure 1.1 concerns strategy. The idea that HRM is a matter of strategic importance requiring the full attention of chief executives and senior management teams is seen as a further distinguishing characteristic. It stems, of course, from the first belief about sources of competive advantage. This belief might lead, in turn, to the proposition that an HR director must have a place on the board in order to influence company policy-formulation at the highest level. But, as long as the chief executive and other senior members are attending to the strategic aspects of HRM the precise functional composition of the board might be regarded as a secondary matter. An associated assumption is that decisions about human resources policies should not stem from a set of *a priori* notions about good professional personnel practice, but should take their cue from an explicit alignment of the competitive environment, business strategy and HRM strategy. Some exponents of strategic HRM would even suggest that HRM policies should not only derive from the corporate plan, but should constructively feed into that plan.

The third element concerns the role of line managers. If human resources really are so critical for business success, the HRM is too important to be left to operational personnel specialists. Line managers are seen as crucial to the effective delivery of HRM policies: conducting team briefings, holding performance appraisal interviews, target-setting, encouraging quality circles, managing performance-related pay, and so on.

In practice there is a further element to this. Much of the drive for HRM came in fact, not from personnel specialists, but from line and general managers (see the evidence in Storey 1992). In some instances, HRM-type policies were pushed through despite the reluctance of personnel professions. In these cases personnel were still clinging to the rationale that they were the privileged mediators between labour and management and that they alone could gauge the feasibility and practicability of new initiatives. Such protestations were cast aside by a newly resurgent managerialism in the 1980s. To this extent at least, the emergence of HRM can be seen as ultimately associated with an upsurge in managerial confidence.

There is a further strand to the idea of a critical role for managers. A great deal of HR activity and energy is directed at managers themselves, rather than shopfloor employees. A disproportionate amount of training and development activity and resources is consumed by management development. Where psychometric testing is used, this is more likely to be directed towards managers – both for selection and promotion purposes. Activity in the realms of target-setting performance management and career planning is again typically geared mainly towards managers. In other words, the panoply of HRM technology is seen in its fullest form in the management of managers.

The fourth distinguishing feature of HRM relates to the key levers used in its implementation. A notable element is the shift of emphasis away from personnel procedures and rules as the basis of good practice, in favour of a new accent on the management of 'culture'. This trend has been remarkable. Just a few years ago the idea of paying regard to something so intangible as 'organizational culture', still less spending senior management time in seeking to manage it, would have seemed implausible. Now, such an aspiration seems to form a critical part of every senior executive's agenda.

So central is this that the twin ideas of 'managing culture change' and moving towards HRM can often appear to coincide and become one and the same project.

Corporate culture management has generated much excitement because it is perceived to offer a key to the unlocking of consensus, flexibility and commitment. These are self-evidently prized objectives. 'Consensus' suggests the achievement of a common set of values and beliefs. It promises an alternative to industrial conflict. Few managers can imagine all disagreements would disappear (even if this were deemed desirable, which is questionable) but many aspire to the securing of consensus about fundamental objectives and priorities. 'Flexibility' is the second prize. If the culture could be changed so as to remove restrictions on movement between erstwhile separate 'jobs', then productivity would be improved. There is, of course, concern that the idea of 'flexibility' is merely a substitute term for greater managerial control. 'Commitment', the third prize in culture change programmes, is seen as potentially carrying labour performance on to an even higher plane. Beyond a simple willingness to work flexibly, there would be an apparent endeavour to succeed. Committed employees would 'go the extra mile' in pursuit of customer service and organizational goals.

These three prizes are obviously highly desirable from an employer's perspective. But how can they be attained? 'Managing' organizational culture is a complex venture. It means altering fundamentally the whole set of ways in which things are routinely done and possibly even seeking a shift in patterns of attitudes, beliefs and values. An array of organizational development (OD) techniques (or 'interventions', as consultants in the OD tradition prefer to term them) is on offer for this purpose.

So much for the idealized model. The question which may legitimately be asked next is whether any of this has actually been put into practice. This brings us to the second area of controversy surrounding HR referred to earlier: the question of practice.

EVIDENCE OF TAKE-UP OF HRM

Is it possible that HRM is simply an elegant theory which has no basis in reality? Until recently there were few studies upon which to draw to allow even an approximate answer to such a question. The early writings and speeches on HRM were concerned solely with American industry. And even here, a few exceptional cases such as Hewlett Packard and Xerox were endlessly cited as exemplars. There was ample room for scepticism about the wider adoption of HRM in America, and even more room for scepticism *vis-à-vis* Britain. The question of its progress in other parts of the world is one we will turn to later. For the moment, it is sensible to concentrate upon Britain alone.

As noted above, the early debate about HRM was conducted largely in the absence of any data about actual practice. While there is still not as much information as would be desirable, the situation has changed considerably during the past two or three years. Data are now available, both from detailed case studies and from large-scale surveys. Here, it is sufficient to note the broad thrust of the findings.

From an in-depth study of fifteen mainstream British employing organizations, it was found that the way in which managers were seeking to manage labour was indeed undergoing extensive and significant change (Storey 1992). This change was evident in a number of ways. Notably, the drive was coming from sources and along paths which were not conventionally regarded as part of industrial relations proper. There had been little sign of outright 'industrial relations reform' of the old kind (following, for example, the nostrums of Flanders (1970), Donovan (1968) or McCarthy and Ellis (1973)). Rather, the recasting had come about as a result of redesigns in production systems, organizational restructuring, quality initiatives and 'culture campaigns'. Notably, many of these initiatives had been devised, as well as driven and delivered, by non-personnel specialists.

To what extent did the important changes which were uncovered amount to evidence of a decisive shift to the human resource management model? This is a very moot point. It is worth quoting directly from the research report:

> The temptation is to seek to measure all change against this 'template'. And an associated danger is the reification of subtle and incomplete tendencies. Both of these divert attention away from extensive and far-reaching changes, which albeit not in themselves constituting HR, are nonetheless of profound significance in shifting the terrain of labour management relations. What seems to have been occurring in the British mainstream is a whole clutch of different, but not divergent, initiatives which range across specialist boundaries. Analyses which attempt to confine themselves within the ambit of conventional frameworks therefore risk a blindness with respect to the changing patterns which emerge from these.
>
> (Storey 1992: 264–5)

The full details of the in-depth studies of the fifteen mainstream UK organizations can be found in the research monograph, *Developments in the Management of Human Resources* (Storey 1992). Here, the main findings will simply be sketched. Using the checklist of items from the HRM model shown in Figure 1.1, it is possible to show that there was an extensive adoption of many of these HRM-style approaches. The four main headings were sub-divided into a twenty-five-item checklist of indicators. This checklist is shown in Table 1.1. Using this checklist, two-thirds of the organizations recorded a positive scoring on at least eleven of the dimensions.

Table 1.1 The twenty-five-item checklist

Dimension	*Personnel and IR*	*HRM*
	Beliefs and assumptions	
1 Contract	Careful delineation of written contracts	Aim to go 'beyond contract'
2 Rules	Importance of devising clear rules/mutuality	'Can do' outlook: impatience with 'rule'
3 Guide to management action	Procedures/consistency control	'Business need'/ flexibility/commitment
4 Behaviour referent	Norms/custom and practice	Values/mission
5 Managerial task *vis-à-vis* labour	Monitoring	Nurturing
6 Nature of relations	Pluralist	Unitarist
7 Conflict	Institutionalized	De-emphasized
8 Standardization	High (e.g. 'parity' an issue)	Low (e.g. 'parity' not seen as relevant)
	Strategic aspects	
9 Key relations	Labour–management	Business–customer
10 Initiatives	Piecemeal	Integrated
11 Corporate plan	Marginal to	Central to
12 Speed of decisions	Slow	Fast
	Line management	
13 Management role	Transactional	Transformational leadership
14 Key managers	Personnel/IR specialists	General/business/line managers
15 Prized management skills	Negotiation	Facilitation
	Key levers	
16 Foci of attention for interventions	Personnel procedures	Wide-ranging cultural, structural and personnel strategies
17 Selection	Separate, marginal task	Integrated, key task
18 Pay	Job evaluation: multiple, fixed grades	Performance-related: few if any grades
19 Conditions	Separately negotiated	Harmonization
20 Labour–management	Collective bargaining contracts	Towards individual contracts
21 Thrust of relations with stewards	Regularized through facilities and training	Marginalized (with exception of some bargaining for change models)
22 Communication	Restricted flow/indirect	Increased flow/direct
23 Job design	Division of labour	Teamwork
24 Conflict handling	Reach temporary truces	Manage climate and culture
25 Training and development	Controlled access to courses	Learning companies

Source: Storey (1992: 35)

The broad pattern of results is shown in Table 1.2. In order to interpret this table, a few points need to be noted. The dimensions listed in abbreviated form in the left-hand column are derived from the ideal-type HRM depiction as shown in Table 1.1. Second, the way the data were derived is of vital significance. The ticks, crosses and dots are not simply the usual record of respondents' replies to a survey. They are the researcher's own summary judgement, based upon multiple sources of information derived from all levels of these organizations.

Two particular problems in devising the table should be noted. The first is the problem of continuity. In many of these cases there would be a particular period of time when one or more of the twenty-five features was clearly being given paramount attention. A year later the emphasis might well have shifted to a new initiative. For the purposes of this figure a tick is recorded where the criterion in question was, at some point during the research, being given clear emphasis. It does not mean that the particular item persisted necessarily for more than a few months as a key feature of the organization's employment management approach. The second difficulty in constructing such a simple summary of complex findings is the way in which, in practice, initiatives may be directed at only one part of the workforce and not another. This in fact was found to be quite a normal state of affairs. Certain levels or certain divisions might be included or excluded for all sorts of different reasons. In these instances a black dot is used to indicate an 'in part' score.

Table 1.2 can be read both horizontally and vertically. Horizontally, one gets a picture of the take-up or neglect of the key HRM dimensions. Reading vertically, the figure reveals those organizations which had adopted, or had experimented with, HRM-style practices with most vigour. The overall pattern, in itself, reveals some fascinating results. Notable first of all is the extensive take-up of HRM-style approaches in the British mainstream organizations. Two-thirds of the companies recorded a definite tick scoring on at least eleven of the dimensions. The level of managerial activity is indicated even more forcefully if one takes into account the 'in parts' scoring device as well as the definite tick. Such has been the apparent level of engagement with these new sets of beliefs, values and practices that the evidence points to a wholesale shift away from the proceduralist recipe in our major employing organizations.

The first section of the table covers prevailing beliefs and assumptions. 'Business need' as a guide to action was the norm. Associated with this was the view that procedures, rules and contractual arrangements were impediments to effective performance. Notably, despite the emphasis given to the 'nurturing' orientation in the idealized portraits of HRM, none of the cases was judged to have unambiguously embraced this.

HRM is said to be fundamentally unitarist. This means that it supposedly has little tolerance for the multiple interest groups and the multiple

Table 1.2 Broad summary of results

	Rover	British Rail	Bradford Council	Eaton Ltd	Ford	ICI	Jaguar	Lucas	Massey Ferguson	NHS	Peugeot-Talbot	Plessey	Rolls-Royce	Smith & Nephew	Whitbread	
Beliefs and assumptions																
'Business need' is prime guide to action	√	√	√	●	√	√	√	√	√	●	√	√	√	√	√	13
Aims to go 'beyond contract'	√	●	√	√	√	√	√	√	√	√	●	√	●	●	√	11
Values/mission	√	●	√	√	√	√	√	√	√	√	√	●	●	●	√	11
Impatience with rules	√	√	√	√	●	√	√	√	√	●	●	√	●	●	√	10
Standardization/parity not emphasized	√	●	√	√	●	√	●	√	√	×	●	√	×	×	√	8
Conflict de-emphasized rather than institutionalized	√	●	√	●	●	√	●	×	●	●	●	√	×	●	√	5
Unitarist relations	●	●	×	×	×	●	●	×	●	×	×	√	×	×	√	2
Nurturing orientation	●	×	●	●	●	●	●	●	●	●	●	●	●	●	●	0
Strategic aspects																
Customer-orientation to fore	√	√	√	×	●	√	√	√	√	●	●	√	√	√	√	11
Integrated initiatives	√	×	√	×	●	●	●	●	●	●	●	×	×	×	√	3
Corporate plan central	√	●	√	×	●	●	●	●	●	×	●	×	●	●	√	3
Speedy decision-making	√	×	●	×	●	●	●	●	●	×	×	●	×	×	√	2

								Line managers								
General/business/line managers to fore	√	√	√	√	√	√	√	√	√	√	√	√	√	√	√	15
Facilitation is prized skill	√	√	√	√	√	√	√	●	√	●	●	●	×	●	√	9
Transformational leadership	√	×	●	●	●	●	●	√	√	√	●	●	●	●	●	4
								Key levers								
Increased flow of communication	√	√	√	√	√	√	√	√	√	√	√	√	√	√	√	15
Selection is integrated key task	√	√	√	√	√	√	√	√	√	●	√	√	●	×	√	12
Wide-ranging cultural, structural and personnel strategies	√	√	√	●	√	√	√	√	√	√	√	√	●	●	√	12
Teamworking	●	●	√	√	√	√	√	√	√	√	●	√	√	●	√	11
Conflict reduction through culture change	√	●	√	√	√	√	√	√	√	√	●	√	●	●	√	11
Marginalization of stewards	√	●	●	●	×	●	√	√	√	√	√	√	●	●	√	8
Learning companies/heavy emphasis on training	√	●	√	×	●	●	√	√	√	●	●	●	√	●	●	6
Move to individual contracts	●	√	●	×	×	×	●	●	●	●	●	√	●	×	√	3
Performance-related pay, few grades	√	●	●	●	×	×	×	●	●	●	●	●	×	●	●	1
Harmonization	√	●	●	×	×	×	●	×	×	×	●	●	×	×	●	1

Key: √ = yes (existed or were significant moves towards) × = no ● = in parts

Source: Storey (1992: 82)

expression of interests which trade unions and the proceduralist traditions make manifest. Yet the pattern of findings shown here reveals that, despite extensive engagement with large parts of the HRM recipe, Britain's large mainstream organizations have placed little emphasis upon disengagement from their pluralist stance.

What was found to be happening on the industrial relations and trade union front was a duality of approach. Trade union recognition and the appurtenances of union relations, such as collective bargaining, were being maintained. But running quite separately from all of this were the new initiatives shown in the tables. In some of the cases this dual dealing was even conducted by separate departments or units, and the communication between them was rudimentary and even hostile. To this extent, what can be said to have been revealed in British industrial relations is the coexistence of two traditions. Whether this dualism can survive long into the 1990s is an issue of some significance.

The second part of Table 1.2 covers strategic aspects. Interestingly, apart from an insistence on a customer orientation, most cases failed to offer much in the way of an integrated approach to employment management, and still less was there evidence of strategic integration with the corporate plan. This finding lends some support to the view that the HRM model is itself not a coherent, integrated phenomenon. Many of the initiatives recorded in the case research, and indicated in summary from here, arose for diverse reasons, and in practice they shared little in common. The fragmentary application of the model could of course be attributed to imperfections in take-up and implementation.

Alternatively, the 'pick-and-mix' way in which these organizations were operating might indicate the true nature of the HRM phenomenon – i.e. that it is in reality a symbolic label, behind which lurk multifarious practices, many of which are not mutually dependent upon each other. If this is so, it would further explain how these largely pragmatic and opportunistic organizations have found it so relatively easy to pick up diverse elements of these 'new' initiatives.

The third part of the table shows how the case studies uniformly revealed the impressive emergence of general 'business managers' and line managers as key players on employment issues. In all fifteen cases there was evidence of these managers devising, driving and delivering new initiatives. The discussion as to whether personnel specialists should 'give human resource management away' will need to be reconsidered in the light of this finding. Are personnel managers in a position to make such a decision? The scoring with regard to 'key levers' produced other surprises. All of the initiatives on the list had been extensively talked about by the mid- to late 1980s in Britain. However, as the figure reveals, there was wide disparity in actual take-up and implementation of these contemporary ideas.

Harmonization of terms and conditions, and performance-related pay, are shown to have been only fractionally introduced at this time. However, continuing contact with most of these organizations up to the present time leads us to the view that, while harmonization continues to make extraordinarily slow progress, performance-related pay would record a much higher scoring today.

Perhaps less surprisingly, the emphasis given to direct communications with the workforce and the increased flow of this form of communication were observed in all cases. Rather more notable, arguably, was the extent to which line managers as well as personnel directors were intent on stressing their engagement with 'culture change' activities. Ten years ago this would have been an extraordinary state of affairs; now it is almost *de rigeur*.

Reading Table 1.2 vertically, the take-up of these initiatives on a company-by-company basis is revealed. It is not part of the intent of this chapter to go into detail on the company comparisons. However, what is notable is the variation in the range of summary scores. Whitbread and Rover score highest on this measure; Smith and Nephew scores lowest. Ironically, this last company, despite (or could it be because of?) its conservative stance in these regards, has consistently been a top-performing company in financial terms.

Perhaps more surprising than the lack of close association between financial performance and the sheer number of human resource initiatives taken, is the similar low correlation between such a score and the quality of working life in these organizations. Employee commitment, trust and satisfaction in the case organizations were not found to be closely associated with scores on this checklist. The reason for this finding may reside in the fact that HRM has, it will be recalled, 'hard' as well as 'soft' dimensions. An emphasis on the former is likely to be associated with a calculative approach to the handling of the labour resource.

The crude scores also say little about the degree of coherence in each company's take-up of these initiatives. Whitbread recorded a high score, and the sense of coherence between the initiatives was also high among the different sites and the levels of the company. Conversely, while Rover and Massey Ferguson also scored highly on the sheer number of initiatives undertaken, the perceived relationship between the various initiatives and the persistence in their application were found to be much lower.

British Rail had launched fewer initiatives, and even for these the degree of coherence and persistence was weak. Ford had, as expected, preserved a connection with its tried and tested constitutionalist approach. Nonetheless, it had also launched a surprising number of initiatives of the modern kind. It played to the advantage of having comparable overseas sites in which to test ideas and applications.

Many factors were found to influence the differential pattern of take-up of initiatives between the case organizations: foreign ownership, the complexity of company structure and the variation from single-product focus to complex multi-product situations, for example.

It has to be recognized, of course, that summation of complex data against a checklist inevitably leads to a rather crude and simplistic representation of reality. The subtle interpretations can only be explored in the full version of the research report. Nonetheless, there is a great value in standing back and taking a summary overview of the kind presented here, because from such a perspective one can capture a unique sense of the overall pattern. What has really been happening to personnel management and industrial relations in Britain is, as was perhaps to be expected, a multi-faceted and complex affair. Typical practice in large organizations in Britain could still be interpreted as being broadly in accord with Sisson's (1989) depiction of it as lacking in strategic integration and, moreover, falling far short of textbook prescription on practically all constituent measures.

However, what clearly emerges is that British managers have been extraordinarily active in relation to labour matters in recent years. There is now evidence that the take-up by mainstream organizations of initiatives of a kind much discussed in connection with 'lead' organizations has been very extensive. It can even be said that there has been indeed a clear aim to go 'beyond contract'. However, what is less clear is the ability of the initiatives taken to deliver this, given the shortcomings in the way in which they have been applied. Further insights on each of these points are to be gained in subsequent chapters in this book.

EVIDENCE FROM SURVEYS

The evidence cited so far concerning the adoption of HRM approaches has concentrated on detailed case studies. These give, by far, the most useful insights into the subtleties and intangibles of developments in human resource management. Inevitably, however, questions need to be asked about how representative such recorded developments are of the situation in the wider economy. In order to access data of a statistically representative kind, it is necessary to look to wide-scale surveys. Fortunately, since the publication in 1989 of *New Perspectives*, three sets of relevant surveys have been conducted and published. We can now proceed to summarize and piece together the evidence about HRM from these three separate sources.

The Leicestershire Training and Enterprise Council survey

What kind of picture would emerge from a study specifically built around the theme of new management practices, covering HRM issues such as winning employee commitment, flexibility, culture change, empowerment and HR strategy, as well as related issues such as changes to the role of managers, total quality management and non-standard forms of employment? This was the central question we tried to answer on behalf of the Leicestershire Training and Enterprise Council (Storey *et al.* 1994).

We surveyed a statistically representative sample of all employing organizations in Leicestershire with more than fifteen employees. This was a telephone survey which covered public and private sector organizations across all the standard industrial classifications (SICs). A total of 560 employing organizations were surveyed, and these were divided into three size bands: small (15 to 24 employees), medium (25 to 199 employees) and large (over 200 employees). In each case the respondents were the most senior figures in the place of work responsible for people-management matters. These included personnel directors, managing directors and works managers.

The headline finding was the remarkable extent to which Leicestershire employers had taken up the new management practices. This was evidenced across all three size bands: small and medium-sized organizations as well as the large organizations reported that they were heavy users of the 'modern' approaches. In the light of the prolonged debate about the extent to which HRM is rhetoric or reality, this is, on the face of it, a significant finding. Obviously some caution must be exercised in interpreting the data, since the survey was built around self-reporting. However, the questionnaire was designed to allow further checking of the initial basic claims. For example, each initiative reported was probed in a number of ways. One significant 'test' was the question about the contribution to organizational effectiveness which each initiative was judged to have made. In the main, initiatives such as team-working and job flexibility were judged to have made a high level of contribution. Moreover, the extent to which the initiatives had been sustained was also reported to be high.

We asked many different questions in order to construct a profile of employment practices. At the heart of the questionnaire, however, was a table which encapsulated eleven critical initiatives. For each of these we sought, in essence, four types of information.

1 Whether an initiative of this type had been launched and implemented within the past five years.
2 In most cases where an initiative had been taken up, information was sought on whether it had been sustained, abandoned or operated only marginally.
3 Whether the initiative had contributed to organizational objectives.
4 Where the organization was part of a larger group, information was sought on the level at which the initiatives had been driven – that is, had they come from a corporate centre or divisional level, or had the location itself introduced the initiative(s)?

Table 1.3 Overview of key HRM initiatives

	Initiative employed %	*Sustained* %	*'Considerable contribution' to objectives* %	*Unit-level driven* %
A *A culture change programme* A conscious and planned attempt to alter the attitudes, values and routine ways of behaving at work.	35	73	65	52
B. *Devolved management* The pushing-down of responsibility to lower management levels.	65	86	71	61
C. *Teamworking* among employees of a non-managerial level.	76	87	74	60
D. *Performance appraisals* for employees of a non-managerial level.	55	78	63	49
E. *A mission statement*	42	85	67	43
F. *Team briefing* where information is transmitted by supervisors to others within the groups.	74	86	74	56
G. *Quality circles*	35	80	63	54
H. *Harmonized terms and conditions*	40	87	68	49
I. *Psychometric tests*	11	45	39	45
J. *De-layering* The removal of one or more tiers in the managerial hierarchy.	19	74	64	54
K. *Increased flexibility between jobs*	75	89	78	58

Base: All organizations (N = 560)

A broad overview of the findings on this core set of questions concerning the 'new management' can be gleaned from Table 1.3. It is evident first of all that the reported take-up of the eleven key initiatives is, on the whole, rather high. In the case of three of these initiatives – teamworking among employees of a sub-managerial level; team briefing, where information is transmitted by supervisors to members of their work teams; and increased flexibility of working between jobs – no fewer than three-quarters of the whole sample base of 560 organizations reported they had adopted them. Given that the question specifically asked about initiatives launched within the past five years, this suggests a very significant movement in managerial practice. It indicates that this set of ideas in particular has now become the virtual orthodoxy.

Also running at a relatively high rate of adoption were initiatives in devolved management – i.e. pushing down responsibility to lower managerial levels; performance appraisal extending across into non-managerial grades; and harmonization of terms and conditions. Each of these initiatives had been adopted by between 40 and 65 per cent of the total sample.

Two initiatives in particular stand out as having been taken up by fewer than 20 per cent of the sample. These were psychometric tests, which had been deployed in the past five years in only 11 per cent of instances, and de-layering (taking out one or more managerial tiers), which had occurred in 19 per cent of cases.

What is also notable about the summary table is the reported high level of maintenance of those initiatives which had been launched. On average, some 80 per cent of respondents claimed that the initiatives adopted within the past five years had been sustained and had neither been abandoned nor even 'operated only at a marginal level'. The top-scoring item here was increased flexibility between jobs: 89 per cent of those organizations adopting this practice claimed to be sustaining their commitment to it. The lowest-scoring item was psychometric tests. Of those few organizations (11 per cent) which had started using psychometric tests for selection purposes in the past five years, only 45 per cent reported that they had sustained their level of commitment to them. In other words, in most cases where psychometric testing had been adopted, its use subsequently declined. There is a pattern here. Psychometric testing also scored lowest when respondents were asked about the extent to which each of the initiatives had contributed to the achievement of organizational objectives. Only 39 per cent replied that it had contributed considerably.

Those establishments which were part of a larger group were also asked whether the different initiatives had been driven from above or had been launched locally. Notably, the sponsorship of psychometric testing had come from outside, in most cases (55 per cent).

Where new initiatives had been launched, we tried to trace correlations with variables such as the presence or absence of trade unions, and the type of sector. Certain hypotheses underlay this activity. Until recently, for example, it was generally assumed that sophisticated HR policies were more prevalent in non-union, high-tech companies. 'Traditional' manufacturing was thought to be non-innovative in its approach to employment management. However, recent studies have shown that it is precisely the unionized manufacturing establishments where innovative techniques such as employee involvement have been most notably installed. One hypothesis is that companies with trade unions are more likely to introduce devices such as team briefings as a way to recapture communication channels from trade union hands.

Our study revealed that there was, in fact, some correlation between the incidence of team briefing and the presence of trade unions in the workplace. Overall, 84 per cent of establishments with trade unions also had team briefing, while for establishments which did not recognize trade unions, the figure was 68 per cent.

Another factor was organizational size. As mentioned earlier, in general, the larger the organization, the more chance there was that each of the new employment initiatives had been launched. The reasons are fairly obvious: the larger organizations had more expertise at their disposal, and the relevance of some of the initiatives (such as delayering or harmonization of terms and conditions) was clearly tied to size.

However, there was an interesting and important new finding. When we looked at the degree to which certain initiatives had been sustained, we found that smaller organizations had enjoyed the greater success. The reason for this is presumably that, once the head of a small enterprise decides to introduce a new approach, it is more likely to be followed through (partly because of evident managerial commitment, and partly because it is easier to make an impact on a smaller organization in a shorter time than to effect change in a large organization).

There is an important implication here. Although it has been generally assumed that the new employment initiatives are mainly a concern of the larger organizations, there is, in fact, a considerable constituency among the far greater number of small and medium-sized enterprises which are willing to experiment with the 'new management' and whose track record, when they do so, would appear to be well above average.

WIRS3

A source of empirical evidence about changing employment practices in Britain which cannot be neglected is the third workplace industrial relations survey (WIRS3), sponsored by the Department of Employment, the Policy Studies Institute and the Economic and Social Research Council (Millward *et al.* 1992). As Sisson notes in his review of this report, WIRS3 on the surface seems to have little directly to say about HRM, even though HRM has been 'the industrial issue of the 1980s and early 1990s' (Sisson 1993: 201). But beneath the surface, Sisson detects some useful indicators of change which shed light on the HRM debate. From just such an analysis Sisson finds that some of the ideas and practices associated with HRM are indeed taking root.

First, there is an evident shift from collectivism to individualism. All the indicators of unionism revealed a marked decline. For example, overall trade union density fell from 58 to 48 per cent between 1984 and 1990. Nor, in the later part of this period, was this due only to structural adjustments in the economy; de-recognition itself became important. Second, the HRM pursuit of employee-commitment through participation and involvement was evidenced in WIRS3. The use of team briefings increased from 36 per cent of workplaces to 48 per cent; regular newsletters were up from 34 to 41 per cent; and the use of employee surveys increased from 12 to 17 per cent. Involvement in the form of quality circles also increased, as did the use of various forms of financial participation. Third, recorded changes to the organization of management itself can be seen as being in line with the HRM thesis. The involvement of general and line managers in activities such as manpower planning and training were shown to be very high. As Sisson (1993: 205) observes: 'All of this suggests that British management is taking its human resources more seriously'. These survey findings by the WIRS team provide confirmation of the case study reports by Storey (1987, 1992) detailing the important phenomenon of increasing line and general manager engagement with human resource management. They also reflect the findings from the Leicestershire survey.

There is a final very significant point arising out of Sisson's review of the WIRS3 data. Contrary to the expectations of many, it was in the unionized rather than the non-union workplaces that the evidence of HR was largely to be found. The non-union sector as a whole was characterized by poor communications, lack of employment security, higher dismissal rates and poorer safety records. Unionized workplaces had managers keen to win 'hearts and minds' by using employee involvement and other HRM methods. To a large extent HRM methods and models offer managers in unionized workplaces an alternative scenario to the 'trench warfare' (Dunn 1990) which they had previously experienced with industrial relations. Managers in unionized workplaces thus had a spur to manage change. In non-union environments, by contrast, there may be a certain measure of complacency. Lacking an effective challenge, managers are more content to allow employee relations to assume a lower rung in their list of priorities. In the unionized settings, HR practices may on occasions be used as a way to prepare the ground for de-recognition. But the evidence would seem to point more convincingly to a less dramatic conclusion. Managers operate in dual fashion – running an attenuated form of collective relations in parallel with the new HRM initiatives. Both can have their uses.

The Warwick company level survey

One final data set is worth reporting. The second company-level survey by the Industrial Relations Research Unit at the University of Warwick gives insight into changing company practices among a representative sample of multi-site companies with over 1,000 employees in the UK. This survey (Marginson *et al.* 1994) was conducted in 1992. The findings help to confirm the picture we have so far constructed about significant change in employment management practices since the mid-1980s. One in five companies had withdrawn recognition wholly or partially from trade unions at one or more sites during the past five years. There were also other indicators confirming a shift from collectivism to individualism. Among the 80 per cent which had opened new sites during the past five years, no recognition had been granted for the largest group of employees in 60 per cent of these cases. Moreover, in 60 per cent of companies the range of matters subject to collective bargaining had decreased during this period, compared with just 14 per cent of cases reporting an increase in the scope of bargaining.

Given the focus of this distinctive survey on company-level activity, it is pertinent to note the findings which relate to personnel's involvement in *strategic* business decisions. Seven main types of strategic management decisions were used as indicators: merger and acquisition; investment in new locations; expansion of existing sites; divestment; closure of existing sites; run-down of sites; and the launch of joint ventures. The overall finding was of only a limited involvement by the personnel function in such decisions. For example, only 13 per cent of personnel respondents claimed that the personnel function was involved in taking the final decision in merger and acquisition cases. As the authors of the report note, the strategic quality of HRM is hardly underscored by these findings. On the other hand, the reported extent to which personnel *issues* are taken into account when such strategic decisions are taken was rather high: 71 per cent in the case of merger/acquisition, 76 per cent for new investment, 79 per cent for divestment decisions and 93 per cent for site run-down.

Finally, the Warwick company-level survey offers further evidence about developments in the area of employee communication and involvement. Overall, 54 per cent of the companies had quality circles or problem-solving groups. For manufacturing, the level was as high as 72 per cent, compared with 41 per cent in service sector companies. Again, notably, it was the companies which recognized trade unions which were the most likely to use a wider range of methods to consult with employees and to communicate with them on issues such as investment plans.

VALUES

The third dimension of the controversy concerns the question of values. Put rather bluntly, is HR generally a good thing or a bad thing? Should whatever progress it makes be applauded or denounced?

The optimistic, benign, face of HRM is evident in many accounts. Thus, Roger Farrance, the then President of the Institute of Personnel Management, writing the foreword to *Handbook of Human Resource Management* (Towers 1992) evidently viewed it in a very positive light. He referred to 'the rejection of corporatism and the definition and projection of individual rights and freedoms . . . the respect of the rights of the individual and for each to have a say in what happens to them' (Farrance 1992: xiii–xiv). He goes on to applaud 'decentralization and devolution of decision-making', accountability being 'pushed-down to the lowest possible levels while hierarchies have been reduced'. In the clearest terms he observes that

> Human resource management must be the route by which companies and employing organizations can come to terms with the new situation. It provides the means by which the fullest potential of employees can be developed and used for the benefit of both themselves and their employers. Good HR practice will ensure that every employee knows that they matter as an individual and a human being while the employer will have the confidence that the workforce will perform to the levels needed and beyond for success in today's competitive world.
>
> (Farrance 1992: xv)

One would expect a backlash against such unalloyed optimism; and yet the most notable feature of the present landscape is the relative paucity of incisive critique – though many of the contributing authors to this present volume help to correct for that neglect. In general, however, the expected backlash has not materialized. One notable exception was the 'unapologetically polemical' assault launched by Hart (1993). He pulled no punches: 'I believe HR to be amoral and anti-social, unprofessional, reactive, uneconomic and ecologically destructive' (1993: 29). The critique is entirely couched in terms of values and ethics. Hart sees HRM as having ousted the decent, welfare and humanistic values of personnel management. The Institute of Personnel Management is castigated for having replaced its classic pronouncement of the mission of personnel management as being essentially about the pursuit of 'efficiency and justice' with a corrupt, totally business-oriented mission. Personnel specialists, it is argued, should rediscover the ambivalence which has long caused much soul-searching within their ranks. This ambivalence Hart views as a positive attribute and certainly a sign of more liberal values than is expressed in the 'ascendancy of HRM and all its amoral practices' (Hart 1993: 36).

As Derek Torrington (1993) observes in his reply to this article, reservations about HRM are not entirely new. Torrington chooses to respond largely in terms of what the controversy means from a personnel specialist's perspective. From this stance, the 'global ecological threat' which HR apparently represents is seen as a hopelessly impractical project for the personnel profession – let alone any individual practitioner. Moreover, Torrington suggests that HRM is not without its positive attributes. He points, for example, to its emphasis on training and development. Torrington suggests that as a consequence of HRM, training budgets have been far better protected in the most recent recession than has happened on previous occasions. He further maintains that the attendant emphasis on 'performance', rather than conformity to rules and formal controls, is of significant value.

Perhaps because Torrington's discussion of the Hart critique is couched in terms of the implications for personnel specialists, he fails to make other potential rebuttals to Hart's polemic. The latter is in truth not so much an attack on HRM as such, but rather a general critique of 'rampant managerialism' in all its forms and of the capitalist market system, to boot.

Hart's lament is that the romanticized version of personnel management as a 'caring profession' has been so utterly displaced by all the talk about sustaining and enhancing market competitiveness. Here he has a valid point. The IPM, however, seemingly remains unrepentant. In a consultative document circulated in early 1994 which sets out three possible 'models' for the development of personnel in the future, in the face of heightened international competition, the IPM offers options which are all variants of the business-need theme (IPM 1994).

In a critique of part of the HRM model, which contrasts it with traditional personnel management, Clark (1993) also takes a values-based stance. He argues that the principles of fairness and consistency 'should be the guide to management action' (ibid.: 80). From such a position he is critical of the 'almost politically correct' tendency to 'downgrade the importance of procedures'. This is not the time to undertake a full analysis of Clark's critique – suffice it to say that HRM is viewed here as highly controversial because it departs from certain cherished values. The two dimensions which Clark selects (clear rules and procedures as a guide to management action) are not the only ones on which a moral stand could be taken. Most of the seven dimensions under the beliefs and assumptions heading could be debated in terms of their ideological purity. For example, the first – the aim to go beyond carefully delineated written contracts – is not without reproach. Likewise, the shift in behaviour referent from norms and customs and practice to values and mission (invariably business-dominated in both instances) is not without its ethical problems. The shift from pluralism is also problematical. But the point to be understood in relation to all of these dimensions is that the analyst who transforms the implicit statements of managers into a more explicit format cannot be criticized as if he is proselytizing these ideas. In the original text of *Developments in the Management of Human Resources*, Storey (1992: 34) writes 'what needs to be clarified is that the "idealized" [model] is not a prescription devised by the author but a representation made by reconstructing the implicit models of the managers interviewed'. Clark equates the departure from procedures with the 'blue-eyed' syndrome. This may in some instances prove to be valid, but if seen *only* in this way, the depiction rather misses the point which many managers were seeking to make. The research unearthed a reaction to the years of detailed reticulation of procedures as a perceived end in itself. Time and time again, managers were keen to emphasize that people-management policies need to stem far more from business developments. There is a dual face to this. On the one side is the idea that trust and empowerment can displace the obsession with rules and procedures. On the other side is the 'hard' dimension to HRM, which Clark neglects to mention. Under this guise, the desire to depart from the regime of pre-ordained rules and procedures stems from a perceived need in highly competive climates to utilize labour in a flexible manner – as business need is seen to dictate. This position is of course close to the anti-pluralist character of certain versions of HRM: the whole point of it, some would say, *is* to escape from joint regulation. Clark is perfectly entitled not to approve of certain elements of HRM (he is by no means alone in this) and heartily to approve of others. The whole point of this section, and of this chapter, and indeed of this whole book, is to bring to light the dilemmas and the 'warts and all' of the new developments in HR. Clark's contribution in this regard is welcome and valuable.

So far in this introductory chapter we have reviewed the three main sources of controversy surrounding HRM – the questions of meaning, evidence and values. In the next section these and other issues which are explored in detail throughout the rest of this book are reviewed in summary form.

THE CRITICAL THEMES EXPLORED IN THIS BOOK

The chapters which follow are arranged in four main parts. The first part of the book attends to the debate about the nature and significance of HRM. The second is concerned with various strategic issues, including, for example, the link between HRM and corporate strategy, the strategic implications for the personnel function, the changing relationship between industrial relations and HRM; and the agenda-setting rule of accountancy logic in the British corporation. The chapters in the third part of the book explore the key practice areas of HRM: planning, recruitment and selection, assessment, training and development, reward, and employee involvement. The fourth part of the book contains three chapters on various aspects of international HRM: the crucial question of the manifestation of HRM in Europe is fully explored, the progress or otherwise of HRM in America is assessed by the most authoritative figures on the subject of 'transformation' – Professors Kochan and Dyer; and the HRM issues arising from the increasing internationalization of business are examined in the penultimate chapter of the book. The final chapter makes an overall assessment of contemporary trends and developments.

There is a common critical thread running through all four parts. The introductory and strategic overview chapters all make the case that there are deep-seated structural constraints which belie the apparent simplicity of implementing the HRM model. These chapters each point out the gap between the broad trends in employment practices and the high principles of the model. Likewise, the chapters which attend in detail to the specific 'practice areas', such as recruitment and selection, training and development and employee involvement, similarly attest to the underlying theme. The recorded activity in each of these areas not only departs in significant ways from the prescription, there are also aspects of practice which run counter to the idea. The chapters in Part III thus provide detailed substantiation to the broader canvas of Part II.

Karen Legge makes an incisive analysis of the HRM phenomenon. Her argument 'is *not* that no new initiatives, that might loosely be labelled HRM, are taking place in UK organizations', rather that the changes are 'thinking but pragmatic responses to the opportunities and constraints afforded by heightened competition, recession and the socio-political-economic changes embodied in notions of the enterprise culture' (p. 54). Given this, the central thrust of her analysis is to seek to explain why the grander rhetoric of something *qualitatively different* in HRM has taken such hold. Her answer hinges around the various stakeholders who find some advantage in this rhetoric in a hostile climate. She points to a fascinating paradox. While at one level HRM represents 'managerial triumphalism', at another the rhetoric of empowerment and 'everyone a manager' raises the awkward question of how those holding conventional managerial posts can lay claim to such special reward and privileges. Might this managerial rhetoric therefore backfire?

The thorough and extensive review of the role of the personnel function made by Keith Sisson in his chapter complements Legge's analysis at many points. In particular, he argues convincingly that the personnel function has not been transformed as one might have expected by all the hype about people as strategic assets and key sources of competitive advantage. For example, the number of personnel directors with a seat on the main board has failed to increase. Moreover, the 'harsh climate' point is echoed: it is the 'hard' rather than the 'soft' dimension of HRM which has been manifest most in recent years. There is a great deal more in Sisson's chapter: indeed, it represents probably the most thorough review of the contemporary state of the art in personnel management so far published.

The question of 'whither personnel?' is also central to Peter Armstrong's chapter on the pervasive influence of accountancy controls and accountancy logic in the typical British corporation. Without a far more imaginative, assertive and radical restatement of its contribution, Armstrong sees little hope for the personnel profession. Recent developments such as benchmarking and falling into line with the logic of quantifiable outcomes seem likely to

> hand over the judgement of [personnel's] effectiveness to managers in other functions. By encouraging cost comparisons, they encourage the contracting out of fragments of personnel work, and by prioritizing easily quantifiable outcomes, they undermine the case for a distinctive 'personnel' approach.
>
> (p. 158)

The way forward is for personnel specialists to learn to promote their projects in terms of the fundamental company objectives and redefining what is pertinent in the operationalizing of these objectives. (It might be argued that this is what much HRM has been about.)

Purcell's searching analysis of the link between corporate strategy and HRM moves the argument on from his distinctive contribution in the *New Perspectives* book. There, he famously noted the incompatibility between the strategic diversification trends in most large multi-dimensional British companies and the ideals of human resource management. In brief, the argument was that the financial control adopted by corporations tended to steer diversified business units towards short-term horizons and that these are inimical to investment in HR strategies, which tend to require a longer-term view. In this new chapter Purcell does not recant his earlier analysis, but he does arrive at a far more optimistic conclusion. Drawing on resource-based models of competitive advantage as outlined by authors such as Barney (1991) and Kay (1993), he traces company success to the skilful construction and handling of firm-specific resources which are valuable, intangible, rare, and not easily copied. Not all such resources derive from the human assets of the firm; but a significant enough proportion do, to make the potential contribution of truly strategic human resource management 'immense'. The role for HR strategy is to steer a path away from the isolationism of diversified, devolved, strategic business unit tendencies which have so far predominated. Instead the role for HR is to develop 'horizontal strategies [which] emphasize intangibles, learning, and skill transfer and the reduction in transaction costs' (p. 84). This carries a clear positive message for corporate HRM strategies. Their challenge is to 'show a link between policy, practice and organizational outcomes that is meaningful to the corporate board' and, beyond this, to 'make a considered contribution to identification and development of particular human resource strengths and contribute to the improvement or replication of distinctive organizational routines that convert resources to competitive advantage (p. 84).

This optimism could even extend into the trade union camp. According to Guest's analysis, the prime thrust in the 1990s from employers has not in fact accorded a high priority to HRM (neither has it, of course, prioritized industrial relations and collective bargaining). The predominant pattern has arguably been a low commitment by employers to both models. Instead, there has been a journey down the 'black hole' of cost-cutting and union de-recognition. Faced with such a scenario, what strategies are open to the trade unions? They have a choice, says Guest (p. 137), 'of either continuing their slow decline, or opting for radical change'. This latter, he suggests, could take the shape of the unions appropriating the HRM model and urging its positive elements on luke-warm employers. 'Unions should also bear in mind that there should be much that is humane and stimulating for the workforce in HRM' (pp. 136–7). A 'distinctively European approach' to HRM is envisaged which contains elements of European Union-inspired legislative support and an emphasis on safety, health, quality and job enrichment. The prospects for mutual benefits are clear: 'People generally feel good working in a successful, positive, high-trust organization' (p. 137).

Chapters 7 to 11 closely examine the main practice areas of HRM. These chapters offer insights into 'best practice' models as well as into actual current practices in UK employing organizations. For example, Sheila Rothwell's review of human resource planning elaborates the main techniques, but additionally she also grounds her analysis in the realities of organizational politics. Ashton and Felstead argue cogently that, while certain survey evidence may reveal marginal increases in training provision in recent years, this has to be put in the context of two key factors. The first of these is that this training seems to have been impelled by the need to satisfy the requirements of health and safety legislation and BS5750 accreditation. It seems less indicative of the influence of an HRM-induced switch to a high-skill strategy. Second, when compared with the acceleration of provision for human capital formation in the Pacific Rim countries such as Singapore, the policies for training and development in Britain look dangerously paltry and short-sighted.

In their chapter on recruitment, selection and assessment, Paul Iles and Graeme Salaman take a rather different line of critique. In a sophisticated and wide-ranging analysis, they present a challenging alternative to the predominant 'efficiency' perspective on these HRM practices. This counterposes an 'emerging European social process model' to the conventional American psychometric model. It reinterprets the sorting, sifting and assessment of individuals as a parallel activity to organizational restructuring. These processes are revealed as meaning systems for reshaping individuals and as expressions of organizational power.

Similarly, Kessler, in reviewing developments in reward systems such as

PRP, notes that in many respects the objectives mirror previous managerial concerns about various pay systems. Yet, at the same time, he argues that there are certain distinctive features about recent PRP schemes (especially the way that they are used to reinforce wider organizational transformation strategies) which render them qualitatively different and which carry long-term implications.

In terms of quantity, the installation of new employee involvement (EI) initiatives, as Marchington demonstrates in his chapter, has been rather impressive. However, in terms of qualitative impact, the analysis made in the chapter suggests a less sanguine conclusion. For the most part the initiatives have been 'faddish' and have rarely been strategically integrated into a wider pattern of HRM change. Perhaps most critically, the impact on employees has been very limited.

The chapters in Part IV each address aspects of the international scene and thus help to put the British debates in a wider comparative context. Kochan and Dyer's analysis of the lack of progress made in the 'transformation' of American employment practices is very significant. This is a far more sober assessment than the celebrated account of *The Transformation of American Industrial Relations* (Kochan *et al.* 1986). The updated argument as developed here fits well within the framework of arguments mounted earlier in the book. The shift from pragmatic, reactive, employment management to the kind of sophisticated strategic model offered by HRM cannot, they now maintain, be brought about by managers alone. Concerted action by other stakeholders and institutional and state support would seem to be necessary. This argument is closely aligned with that made by Sisson (1994).

Chris Brewster in Chapter 12 argues that it is possible and beneficial to clarify a distinctively 'European' version of HRM. Drawing upon data from the extensive Cranfield/Price Waterhouse three-year survey of fourteen countries, he of course recognizes the variants (both country-specific and regional clusters) within Europe but the main thrust of his analysis is directed towards the idea of a 'European' model. This acknowledges, in a way that the original American model arguably failed to do, that one needs to take into account different degrees of scope for the exercise of independent managerial 'strategic choices'. Significantly, in their review of the American scene in Chapter 13, Kochan and Dyer also put this issue increasingly to the fore. Further, the European model builds in to the model a larger role for the State and for trade unions. Brewster sees in this European version of HRM a greater chance of partnership and a balance between efficiency and justice: organizational requirements and a concern for people.

Finally, Scullion in Chapter 14 takes the debate beyond Britain and Europe, on to the truly international level. In particular, his review is useful in summarizing the issues and the research on the topic of strategic international human resource management. This is carried forward in the context of increasing internationalization of business and the emergence of arrangements such as joint ventures and strategic alliances which transcend the national state. As Scullion readily acknowledges, a great deal of further research still needs to be done in these areas. At the same time, he also rightly points out that considerable progress has been made in recent years in developing understanding about the international dimensions of HRM. The same two points can aptly be made about HRM in general – as all the chapters in this book attest.

REFERENCES

Barney, B. (1991) 'Firm resources and sustained competitive advantage', *Journal of Management* 17(1): 99–120.

Beardwell, I. and Holden, L. (1994) *Human Resource Management: A New Contemporary Perspective*, London: Pitman.

Beaumont, P.B. (1993) *Human Resource Management: Key Concepts and Skills*, London: Sage.

Blyton, P. and Turnbull, P. (1992) 'HRM: debates, dilemmas and contradictions', in P. Blyton and P. Turnbull (eds) *Reassessing Human Resource Management*, London: Sage.

Bratton, J. and Gold, J. (1994) *Human Resource Management: Theory and Practice*, Basingstoke: Macmillan.

Clark, J. (1993a) 'Procedures and consistency versus flexibility and commitment in employee relations: a comment on Storey', *Human Resource Management Journal* 3(4).

—— (ed.) (1993b) *Human Resource Management and Technical Change*, London: Sage.

Donovan, Lord (1968) *Report of the Royal Commission on Trade Unions and Employers' Associations*, Cmnd. no. 3623, London: HMSO.

Dunn, S. (1992) 'Root metaphor in the old and new industrial relations', *British Journal of Industrial Relations* 28: 1–31.

Farrance, R. (1992) 'Foreword', in B. Towers (ed.) *The Handbook of Human Resource Management*, Oxford: Blackwell.

Flanders, A. (1954) *The Fawley Productivity Agreements*, London: Faber & Faber.

—— (1970) *Managerial Unions: The Theory and Reform of Industrial Relations*, London: Faber.

Gallie, D. and White, M. (1993) *Employee Commitment and the Skills Revolution: First Findings from the Employment in Britain Survey*, London: Policy Studies Institute.

Goss, D. (1994) *Principles of Human Resource Management*, London: Routledge.

Hall, R. (1992) 'The strategic analysis of intangible resources', *Strategic Management Journal* 13: 135–44.

Harrison, R. (1993) *Human Resource Management: Issues and Strategies*, Wokingham: Addison-Wesley.

Hart, T.J. (1993) 'Human resource management: time to exercise the militant tendency', *Employee Relations* 15(3): 29–36.

IPM (1994) *Managing People: The Changing Frontiers*, an IPM Consultative Document, London: IPM.

Kay, J. (1993) 'The structure of strategy', *Business Strategy Review* 4(2): 17–37.
Keenoy, T. (1990) 'HRM: a case of the wolf in sheep's clothing?', *Personnel Review*.
Keenoy, T. and Anthony, P. (1992) 'HRM: metaphor, meaning and morality', in P. Blyton and P. Turnbull (eds) *Reassessing Human Resource Management*, London: Sage.
Kochan, T.A., Katz, H.C. and McKersie, R.B. (1986) *The Transformation of American Industrial Relations*, New York: Basic Books.
Kravetz, D.J. (1988) *The Human Resource Revolution: Implementing Progressive Management Practices for Bottom-Line Success*, San Francisco: Jossey-Bass.
Legge, K. (1989) 'Human resource management: a critical analysis', in J. Storey (ed.) *New Perspectives in Human Resource Management*, London: Routledge.
—— (forthcoming) *From Personnel Management to HRM: Rhetoric or Reality?*, Basingstoke: Macmillan.
McCarthy, W.E.J. and Ellis, N.D. (1973) *Management by Agreement*, London: Hutchinson.
Mahoney, J.T. and Pandian, J.R.C. (1992) 'The resource-based view within the conversation of strategic management', *Strategic Management Journal* 13: 363–80.
Marginson, P., Armstrong, P., Edwards, P., Purcell, J. and Hubbard, N. (1994) 'The control of industrial relations in large companies: an initial analysis of the second company level industrial relations survey', *Warwick Papers in Industrial Relations*, No. 45, Coventry: University of Warwick.
Millward, N., Stevens, M., Smart, D. and Hawes, W.R. (1992) *Workplace Industrial Relations in Transition*, Aldershot: Dartmouth.
Noon, M. (1992) 'HRM: a map, model or theory?', in P. Blyton and P. Turnbull (eds) *Reassessing Human Resource Management*, London: Sage.
Parker, S.K., Mullarkey, S. and Johnson, P.R. (1994) 'Dimensions of performance effectiveness in high-involvement work organizations', *Human Resource Management Journal* 4(3).
Prahalad, C.K. and Hamel, G. (1990) 'The core competence of the corporation', *Harvard Business Review* May–June.
Quinn, J.B. (1992) *Intelligent Enterprise: A Knowledge and Service Based Paradigm for Industry*, New York: Free Press.
Sisson, K. (1989) 'Personnel management in perspective', in K. Sisson (ed.) *Personnel Management in Britain*, Oxford: Blackwell.
—— (1993) 'In search of HRM', *British Journal of Industrial Relations* 31(2): 201–10.
—— (1994) 'Personnel management: paradigms, practice and prospects', in K. Sisson (ed.) *Personnel Management: A Comprehensive Guide to Theory and Practice in Britain*, Oxford: Blackwell.
Stalk, G., Evans, P. and Shulman, L.E. (1993) 'Competing on capabilities: the new rules of corporate strategy', in R. Howard (ed.) *The Learning Imperative: Managing People for Continuous Innovation*, Cambridge, MA: Harvard University Press.
Storey, J. (1987) 'Developments in human resource management: an interim report', *Warwick Papers in Industrial Relations*, No. 17, Coventry: University of Warick.
—— (ed.) (1989) *New Perspectives in Human Resource Management*, London: Routledge.
—— (1992) *Developments in the Management of Human Resources*, Oxford: Blackwell.
Storey, J., Ackers, P., Bacon, N., Buchanan, D., Coates, D. and Preston, D. (1994)

Human Resource Management Practices in Leicestershire: A Trends Monitor, Loughborough: Training and Enterprise Council in Association with Loughborough University Business School.

Torrington, D. (1993) 'How dangerous is HRM?: A reply to Hart', *Employee Relations* 15(5): 40–53.

Towers, B. (ed.) (1992) *The Handbook of Human Resource Management*, Oxford: Blackwell.

Wood, S. (1993) 'High commitment work organisations', paper presented to the British Universities Industrial Relations Association conference, University of York, July.

Chapter 2

HRM: rhetoric, reality and hidden agendas

Karen Legge

INTRODUCTION

In an earlier collection, edited by John Storey (1989), I commented on how the vocabulary for managing the employment relationship had undergone a change: ' "Personnel management" is giving way to "human resource management" or better still to "strategic human resource management" ' (Legge 1989: 19). In the UK, early straws in the wind were the special issue of *Journal of Management Studies* in 1987, entitled 'Managerial Strategy and Industrial Relations' and in the series of papers by Pettigrew, Hendry and Sparrow (e.g. Hendry and Pettigrew 1986, 1987, 1988; Hendry, Pettigrew and Sparrow 1988; Sparrow and Pettigrew 1988; Pettigrew *et al.* 1988) not to mention, in January 1988, *Personnel Management* adopting a new subtitle: 'The Magazine for Human Resource Professionals'. By the end of the 1980s and beginning of the 1990s the floodgates were opened. Not only are job advertisements in the professional magazines and in the appointments pages of the quality press as likely to ask for a 'Human Resource Manager' as a 'Personnel Manager' (particularly for senior posts), but erstwhile 'personnel management' courses are being retitled and the content refocused, new courses in HRM are being set up (see, for example, the Open University's 'Human Resource Strategies' module on the MBA), guided by incumbents of newly established professorships in HRM, and a large literature is emerging exploring both the theoretical debates and empirical manifestations that are associated with this term (see, for example, Guest 1990, 1991; Keenoy 1990a, 1990b; Hendry and Pettigrew 1990; Storey 1992; Blyton and Turnbull 1992; Starkey and McKinlay 1993; Mabey *et al.* 1993; Beaumont 1993). Recent titles are interesting. They suggest not only that HRM is the new orthodoxy: *Strategy and the Human Resource* (Starkey and McKinlay 1993), *Strategic Human Resource Management* (Mabey *et al.* 1993), but that the subject is mature enough to be re-evaluated: *Reassessing Human Resource Management* (Blyton and Turnbull 1992). Reflecting and reinforcing this interest in HRM has been the emergence, in 1990, of two new academic journals, entitled respectively *Human Resource Management Journal* and *International Journal of Human Resource Management*, eclipsing the long-established specialist journal *Personnel Review*. The new language for managing the employment relationship seems to be here to stay – or is it?

This shift in language from 'personnel management' to 'HRM' in the 1980s in the US and, more markedly, in the UK, must be seen against a background of changes, experienced in both countries, in both product and labour markets, mediated by new technologies and a swing to right-wing political ideologies. A cluster of symbiotic buzz-words signify these changes and form part of the baggage of HRM: intensification of international competition, globalization, the Japanese Janus (threat/icon), cultures of excellence, information technology, knowledge working, high value added, JIT and TQM, customer care, the enterprise culture. The phrase that encapsulates the essence of this language is 'the search for competitive advantage'.

To what extent does the development of such language signify practices and behaviours radically different from traditional personnel management? In this chapter I will argue that although, undoubtedly, some changes, in some sectors of industry, have taken place in the management of the labour process and in employment relationships, this largely reflects a pragmatic response to opportunities and constraints in the present socio-politico-economic environment, rather than constituting expressions of a coherent new employment philosophy. The hyping of HRM as a 'new' approach does not square with the lack of distinctiveness of the 'soft' model from the traditional normative models of personnel management; with the conceptual confusion surrounding the 'soft' model's lack of internal consistency and with the potentially conflicting epistemological and practical assumptions implicit in the competing 'hard' and 'soft' models; or with the patchy and sometimes contradictory evidence on implementation. Rather, the use of the language of HRM to express new orthodoxies, it is suggested, owes much to the functions it serves for interested parties seeking legitimacy and survival in a changed and increasingly competitive world. As such, does the reality of HRM lie as much in the rhetoric and hype as in its practice?

THE 'HARD' AND 'SOFT' MODELS OF HRM

Before I explore the above issues, it is necessary to clarify and elaborate Storey's (1987) distinction between 'hard' and 'soft' normative models of HRM, the former reflecting a 'utilitarian instrumentalism' and the latter more reminiscent of 'developmental humanism' (Hendry and Pettigrew 1990).

The 'hard' model stresses HRM's focus on the crucial importance of the close integration of human resources policies, systems and activities with business strategy, on such HR systems being used 'to drive the strategic objectives of the organization', as Fombrun *et al.* (1984: 37) put it. This requires that personnel policies, systems and practices are not only logically consistent with and supportive of business objectives, but that they achieve this effect by their own coherence (Hendry and Pettigrew 1986). From this perspective the human resource, the object of formal manpower planning, can be just that – largely a factor of production, along with land and capital and an 'expense of doing business' rather than the 'only resource capable of turning inanimate factors of production into wealth' (Tyson and Fell 1986: 135). This perception of 'resource' appears to underlie Torrington and Hall's (1987: 16) model of HRM, with its reference to appropriate factors of production ('numbers' and 'skills') at the 'right' (implicitly the 'lowest possible') price. In their model, too, the human resources appear passive ('to be provided and deployed') rather than (to quote Tyson and Fell) 'the source of creative energy in any direction the organization dictates and fosters'. In essence, then, the 'hard' model emphasizes the 'quantitative, calculative and business strategic aspects of managing the headcount resource in as "rational" a way as for any other economic factor' (Storey 1987: 6). Its focus is ultimately human *resource management*.

In contrast, the soft 'developmental humanism' model, while still emphasizing the importance of integrating HR policies with business objectives, sees this as involving treating employees as valued assets, a source of competitive advantage through their commitment, adaptability and high quality (of skills, performance and so on) (see Guest 1987). Employees are proactive rather than passive inputs into productive processes; they are capable of 'development', worthy of 'trust' and 'collaboration', to be achieved through 'participation' and 'informed choice' (Beer and Spector 1985). The stress is therefore on generating commitment via 'communication, motivation and leadership' (Storey 1987: 6). If employees' commitment will yield 'better economic performance', it is also sought as a route to 'greater human development' (Walton 1985). In this model, then, the focus is on HR policies to deliver 'resourceful' humans (Morris and Burgoyne 1973) – on *human resource* management.

Clearly, these rather different emphases are not *necessarily* incompatible. Indeed, most of the normative statements of what constitutes HRM (see Legge 1989) contain elements of both the 'hard' and 'soft' models. Where an organization pursues a strategy of producing high value-added growth, rather than asset management (Cappelli and McKersie 1987: 443–4), treating (at least its core) employees as resourceful humans to be developed by humanistic policies makes good business sense. This is conveyed in the definitions of HRM of Hendry and Pettigrew (1986) and of Beer and Spector (1985), Walton (1985) and by Guest (1987). But what of the organization that, as part of its asset management, chooses to compete in a labour-intensive, high-volume, low-cost industry, generating profits through increasing market share by cost leadership? For such an organization the

HR policies that may be most appropriate to 'driving strategic objectives' are likely to involve treating employees as a variable input and as a cost to be minimized. This is a far cry from the employee relations philosophy embodied in the models of Beer and Spector (1985), Walton (1985) and Guest (1987).

HRM: WHAT IS THERE TO HYPE?

Why has a rhetoric of HRM been as widely touted in both academic and managerial circles? At first sight this appears surprising, as:

- The 'soft' models of HRM and the normative models of personnel management appear very similar, if with some shifts in emphasis.
- Both 'hard' and 'soft' models can be readily identified with various of the employee relations management styles identified in Purcell and Sisson's (1983) pre-HRM classificatory schema.
- The 'hard' and 'soft' models contain potentially conflicting epistemological assumptions and implications for action.
- The 'soft' model is riddled with internal contradictions.
- There is only patchy and sometimes contradictory evidence on HRM's strategic implementation.

To mix the epithets of a great transformational leader and of a great philosopher, this looks suspiciously like a case of 'old wine in new bottles' (Armstrong 1987) or of 'all that is solid melts into air'.

Old wine in new bottles?

The argument here is that if we compare the 'soft' normative model of HRM with the normative models of personnel management, we may be struck more by the similarities than the differences. As I have rehearsed the arguments elsewhere (Legge 1989), a brief summary may suffice. Both models emphasize the importance of integrating personnel/HRM policies and practices with organizational goals; both models vest personnel/HRM firmly in line management; both emphasize the importance of individuals fully developing their abilities for their own personal satisfaction to make their 'best contribution' to organizational success; both models identify placing the 'right' people into the 'right' jobs as an important means of integrating personnel/HRM practice with organizational goals, including individual development. The sharp contrasts which both Guest (1987) and Storey (1992) elicit in their comparisons of personnel management and human resource management stereotypes appear to owe much to an implicit comparison of the *descriptive* practice of personnel management with the *normative* aspirations of HRM, rather than comparing like with like – as both authors acknowledge.

Similarities are evident, too, when we compare the normative models of HRM with those of employee relations style associated with the enactment of personnel management (Purcell and Sisson 1983; Purcell and Gray 1986; Purcell 1987; Marchington and Parker 1990). The 'soft' 'developmental humanism' model of HRM is reminiscent of Fox's (1966, 1974) unitary frame of reference (with the emphasis on compatibility of stakeholders' interests, shared vision and culture) and of styles based on an individualistic, investment orientation to employees. There seems little difference, for example, between the Beer and Guest 'soft' models and 'sophisticated human relations'. In contrast, the 'hard' 'utilitarian-instrumentalism' model of HRM, emphasizing as it does the close integration of human resource policies, systems and activities with business strategy, could resemble *any* of the conventionally identified employee relations styles (except the opportunistic 'standard modern'), depending on the strategy chosen to achieve competitive advantage. And, in enacting either 'soft' or 'hard' models of HRM, the role of management points to Tyson and Fell's (1986) 'architect' model of personnel management.

But if HRM (at the level of normative modelling) is essentially the same wine in a new bottle, does the relabelling highlight new, previously dormant characteristics? As I have already argued (Legge 1989) the rhetoric, at least, of HRM seeks to secure new meanings and emphases as compared to the normative personnel management models. It presents HRM as aimed at managers and 'core' workers, rather than at the non-managerial workforce as a collective; it is vested in line management not as 'people managers', but as business managers responsible for coordinating and directing all resources in the business unit in pursuit of bottom-line results; most HRM models emphasize the management of the organization's culture as a central activity for senior management. The three differences in emphasis all point to HRM, in theory, being essentially a more central strategic management task than personnel management, in that it is experienced by managers, as the most valued company resource to be managed, it concerns them in the achievement of business goals and it expresses senior management's preferred organizational values.

From this perspective it is not surprising that Fowler (1987) identifies the real difference between HRM and personnel management in terms of language use: 'not what *it is* but who *is saying it*. In a nutshell HRM represents the discovery of personnel management by [strategically-oriented] chief executives' (ibid.: 3; added emphasis). This raises the question: what factors stimulated such a belated discovery, and if it was just the discovery of personnel management, why was a new language required? I return to this point later.

'All that is solid melts into air'

The conflicting epistemological assumptions and implications for action embedded in the 'hard' and the 'soft' model, give an air of insubstantiality to the HRM normative models generally. A short introduction to some of the tensions in the 'soft' model may be found in Legge (1989). Suffice it to say here that the normative models of HRM are problematic at two levels. First, at the surface level, there are the problems stemming from ambiguities in the conceptual language of both the 'hard' and 'soft' models (see Keenoy 1990a: 9–10). The key concept in the 'hard' model is that of integration. But 'integration' appears to have two meanings: integration or 'fit' with business strategy, and the integration or complementarity and consistency of 'mutuality' employment policies aimed at generating employee commitment, flexibility, quality and the like. The double meaning of integration has been referred to also as the 'external' and 'internal' fit of HRM (Baird and Meshoulam 1988). The epistemological – and potentially practical – problem is that while 'fit' with strategy would argue a *contingent* design of HRM policy, internal consistency – at least with the 'soft' human resource values associated with mutuality – would argue an *absolutist* approach to the design of employment policy.

Can this contradiction be reconciled without stretching to the limit the meaning of HRM as a distinct and 'different' approach to managing people at work? Indeed, should we consider HRM as a 'special variant' of personnel management, reflecting a particular discipline or ideology about how employees should be managed? Or should we regard it as a variety of different policies and practices designed to achieve the desired employee contribution, judged solely 'against criteria of coherence and appropriateness (a less rigid term than "fit")'? But has not personnel management, in theory, *always* tried to do this? And, in which case, would we be treating HRM as a 'perspective on personnel management, not personnel management itself'? (Hendry and Pettigrew 1990: 8–9; Guest 1989a).

The problems inherent in this double meaning of 'integration' find echoes in similar ambiguities – and resultant contradictions – in the conceptual scaffolding used to buttress the 'soft' model of 'developmental humanism'. 'Flexibility', for example, can express values of employee upskilling, development and initiative (as in functional flexibility of 'core' employees) or the numerical and financial flexibility to be achieved by treating labour, not as resourceful, but as a variable cost-to-be-minimized resource input (Atkinson 1984). Is the right quality of an organization's workforce, or its product or service, to be judged against absolutist standards ('zero-defect') or relative to business strategy? (Note the qualifications to 'customer care' in any of the 'Citizen's Charters' – particularly British Rail's.) What is the precise meaning of commitment? Does it refer to an individual's 'affective attachment and identification' (Coopey and Hartley 1991: 19) – that is, the relative strength of an individual's involvement with, and in, a particular organization? Or, following Becker (1960), Kiesler (1971) and Salancik (1977, 1982), does it refer to 'the binding of the individual to behavioural acts'? The implications for HRM strategy differ markedly depending on the conceptualization adopted. Implicit in the 'affective identification' conceptualization is the assumption that attitudes are prior to and influence behaviour, with the implication that appropriate strategies to achieve commitment are re-educative (development and training, persuasive communications, role-modelling, counselling) or replacement strategies (recruitment, selection, intensive socialization) designed to change beliefs (or to recruit compatible beliefs) in the assumption that appropriate behaviour will follow. In contrast, if the 'behavioural acts and consistencies' (Coopey and Hartley 1991: 19) conceptualization is adopted, the preferred strategy might be to induce behavioural change, but through minimal use of material rewards (to inhibit behavioural compliance rationalized through instrumentality) and to rely on the individuals involved developing attitudes consistent with, and hence reinforcing, their new desired behaviours. A danger here is that confusion in conceptualization may result in an inappropriate use of rewards and sanctions that serves only to induce behavioural compliance (the so-called 'personnel management' approach), rather than to change deep-seated existent attitudes (see Ogbonna 1992). In any case, what exactly is the employee to be committed to: job, career, profession, department, trade union, organization?

Leaving aside such ambiguities in the conceptual scaffolding of the 'soft' model of HRM, what of the potential tensions, not to say contradictions, *between* policies aimed at enhancing these different values? Some of these have been outlined in an earlier publication (Legge 1989) and will not be repeated here. Suffice to say that, leaving aside those between external and internal integration, major tensions may be discerned, both logically and empirically, between commitment and flexibility, between flexibility and quality, between individualism and teamwork, between strong culture and flexibility and even, somewhat paradoxically, between quality and commitment. In part, these contradictions may account for the evidence of the somewhat patchy implementation of these values central to the 'soft' HRM model. Let us turn, then, to evidence of the implementation of HRM.

O, brave new world?

Given the evidence we have from exemplar case studies (e.g., Wickens 1987) and the WIRS surveys (Millward and Stevens 1986; Millward *et al.* 1992), it has often been suggested that foreign-owned companies setting up greenfield site plants in the UK are the most fertile soil for fostering 'soft' model HRM initiatives (Guest 1989b: 47; Storey 1992). This raises two points: what is the empirical status of HRM if the evidence shows that, even in the most conducive environment, the implementation of HRM values is patchy and incomplete? Further, even if there is evidence of HRM strategy implementation in foreign-owned greenfield sites, what of implementation in 'mainstream', unionized, multi-site UK organizations (Storey 1992)? Are HRM values being pursued strategically, or are HRM associated 'fads' being adopted as the 'flavour of the month', pragmatically and opportunistically? Clearly there is not space here to undertake a systematic evaluation of all the evidence pertaining to the implementation of HRM, but if we assume for the moment that HRM initiatives *are* being implemented, it is worth looking at some of the moderating or disconfirming evidence.

Flexibility

Are numerical and functional flexibility being adopted as conscious strategies to drive business goals? What is going on out there?

The evidence we have derives from two sources: surveys (in particular, WIRS 1, 2, and 3, the Warwick company-level survey, that of ACAS, the Employers' Labour Use surveys (ELUS) and the Labour Force survey (LFS), the Labour Research Department survey (LRD) and the IMS panel study of large firms (Daniel and Millward 1983; Millward and Stevens 1986; Millward *et al.* 1992; Marginson *et al.* 1988; Hakim 1990; Casey 1991; Atkinson and Meager 1986)) and case studies (e.g., Newell 1991; Geary 1992; Storey 1992; Hendry 1993; Clark 1993; Preece 1993). By their nature, surveys tend to reveal continuity, while case studies highlight change (Legge 1988; Morris and Wood 1991). In summary, the evidence would broadly point to the following (see Legge, forthcoming, for more detail):

- That while there is some increase in the use of *numerical* flexibility (mainly through rises in part-time working and subcontracting) this reflects sectoral changes, or is often building on practices of long standing, and is undertaken pragmatically and opportunistically, rather than as part of a coherent strategy of adopting any flexible firm ideal type.

  The one exception to this rule is not foreign-owned, greenfield site plants, or even out-of-town supermarkets (which traditionally have recruited largely part-timers) but public sector services, primarily through their adoption of subcontracting via competitive tendering and contracting out. Here the Conservative government, as legislator and paymaster, has the power and the will to translate espoused policy into action to an extent unfeasible among private sector organizations. Rather than such policies being opportunistic and pragmatic, they comprise part of a coherent strategy promoting the primacy of the free market, buttressed by a rhetoric advocating reduction in public expenditure, the introduction of 'business principles' into the management of public sector services, in the interests of efficiency for the client as customer and taxpayer. Arguably, the 'hard' rather than the 'soft' HRM model is being pursued here.

- Such *functional* flexibility as has occurred is a modest and incremental change towards job enlargement and overlapping job descriptions and functions, but with little multi-skilling (see Elger 1991; Storey 1992; Clark 1993).

To elaborate on this point, while there is plenty of evidence (particularly from case studies that focus largely, but not exclusively, on the motor industry – Holloway 1987; Starkey and McKinlay 1989; Marsden *et al.* 1985; Smith 1988; Garrahan and Stewart 1992) to suggest a fairly widespread movement towards enhanced task flexibility, the degree of flexibility both sought for and achieved in the vast majority of cases appears more modest than celebratory accounts of multi-skilled team working or craft-based flexible specialization might imply. Elger's (1991: 51) analysis of IMS data, for example, indicated that 'the extent of the change appeared largely determined by managerial juggling of technical, organizational and training cost considerations' and the emphasis on flexibility was qualified by managerial awareness of the continuing advantages of retaining specialist skills. Storey (1992), on the basis of his case study research, comes to the same conclusion:

> Management may expressly want a limited number of experienced workers to remain dedicated to a particular task – swapping and changing round would be regarded as wasteful and even dangerous. Similarly the costs of achieving flexibility – whether incurred through training or through extra payment for skill attainment – may also deter.
>
> (Ibid.: 91)

- As a result, many managers' objectives were relatively modest. Elger (1991) cites such concerns as the reduction of 'porosity' and the intensification of effort, as much by cutting down pauses and waiting time as by increasing the pace of work directly.
- The intent of the changes, as a result, has rarely involved radical skill enhancement. More characteristic is the achievement of limited craft overlap, sometimes requiring retraining, or the small enlargement of a craftsman's job, but without 'violation of any group's "core trade"' (NEDO 1986: 45, cited in Elger 1991: 50). Some firms' attempted moves towards the 'super craftsman' or the spanning of core trade boundaries have come unstuck through union resistance (see, for example, Storey's (1992: 87) account of the problems in achieving mechanical-electrical/electronic teams of maintenance engineers at Bird's Eye Walls). Sometimes crossover between electrical and mechanical skills is seen as not attainable, for technical reasons, other than at the margins, although

flexibility between mechanical craftsmen may be sought, as at Ford at Dagenham and Halewood (Storey 1992: 91–5). Where multi-trade working for craftsmen is sought (as at Peugeot-Talbot), it may be for only a small elite, 'the brighter of the toolmakers', management not requiring more extensive upskilling, nor wanting to pay for it (Storey 1992: 96).

Widespread change, however, of a job enlargement rather than job enrichment nature, has taken place for semi-skilled operatives, particularly in the motor industries (Elger 1991). Typically, this has involved some relaxation and reorganization of job boundaries among operatives, involving inspection and routine maintenance, often capitalizing upon the self-diagnostic capabilities of modern equipment.

- The extent of the flexibilities sought and achieved depends much on prior technological choices and discussions about investment, head counts and labour costs. Thus while Plessey Naval Systems' 'Flexibility Agreement' with the (then) EETPU contains the rhetoric of total flexibility, in practice this pointed more to the use of managerial prerogative over labour deployment in a Tayloristic work system, for, as Storey (1992: 90) suggests, 'as the bulk of the work was becoming more standardized and deskilled the implied necessity for staff enhancement proved to be somewhat illusory'. Similarly Peugeot-Talbot's requirement for multi-skilled 'A+ grade' craftsmen was seen to vary across plants, depending on technological investment and sophistication (Storey 1992: 96). In contrast, much functional flexibility via job enlargement and labour intensification, coupled with management effort to enhance its control over resulting flexibility, has occurred almost by the back door as reductions in head count as part of cost-cutting exercises have resulted in smaller numbers of employees covering an unchanged – or enhanced – set of production requirements. Flexibilities achieved informally by headcount reductions may subsequently be formalized, as concessions are bargained from employees eager to attract investment as a guarantee against potential plant closure.

The equivocal messages of the research cited above are underlined by recent case studies of greenfield sites. At Pirelli's greenfield site at Aberdare, Clark (1993) found that in spite of a negotiated agreement that all non-managerial staff could be deployed totally flexibly between tasks and different areas of the factory (within the constraints of their level of training) in practice full flexibility was neither achieved nor sought. Furthermore, by mid-1990 there was some contractual retreat from the notion of full flexibility, by agreement to 'cap' the number of staff modules an employee could undertake and by prescribing 'primary' and 'secondary' areas of responsibility. Newell's (1991) findings at 'Brewco' and 'Grimco' point also to the limitations in the amount of flexibility sought and achieved. At 'Brewco', management did not seek flexibility between the eight manufacturing units, only job enlargement within each unit. At 'Brewco', process operators undertook minor engineering work, or assisted a multi-skilled tradesman with more major engineering work, while such tradesmen assisted operators to run the line as required. However, the feasibility of process operators undertaking engineering tasks, in an environment where post-commissioning training was perceived as inadequate, was called into question by an error in valve replacement that resulted in an explosion that halted the process for three days. Experience of functional flexibility, even on a greenfield site, can result in ambitious plans being tailored to the practicalities of operational constraints. Garrahan and Stewart's (1992) study of Nissan's greenfield site at Washington suggests that the much-vaunted common grading and teamworking, in practice, involved only limited flexibility, and focused primarily on switching among related work routines within the team. Instead, they argue, productivity is mobilized through stress via reductions in buffer stocks, the elimination of off-line inspection and rectification, and the maximization of line speeds, underpinned by 'a compelling ethos of competitive team working' (Elger 1991: 62).

If the degree of functional flexibility sought and achieved is more modest than the normative 'soft' model and celebratory accounts might imply, it is just about consistent with what might be implied by the 'hard' HRM model: functional flexibility is sought to the degree that it will optimize business objectives (including cost minimization). The reason it is not sought (or achieved) to the degree the messianic 'flexible specialization' manifestos might imply is precisely *because 'flexibility' (both numerical and functional) is often in contradiction to notions of commitment and quality.*

For example, with reference to numerical flexibility, Geary (1992) points out, in his case studies of three electronics factories, how management's preferred strategy was to minimize its dependence on temporary employees wherever possible, using them in the traditional fashion to meet production peaks and as a buffer against changes in demand. The disadvantages of temporaries were seen in terms of commitment, teamwork and quality. First, high levels of temporaries were considered to lead to animosity between temporaries and permanent employees, which impacted negatively on sought-for teamwork. Second, such conflicts as arose required time-consuming intervention from supervision, taking them away from more productive tasks. Third, there was concern among line managers that unsuitable candidates were recruited, resulting in a loss of product quality. Management was concerned, too, that temporaries were inhibited from 'speaking out' in suggesting improvements to the production process, or in wishing to rotate between tasks, or in expressing dissatisfactions, believing that it ruined their chances of gaining permanency. In essence, as Geary (1992: 267–8) points out, a policy of large-scale employment of temporaries, by creating a new status divide, paradoxically, resulted in a new rigidity, rather than flexibility. As a result 'when management themselves came to see employment flexibility as a rigidity, when it was defined as dysfunctional to their interests, they sought to establish more *rigid* and *stable* forms of employment'.

Similarly Clark (1993) argues that Pirelli's concerns about quality (and cost of training) were largely behind its abandonment of full functional flexibility at its greenfield site at Aberdare. The importance of specialist knowledge for producing good quality work, and of maintaining a personal relationship with industrial customers, was recognized as an inhibitor on full flexibility. Further, there was strong management and employee interest in the latter's 'ownership' of particular work areas, with the greater possibility of commitment to, and achievement of, high-quality work. Additionally, quality issues were raised by problems of skill acquisition and retention. Many employees were more suited to, and interested in, some areas of work rather than others. Skills were often forgotten if there was too great a gap between skills acquisition, putting them into practice and regularly reinforcing them by practice.

Commitment and quality

In the theory of HRM these concepts are seen as symbiotic. Employees, through careful selection and intensive socialization, become committed to the values that drive business strategy. Pre-eminently, *cultural* change programmes over the last decade have promoted the values of quality (of product or service) and the pre-eminence of the market-place, sanitized into customer sovereignty or 'customer awareness/customer care' (Keat and Abercrombie 1990; Fuller and Smith 1991; du Gay and Salaman 1992; Legge, forthcoming). (The other major values of cost effectiveness and flexibility – read 'labour intensification'? – are promoted largely through systems of bureaucratic control, although their rhetoric may enter cultural change programmes) (Legge, forthcoming).

The values of quality and customer awareness come together in the much-touted adoption of systems of JIT and TQM, principally in car and electronics assembly manufacturers (Caulkin, 1988, 1990; Ferguson 1989; Womack *et al.* 1990). JIT rests on the notion of both external and internal customers as production is pulled through the factory in response to the configuration of final market demand, with each stage in a linear production process acting as both salesman and customer to the next and preceding stages of production. Quality is an equal driver in the system, as any defective components, in the absence of stocks, would halt the system (and thereby create waste of time and labour, not to mention materials – in contradistinction to the rationale of a waste-eliminating 'lean' system) and internal as well as external customers have the right (obligation?) to accept only defect-free goods. In theory, JIT and TQM systems encapsulate the values of the 'soft' HRM model: of 'shop-floor empowerment, trust and mutual dependency' (Sewell and Wilkinson 1992: 98). In other words, job enrichment occurs as teams take responsibility for quality, routine maintenance and 'fine tuning of the production schedule', receiving resources necessary to achieve goals and continuously to increase their effectiveness within the domain of their delegated (hence empowered) responsibility. Hence, in theory, 'through giving employees more responsibility, they will become increasingly committed to the organization' (Sewell and Wilkinson 1992: 102).

However, case study material, drawn from 'Japanese-style' (and often owned) organizations – supposedly test-beds for 'soft' model HRM – paints a rather different picture (Delbridge and Turnbull 1992; Sewell and Wilkinson 1992; Garrahan and Stewart 1992). Sewell and Wilkinson (1992), in their description of the electronic 'traffic light' system of quality monitoring at Kays, show how the identification of individual members' performance in relation to the team in fact constitutes a 'panoptic gaze' (Foucault 1977) of shopfloor surveillance, that facilitates the social disciplining force of the team. Delbridge and Turnbull (1992) analysing the logic and empirical evidence about JIT and HRM systems, argue that, contrary to achieving effectiveness through shopfloor empowerment,

> The management of labour under a JIT regime is based squarely on compliance, blame and stress, producing an oppressive working environment accessible only to the young and/or the fit. Moreover the system is dependent on some variant of enterprise (or non-) unionism, and contingent on superimposing collaborative goals over the distinct interests of the workers. Conformity with the goals of the organization takes precedence over any form of worker emancipation or industrial democracy (management through compliance); apparently high-trust employment relations are contradicted by tight surveillance, strict discipline and quality control procedures which seek to identify (and often publicly humiliate) the 'guilty' workers (management through blame); and the extreme standardization of jobs, with no individual variation, belies any notion of worker empowerment or multi-skilling as work is continually intensified (management by stress).
>
> (Ibid.: 60)

The picture these studies present reveals a contradiction between the rhetoric of the 'soft' HRM model and the realities of the 'hard' model, and of tensions between the values embedded in the 'soft' model. For example, in Delbridge and Turnbull's and Sewell and Wilkinson's work the techniques used to achieve quality, involving as they do an oppressive and potentially humiliating form of surveillance, could be argued to undermine employee commitment to both task and organization. Rather than the individual being empowered through the support of the team, the team, through acting as a vehicle for peer group pressure, in the context of labour intensification, is primarily an instrument of management surveillance and control. Individualism is emphasized in order to hold responsible and accountable the smallest unit within the organization, but these individuals are expected to conform to the pressure of a peer group that in turn conforms to managerially imposed values. Rather than being a system to encourage creativity and resourcefulness in individuals, the necessity to eliminate all variation within production creates a work pattern, when combined with flexibility and job rotation, 'characterized by routine variety, such that while jobs are not homogenized, the abilities of the workers are' (Delbridge and Turnbull 1992: 67). This is consistent with the recruitment, selection, induction and appraisal policies that are designed to yield a homogeneous workforce of 'docile bodies', amenable to peer group pressure and unquestioning of management control as 'just another part of the job' (Sewell and Wilkinson 1992: 110; Townley 1989).

Tensions between quality and commitment (and the latter's different conceptualizations) have also been identified in Ogbonna and Wilkinson's (1988) and Ogbonna's (1992) studies of supermarkets. They point to the likelihood that, rather than employees showing an attitudinal commitment to the espoused managerial values of the 'customer is king', 'quality and service', 'service with a smile', 'resigned behavioural compliance' is all that may result when the 'customer care' rhetoric is at odds with their experience of work as involving rude customers, monotony and intense pressure for speed combined with managerial surveillance. While employees take pride in their ability to act out the espoused values of 'service with a smile' ('We are told to smile all the time . . . sometimes it's very hard . . . I succeed because I try to put on an act . . . my mother thinks I'm very good at it and that I should have been an actress'), Ogbonna and Wilkinson (1990) claim that rarely do such values appear internalized. On the contrary,

> the motives behind the behaviour patterns displayed on the shopfloor were almost invariably either instrumental ('this disarms the customer') or under threat of sanction ('I smile because I'm told to'; 'you have to be very careful and polite because they can report you to the manager'). The check-out operator's job is, of course, highly visible and not smiling or even 'putting on a false smile' can result in being 'called into a room for a chat' with the supervisor. Random visits by bogus shoppers and head office management reinforce the threat of sanctions for undesirable behaviour or expressing one's true feeling to difficult customers.
>
> (Ibid.: 13)

Following Salancik's (1977) conceptualization of commitment, not as 'affective identification', but as 'binding the individual to behavioural acts', this account raises two contradictory possibilities. First, does continuous acting finally internalize the values being enacted (i.e., generate an affective identification to them)? Storey (1992: 241) cites the case of supervisors at Whitbread who had 'caught the management bug' and who eagerly changed their name plates to 'first line managers'. In this case the answer might be 'yes', as the behaviour was voluntary. Or does the process of acting out a part at odds with perceptions of reality merely enhance cynicism and, paradoxically, a deeper rejection of the newly proselytized values? This may well be true for Ogbonna and Wilkinson's check-out operators, where old-fashioned compliance to management's directives, rather than any commitment to quality, might better represent the state of employee relations.

Some reflections on the evidence

Space constraints preclude further examination of evidence for the implementation of HRM. Certainly there are indicators of changing working and employee relations practices, but most fall far short of the long-term developmental philosophy of 'soft' models of HRM. What evidence we have is of a patchy implementation of practices designed to achieve flexibility, quality and commitment, often constrained by the contradictions inherent in enacting these slippery concepts, and motivated more by the opportunities afforded by high levels of unemployment and the constraints of recession and enhanced competition, than by any long-term strategic considerations. As far as the 'soft' model goes, the comment by Kirkpatrick *et al.* (1992: 146) about the relationship between HRM and decentralization rings true: 'Can the long-term aspects of HRM so central to its whole philosophy survive in a decentralized line environment dominated by short-term pressures? Our analysis suggests not.'

This is not to suggest that such HRM-associated practices that are implemented are done so with an unthinking pragmatism. The policies are adopted to drive business values and are modified in the light of changing business objectives and conditions. It is a *thinking* pragmatism. Insofar that any one model is being implemented, the evidence would suggest more support for the 'hard' rather than the 'soft' model. There is little evidence for the widespread implementation of the long-term developmental 'soft' model, *yet it is the latter that is supposed to be distinctly different from the stereotypes of personnel management practice, not the former.* Is what we are seeing, in reality, the implementation of the old-style 'standard modern' personnel management, asserting an opportunistic exercise of managerial prerogative, but dressed up in a 'soft' HRM rhetoric? Certainly the evidence of the realities of JIT and TQM systems might support this interpretation. Further, in relation to flexibility, as Clark (1993) points out, where enhanced flexibility has been sought, if not fully achieved, or modified in the light of experience, the rhetoric surrounding it, combined with other initiatives (such as single status, single unionism, more selective recruitment, enhanced commitment to training and communications) can have a climate-changing effect. Particularly on greenfield sites, employees may increasingly take it for granted that, within the limitation of their training and capabilities, they will be as flexible as operations – and business plans – require. Many small changes 'at the margin' may nevertheless add up to substantially increased managerial control over the workforce and, in conditions of high unemployment, a workforce prepared to show behavioural compliance to such changes. Are we then seeing 'macho management' dressed up as a benevolent paternalism – or perhaps we should say, as the samurai warrior? But the question remains as to why behaviours that seem similar to the opportunistic 'standard modern' practice of 'traditional' personnel management require a new and consumer-friendly packaging? To answer this, in an age of consumer sovereignty, we need to ask who are the 'buyers' and 'sellers' of HRM, and what exactly is the product?

STAKEHOLDERS OF HRM

I would identify three groups as being the major stakeholders of HRM: academics, line managers and, more ambiguously, personnel managers themselves. (As with any fad, consultants may also be included.) All three can act variously as 'buyers' or 'sellers' (as will be discussed below). What is being bought is higher education and research funding, work intensification and competitive survival and managerial legitimacy. In such transactions the rhetoric of HRM is the reality of the commerce.

Academics

It has already been pointed out in the introduction to this chapter that HRM has become big business in institutions of higher education, spawning new chairs, new journals and new degree courses, not to mention a burgeoning number of HRM texts, collections of critical papers and so forth. Why has this occurred? Without intending to be unduly critical, the following speculation, resting on little evidence save absorption of academic culture over the last two decades, may be offered. Interest in, and financial support for old style institutional industrial relations studies has been dealt a death blow, throughout the 1980s, by successive Conservative governments' programmes of restrictive legislation. These were designed to curb the unions, and by the fall in union membership and militancy occasioned by sectoral changes, combined with two major recessions and high residual unemployment. The 'new realism' of industrial relations, it might be said, is matched by a new realism among academic staff. The beauty of HRM is that it allows discipline-based research in organizational behaviour and industrial relations to achieve research funding for projects, which, while conceptually interesting from their disciplinary point of view, can be given the commercial gloss of relevancy demanded by most funding bodies. Hence, for example, the titles of three projects which I have recently refereed, that successfully achieved funding from the Leverhulme Trust: 'HRM in a Professional Partnership Firm'; 'HRM and JIT in Japanese Manufacturing Plants'; 'When Greenfield Sites Turn Brown: The Evolution of HRM'.

Further, most funding bodies these days require evidence that the researcher has some promise of access. How much easier to gain access to look at an interesting organizational experiment (JIT? TQM? Team-building?) in a greenfield site owned by an exemplar organization than to seek access to research an industrial relations' 'problem' in a brownfield, unionized manufacturing organization engaged in exercises of plant closure and downsizing? An added bonus for the hard-pressed academic is that, as far as teaching goes, discipline-based teaching material can be repackaged into a form more in tune with the interests and relevancy requirements of increasing numbers of self-funded business studies undergraduates and MBA students. Indeed, the academic's own marketability in consultancy arenas can be further enhanced by extending organizational behaviour interests into areas of business strategy via the wonderfully inclusive umbrella of researching organizational change – and we all know that *strategic* integration is integral to HRM. Indeed, the utility of HRM to academics, struggling to meet the various demands of government-inspired research selectivity exercises, student-led funding and the teaching quality audits (not to mention the miserly pay awards that might propel some towards consultancy activities) is such that if it did not exist, we would have had to invent it. Certainly, in our roles as writers and consultants, I sometimes think that we have!

But what of the product academics have sold? To the funding councils and MBA students, the relationship between HRM and competitive advantage, wrapped up in the paper of quality and the string of flexibility, has been the product on offer. But that is not all. Nostalgia for our discipline origins, not to mention the labour process hey-day of the later 1970s and early 1980s, made some academics more prone to seeing HRM as one or more variant on personnel management's old function as a mediator of the contradictions of capitalism, rather than as the key to competitive advantage. Additionally, academic careers can be forwarded by a critical dissection (or, in these post-modernist days, perhaps I should say 'deconstruction?') of new orthodoxies. Hence a large critical literature has emerged that has focused on deconstructing the contradictions and rhetoric of HRM (see, for example, Legge 1989; Keenoy 1990a, 1990b; Guest 1990; Delbridge and Turnbull 1992; Sewell and Wilkinson 1992; Keenoy and Anthony 1992). Nor should it be assumed that academics adopting a critical stance represent a different group from those successful with the research funding bodies. Quite the contrary: as even the most passing acquaintanceship with actor network theory would suggest, successful academics have to develop an entrepreneur's sensitivity to consumer taste and market niches (Callon 1986; Latour 1987) – and an awareness that research proposals will be reviewed by academics of a radical as well as managerialistic predisposition. Hence they know well that the secret of obtaining research funding (apart, of course, from proposing a methodologically sound study) is to construct a proposal that will enrol the very different potential actors in their support. Academics, in developing and marketing the product of HRM, have had to be as customer-oriented in their product development and marketing as any other competitor in the enterprise culture.

Line managers

Earlier in this chapter I referred to Fowler's (1987) comment that HRM represents the discovery of personnel management by chief executives. Recent research by Storey (1992), comprising a core of fifteen case studies of large, multi-site, multi-divisional, unionized private sector manufacturing and key public sector service organizations, to some extent, bears this out (see, especially, Chapter 7). In Smith and Nephew, Ford, Bradford Council and Peugeot, senior management were increasingly giving 'HRM issues' a high profile in their general deliberations on business strategy, while, at the same time, maintaining that personnel policy itself had been taken over by the executive (Storey 1992: 172, 204). Two quotations cited by Storey (1992) are indicative:

> Every month the Executive Committee of Ford of Europe (i.e., the vice president's board of directors) moves, in the afternoon, from the board room to a more relaxed atmosphere to discuss the 'people' issues of involvement, appraisal, employee relations, etc. . . . In total it adds up to a very considerable proportion of the board's time.
> (Director, Ford of Europe)
>
> The central personnel function is now basically a coordinating activity. The personnel director leads for us in the final negotiations with the trade unions. But on the major policy shifts in areas such as communications, man-management, quality, team-building, problem-solving teams and the like, these are matters for the executive.
> (Director of Manufacturing, Peugeot UK)
>
> (Ibid.: 203, 204)

Further, the major initiatives to achieve competitive advantage appear to have taken two forms: those rooted in operational management (such as JIT, TQM, MRP and CAM) and those in organizational design (not just the development of new team-based work systems, consequent on the operations management changes, but strategic initiatives such as decentralization to single business units and the 'de-layering' of swathes of middle management 'support' staff, redefined as 'overhead'). Both types of change are designed to serve similar, if potentially incompatible (as we have seen) ends: cost-cutting, quality enhancement, and increased flexibility and customer awareness, both inside and outside increasingly permeable organizational boundaries. Such changes, where undertaken strategically rather than pragmatically, are consistent with the 'hard' model of HRM. And, according to Storey, line managers are not only central to such initiatives but may use them to enhance their roles and career prospects.

The argument goes as follows. The reasons surrounding the vesting of HRM initiatives, rooted in operations management and organizational design, in line management, reflect the 'crucial fusion' of devolved management and the non-proceduralized approach of HRM, with its emphasis on direct communications with employees, participation and involvement, hands-on management style, on-the-job coaching and development.

On the one hand, the creation of cost and profit centres (SBUs) at lower levels within organizations has given the line management both a broader remit and enhanced legitimacy as the key contributor to the 'bottom line'. The old-style, technically oriented, reactive 'progress chasing' production manager, in many of Storey's case study organizations, has been transformed into a proactive (albeit technically oriented) 'manufacturing manager' 'actively seek[ing] to find new ways of reducing costs, or improving quality and of deploying labour, materials and plant in new configurations which will add value to the processes in hand' (Storey 1992: 198). In some cases this transformation has gone one step further, with the manufacturing manager evolving into a proactive, but commercially oriented 'business manager', aware of the total organization and its interface with the wider environment of customers and suppliers 'competent in SWOT analysis, planning, target setting, finance, marketing and the management of change' (Storey 1992: 198). In both cases, line managers increasingly have become generalists, directing a team of support functions, towards the achievement of business goals. As Storey (1992: 202) quotes the director of manufacturing at Peugeot-Talbot, 'The manufacturing manager is king'.

This transformation, in itself, has given line management the responsibility for a wider matrix of employees and for the management of change. This in turn brings human resource issues higher up the line manager's agenda, as the new initiatives in operations management and organizational design, already referred to, have implications for a whole host of HRM issues such as recruitment, selection, training and achieving attitudes and behaviours that deliver the required quality and flexibility. Further, as Storey (1992) points out, line management is both the object of HRM-inspired initiatives in such areas as well as the designer and deliverer of its repercussions to the shop floor.

The upshot of all this is that line management has a vested interest in the rhetoric of HRM. If the line manager is to demonstrate that she has graduated from being an old-style reactive 'mere' production manager, to a new proactive manufacturing (or better still 'business') manager, she must demonstrate that she is responsible for coordinating and directing *all* resources in the business unit, including people, in pursuit of 'bottom-line' results. The language of HRM is a most appropriate vehicle to demonstrate optimum resource utilization in pursuit of the bottom-line – yet with an acceptable face. Again, to quote one of Storey's (1992) departmental managers, in a process company, in response to a question on changes in his role:

> 'Oh [it has changed] quite significantly. The old progress chasing game has gone, I am much clearer about what my contribution is. I look outwards to the customer but I also get involved with the motivation of teams. In a sense what is new is that employee relations now have to be seen to make sense in a market context.'
>
> (Ibid.: 201)

In these few lines the rhetoric of commitment, customer care and strategic integration trip neatly off the tongue.

Munro and Kernan's (forthcoming) in-depth case study research on rhetorics employed by middle-ranking line managers is consistent with this view. Embedded in a broader, sophisticated argument about governmentality effects and surveillance, they argue that middle managers are enrolling 'quality', that cornerstone of the 'soft' HRM model, as an expertise and rhetoric to protect themselves and their status as their traditional position is eroded via de-layering, outsourcing, and so on. Munro and Kernan argue that professionalizing over quality enables managers to represent themselves as the 'voice of the customer' and hence as representing the 'real' bottom-line interests of the company in a competitive environment. Further, surveillance paths can be constructed around concepts of quality rather than standard costs, and

> if control over the lines of surveillance is likely to remain in the hands of middle managers, as the holders of the expertise of quality, then the result is likely to create a new province ruled by middle managers and radiate a governmentality effect over employees, through talk of 'empowerment' and the like . . . re-representing the customer affirms the governing rights of middle managers.
>
> (Ibid.)

Personnel managers

Traditionally, personnel managers have suffered from problems of achieving credibility, recognition and status in the eyes of other management groups and employees (Watson 1977; Legge 1978; Thurley 1981). This has resulted in a willingness to adopt different roles and rhetorics to suit the contingencies of the times and to exploit possible bases of power (Legge 1978; Tyson and Fell 1986; Torrington 1989). The post-war consensus on full employment, combined with an upsurge in union membership and militancy, and the development of supportive employment law in the 1970s, gave rise to a valuable but ambiguous source of legitimacy for personnel managers, as mediators, not to say shock absorbers of trades union pressure, and policemen of line managers' propensity to *ad hoc* decision-making that, in the multi-site organizations, might upset the apple cart. This role has been variously referred to as the 'contracts manager' (Tyson and Fell 1986), the 'consensus negotiator' (Torrington 1989) and, more recently, 'the regulator' (Storey 1992). That this was an ambiguous source of legitimacy stemmed from two interrelated factors. First, such personnel managers were perceived as having a symbiotic relationship with the unions – the 'enemy within', and as such were not truly part of the management team (Batstone 1980). Second, they were regarded as performing a gate-keeping function, a barrier between trade unions and access to strategic management considerations – with the result that such personnel specialists themselves became segmented into an isolated department and excluded from strategic management decisions (Marginson *et al.* 1988).

However, 'managing the unions' as a source of even an ambiguous legitimacy, has become increasingly vulnerable following two major recessions, persistently high levels of residual unemployment, falling union membership and restrictive labour legislation. By the late 1980s the most perspicacious personnel managers realized the need for a new rhetoric to assert credibility, one that would perform the dual, if paradoxical, function of highlighting a new specialist contribution, while simultaneously locating themselves unequivocally within the management team. At first glance, HRM hardly fits the bill – after all, a key emphasis is the vesting of people management in line management, of 'having to "give HRM away" in order to maintain a presence' (Storey 1992: 186). But skilful interweaving of the rhetorics of the 'hard' and 'soft' models maintains the paradox. While the 'hard' model uses the rhetoric of strategic integration, 'the subsumption of personnel under the prevailing (usually management accounting) business logics of the senior team', the latter 'emphasizes the unique qualities of the human resource and thus seeks to unlock its potential through the use of an altogether distinctive set of techniques' (ibid.: 169). HRM, in other words, has the potential for personnel managers to have their cake and eat it. The subtle shifts of emphasis in backgrounding or highlighting the 'team member' or 'distinctive contribution' aspects of HRM are conveyed in two attributions of personnel directors' special qualities (made by line colleagues) cited by Storey:

> 'DT [the personnel and corporate affairs director] is very much a team-player. As for a "distinctive personnel contribution", as you put it, I don't know. In fact, I'm not really sure what these personnel people actually do. But if we didn't have [DT] we would certainly miss him, well I would. . . . We've got a very good manpower planning system in place now, we used to have chronic overmanning – that's now a thing of the past. We have cut the number of locations by half and that was achieved without a single dispute; our people are now fully flexible.'
>
> 'Chris has brought a breath of fresh air to the board. Our "analysis" of people-management issues in the past was clouded by our obsession with relative remuneration packages and the like. We now have a much wider vista; talk of retention, development and career planning has become more meaningful and more serious. Oddly our people-management policies now seem to make far more business sense. The board feels more in control of the massive culture change which we are undoubtedly undergoing.'
>
> (Ibid.: 182–3)

Shifts of emphasis there may be, but integration with business strategy is a common theme in both discourses.

Storey (1992), with reference to his sample of 'mainstream' UK organizations, is the first to admit that a fully fledged adoption of HRM rhetoric and values was evident in only two of his fifteen core cases (although more widespread in his panel firms). A continuing commitment to the 'regulator' role was evident among a hard core that could dismiss HRM initiatives as a passing fad. As Storey (1992: 187) points out, this might be accounted for by the nature of the organizations involved: large, unionized and proceduralized. Nevertheless, even in this context, the writing is on the wall. Storey suggests that at least half the personnel managers and directors had aspirations to move towards the HRM changemaker role.

CONCLUSION

The argument of this chapter is *not* that no new initiatives, that might loosely be labelled HRM, are taking place in UK organizations. Clearly research into the motor manufacturing and electronic assembly, not to mention public sector organizations shows that the times they are a-changing. The argument here is that the changes observed are thinking but pragmatic responses to the opportunities and constraints afforded by heightened competition, recession and the socio-politico-economic changes embodied in notions of the enterprise culture. Many of the initiatives undertaken appear to be 'old wine in new bottles' and/or to be not inconsistent with the opportunistic standard modern style of employee relations traditional in UK industry in the 1970s and earlier. Why, then, the hyping of

HRM as something new in theory and practice 'different' from the theories and practice of personnel management?

My argument has been that the rhetoric of HRM as something new and consistent with the demands of the enterprise culture has served the purposes of three groups seeking legitimacy in a hostile climate. It has been in their interests to 'talk-up' HRM as a coherent new strategy of employee relations that paves the ways to achieving competitive advantage. The 'brilliant ambiguity' (Keenoy 1990b) of the language of HRM has facilitated their endeavours.

But herein lies a danger. Without doubt, the language of HRM – and its close cousin, the language of excellence – is that of managerial triumphalism. Managers create missions for their organizations, they change their cultures, they act as transformational leaders that gain the commitment of employees to the values of quality, service, customer sovereignty, that is translated into bottom-line success. In the interests of achieving these values, employees must take responsibility, become empowered – as also are the supreme arbiters, the customers.

So, what do we have? The rhetoric, if not practice, asserts that we are *all* managers: the employee becomes 'responsibly autonomous' to manage the operational variances in JIT and TQM systems; in service sector industries, 'customers are made to function in the role of management' (du Gay and Salaman 1992: 621) by their perceived needs and demands being used to control employee behaviour; in higher educational institutions, there is much talk of student-managed learning. Now, at one level, we might recognize this as a rhetoric masking the intensification and commodification of labour (Keenoy and Anthony 1992), but at another level it raises the question of who are the 'real' managers? If we are all managers now, why is it that those holding conventional management positions lay claim to power, privileges and material returns far in excess of those received by these new management stakeholders in the organization?

Paradoxically, then, a rhetoric adopted to enhance managerial legitimacy might prove the thin end of the wedge for at least some of its advocates.

REFERENCES

Armstrong, M. (1987) 'Human resource management: a case of the emperor's new clothes?', *Personnel Management* 19(8): 30–5.

Atkinson, J. (1981) 'Manpower strategies for flexible organisations', *Personnel Management* 16(8): 28–31.

Atkinson, J. and Meager, N. (1986) *New Forms of Work Organisation*, IMS Report No. 121, Brighton: Institute of Manpower Studies.

Baird, L. and Meshoulam, I. (1988) 'Managing the two fits of strategic human resource management', *Academy of Management Review* 13(1): 116–28.

Batstone, E. (1980) 'What have personnel managers done for industrial relations?', *Personnel Management* 12(6): 36–9.

Beaumont, P. (1993) *Human Resource Management*, London: Sage.
Becker, H.S. (1960) 'Notes on the concept of commitment', *American Journal of Sociology* 66: 289–96.
Beer, M. and Spector, B. (1985) 'Corporate wide transformations in human resource management', in R.E. Walton and P.R. Lawrence (eds), *Human Resource Management Trends and Challenges*, Boston, MA: Harvard Business School Press.
Blyton, P. and Turnbull, P. (eds) (1992) *Reassessing Human Resource Management*, London: Sage.
Callon, M. (1986) 'The sociology of an actor network', in M. Callon, J. Law and A. Rip (eds) *Mapping the Dynamics of Science and Technology*, Basingstoke: Macmillan.
Cappelli, P. and McKersie, R.B. (1987) 'Management strategy and the redesign of work', *Journal of Management Studies* 24(5): 441–62.
Casey, B. (1991) 'Survey evidence on trends in "non-standard" employment', in A. Pollert (ed.) *Farewell to Flexibility?*, Oxford: Blackwell.
Caulkin, S. (1988) 'Britain's best factories', *Management Today* September: 58–80.
—— (1990) 'Britain's best factories', *Management Today* November: 60–89.
Clark, J. (1993) 'Personnel management, full flexibility and self-supervision in an automated factory', in J. Clark (ed.) *Human Resource Management and Technical Change*, London: Sage.
Coopey, J. and Hartley, J. (1991) 'Reconsidering the case for organizational commitment', *Human Resource Management Journal* 1(3): 18–32.
Daniel, W.W. and Millward, N. (1983) *Workplace Industrial Relations in Britain. The DE/PSI/SSRC Survey*, London: Heinemann.
Delbridge, R. and Turnbull, P. (1992) 'Human resource maximisation: The management of labour under just-in-time manufacturing systems', in P. Blyton and P. Turnbull (eds) *Reassessing Human Resource Management*, London: Sage.
du Gay, P. and Salaman, G. (1992) 'The cult(ure) of the customer', *Journal of Management Studies* 29(5): 615–33.
Elger, T. (1991) 'Task flexibility and the intensification of labour in UK manufacturing in the 1980s', in A. Pollert (ed.) *Farewell to Flexibility*, Oxford: Blackwell.
Ferguson, A. (1989) 'Britain's best factories', *Management Today* November 68–96.
Fombrun, C., Tichy, N.M. and Devanna, M.A. (1984) *Strategic Human Resource Management*, New York: Wiley.
Foucault, M. (1977) *Discipline and Punish: The Birth of the Prison*, London: Allen Lane.
Fowler, A. (1987) 'When chief executives discover HRM', *Personnel Management* 19(1): 3.
Fox, A. (1966) *Industrial Sociology and Industrial Relations*, Research Paper 3, Royal Commission on Trade Unions and Employers' Associations, London: HMSO.
—— (1974) *Beyond Contract Work: Trust and Power Relations*, London: Faber & Faber.
Fuller, L. and Smith, C. (1991) 'Consumers' report: management by customers in a changing economy', *Work, Employment and Society* 5(1): 1–16.
Garrahan, P. and Stewart, P. (1992) *The Nissan Enigma*, London: Mansell.
Geary, J. (1992) 'Employment flexibility and human resource management', *Work, Employment and Society* 6(2): 251–70.
Guest, D.E. (1987) 'Human resource management and industrial relations', *Journal of Management Studies* 24(5): 503–21.

—— (1989a) 'Personnel and HRM: can you tell the difference?', *Personnel Management* 21(1): 48–51.
—— (1989b) 'Human resource management: its implications for industrial relations and trade unions', in J. Storey (ed.) *New Perspectives on Human Resource Management*, London: Routledge.
—— (1990) 'Human resource management and the American dream', *Journal of Management Studies* 27(4): 378–97.
—— (1991) 'Personnel management: the end of orthodoxy?', *British Journal of Industrial Relations* 29(2): 149–76.
Hakim, C. (1990) 'Core and periphery in employers' workforce strategies: evidence from the 1987 ELUS survey', *Work, Employment and Society* 4(2): 157–88.
Hendry, C. (1993) 'Ten years of change at Hardy Spicer: personnel leadership in technical and human resource change', in J. Clark (ed.) *Human Resource Management and Technical Change*, London: Sage.
Hendry, C. and Pettigrew, A. (1986) 'The practice of strategic human resource management', *Personnel Review* 15(5): 3–8.
—— and —— (1987) 'Banking on HRM to respond to change', *Personnel Management* 19(11): 29–32.
—— and —— (1988) 'Multiskilling in the round', *Personnel Management* 20(4): 36–43.
—— and —— (1990) 'Human resource management: an agenda for the 1990s', *International Journal of Human Resource Management* 1(1): 17–44.
Hendry, C., Pettigrew, A. and Sparrow, P. (1988) 'Changing patterns of human resource management', *Personnel Management* 20(11): 37–41.
Holloway, J. (1987) 'The red rose of Nissan', *Capital and Class* 32: 142–64.
Hyman, R. (1989) 'Why industrial relations?' in R. Hyman (ed.) *The Political Economy of Industrial Relations. Theory and Practice in a Cold Climate*, Basingstoke: Macmillan.
Keat, R. and Abercrombie, N. (eds) (1990) *Enterprise Culture*, London: Routledge.
Keenoy, T. (1990a) 'HRM: a case of the wolf in sheep's clothing', *Personnel Review* 19(2): 3–9.
—— (1990b) 'HRM: rhetoric, reality and contradiction', *International Journal of Human Resource Management* 1(3): 363–84.
Keenoy, T. and Anthony, P. (1992) 'HRM: metaphor, meaning and morality', in P. Blyton and P. Turnbull (eds) *Reassessing Human Resource Management*, London: Sage.
Kiesler, C.A. (1971) *The Psychology of Commitment: Experiments Linking Behavior to Belief*, New York: Academic Press.
Kirkpatrick, I., Davies, A. and Oliver, N. (1992) 'Decentralization: friend or foe of HRM?' in P. Blyton and P. Turnbull (eds) *Reassessing Human Resource Management*, London: Sage.
Latour, B. (1987) *Science in Action*, Milton Keynes: Open University.
Legge, K. (1978) *Power, Innovation and Problem-Solving in Personnel Management*, London: McGraw-Hill.
—— (1988) 'Personnel management in recession and recovery: a comparative analysis of what the surveys say', *Personnel Review* 17(2) (monograph issue).
—— (1989) 'Human resource management – a critical analysis', in J. Storey (ed.) *New Perspectives on Human Resource Management*, London: Routledge.
—— (forthcoming) *Deconstructing HRM*, Basingstoke: Macmillan.
Marchington, M. and Parker, P. (1990) *Changing Patterns of Employee Relations*, Brighton: Harvester Wheatsheaf.
Marginson, P., Edwards, P.K., Martin, R., Purcell, J. and Sisson, K. (1988)

Beyond the Workplace: Managing Industrial Relations in Multi-Plant Enterprises, Oxford: Blackwell.

Marsden, D., Morris, T., Willman, P. and Wood, S. (1985) *The Car Industry: Labour Relations and Industrial Adjustment*, London: Tavistock.

Millward, N. and Stevens, M. (1986) *British Workplace Industrial Relations – 1980–1984*, the DE/ESRC/PS1/ACAS survey, London: Gower.

Millward, N., Stevens, M., Smart, D. and Hawes, W.R. (1992) *Workplace Industrial Relations in Transition*, the ED/ESRC/PS1/ACAS survey, Aldershot: Dartmouth.

Morris, J. and Burgoyne, J.G. (1973) *Developing Resourceful Managers*, London: Institute of Personnel Management.

Morris, T. and Wood, S. (1991) 'Testing the survey method: continuity and change in British industrial relations', *Work, Employment and Society* 5(2): 259–82.

Munro, R. and Kernan, D. (forthcoming) 'Governing the new province of quality: from representations of economic reality to re-presenting the customer'.

NEDO (1986) *Changing Working Patterns: How Companies Achieve Flexibility to Meet New Needs*, London: NEDO.

Newell, H.J. (1991) 'Field of dreams: evidence of "new" employee relations in greenfield sites', D.Phil. dissertation, University of Oxford.

Ogbonna, E. (1992) 'Organization culture and HRM: dilemmas and contradictions', in P. Blyton and P. Turnbull (eds) *Reassessing Human Resource Management*, London: Sage.

Ogbonna, E. and Wilkinson, B. (1990) 'Corporate strategy and corporate culture: the management of change in the UK supermarket industry', *Personnel Review* 19(4): 9–15.

Pettigrew, A., Sparrow, P. and Hendry, C. (1988) 'The forces that trigger training', *Personnel Management* 20(12): 28–32.

Preece, D.A. (1993) 'Personnel specialists and human resource management at greenfield sites', in J. Clark (ed.) *Human Resource Management and Technical Change*, London: Sage.

Purcell, J. (1987) 'Mapping management style in employee relations', *Journal of Management Studies* 24(5): 533–48.

Purcell, J. and Gray, A. (1986) 'Corporate personnel departments and the management of industrial relations: two case studies in ambiguity', *Journal of Management Studies* 23(2): 205–23.

Purcell, J. and Sisson, K. (1983) 'Strategies and practice in the management of industrial relations', in G.S. Bain (ed.) *Industrial Relations in Britain*, Oxford: Blackwell.

Salancik, G.R. (1977) 'Commitment and control of organizational behavior and beliefs', in B.M. Staw and G.R. Salancik (eds) *New Directions in Organizational Behaviour*, Chicago, IL: St Clair Press.

—— (1982) 'Commitment is too easy', in M.L. Tushman and W.L. Moore (eds) *Readings in the Management of Innovation*, London: Pitman.

Sewell, G. and Wilkinson, B. (1992) 'Empowerment or emasculation? Shopfloor surveillance in a total quality organization', in P. Blyton and P. Turnbull (eds) *Reassessing Human Resource Management*, London: Sage.

Smith, D. (1988) 'The Japanese example in south west Birmingham', *Industrial Relations Journal* 19(1): 41–50.

Sparrow, P. and Pettigrew, A. (1988) 'Strategic human resource management in the computer supplier industry', *Journal of Occupational Psychology* 61: 25–42.

Starkey, K. and McKinlay, A. (1989) 'Beyond Fordism? Strategic choice and Labour relations in Ford UK', *Industrial Relations Journal* 20, summer: 93–100.

—— and —— (1993) *Strategy and the Human Resource*, Oxford: Blackwell.
Storey, J. (1987) 'Developments in the management of human resources: an interim report', *Warwick Papers in Industrial Relations*, No. 17, IRRU, School of Industrial and Business Studies, University of Warwick, November.
—— (ed.) (1989) *New Perspectives on Human Resource Management*, London: Routledge.
—— (1992) *Developments in the Management of Human Resources*, Oxford: Blackwell.
Thurley, K. (1981) 'Personnel management in the UK: a case for urgent treatment', *Personnel Management* 13(8): 24–9.
Torrington, D. (1989) 'Human resource management and the personnel function', in J. Storey (ed.) *New Perspectives on Human Resource Management*, London: Routledge.
Torrington, D. and Hall, L. (1987) *Personnel Management, A New Approach*, London: Prentice-Hall.
Townley, B. (1989) 'Selection and appraisals: reconstituting "social relations"?', in J. Storey (ed.) *New Perspectives on Human Resource Management*, London: Routledge.
Tyson, S. and Fell, A. (1986) *Evaluating the Personnel Function*, London: Hutchinson.
Walton, R.E. (1985) 'Toward a strategy of eliciting employee commitment based on policies of mutuality', in R.E. Walton and P.R. Lawrence (eds) *Human Resource Management, Trends and Challenges*, Boston, MA: Harvard Business School Press.
Watson, T.J. (1977) *The Personnel Managers: A Study in the Sociology of Work and Industry*, London: Routledge & Kegan Paul.
Wickens, P. (1987) *The Road to Nissan*, London: Macmillan.
Womack, J.P., Jones, D.T. and Roos, D. (1900) *The Machine that Changed the World*, New York: Rawson Associates.

Part II

Strategic issues

Chapter 3

Corporate strategy and its link with human resource management strategy

John Purcell

All definitions of human resource management agree on one point: that there must be a link between a firm's strategy and the deployment and utilization of the human resource. Quite what that link is, where it is realized and how it is developed, are separate matters. It may be no more than a self-evident truth. The type of market a firm chooses to enter will deeply influence the design of jobs, the skills required, the number of people to be engaged, and so on. In this sense, policies toward people will ultimately derive from a wider set of strategic decisions taken earlier. The assumption behind the term 'strategic human resource management', however, is more ordered and rational, evoking a world of deliberate policy-making where decisions on the long-term direction of the firm and its mix of activities are taken with due cognisance of personnel issues, and where choices within human resource management flow, in a deliberate way, from the wider strategic requirements and decisions of the firm.

It is relatively easy, but ultimately highly deceptive, to generate normative statements of what ought to happen and the way in which policies toward people at work should be constructed to maximize productivity, performance and ultimately profits. Best practice is garnered from around the world and honed into policy prescriptions without regard to the context in which the firm is set, or to the capability of the organization to implement or respond to the 'new' ideas. Students learning about personnel management in this way are ill-equipped to deal with uncertainty, complexity and intra-organizational conflicts which provide the setting for managerial decision-making (Amit and Schoemaker 1993). All three of these features of decision-taking are made more complex in large, multi-level and multi-product firms. It is here that the distinction between corporate strategy and business strategies becomes critical.

The central focus of this chapter is with the big decisions taken in the corporate office, and the way these impact on human resource management. The chapter starts by drawing the crucial distinction between corporate and business strategies. It goes on to review some of the recent evidence on the extent to which corporate decisions and strategies are linked to human resource management activities, both directly and indirectly. In so doing, it utilizes the model of three levels of strategy developed in *New Perspectives on Human Resource Management* (Purcell 1989). It then seeks to provide a number of explanations for the general hypothesis that as firms grow and diversify, it becomes harder to maintain a deliberate link between corporate strategy and human resource management. Explanations on offer range from the image of the corporate personnel function, the requirement for representation in the corridors of power and the boardroom, to shifts in the logic and form of corporate control and the restricted view of the market-positioning view of strategy. The concluding section is more optimistic, utilizing the emerging ideas of the resource view of the firm. This posits that

> when the external environment is in a state of flux, the firm's own resources and capabilities may be a much more stable basis on which to define its identity. Hence, a definition of a business in terms of what it is capable of doing may offer a more durable basis for strategy than a definition based upon the needs (e.g. markets) which the business seeks to satisfy.
>
> (Grant 1991a: 116)

This places value on intangible assets such as people, culture, style and the way organizations develop routines which order resources and convert them into capabilities. This will allow us to return to our normative starting point by suggesting not that there ought to be a link between strategy and human resource, but that the most pressing human resource issue facing the firm is to identify its unique (human) resource capabilities.

THE DISTINCTION BETWEEN CORPORATE AND BUSINESS STRATEGIES

One of the most distinctive features of the British economy is the dominance of large, multi-product firms, usually organized along multi-divisional lines. Channon (1982) made a crucial distinction between types of firm based on degrees of relatedness of the business portfolio held by the enterprise. In 1950 around one-third of the largest 200 firms in the UK in the private sector were single businesses where not less than 95 per cent of sales came from one basic business. Typical here in modern Britain would be the major retailers who have stuck to their core business. In 1950 a further two-fifths of firms were classified as 'dominant businesses', where less than 95 per cent but more than 70 per cent of sales came from one major business. A further fifth of firms were 'related businesses' – firms with sales distributed among a series of related businesses such that none accounted for 70 per cent of sales. An example of such an enterprise might be a food company with operating subsidiaries covering frozen, chilled, baked, fresh picked, snacks and so on but also with packaging and distribution companies. Relatedness here can be defined in terms of commodities in supply, or a linked supply chain process, or in terms of the ultimate market. Finally, in 1950 there was a miniscule number of 'conglomerate businesses' where sales were distributed among a series of unrelated businesses, such that none accounted for 70 per cent of sales. Channon recorded shifts in structure up to 1980. By then the single business category had declined to less than 10 per cent; a quarter of firms were 'dominants', but 'relateds' and conglomerates had both expanded substantially. In other words, most large British firms changed in the post-war period by diversifying beyond their original core business.

A number of highly significant features of modern organizations and organizational analysis flow from this. These range from means used to diversify (by acquisition or organic development); the changing nature of the relationship between parts of the business and the head or corporate office; the development of intermediary structures commonly called divisions (and thus the multi-divisional, or M-form company), and the emergence of a distinction between corporate and business policy. Much of this comes to be subsumed in the strategy–structure debate, which has flowed from the famous distinction first made by Chandler (1962) that the structure of the firm follows or flows from its strategy. A strategy to diversify, especially by acquisition, has profound implications for the structuring of the enterprise, if only because a decision has to be made on how to handle the post-acquisition phase: to integrate the two organizations, or to keep them separate?

More recent data than Channon's, quoted by Whittington (1993: 91) shows that by 1990 among the top 100 companies, none were single businesses, while just under 20 per cent were conglomerates, or what Whittington terms more accurately as 'unrelated diversifiers', and just over 40 per cent were 'related diversifiers'. The 1992 company-level industrial relations survey (Marginson, Armstrong, Edwards and Purcell 1993) provides a different, but not inconsistent picture, based on a representative sample of firms in the private sector with 1,000 or more employees in the UK. At the time of the survey there were 978 such companies, of which all but three had employees spread over more than one site. The survey covered 176 of these multi-site companies and was weighted to be representative of the population of large firms. In this survey just under half of the companies claimed to be single businesses, 16 per cent were 'dominants', 24 per cent 'relateds' and 12 per cent 'unrelated'. Part explanation for the difference with the Channon data is the wider coverage of firms – near enough the top 1,000 in employment terms. These also included recently privatized firms, most of which had been single businesses since they were prohibited, while in public ownership, from diversifying. It was the smaller firms in the sample which were most likely to be single-industry focused. Many of these were 'domestic' firms – that is, they had no significant levels of employment outside the UK. Diversification is thus often associated with the development of multi-nationality, itself a course of action with profound implications for the role of the centre, and for human resource management.

The Industrial Relations Research Unit at Warwick University looked at European large firms to see how many would fall within the criteria for a European Works Council (headquarters in the EC, 1,000 or more employees and 100 plus in two or more member states). This showed that 332 of the 880 companies that meet these criteria have their headquarters in the UK – a much higher proportion (38 per cent) than any other member state, with Germany next with 257 companies and then France with 117. Forty-eight of the 100 largest European companies are British-based (Sisson, Waddington and Whitson 1992). No country has such a concentration of large firms, most of which are diversified, as the UK. It is this distinctiveness which justifies a concentration on corporate strategies.

The 1992 company-level survey provided further interesting information on the structure of large companies. It showed, for example, that just over a quarter produce the same goods or services in all sites in the UK. Not surprisingly, forty-one of these forty-nine companies claimed to be single businesses. Just under half produced the same goods or services in some but not all UK sites, while 28 per cent produced different goods and services on each site. This type of connection between businesses owned by the same firm is reflected in the type of organization firms seek to create at the intermediary divisional level. Sixty-two per cent of companies said they had an intermediary level between the business unit (defined as the lowest level of organization) and the UK corporate office. Half of the companies with this type of divisional, intermediary layer had some form of integrative activity linking divisions together. This might be internally organized supply chains, or service provision when the benefits of 'relatedness' can be realized. The others claimed each division was independent.

At the lowest level, the business unit, the majority of companies reported that these were organized on business lines, rather than as geographical or territorial units. This meant that the business unit had a particular product dissimilar from those produced by other units in the same firm. It is likely, therefore, that the specific marketing, sales, production and buying decisions – the functional business strategies concerned with how best to meet the market and respond to competition – will have to be taken at this level of business. This separation of business strategies would not apply so obviously to firms where there is a form of integration organized between divisions or business units.

Multi-product and multi-divisional firms have to make a distinction between corporate and business strategies; between those taken at the centre covering the whole enterprise, and those taken lower down at division or business-unit level and related to the products made and the market served.

The nature of this distinction and the way it comes to be drawn is far from straightforward. There is no obvious, clear-cut rule determining either the level where business strategies are developed, or the relationship between business and corporate strategies. Hill and Pickering (1986) made the assumption that personnel and industrial relations were operational decisions. They concluded that those companies whose head offices or divisional centres intervened in business-unit decisions, especially in personnel and industrial relations matters, were likely to be less profitable.

The business unit, or operating subsidiary company, will need to determine the human resource policies which are best suited to its needs and requirements in the light of product and labour markets, work processes and technology. It would be at this level that we should, most obviously, start to search for 'strategic human resource management' and try to find the connection with the wider business strategies developed by the subsidiary company. We cannot, however, treat the subsidiary company as though it were independent and wholly responsible for its own future. The relationship with the owners, the corporate office and the links with other units in the same firm will be crucial. It is the corporate human resource decisions and more profoundly broader decisions on strategies and structures which provide the framework for functional business strategies and localized initiatives in human resource management.

CORPORATE STRATEGIES AND THEIR INFLUENCE ON HUMAN RESOURCE MANAGEMENT

Three critical features of corporate strategy have profound effects on the degree of freedom of business units to determine their own policies. These relate to decisions on the scope and range of activities – what are termed here as first-order strategies; the type of interrelationships and control systems employed by the centre – second-order strategies; and the choice of types of control systems to utilize.

Table 3.1 utilizes the second company-level survey data to illustrate the degree of change taking place among large firms in their first-order strategies. First-order strategies relate to the decisions taken from time to time on the long-run aims or 'mission' of the firm and the scope of its activities (the markets to be served). We do not have comparable British data to judge whether the volume of change has increased, but certainly virtually all these large firms engaged in first-order strategic decisions in the five-year period 1987–92. Two-thirds had at least one merger or acquisition experience, or invested in a new location or expanded an existing site. Half had divested a business in the period. Divestment was especially likely to occur in those companies which also engaged in a merger or acquisition. It is obvious that decisions such as these have human resource implications in terms of the impact on job security, career expectations, trade union organization, level of collective bargaining, training and development, types of integrated reward systems such as share option schemes and pensions, etc. We will look later at the evidence on the extent to which the personnel function is involved in the making and taking of these big decisions like mergers.

Table 3.1 Changes in corporate strategy of large companies over previous five years

65%	had merger or acquisition
68%	had invested in new locations
66%	had expanded on existing sites
48%	had divested out of existing businesses
62%	had closed existing sites
40%	had run down existing sites
35%	had entered a joint venture

(Of the two-thirds of companies which engaged in merger and acquisition, 85 per cent also divested in the period.)

Base: All Companies N = 176

Source: Marginson *et al.* (1993).

The significance of the volume of corporate strategic change is its link with second-order strategies determining the internal shape and behaviour of the firm. This raises the critical issue of the type of economic return that the firm is trying to achieve. Economists would require that the centre adds value; that the subsidiary company is made more efficient (however that is defined) by being owned by a larger parent firm, than by being independent. The rise in management buy-outs and the flotation of parts of businesses as independent firms is a testimony to the usefulness of the requirement that the centre adds value. But the way the centre adds value is far from straightforward, and will have considerable consequences for the type of corporate personnel roles that are possible. This takes us into the debate on the nature of synergies.

Marginson (1993) uses the work of Hill and Hoskisson (1987) and Hoskisson (1987) to argue that the 'true' multi-divisional firm requires an almost complete separation between operating and strategic decisions. He quotes Williamson (1970: 148), the leading early theorist on M-form companies: 'the M-form structure is thoroughly corrupted when the general management involves itself in the operating affairs of divisions'. This derives from the premise that the prime advantage of corporate ownership is the maximization of the internal financial information system which informs capital allocation decisions taken exclusively by the centre. In this way the internal capital market is more efficient than the external market (Goold and Campbell 1987). These pure M-form companies tend to focus on the achievement of financial economies. Tough budget-setting is linked with weekly or monthly monitoring of rates of return on capital and sales. The driving force is a requirement to maximize earnings per share as a measure of aggregate efficiencies. For the internal capital market to work properly, it is necessary to decentralize profit responsibility to the lowest possible level and to emphasize short-term financial performance goals (Goold and Campbell 1987). It is above all necessary to be able to identify the profit contribution that each business makes. This then leads to the break-up of divisional intermediary layers (or their decomposition, as Hill and Hoskisson put it). It follows that the centre manages each subsidiary company as separate parts of the corporate portfolio. Judgements of profit potential are made on the basis of the position of each unit in its market and the attractiveness of that market in terms of its growth potential and the barriers that protect it from competitor action. Thus portfolio planning, the pursuit of financial economies, the assumption of unrelatedness and the separation of businesses all combine together to form a distinctive type of company. These are most likely to be conglomerates. The implication for human resource management was explored in the *New Perspectives* book (Purcell 1989).

These firms are often known as predator acquirers, identifying profit potential by reducing labour costs, decimating head offices and introducing financial incentives for business unit chiefs who succeed, and an uncertain future for those who fail. In this way their behaviour is consistent with their strategy and structure.

Few firms are like this; most, when they acquire, justify their action on the grounds that they will achieve 'synergy'. This is described at its simplest as 2+2=5, where the ability to mould the parts of the new, combined firm leads to productivity improvements and positive gains. The fact that around half of acquisitions fail to achieve their synergistic aims (Chatterjee 1986) raises important questions on the nature of synergies and how best to maximize resource strengths. There are different sorts of synergies and thus synergistic economies to be achieved. These might be vertical, horizontal or spatial. The economic benefits of vertical integration (from raw material supply to the end customer, the supply chain):

> lie in economies of scale or integration, and in the minimisation of transactions costs. . . . Realizing these economies means ensuring that the recipient division becomes a captive customer for the supplying division to achieve advantages arising from investment in specialized assets and in joint production scheduling. This in turn requires the establishment of inter-divisional linkages and central co-ordination by corporate office. Divisional autonomy is thereby compromised.
>
> (Marginson 1993: 6)

In contrast, horizontal economies are achieved when diversification allows for economies of scope:

> [These are] achieved through the use of a shared input, such as a technology or distribution network across divisions. Realizing such economies requires a detailed knowledge of the processes involved and inter-divisional co-ordination by the corporate office. Again divisional autonomy is compromised.
>
> (Ibid.)

Spatial diversification is where the same task is carried out in each division, with the divisions likely to be geographically organized, for example on a country-by-country basis. Here:

> economies of scale can be achieved by central purchasing of inputs and services, and economies of replication secured by the adoption of standardised operating decision-rules across the divisions. Corporate office becomes involved in regulating and co-ordinating operational matters, and divisional autonomy is circumscribed.
>
> (Ibid.)

The problem for corporate management is that it cannot simultaneously seek to achieve the financial economies of separation and decentralization, and the achievement of vertical, horizontal or spatial synergies.

> Companies engaged in related business activities must choose which kind of economic benefit they are trying to secure – the incompatible nature of the internal management organization to secure one kind of benefit rather than the other means that such companies cannot obtain both.
>
> (Marginson 1993: 7)

It is here that the logical connection between strategy and structure breaks down, or rather that second-order decisions on internal operating procedures and relationships cannot be assumed to flow without difficulty from the first-order strategies. Few firms are straightforwardly structured to maximize just one type of economy, and the balance of costs and benefits of achieving a mix or preferring one over the other are hard to quantify and cannot be assumed to remain unchanged throughout the trade cycle. This is where the problem of managerial decision-making in conditions of uncertainty, complexity and intra-organizational conflict comes to be important. A political process model of decision-making is more convincing than a rational weighing of probabilities, costs and benefits. In these circumstances it is likely that there will be continuous shifts as the environment changes, competitors reposition themselves, and different coalitions of management come to power, and in response to fashion or fad in organizational design. The pendulum between centralization and decentralization is never still.

Table 3.2 shows the volume of internal organizational changes that occurred in the companies in the second company-level survey in the five years prior to the survey in 1992. Market-related strategies are those of internal growth of the business, acquisition and diversification, but these, our respondents said, had led to internal organizational change. Internal reasons, directly allied to second-order strategic decisions, were for the most part linked to questions of decentralization, de-layering, accountability and refocusing. Each of these happened in between a quarter and a half of companies. Each of these types of structural decision has a direct impact on human resource management, especially concerning levels of responsibility and decision-making, relationhips between managers and employees and the role of head offices.

Table 3.2 Changes in internal structure of large companies over previous five years

Source of change	%
Internal growth of business	53
New acquisition	40
New diversification	16
Shift from production to market logic	25
Increased accountability to business units	53
Simplification of business (delayering)	37
Decentralization of business decision-making	26
Other	13
Any change	94
No internal change	6

Base: All companies N = 176

Source: Marginson *et al.* (1993)

Whatever the nature of corporate decision-making, it is clear that the type of economies a firm tries to achieve will have far-reaching consequences for the structure of divisions, their relationship with head office and thus the type and range of human resource policies to be pursued. For example, if economies of replication are based around known organizational routines, as in a top-quality hotel chain or a retail store, and where service is delivered by employees to customers, then, to quote *In Search of Excellence* 'customer relations [will] simply mirror employee relations' (Peters and Waterman 1982). In such firms it is very probable that the group HR function will play a major role, and it is liable to be well-staffed. Sisson and Scullion (1985) have described this in terms of a 'critical function'. They ask what critical activity or function drives the organization. Human resources may either be defined as the critical function itself (this would be unusual) or be closely allied to the dominant interest group (e.g. operations in a hotel or retail store).

The critical function in those companies pursuing financial economies is almost certain to be finance. Indeed, it will be probable that finance is the only functional area represented on the board, and usually it is only finance managers who experience career mobility between operating subsidiaries within the enterprise. There will be a very small central personnel unit.

The critical function in horizontal and vertical economy firms will depend on the nature of the synergies expected. In some it may be that managerial talent is seen as critical, with emphasis paid to graduate recruitment and management development. This might be the main corporate office function in personnel, while responsibility for non-managerial staff is seen very much as an operating responsibility. In other firms, brand image and goodwill might be seen as a form of competitive advantage (something others cannot easily copy) and standards of service to customers and the quality of staff relations might be valued and protected. In yet another case of a firm in a rapidly moving sector, it might be the ability of the organization to adapt and learn that is the most highly valued intangible asset. This might then lead on to emphasis being placed on training and development and strong steers from the corporate office on management style in managing change. It is here that the historical pattern of behaviour in the firm, its culture ('the way we do things around here'), comes to be important as an explanatory variable. There are, after all, no convincing ways of determining scientifically the link between strategy, structure and behaviour, and from first to second to third levels of strategy.

The second company-level survey throws an interesting light on the link between degrees of diversification and the role and structure of the corporate personnel office. Table 3.3 uses two different sorts of measure to illustrate this. The index of IR autonomy is a composite measure made up of eleven areas of policy in personnel and industrial relations. In each item, the personnel executive in the corporate office was asked whether the centre issued instructions, provided advice, gave loose guidelines or complete autonomy to divisions and business units. The responses to all eleven were aggregated to form the IR autonomy index. Average scores were derived: four is complete autonomy and one means absolute head office instruction. The second measure is the number of management staff working full-time in personnel in the corporate office, expressed as a ratio per thousand employees.

The expected relationship between degrees of diversification and corporate personnel is evident. The greater the diversification and the more unrelated parts of the firm are, the more likely it is that there will be a small corporate personnel department and that business units will be given greater freedom to determine their own policies. This applies even to policies such as the recruitment, training and development of senior managers. In decentralized diversified firms, decisions in these areas are likely to be handed to divisions to manage themselves.

In summary, first- and second-order strategies determining the long-term

Table 3.3 Degrees of diversification and the corporate personnel office: index of autonomy and HQ personnel managers per 1,000 employees

	Index of autonomy	*Ratio of personnel managers per 1,000*	*N* =
Single business	1.96	2.12	84
Dominant business	2.05	1.73	28
Related business	2.23	1.55	42
Conglomerates	2.51	1.46	22

Source: Marginson *et al.* (1993)

aims of the enterprise and the mix of activities, the way the firm is organized and the relationship between units, divisions and the centre all play a dominant role in shaping the internal environment where third-order human resource decisions are taken. The key issues are the type of growth (whether organic or by acquisition), the way in which the centre views and manages the portfolio of businesses it owns, the type of economies the firm wishes to maximize, and the form that synergies take and are managed. Historically derived expectations and cultural assumptions overlay these factors such that there is no single straightforward pattern or relationship to explain either differences or outcomes. Personnel, especially in the corporate office, is an area where the role performed is shaped by what they are invited to do by the board and especially the chief executive. This is explored in the next section looking at the role of corporate personnel in the making of strategic decisions.

THE ROLE OF CORPORATE PERSONNEL IN POLICY AND STRATEGY

There are no obvious roles for a corporate personnel department. Indeed, in the second company-level survey sample of companies, 6 per cent claimed to have no managers working full-time in personnel and industrial relations in the corporate office. This did not stop them from having policies – for example, on equal opportunities. In fact they were more likely to claim to have such a policy than firms with a small number of headquarters managerial staff in human resources. This points to the difficulty of interpreting the way in which companies develop corporate-level policies and practices in personnel. It is quite possible, as the first company-level survey showed (Marginson *et al.* 1988), for there to be a well-staffed central office with little influence over or involvement in strategy. Their function was primarily the maintenance and monitoring of personnel systems, or third-order strategies, in the terms used here. Other large firms, albeit a very small number, chose to emphasize the importance of the function, without employing functional specialists at this level. They may have a personnel policy committee made up of line managers, divisional heads and someone from finance. Here the lack of any personnel specialist could mean that *more* attention is paid to human resources than where there is a department. Alternatively it could mean that personnel is ignored at the corporate level, but given full attention in the work unit. Or again, it might be ignored there as well. We have to look for outcomes and patterns of influence, rather than just structures.

The strong connection between strategy and structure helps to explain variety in the extent to which head offices expect personnel to be an operational responsibility. Unrelated diversifiers, or more accurately, perhaps, those companies seeking to maximize financial economies (since this behaviour can occur in firms with related businesses choosing to manage them as separate units), are more likely to see personnel as an operational matter, the responsibility of subsidiary companies. This was shown in the index of IR autonomy in Table 3.3. The process of achieving diversification, of the introduction of tougher financial measures and of decentralization, will be likely to involve major changes to the role of the corporate personnel office, especially when these require a dismantling of corporate-wide systems for job evaluation, collective bargaining and consultative machinery. (For case study material and a wider debate on these issues, see Purcell and Ahlstrand 1994.) One option is to reorganize the corporate personnel department as a quasi-independent profit or revenue centre where it charges for its services to operating companies.

In the most 'market-tested' models, the subsidiaries are free to seek advice from a lower-cost or higher-quality provider, or not to seek advice at all, if the budget gets tough. The hidden assumption in this approach is that it is the job of corporate personnel to develop the best possible systems of personnel administration and to work with line colleagues in divisions and operating units. Here, personnel conforms with the view that it is an operating management activity, with no part to play in the formulation of corporate strategies and policies which control unit behaviour. Yet it is the corporate decisions on strategy, the way in which budgets are determined and compliance monitored, that critically affects what sort of personnel and human resource policies can be and are applied by operating subsidiaries. The extent to which personnel people are involved in these first- and second-order decisions also sends symbolic messages to operating units on the importance attached to personnel. Thus 'market testing' of corporate personnel staff reflects an attentuated view of what personnel is, both in the corporate office and the workplace. Logically it will be cheaper to hire people on a daily basis. The assumption of a personnel administration function also helps to explain why the search for a strategic role for personnel has proved so elusive.

RETHINKING THE STRATEGIC ROLES OF CORPORATE PERSONNEL

There are three types of corporate activity where, if human resource management really were strategic, personnel issues would be taken into account probably through the presence of a personnel specialist in the appropriate decision-making forum. These are:

1 the making of strategic first-order decisions
2 the determination of budgets and control activities
3 the management of the careers of business unit managers.

In the first, the major human resource implications would have to be considered as part of the decision-making process, rather than as an afterthought, as is more usually the case, for example in acquisitions (Hunt and Turner 1987). Budget formulation and control constitute one of the most important regular activities that corporate offices have to undertake. It is probable that more consistent, planned management time is spent on budgeting and budget review than on any other activity. It dominates the work of divisional and unit heads months before the intense period of budget presentation and debate at the corporate office. Once agreed, it sets the agenda for the next year (and probably the next five years, if rolling five-year forecasts are used), it establishes the level of capital expenditure and, as Armstrong shows in his chapter in this volume, by using a battery of measures, most of which include labour cost and performance data, it determines the boundaries for human resource management initiatives. It is in budget review meetings also that corporate chiefs get to meet their senior divisional and unit executives in action. This experience is inevitably linked with the central role of succession planning and senior management career development. A key role thus often ascribed to corporate personnel is the management of managers.

The new second company-level survey throws some light on each of these activities. Table 3.4 needs to be examined carefully, since it is an amalgam of data from two questionnaires covering a variety of strategic management decisions. The first row of data come from asking the personnel management respondents about whether personnel issues were taken into account by the board, or the senior executives concerned, when seven different types of decision (shown in Table 3.1) were listed. Not all companies embarked on all of these changes, and respondents were only asked to talk about four such incidents. This explains the differing number of cases listed in italics as the (*N*) figure. The table shows that in three-quarters of cases of major change, with the exception of mergers and acquisitions where it is 70 per cent, personnel matters, it is claimed, were taken into account. In cases where there is an obvious direct impact on the existing workforce (run-down and closure of sites) personnel issues are more likely to be taken into

Table 3.4 Role of personnel function in strategic management

	(Percentage of cases)													
	Merger/ acquisition		*Invest in new location*		*Expand existing sites*		*Divestment of existing businesses*		*Closure of existing sites*		*Run-down of sites*		*Joint venture*	
Personnel *issues* taken into account (a)	71		76		76		79		86		93		76	
(N)	*(66)*		*(123)*		*(126)*		*(34)*		*(108)*		*(83)*		*(21)*	
Personnel *function* involved:	(a)	(b)	(a)	(b)	(a)	(b)	(a)	(b)	(a)	(b)	(a)	(b)	(a)	(b)
– In drawing up proposals	51	33	51	42	72	37	59	42	67	58	73	54	75	42
– Evaluating financial consequences	28	30	22	41	27	35	30	24	26	39	27	44	19	29
– Taking final decision	13	18	23	23	22	17	41	15	26	19	25	23	31	12
– Implementation	64	55	66	40	48	42	67	42	56	50	51	39	50	41
(N)	*(47)*	*(60)*	*(93)*	*(103)*	*(96)*	*(94)*	*(27)*	*(33)*	*(93)*	*(88)*	*(93)*	*(57)*	*(16)*	*(17)*

(a) *Source*: Personnel respondents
(b) *Source*: Finance respondents

Base: The number of responses is given in each column as respondents were only asked to comment in detail on four of the seven corporate changes listed.

Source: Marginson *et al.* (1993)

account. The second set of data are derived from questions posed to both the personnel (a columns) and the finance executives (b columns). They were asked whether in each of these changes the personnel function was involved in the four stages of decision-making: drawing up proposals, evaluating financial consequences, taking the final decision, and implementation. This is a much more focused question and allows us to avoid the halo effect sometimes encountered when professionals are asked to evaluate their own role in history.

We can view these data in a number of ways. First, according to both finance and personnel people, it is in the implementation of decisions that the personnel function is most likely to be involved. They are least likely to play a role in actually taking the final decision. The most important part of the decision-making process is the drawing up of the proposals. Here personnel claimed to be involved in over half, and in some cases over three-quarters, of the cases. In contrast, the finance respondents' views of personnel involvement show that this occurred in only a third to half of the cases. Thus, according to the finance respondents, in merger and acquisitions decisions, personnel were *not* involved in drawing up the proposal in two-thirds of the cases; in 70 per cent there was *no* personnel involvement in evaluating the financial consequences, and in 82 per cent, personnel did *not* have a role in making the final decision. In a separate question the finance respondents showed that in half the cases where they were asked to estimate benefits that could come from improved productivity in the acquired company (61 per cent of all cases), personnel were asked for advice half of the time. But half of 61 per cent still means that *no* personnel advice was sought in a majority of cases. Even in implementation, in five out of seven of the types of decisions listed, the majority of finance respondents had not experienced personnel involvement. The interim analysis of the CLIRS data concludes that 'if one of the defining characteristics of human resource management is the explicit link with corporate and business strategies then this survey has failed to find it for the majority of large companies' (Marginson *et al.* 1993: 71).

Corporate personnel took part in the critical business unit review meetings in only just over a third of cases. They were much more likely to be involved in decisions on the career development of senior managers. On average this was the case in two-thirds of the companies, but there was a very marked difference according to the size of the department. Thus, where there were small departments of between one and three managers, just under half were involved in career development. In the largest departments, with ten or more personnel managers, the proportion rose to 93 per cent (but only 17 per cent of companies had these huge departments). Other data from the same survey tend to confirm this picture of a relatively low level of involvement by corporate personnel in forms of head office decision-making. For example, another area tested was the design of performance-related pay schemes for business unit managers. Here, according to the finance respondents, corporate personnel play a more important role in the design of the scheme than finance in 29 per cent of the cases, while finance is more important in 44 per cent of companies. Performance-related pay is far from straightforward in the behavioural assumptions that govern design and execution, as Kessler points out in his chapter. It is not a mechanical financial exercise. The same type of picture is drawn by looking at the design of share and profit schemes, and in the extent to which corporate personnel are involved in providing information on pay determination. Finance people see themselves as most important in over half of the firms in the survey, with the remainder split between cases where there is an even influence and those where personnel dominates. These are where there is a large department.

Explanations for this relatively modest role for corporate personnel are easy to find but difficult to test. Many authors have suggested that there is a prime need for personnel people to be able to make a positive contribution to the performance of the firm, by focusing less on policies of fairness and equity, and more on the link output and productivity (Brewster and Connock 1985). Second, it is suggested that the need is to adopt a more strategic perspective – what Tyson calls the 'architect model', in comparison with the more limited 'contracts manager role', or the baleful but well-described job as 'clerk of the works', engaged in reactive, routine administration (Tyson and Fell 1986). All such calls trigger yet further soul-searching in the professional journals, in the institutes and among lead bodies. The strategy and structure debate in diversified companies, however, would point to the conditions under which a corporate role might be expected. Under what conditions might it be expected that a major role could be played? To put this another way, personnel has been limited both by what it has often been asked to do (the legacy of welfare administration) and by the management decisions from which it is excluded. A strong corporate role, of sorts, can come about when there is an interventionist government backed by powerful trade unions (Purcell and Gray 1986), but this type of power-base, which has not been seen for twenty years, would merely serve to perpetuate the 'gamekeeper' role where the prime function is to keep external threats at bay. It would not lead on to participation in the corridors of corporate power.

There is clear, unambiguous evidence from the second company-level survey that the presence of a personnel director on the main board makes a considerable difference to the role played in corporate strategy. Overall, only 30 per cent of companies had a full-time personnel director in membership of the board. There was no association with enterprise size or other structural variables, except for ownership: large overseas-owned firms in the UK were much more likely to have a personnel director (54 per cent) than their UK counterparts. The importance of these data is that the decision to have a main board personnel director is a matter of choice unrelated to size, structure or strategy. Almost certainly it is linked to the views of the chief executive, the non-executive directors and the historical experience of the firm.

An example of the effect of a personnel director is the extent of representation of the personnel function in business unit review meetings. This occurred in 30 per cent of the cases where there was no director, but rose to 48 per cent where there was a director. What was even more interesting was the finding that the local unit personnel manager was more likely to be involved in the review meetings too in these companies with a main-board personnel director. This provides credence to the symbolic importance of a personnel director. Elsewhere, the presence of a personnel director had a marked effect in reducing the exclusive role of the finance function in the design and administration of profit and share schemes, the provision of information on pay determination, performance-related pay for unit managers and for staff (for details, see Marginson *et al.* 1993).

Two more pieces of data raise further issues. These relate to the role of personnel in career management, and the building of links throughout the enterprise. Both issues can be related back to the question of synergies, and forward to the final section on the importance of recognizing organizational resources and capabilities. In the first case, career development for senior managers, the presence of a personnel director increases the likelihood of a decision-making role for personnel, from 59 to 78 per cent. Second, if the corporation is seeking to maximize synergistic economies of one sort or the other, then relationships between senior managers at unit and divisional level become more important than where managers are isolated one from another, as would be expected in pure financial economy, portfolio companies. In these companies, succession planning (if it occurs at all) is designed to fill gaps if and when they occur, but otherwise relationships between business units are purely commercial and contractual. In the 'synergy' companies, questions of team and corporate culture and suchlike intangibles become valued, and career planning becomes a more important corporate activity, since managers often possess knowledge of markets and operational processes that can be applied through the value chain, to use Porter's (1985) term.

Table 3.5 looks at the extent to which regular meetings are held within the corporation between personnel managers in the field and those at the centre. Again, the more interrelated the enterprise along synergistic lines, the more we would expect coordination meetings to be held. In practice, it was not possible to find statistically robust data to confirm this. The key associations were with the size of the department and the presence of a personnel director. Thus Table 3.5 shows that where there is no personnel director, regular meetings are held in less than half of the companies. With a personnel director in place, this rises to just under three-quarters. The proportion of firms which hold no meetings at all varies inversely with the presence of a personnel director.

Table 3.5 Regular meetings of personnel managers by size of personnel department and presence of a personnel director

	No department	*Small*	*Medium*	*Large*	*Personnel director*	*No personnel director*	*All*
	%	%	%	%	%	%	%
Regular meetings held	37	37	64	81	73	45	54
Ad hoc meetings	26	22	20	11	14	22	19
No meetings held	37	41	16	8	13	33	27

Base: All enterprises (N = 176)

Source: Marginson *et al.* (1993)

We have here pointers to a set of propositions: first, that the presence of a personnel director on the main board will make it more likely that human resource issues are considered in corporate strategy. Second, that the enterprise will be more able to develop connections between business units based on the exploitation of synergistic strengths when there is a main-board personnel director. Third, the choice to have a main-board director or not is unrelated to strategies and structures, and cannot be satisfactorily explained in terms of business rationality. Clues as to why some firms value human resources more than others (or at least some suggestions for future research) may be gleaned from shifts in strategic thinking in the last few years. Many strategy analysts have come to place greater value on internal strengths than on external market positions as a source of competitive advantage. This might provide a new way of linking human resource management to strategy.

FROM MARKET POSITIONING TO RESOURCE CAPABILITIES

> The idea that combining different but related businesses could create value through synergy was widely accepted and used as a justification for the extensive diversification that took place in the United States in the 1960s and early 1970s. Statements describing hoped-for areas for synergy accompanied many merger announcements, and were common in annual reports. By the late 1970s, however, the enthusiasm for synergy had waned. Synergy, it seemed, was a nice idea *but rarely occurred in practice*. Instead . . . the answer seemed to lie in decentralization, where business unit managers would be given authority and responsibility and

> rewarded based on results. . . . Decentralization, coupled with disenchantment with synergy, has reinforced the view that portfolio management is the essential task of corporate strategy.
>
> (Porter 1985: 318)

These ideas of decentralization and separation are still very much in vogue in Britain and are being applied in the public service sector, based around the advantages of reducing costs, increasing efficiency and the close monitoring of business unit financial performance. Although the original and best-known approach to portfolio planning, the Boston Consulting Group's growth–share matrix with its cats, dogs, cows and stars, is very dated, the corporate requirement to achieve a balance between business units over time remains. This involves allocating resources, formulating business unit strategy ('grow, hold, harvest', according to the McKinsey matrix: see Grant 1991b: 340), setting performance targets and analysing portfolio balance. In effect, the dominant logic for diversified companies, whatever the nature and degree of the relatedness between business units, has been the management of the portfolio from the centre. In *New Perspectives on Human Resource Management*, I quoted from Hill and Hoskisson to the effect that:

> as firms grow by vertical integration or related diversification, they will become increasingly constrained by information processing requirements to focus on attaining financial economies . . . [and that] under conditions of either high or increasing uncertainty, vertically integrated firms will focus on realizing financial economies.
>
> (Hill and Hoskisson 1987: 338, 340)

The implication of these propositions was that there was an inevitability toward a focus on financial economies, even in vertically integrated firms. This led me to conclude that 'current trends in corporate strategy in many large diversified companies render the ideals of human resource management . . . unobtainable' (Purcell 1989: 90). Since then, strategy theorists have turned their attention away from market positioning and more toward a resource view of the firm. In the crude terms of a SWOT analysis, emphasis is switching from external market-related opportunities and threats, to internal strengths and weaknesses. In practice, too, firms have been divesting unrelated parts of their portfolio, on the grounds that there is a need to return to the core business and in effect to learn to maximize synergistic strengths.

The question of resource-relatedness and of seeking to build around synergies – what Porter calls horizontal strategies – is emerging as a new approach to strategy. This should have profound implications for the practice and study of human resource management and its links with corporate strategy. At the simplest level, the resource view is based around a number of linked or sequential questions: what is the firm good at? Does this derive from a unique set of resources and/or a particular set of capabilities? Can the firm utilize its resources more effectively than its competitors? Can these strengths be easily copied by others? (In which case there is little competitive advantage to be obtained.) Is the firm able to keep its resources from depreciating rapidly? Is it able to reproduce and develop resource strengths and capabilities for future benefit? Behind all of these questions is the requirement that the firm is able to exploit these competitive advantages in the form of increased rent (Amit and Schoemaker 1993) and gain sustained competitive advantage (Barney 1986). This is allied to the requirement that any given strengths are difficult to imitate, and therefore are both rare and able to generate higher rent – or to use a different term, greater added value.

It is not difficult to see where the potential links with human resource management can be made. Cappelli and Singh (1992: 186) propose that once the perspective is adopted that competitive advantage arises from firm-specific, valuable resources which are difficult to imitate, 'an important research question relates to the role of human resource policies in the creation of valuable, firm specific skills'. It also follows that the potential exists for a much more fruitful integration between human resource management practice and theory with corporate and business strategy. For example:

> the resource-based model suggests that sources of sustained competitive advantage are firm resources that are valuable, rare, imperfectly imitable, and non-substitutable. These resources include a broad range of organizational, social, and individual phenomena within firms that are the subject of a great deal of research in organization theory and organizational behaviour.
>
> (Barney 1991: 116)

This may mean no more than that economic models of the behaviour of the firm in the context of markets have proved less than satisfactory, and attention is now turned to intangible qualities of the firm. It is necessary to be able to find a means of identifying these rare, valuable, imperfectly imitable and non-substitutable resources both in theory and practice. Kay (1993) sees 'the creation and maintenance of distinctive capabilities [to be] at the heart of successful strategy', so the potential contribution could be immense. Not all resources, by any means, fall within the ambit of human resource management. Some refer to tangible physical or financial assets, and proprietary technology. Patents, brand reputation and 'goodwill' are other forms of intangible resources. It is also important to recognize that the search here is for what is unique in the firm's selection and utilization of human resources that gives it an advantage over others. This advantage has to be something which cannot be easily copied (is 'imperfectly imitable'), rather like Japanese management. As a result, the potential for generalizing to universal propositions in HRM must be highly restricted, in the same way the 'Lessons' in books such as *In Search of Excellence* were of little value to the large number of ordinary, humdrum firms.

A study by Hall, of UK chief executive officers, tried to operationalize some of the ideas in the resource view of strategy by asking them to rate the relative contribution of twelve different types of resources to organizational success, and within the category of 'employee know-how' the type of knowledge most highly valued. Questions were also asked as to the speed at which a given resource could be replaced.

> All CEOs rated company reputation, product reputation and employee know-how as the most important contributors to overall success . . . [these] were also identified as the resources which would take longest to replace if they had to be replaced from scratch.
>
> (Hall 1992: 143)

The most valued employee know-how, according to the CEOs, was operations – 'the way things are done'. These operational skills relate closely to the concept of 'organizational routines' used by Grant (1991b) to provide the critical bridge between resources and competitive advantage. Thus, 'the way we do things here' as an operational definition of culture can come to provide a powerful means of establishing and reproducing operational or organizational routines. Economies of both scale and scope, or of replication, in multi-plant firms are very much bound up with the capacity to reproduce routines. Routines are more than instructions in a manual, and more even than skills, and may well require cooperation between individuals, to gain maximum value. A talented football player, for example, in a disorganized, ill-coordinated team can do little to improve the performance of the team as a whole. Such a talented person is able to command a premium price and has little incentive to stay in terms of social satisfaction, or intangible rewards of team play. Organizations with excellent routines are more able to get their scarce skills embedded in the organizational culture. As a result they are less vulnerable and harder to copy or poach from. It is the *combination* of skills and routines that is most likely to be the source of human resource-based competitive advantage. Routines allow skills to be made specific to the organization. This is closely allied to the distinction between the core and periphery used as a means to differentiate types of human resource policies appropriate to different types of employee. The core is closely associated with the development of an internal labour market and firm-specific skills.

Once these questions are asked of multi-divisional firms – the identification of key resources and the means needed to convert them into sources of sustained competitive advantage – it is no longer obvious that the operating subsidiary is the most appropriate unit of organization. Organizational learning of unique attributes which make up the synergies, resources and capabilities comes to be valued across the firm, as in Porter's horizontal strategies. To the extent that these attributes or competences reside in people, a premium comes to be placed on the valuing of human resources. In these cases the firm needs to be able to determine the durability of these resources and capabilities, how easily they are transferred within the firm (but made hard for others to acquire), and how they come to be replicated over time. This in turn raises questions on training and development, mobility between constituent parts of the firm and reward strategies that seek to bind employees with know-how into the firm. In short, the resource view of the firm allows for a different set of questions to be posed at both the first and second levels of strategy formation. Rather than an exclusive concern with market growth and attractiveness, niches and segmentation, the language becomes one of maximizing strengths of resources and capabilities to achieve synergy – the development of a core competence. Instead of isolating each component unit of the firm in order to find its precise contribution to profits and growth (or loss and decline), horizontal strategies emphasize intangibles, learning, and skill transfer and the reduction in transaction costs.

Grant (1991b: 101) lists the main characteristics of human resources in his general classification of a firm's potential resources as follows:

- The training and expertise of employees determine the skills available to the firm.
- The adaptability of employees determines the strategic flexibility of the firm.
- The commitment and loyalty of employees determines the firm's ability to maintain competitive advantage.

This could be seen as no more than a familiar litany of normative statements defining the 'soft' side of human resource management (Guest 1987). The value here, however, is that it reflects thinking within the emerging resource capability school. It provides grounds for some optimism that the contribution that human resource management can make to corporate as well as business strategies will come to be recognized as enterprises seek to build more on synergies and less on portfolios. If this happens, senior executives may ask more of their personnel colleagues. The challenge for human resource management is to show a link between policy, practice and organizational outcomes that is meaningful to the corporate board. To be taken seriously, they must be able to make a considered contribution to identification and development of particular human resource strengths, and contribute to the improvement or replication of distinctive organizational routines that convert resources to competitive advantage.

REFERENCES

Amit, R. and Schoemaker, P.J.H. (1993) 'Strategic assets and organizational rent', *Strategic Management Journal* 14: 33–46.

Barney, J.B. (1986) 'Organizational culture: can it be a source of competitive advantage?' *Academy of Management Review* 11(3): 656–65.

—— (1991) 'Firm resources and sustained competitive advantage', *Journal of Management* 17(1): 99–120.

Brewster, C. and Connock, S. (1985) *Industrial Relations: Cost-Effective Strategies*, London: Hutchinson.

Cappelli, P. and Singh, H. (1992) 'Integrating strategic human resources and strategic management', *Research Frontiers in Industrial Relations and Human Resources*, Industrial Relations Research Association Series.

Chandler, A. (1962) *Strategy and Structure*, Cambridge, MA: MIT Press.

Channon, D.F. (1982) 'Industrial structure', *Long Range Planning* 15(5).

Chatterjee, S. (1986) 'Types of synergy and economic value: the impact of acquisitions on merging and rival firms', *Strategic Management Journal* 7.

Goold, M. and Campbell, A. (1987) *Strategies and Styles: The Role of the Centre in Managing Diversified Corporations*, Oxford: Blackwell.

Grant, R.M. (1991a) 'The resource based theory of competitive advantage: implications for strategy formulation', *California Management Review* 33(3): 114–35.

—— (1991b) *Contemporary Strategy Analysis: Concepts, Techniques, Applications*, Cambridge, MA: Blackwell.

Guest, D. (1987) 'Human resource management and industrial relations', *Journal of Management Studies* 24(5).

Hall, R. (1992) 'The strategic analysis of intangible resources', *Strategic Management Journal* 13: 135–44.

Hill, C.W.L. and Hoskisson, R.E. (1987) 'Strategy and structure in the multiproduct firm', *Academy of Management Review* 12(2).

Hill, C.W.L. and Pickering, J.F. (1986) 'Divisionalisation, decentralisation and performance of large United Kingdom companies', *Journal of Management Studies* 23(1).

Hoskisson, R.E. (1987) 'Multidivisional structure and performance: the contingency of diversification strategy', *Academy of Management Journal* 30(4): 625–44.

Hunt, J. and Turner, D. (1987) 'Hidden extras: how people get overlooked in takeovers', *Personnel Management*.

Kay, J. (1993) 'The structure of strategy', *Business Strategy Review* 4(2): 17–37.

Marginson, P. (1993) 'The multi-divisional structure and corporate control: explaining the degree of corporate coordination over decisions on labour relations', *Papers in Organization*, No. 12, Institute of Organization and Industrial Sociology, Copenhagen Business School.

Marginson, P., Edwards, P.K., Martin, R., Purcell, J. and Sisson, K. (1988) *Beyond the Workplace: Managing Industrial Relations in Multi-Plant Enterprises*, Oxford: Blackwell.

Marginson, P., Armstrong, P., Edwards, P.K. and Purcell, J. (1993) 'The control of industrial relations in a large company: initial analysis of the 2nd company-level industrial relations survey, *Warwick Papers in Industrial Relations*, No. 45, Industrial Relations Research Unit, School of Industrial and Business Studies, University of Warwick.

Peters, T.J. and Waterman, R.H. (1982) *In Search of Excellence: Lessons from America's Best Run Companies*, New York: Harper & Row.

Porter, M.E. (1985) *Competitive Advantage Creating and Sustaining Superior Performance*, New York: The Free Press.

Purcell, J. (1989) 'The impact of corporate strategy on human resource management', in J. Storey (ed.) *New Perspectives on Human Resource Management*, London and New York: Routledge.

Purcell, J. and Ahlstrand, B. (1994) *Human Resource Management in the Multi-Divisional Firm*, Oxford: Oxford University Press.

Purcell, J. and Gray, A. (1986) 'Corporate personnel departments and the management of industrial relations: two case studies in ambiguity', *Journal of Management Studies*, March: 205–23.

Sisson, K. and Scullion, H. (1985) 'Putting the corporate personnel department in its place', *Personnel Management*, December.

Sisson, K., Waddington, J. and Whitston, C. (1992) 'The structure of capital in the European Community: the size of companies and the implications for industrial relations', *Warwick Papers in Industrial Relations*, No. 38.

Tyson, S. and Fell, A. (1986) *Evaluating the Personnel Function*, London: Hutchinson.

Whittington, R. (1993) *What is Strategy and Does it Matter?*, London: Routledge.

Williamson, O.E. (1970) *Corporate Control and Business Behaviour*, Englewood Cliffs, NJ: Prentice Hall.

Chapter 4

Human resource management and the personnel function

Keith Sisson

In the late 1980s, there was much debate among practitioners and academics alike about the implications of human resource management (HRM) for the personnel function. Even if some found it difficult to understand what the fuss was about (HRM looked very much like the personnel management they thought they were practising), many practitioners welcomed the new paradigm (Armstrong 1987; Fowler 1987). It seemed to offer a guide to best practice which was far better grounded and integrated than ever before: here was an extremely optimistic model that appeared to be able to square the circle – it met the demand for economic efficiency and yet also promised to make a significant contribution to improving the quality of working life. Perhaps more important still, as Torrington (1989: 64) suggested in *New Perspectives*, the stress on the significance of the management of human resources to the competitive advantage of the organization appeared to give the personnel function the status which so many commentators had been seeking. Personnel could no longer be equated with 'a collection of incidental techniques without much internal cohesion . . . a hodge podge' (Drucker 1961: 243). Rather it became the very essence of management.

Others were much more cautious. Thus, while the stress on the significance of the management of human resources to the competitive advantage of the organization was welcomed, the suggestion that the burden of responsibility for personnel management should be assumed by line managers went down less well with some personnel specialists. There were also concerns that the personnel function would be 'subject to increasing encroachment from external consultancies . . . poaching their day-to-day activities' (Adams 1991: 40) and that it might itself turn into a peripheral function.

These linked with other concerns, in many respects more significant, stemming from the welfare and professional tradition of personnel management in the UK. As Storey (1989) observed in *New Perspectives*, there were considerable ambiguities surrounding HRM, and at least two main versions:

> The hard one emphasizes the quantitative, calculative and business-strategic aspects of managing the headcounts resource in as 'rational' a way as for any other economic factor. By contrast, the 'soft' version traces its roots to the human-relations school: it emphasizes communication, motivation and leadership.
>
> (Storey 1989: 8)

The worry was that in the UK it was more likely to be the 'hard' rather than the 'soft' verson that would be introduced. By definition, the 'hard' version sat uneasily with the view that personnel management was 'different from other staff jobs' (Miller 1975); that employees as well as employers were to be seen as the 'clients' of the professional personnel specialist and, in maintaining the highest standards of integrity – often based on codes of ethics – he or she also performed an important public service which earns the right to claim some of the independence which went with the traditional professions. Not only that: the contingent nature of the 'hard' model – policies and practices were to be tailored to suit particular circumstances – was at odds with the pursuit of the universally applicable 'best' practice to which many personnel managers had been encouraged to aspire. Worse still was the fear that some organizations might be encouraged to introduce the 'hard' version under the guise of the 'soft' version. This was especially so as many presentations of the 'soft' version were either ambivalent or silent about such key issues as trade union recognition and collective bargaining.

So how does the personnel function in the UK look after nearly a decade in which the ideas of HRM have held sway? Have there been major changes in the function as a result of the impact of HRM? Or is it largely a question of many changes, but little that is fundamentally different? If so, what does this tell us about the personnel function and the prospects for the widespread adoption of HRM in the UK?

This chapter begins to answer these questions by considering what has happened to the numbers and qualifications, activities, organization and influence of personnel managers in the UK in the 1980s. It then considers the variations on the major themes and, in particular, the contrasts between UK and foreign-owned companies. It goes on to look at the profession of personnel management and the activities of the Institute of Personnel Management (IPM). It concludes by considering the implications of the findings for the likelihood of the adoption of a more strategic approach to the management of people. Personnel managers and the IPM, it is argued, must speak out if there is to be any prospect of the adoption of such an approach in more than a handful of organizations.

THE PERSONNEL FUNCTION IN PROFILE

The reality of the personnel function in the UK has always been in strong contrast to the picture which appears in the textbooks and practitioner journals. The latter have been dominated by what Torrington (1989), drawing on a medical analogy, has termed the 'general practitioner' model, i.e. personnel managers are (and, by implication, should be) 'professionals', involved in a wide range of activities. In practice, however, as the author Sisson (1989: 11–14) and others (see below) have argued, things have been very different. Thus, in the early 1980s:

- Large numbers of personnel managers – more than half – did not belong to the IPM and were not 'qualified' (Daniel 1983: 26; Millward and Stevens 1986: 25–7). Even many that were did not see themselves as 'professional' in the sense of owing their prime loyalty to the occupation. Most were 'managers first and personnel people second' (Mackay and Torrington 1986: 161–2).
- Personnel management, far from being a single homogeneous occupation, involved a variety of roles and activities which differed from one organization to another and, perhaps even more importantly, from one level to another in the same organization. The range extended from 'clerks', who made up the majority, through 'contract managers', who were responsible for negotiations with trade unions, to a small number of 'architects' at the pinnacle (see list below).
- Personnel management was highly 'balkanized' (Tyson 1987: 530). Not only was there a variety of roles and activities, in other words, but these tended to be relatively self-contained, with little passage between them. Many of the 'architects' referred to in the list below came from the ranks of line managers, rather than personnel managers.
- Personnel management was highly structured on gender lines. Women made up the great majority of personnel managers, yet they tended to be employed in lower-level and less well-paid jobs than their male counterparts, which helped to reinforce the 'cinderella' image of the function as a whole (Long 1984a, 1984b; Legge 1987).

With these corrections in mind, the aim here is to give an impression of what has been happening to the personnel function in the UK in recent years on a number of dimensions: number and qualifications, activities, organization, and influence. Each of these dimensions, it might be thought, would have been significantly affected by HRM thinking and practice.

Types of personnel manager

- *'Clerk of the works'*. Largely involved in routine matters; record-keeping, preparing letters and documents on instructions, first-interviewing of some applicants for employment, and welfare matters, e.g. visiting the sick. Reports to a senior line manager or personnel manager.

- *'Contracts manager'*. Most likely to be found in organizations with strong trade unions and a traditional industrial relations background. Involved in policy-making but of a relatively short-term time-scale; main activity is likely to be the making and interpretation of procedures and agreements. In some organizations may exercise considerable power and authority which comes from ability to resolve day-to-day problems, and from their intimate knowledge and personal relationships with shop stewards and trade union officers, as well as senior line managers.
- *'Architect'*. Likely to be intimately involved in policy-making as a member of the senior management team and/or have a seat on the board of directors. Will regard him or herself as 'business manager' first and 'personnel manager' second and will have a broad portfolio which encompasses not just dealing with trade unions but the organization's entire human resources. Also likely to be involved in the design of the structure of the organization. Probably qualified, both academically and in experience, although may not be member of the IPM; may have considerable experience as a line manager or consultant at some time in their career.

(Based on Tyson and Fell 1986: 21–7)

Numbers and qualifications

The third Workplace Industrial Relations Survey (WIRS), carried out in 1990, contains two surprises in terms of the debates about the impact of HRM on the personnel function. First, there does not appear to have been a move to include 'human resource' in job titles. Indeed, the number of specialists calling themselves 'human resource managers' turned out to be less than 1 per cent (Millward *et al.* 1992: 29). Second, there does not appear to have been any reduction overall in the number of workplaces with specialist managers, i.e. those with 'personnel' or 'industrial' or 'human resource management' in their title. Workplaces were as likely to have a specialist manager as in earlier years; these were also no less likely to have support staff. Indeed, there was a slight increase in the second half of the decade (see Table 4.1), which was particularly evident among medium-sized enterprises with between 100 and 999 employees (Millward *et al.* 1992: 27–38). An important point not to be missed is that the number of workplaces with specialist personnel managers remained very small. Overall, only 17 per cent had such a manager. It was only in the larger workplaces, i.e. those with more than 200 employees, that a personnel specialist was likely to be employed.

As for the qualifications, there was a substantial increase in the number of workplace personnel specialists with them from 1980 to 1984. In the light

Table 4.1 The presence of designated personnel managers by size of establishment, 1980, 1984 and 1990 (percentages)

		Size of establishment					
	All establishments	*25–49*	*50–99*	*100–199*	*200–499*	*500–999*	*1,000 or more*
Whether personnel in job title							
1980	15	5	12	25	52	74	88
Unweighted base	*1868*	*340*	*339*	*353*	*343*	*233*	*260*
Weighted base	*1831*	*936*	*456*	*239*	*138*	*38*	*26*
1984	15	4	12	29	54	68	88
Unweighted base	*1794*	*311*	*315*	*313*	*321*	*267*	*267*
Weighted base	*1779*	*933*	*432*	*229*	*130*	*36*	*21*
1990	17	6	12	34	64	81	87
Unweighted base	*1697*	*286*	*292*	*296*	*272*	*219*	*332*
Weighted base	*1644*	*866*	*423*	*203*	*108*	*29*	*16*

Bases: managers interviewed at sampled establishment.

Source: Millward *et al.* 1992

of this, the WIRS team expected to see a further increase between 1984 and 1990 (Millward *et al.* 1992: 37). In the event, they were disappointed. As Table 4.2 confirms, there was a reduction in the number of specialists with qualifications: the proportion was down from 54 per cent to 50 per cent.

Table 4.2 Qualifications, experience and support of managers, 1980, 1984 and 1990 (percentages)

	Designated personnel managers			*Non-designated managers spending a quarter or more of their time on personnel or industrial relations matters*		
	1980	*1984*	*1990*	*1980*	*1984*	*1990*
Professional, educational qualifications	49	58	54	16	19	28
Support staff	48	54	50	57	50	54
Two or more years' experience in the work	89	95	95	82	95	98
Base: managers interviewed at sampled establishments spending a major part of their time on personnel in 1980, a quarter or more of their time in 1984 and 1990						
Unweighted	*711*	*786*	*657*	*344*	*493*	*515*
Weighted	*244*	*259*	*198*	*364*	*635*	*574*

Source: Millward *et al.* 1992

The nature of the qualifications of specialist or designated personnel specialists, which the WIRS explored in a parallel survey, also makes interesting reading. Only 12 per cent were educated to degree level, and only 7 per cent had a degree or postgraduate diploma in personnel/IR/trade union studies. The great majority (72 per cent) simply had a professional qualification with little change over the 1980s.

It is the growing significance of line management involvement which catches the eye, however. Not only were an increasing number of line managers spending a large part of their time on personnel matters, but they were also better qualified in personnel: the proportion of non-specialists who only spent part of their time on personnel matters with qualifications in the area was up from 19 per cent in 1984 to 28 per cent in 1990.

Although the position is not so clear-cut at corporate level, because the survey data are not strictly comparable, the signs are that there has not been a dramatic change at this level either. In the first company-level industrial relations survey (CLIRS) carried out by the Industrial Relations Research Unit in 1985, 81 per cent of companies claimed to have a corporate function (Marginson *et al.* 1988: 55); in the second survey undertaken in 1992, the figure was 78 per cent (Marginson *et al.* 1993b: 30). The major change, which might have been expected in view of some of the much-publicized examples (such as that of the Post Office (Hilton 1993)), was in the size of department: in 1985 up to a half reported having three or four staff, whereas in 1992, this figure was down to 36 per cent. Significantly, however, this change seems to have been as much a reflection of the reduction of the overall number of employees as a reduction in the size of the personnel department. In 1985, the ratio of corporate personnel staff to employees was 1:1,250 and 1:357 for UK-owned and foreign-owned companies respectively (Marginson *et al.* 1988: 57); in 1992, it was 1:1,800 overall (Marginson *et al.* 1993b: Table 4.2). Last, but by no means least, headquarters personnel managers seemed to be no more taken with the term 'human resources' than their workplace counterparts: in 1992 only 9 per cent of the respondents in the companies surveyed used the phrase in their job titles, and there was no main-board director using this designation.

Both the 1985 and 1992 CLIRS confirmed that corporate personnel managers were more likely to be qualified than their workplace counterparts. In two other respects, however, the findings at the higher level were very similar to those at the lower. There was little or no change in the proportion of corporate level personnel managers with qualifications; it was around two-thirds in both surveys. Also the main qualification was that of the IPM. Like their workplace counterparts, relatively few corporate personnel managers had a degree.

Activities

Those expecting strong evidence of the demise of the 'contracts manager' will also be surprised. In the first half of the decade, the WIRS team (Millward *et al.* 1992: 39) found some evidence of a widening in the scope of the activities of those managers responsible for personnel, with a 'substantial increase in the proportion indicating that they dealt with procedures for grievances, discipline and disputes, with settling and negotiating terms of employment and with job evaluation'. In the second half, however, taking specialists and non-specialists together, there was little change overall. At the margin, there was some evidence that dealing with disciplinary cases was less important, whereas recruitment and selection and setting terms and conditions became more important.

At first sight, this continued high level of involvement in settling pay seems difficult to square with the considerable reduction in trade union membership and the coverage of collective bargaining reported elsewhere in the WIRS findings. Two points can be made. First, there has been a considerable decentralization in the levels of collective bargaining throughout the 1980s; many more workplaces were responsible for pay determination in 1990 than in 1980. Second, pay determination was a major activity whether or not there was collective bargaining.

A major finding which is more difficult to explain relates to what Millward and his colleagues refer to as the 'growing differences' between specialists and non-specialists. Significantly, whereas there was no change in the number of non-specialists with responsibilities for training, there was a sizeable fall in the number of specialists who continued to enjoy this responsibility, from 78 per cent to 67 per cent. Likewise, specialist personnel managers were less involved in job evaluation and pay systems than non-specialists. Further insights come from the survey of most important activities carried out for the first time in the 1990 WIRS. This suggests a substantial involvement of specialists in recruitment and selection and in settling terms and conditions; but less involvement in training and in staffing/manpower planning.

An important consideration here, the WIRS team suggests (Millward *et al.* 1992: 39), is the increasing 'balkanization' or fragmentation of the personnel function, which is discussed later. Many key personnel activities, it seems, are being undertaken by non-specialists or by other groups such as training departments. Many specialist personnel managers are being left with relatively routine systems maintenance functions, such as recruitment and selection and pay determination. The only substantial difference is that there is less involvement of trade unions.

The situation at corporate level is more complex because of the variety of organization types discussed in the next section. One point is worth emphasizing, however. There had been, as might have been expected from the highly publicized case studies, a marked, although by no means universal, trend towards the decentralization of the pay negotiation process to lower levels such as divisions and individual business units. This did not necessarily mean as dramatic a change in activities as at first sight might appear. Significantly, as in 1985, in the great majority of companies headquarters managers continued to be involved in the pay determination process at lower levels. In about a third of the companies there was direct involvement; elsewhere the involvement was indirect, and most commonly took the form of the issuing of guidelines.

Organization

As well as a general trend towards the greater involvement of line managers, three related developments might be supposed to have had an effect on the organization of the personnel function in the 1980s. One was the break-up of centralized functional bureaucracies into quasi-independent businesses and units. The second was the reduction in the number of tiers of managers as a result of the flattening, or de-layering, of job hierarchies. The third was the development of internal markets in which goods and services are traded between business and units, as well as between headquarters and divisions. In this latter case the questions increasingly being asked relate to the balance between 'hierarchy' and 'market' in the handling of activities.

Here our main source of information is the survey of nearly one hundred of the largest organizations carried out by the *Recruitment and Development Report* in 1991 (RDR 1991). On the basis of this, Adams (1991) has identified no fewer than four main ways of delivering personnel activities, besides the traditional department:

1 The 'in-house' agency, in which the personnel department, or some of its activities – for example, graduate recruitment – is seen as a cost centre and its activities are cross-charged to other departments or divisions.
2 The 'internal consultancy', in which the personnel department sells its services to the parent organization or its units – the implication being that managers in the parent organization will enjoy some freedom in deciding to go elsewhere if they are not happy with the service that is being provided.
3 The 'business within a business', in which some of the activities of the function are formed into a quasi-independent organization which may trade not only with the parent organization and its units, but also externally.
4 'External consultancy', in which the organization and its units go outside to completely independent businesses for help and advice on IR and HR matters.

As Adams (1991: 44) points out, each of these four alternatives to the traditional department can be seen as representing a 'kind of scale of increasing degrees of "externalisation", understood as the application of market forces to the delivery of personnel activities'. Common to each of them, however, is some kind of service contract in which there is charging for the services delivered.

Figure 4.1, which summarizes the results of the survey, confirms that there have been significant shifts away from the traditional personnel department. Contrary to some fears, however, it is not a straightforward question of an increase in externalization. Clearly there has been an increase. Not only is it more marked for some activities, such as executive search and selection and training, than for others, however; the activities in which the increase has been greatest are those where externalization has traditionally been most used. Just as striking were the increases in the other forms of managing the activities involved; in the case of training this was as great as, if not greater than, external consultants. Indeed, there were some instances of a return to in-house activity – a point which receives some confirmation from the WIRS findings: more and more managements seemed to be assuming responsibility for their own industrial relations, rather than delegating them to employers' organizations as they have done in the past (Millward *et al.* 1992: 45–8).

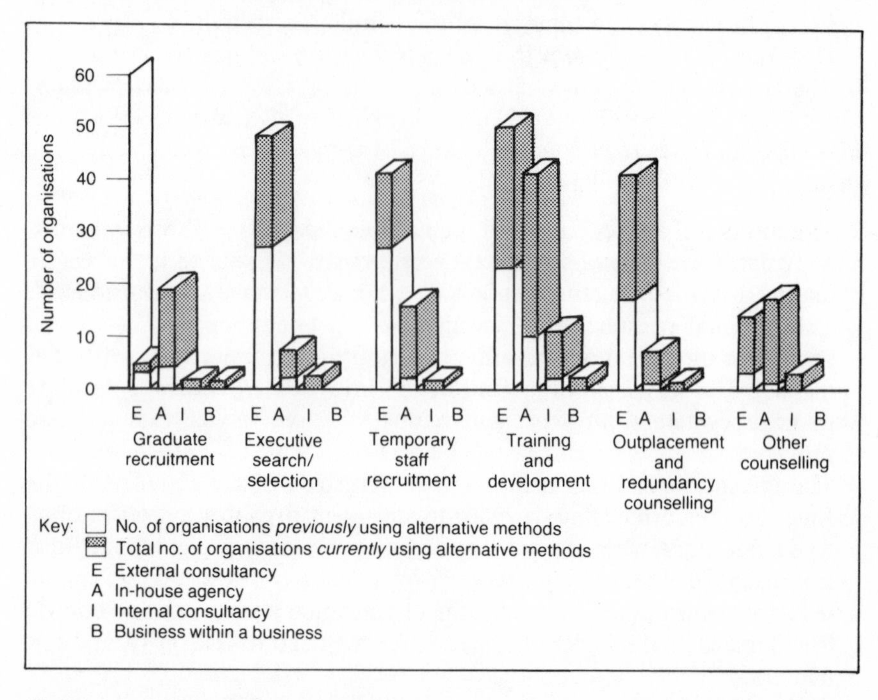

Figure 4.1 Comparison of organizations *previously* and *currently* using alternative ways of managing six HR functions

An equally important finding of the *Recruitment and Development Report* is that there is 'clear indication of the increasing specialization and fragmentation or "balkanization", to use Tyson's (1986) term, involved in personnel work'. As Adams (1991: 51) argues, each of the organizational forms identified can be seen as different ways of 'parcelling up' a different personnel activity. Not only that. In some cases, such as recruitment, where there were separate units looking after executive search and selection, graduate recruitment and temporary staff, even the one activity is being subdivided. In others, such as training and development, where organizations appear to be using two or three different methods of organization, there is some evidence of even more minute fragmentation. Here too, confirmation comes from the WIRS findings: Millward *et al.* (1992: 39) suggest that 'a greater division of labour between designated [personnel] managers, training managers and others concerned with sub-sets of the broad employee relations area arose over the second half of the 1980s'.

Influence

Both workplace and corporate personnel managers in WIRS and CLIRS reported an increase in their influence; this was also corroborated by financial managers. An increase in influence within a relatively narrow range of activities is only of marginal significance, however. The acid test, so far as the impact of HRM is concerned, might be thought to be the involvement of the personnel function in the highest levels of management decision-making. Representation at the very highest levels of the organization is not only massively symbolic of the status with which personnel issues are seen. If there is one thing which united the many different models and interpretations of HRM, it is an emphasis on the key role of strategy and the need to integrate the management of human resources into the strategic management processes. If personnel specialists are not even present when key decisions are taken, this effectively means that personnel issues will almost inevitably be condemned to second-order status: the input the personnel function can make is inevitably limited to dealing with the implications of implementing such decisions. The chances of developing coherent and consistent policies would also appear to be pretty slim.

In the event, the picture could hardly be more disappointing. The WIRS survey, for example, found virtually no change in the proportion of independent establishments in the trading sector with someone with specific responsibility for personnel and industrial relations work on the senior management committee. Overall, only half reported such representation, with the proportion increasing with size; such representation was also more likely in manufacturing than in services (Millward *et al.* 1992: 50–1).

In the case of multi-establishment organizations, WIRS offers two figures for personnel management involvement at the highest levels of the organization. One is for any representation of the personnel function on the top governing body, which is roughly comparable to the measure for independent establishments mentioned above. The other, which gives a more accurate reflection of influence, is for specialist representation, i.e. where personnel was the main job for the incumbent.

Two things are clear from the results shown in Table 4.3. First, no more than two in five workplaces had specialist representation. Second, there was virtually no change throughout the 1980s in either of the two measures.

A second source of information is the two company-level industrial relations surveys (CLIRS) quoted earlier. In this case the respondent was an executive responsible for personnel and industrial relations at corporate level. This is important, because such individuals might be expected to have more accurate knowledge of board-level matters than their workplace counterparts. Confusingly, the title 'personnel director' does not necessarily mean that the individual sits on the main board; it may simply denote that he or she is responsible for the corporate personnel function. Although the two samples are not strictly comparable, they nonetheless would seem to confirm the WIRS findings: not only was specialist board representation restricted to a minority of companies (30 per cent), but also there was no change between 1985 and 1990.

Table 4.3 Representation of the personnel function on the board, by size of organization, 1980, 1984 and 1990 (percentages)

	All establishments	*Size of organization* 25–499	500–1999	2000–9999	10,000 or more
Any representation on board					
1980	71	59	71	76	79
1984	73	66	68	68	85
1990	69	61	65	70	74
Specialist representation					
1980	42	11	39	46	64
1984	43	8	40	49	70
1990	40	10	21	43	60
Base[1]: trading sector establishments that were part of multi-establishment organizations					
Unweighted	*1271*	*140*	*85*	*158*	*474*
Weighted	*1039*	*250*	*83*	*107*	*351*

[1] Only 1990 bases are given, for presentational reasons.

Source: Millward *et al.* 1992: 49

It is difficult to exaggerate the significance of these findings. The continued absence of boardroom representation in something like two-thirds of even large organizations, and the fact that there appeared to be virtually no change throughout the 1980s, is little short of remarkable, given the debate which HRM engendered among personnel practitioners as well as academics. Surely it might be expected, if there was going to be any impact it would be at the highest levels. Yet the survey evidence suggests there has been no growth whatsoever.

Moreover the CLIRS results confirm that the lack of representation at the very highest levels of the organization was not just symbolic of the status with which personnel issues were seen. Companies with a main board personnel director were, according to both the personnel and financial respondents to the survey, more likely to take personnel matters into account in strategic business decisions. They were also more likely to accord personnel a role in the monitoring and control of business units.

Board-level representation was also correlated with a number of other significant features. Personnel policy committees, bringing together management functions at corporate level, were reported in over 40 per cent of companies. Regular meetings – more than once a year – were held between corporate personnel managers and those in business units in just over one-half of cases. This proportion rose to three-quarters in companies with a main board director for personnel. Company-wide policies were strongly associated with the existence of a corporate personnel policy committee: the implication is that such committees were primarily concerned with developing guiding principles, rather than specific policies.

Such information also bears on the relationship between personnel managers and line managers. Most commentators agree that there was a general trend towards the greater involvement of the latter in personnel work in the 1980s. The key issue is the nature of the relationship. As Fowler (1992: 22) points out, there are two possible approaches. One reduces the personnel function to largely administrative support to managers, who handle their own operational personnel work. The other, while devolving much operational decision-making to managers (e.g. for selection), sees a key role for personnel managers in setting and monitoring standards of personnel practice.

The strong suspicion must be that it is the first approach which dominates in the UK. The main reason, as Fowler (1992: 23) recognizes, is that the second approach requires that the personnel function is represented on the top management team. Such representation, as WIRS and CLIRS clearly demonstrate, is all too often missing.

Still a Cinderella function?

How far this state of affairs links with the gender structure of the personnel function in the UK, touched on earlier, is difficult to say. There has been no attempt to repeat the detailed analysis which Long (1984a and 1984b) undertook a decade ago. The little evidence that is available, however, suggests that not a great deal has changed. The majority of the membership of the IPM is female, and women continue to make up the bulk of the new recruits. Yet very few occupy the senior positions, even among the 'clerks' and the 'contract managers', let alone fill the seats on the main boards. Thus, as one of the architects of the third WIRS – Neil Millward – explained to the author, there did not seem to be much point in registering the gender of the respondents in the 1990 WIRS, since the great majority were men. Likewise, only 18 per cent of the respondents to the second CLIRS were women, and only 13 per cent were the most senior personnel executive in their organizations. In short, as Legge (1987: 52) suggested, it does seem to be a question of 'Heads I win, tails you lose.' There has been a decline in the activities, such as negotiating with trade unions, in which men predominated; yet there does not seem to have been an increase in the influence of women.

Conclusion

Clearly there have been changes in the profile of the personnel function in the UK in recent years. This is above all true of the activities and organization of the personnel function. Personnel managers are much less involved in dealing with trade unions now than was the case a decade or so ago, and are much more likely than they were to work on the basis of some form of service contract. Both, it can be argued, are consistent with HRM thinking, although they probably have more to do with the finance-driven preferences of senior managers for 'markets' over 'hierarchy' in decision-making about organization structures.

It is the continuities that are as impressive as, if not more impressive than, the changes, however. The picture is hardly flattering, and must be extremely disappointing for those hoping that HRM thinking would have had an impact. Personnel remains a highly fragmented occupational grouping; the image of the personnel manager as the general medical practitioner seems far removed from reality. Personnel management in the UK, it can be argued, remains largely made up of 'clerks' and 'contract managers', performing relatively routine administrative functions. The number of 'architects' is relatively small. The number of companies, even very large companies, with such people in the highest levels of decision-making is remarkably small. Critically, as the next section will demonstrate in more detail, this stands in marked contrast to overseas-owned companies, which are twice as likely to have such representation. The influence of the personnel function over budgetary and strategic decisions is correspondingly greater in overseas-owned as compared to UK-owned enterprises.

VARIATIONS ON A THEME

So far, the concern has been with the general profile of personnel management in the UK. Patterns differ from workplace to workplace and from company to company. Such differences are not entirely random, however. Two sets of variables are especially significant in making sense of the diversity. One reflects the choices that senior managers make about the strategy and structure of the organization. The other is ownership: Millward and his colleagues (1992: 33) say that the contrast between UK and foreign-owned organizations is 'striking'.

Strategy and structure

One decision which has a substantial influence is the strategy for growth. Thus, in the case of establishments it has already been shown that there is a very significant correlation between size and the presence of a specialist personnel manager: the larger the workplace, the more likely it is that there will be such a manager. The level of technology is also important: a personnel manager is more likely to be present where there is advanced technology (Millward *et al.* 1992: 33).

In the case of multi-establishment organizations, three significant axes of differentiation are diversification, divisionalization and strategic style. Diversification concerns whether companies are involved in related activities, and the associated degree of integration between different activities, or in unrelated activities, or whether they are spatially diversified but undertake the same kind of activity in many different locations. Divisionalization primarily concerns whether internal lines of differentiation within companies are primarily territorial (i.e. segmented according to regions or districts) or business-based (i.e. segmented into product or service divisions). Strategic style concerns the level at which strategic business decisions are taken (business unit, division, national subsidiary or corporate headquarters), the role of corporate headquarters in business development (planning, reviewing, monitoring) and the degree to which it stresses 'numbers-driven' rather than 'issue-driven' planning (for further details, see Marginson and Sisson (1994) and Sisson and Marginson (1994)).

Differences along these three axes generate differences in the extent to which companies are centralized or decentralized in their overall management approach, with consequent implications for the organization of the personnel function. Variations in the size of corporate personnel departments, for example, are only partially accounted for by the employment size of companies (Marginson *et al.* 1993: 5). The largest corporate personnel functions tend to be found among single business enterprises, such as the automobile manufacturers (Ford, General Motors (Vauxhall), Peugeot-Talbot and Rover), the main clearing banks (Barclays, Lloyds, National Westminster and Midland) and the multiple retailers (e.g. Sainsbury and Tesco), and among strategic planners; whereas diversified conglomerates and financial controllers, such as Lonrho or BTR, tend to have small numbers of corporate specialist staff, or none at all.

Ownership

A key variable in explaining major differences between organizations is whether they are UK- or foreign-owned:

> Twice the proportion of foreign-owned establishments as indigenous employed designated personnel specialists: as many as a third (32 per cent) did so compared with only 15 per cent of UK-owned establishments. As in 1984 the differences remained substantial when we compared establishments of similar size and they provided a first indicator of the continuing differences between UK and foreign-owned establishments which we describe at a number of points in this report.
>
> (Millward *et al.* 1992: 33)

The reference is to such differences as the structure of collective bargaining (foreign-owned establishments were more likely to deal with trade unions independently, than through the agency of an employers' organization), communication practice (foreign-owned establishments collected more information and disseminated more of it to their employees), and pay systems (foreign-owned establishments were more likely to use some form of incentive pay).

The two CLIRS also confirm that there were major differences between UK and foreign-owned companies. Foreign-owned companies were more than twice as likely to have a personnel director on the main UK board as their UK-owned counterparts. They were also more likely to have a corporate personnel policy committee comprised of senior managers from a range of functions and to hold meetings of personnel managers from different locations (Marginson *et al.* 1993b).

It also emerged that, although there was little difference in approach to trade unions and collective bargaining, there were significant differences in a range of other aspects:

> Overseas-owned companies were distinctive in their approaches to employee development, communication and involvement. As compared with UK-owned companies, they tended to have relatively high levels of expenditure on employee training; employed a wider range of methods of employee communication; were more likely to use upwards and two-way forms of communication; were more likely to provide information on investment plans to employees; and were less likely to utilise forms of financial participation.
>
> Overseas-owned companies were also distinctive in their policies towards managerial employees. Overseas-owned multinationals were more likely to move managerial staff between countries, to use a common job grading scheme for senior managers (such as Hay-MSL) across their worldwide operations and to have a separate head office department responsible for the training and development of managers in their subsidiaries overseas, than were UK-owned multinationals.
>
> (Marginson *et al.* 1993a: 13–14)

The presence of a personnel director – or, for that matter, a personnel manager in the case of the WIRS findings – makes many of these developments possible. It is not a straightforward issue of cause and effect, however. The presence of a personnel specialist and an array of personnel policies is to be seen as part and parcel of a general commitment to the management of human resources. It is this commitment which seems to distinguish UK from foreign-owned companies.

These findings can in turn be related to fundamental differences in systems of corporate governance. Two main types have been identified: the 'outsider' system, exemplified by the UK and the USA, and the 'insider' system associated with Germany and the Nordic countries (Franks and Mayer: 1992). Differences in the nature of the institutional shareholding and exposure to hostile takeover result in a greater concentration on short-run financial performance in the case of the 'outsider' system, whereas the 'insider' system allows greater emphasis on longer-run performance. Under 'outsider' systems, it can be argued, there is a stronger incentive to see employees as costs to be minimized, rather than assets to be developed, whereas the opposite is true of 'insider' systems. This is especially so in countries such as Germany, where employees or their representatives also have considerable rights as stakeholders. A corollary is that the management of human resources is more likely to be regarded as a strategic concern to headquarters under 'insider' systems than in 'outsider' systems, where responsibility is likely to be left to operating units (for further details, see Marginson and Sisson (1994)).

PERSONNEL MANAGEMENT AS A PROFESSION

The tendency for most of the functions into which management can be divided to seek to be regarded as 'professions' akin to medicine or the law is especially pronounced in Britain (Armstrong 1984). Personnel management is no exception. As Torrington and Hall (1987: 17) point out, personnel management in Britain has long exhibited many of the hallmarks of the profession listed by Millerson (1964): a permanent organization (the permanent headquarters staff of the IPM totalled just over 100 in 1994; skills based on theoretical knowledge; education and training provisions – the IPM is responsible for two major education programmes, the Certificate in Personnel and the Professional Education Scheme, as well as the provisions for continuing professional development discussed below; qualifying examinations – success in the examinations of the Professional Education Scheme is the main route into membership; codes of ethics; and a claim to be in the public good. The two regular monthly publications which the IPM supports, *Personnel Management* and *Personnel Management Plus* (which incorporates the *IPM News*) are not only an important source of general information, but also play a key role in the IPM's appointments service, which makes a significant contribution to the IPM's income.

As with the profile of the personnel function presented earlier, although there have been significant developments in the organization and activities of the IPM, it is the continuity which is most striking. Thus, membership continues to be restricted in two senses of the word. First, it remains restricted by design. There has been little concession to demands for greater opening. By far the most important route is by qualifying examination under the Professional Education Scheme. A so-called management entry route, which is based on an assessment of learning and experience, is available, but the numbers coming through it are relatively small. Significantly, too, even the prospect of merger with the Institute of Training and Development (ITD), which many have seen as a major way of raising the profile of the management of human resources (see, for example, the views expressed in Lawrence 1993), raised the ire of members, as the letters columns in *Personnel Management* regularly confirm.

The second sense in which IPM membership remains restricted is a direct result of the first. Even though the membership of the IPM has been growing throughout the period, it probably still represents only a minority of personnel managers in the UK. A significant proportion of the personnel managers employed in the corporate and divisional headquarters of the larger enterprises in the private sector is also not IPM-qualified (Marginson *et al.* 1988: 54; Marginson *et al.* 1993b: 29).

In the case of education and training, there have been major initiatives in continuous professional development (CPD), following an investigation of the activities of other professional bodies such as the Law Society. The IPM has not only made considerable investments in flexible training and learning packages, but has also drawn up guidelines to help members to develop themselves on the job. This also links with the work that IPM is undertaking in cooperation with the so-called Personnel Standards Lead Body for developing national qualifications for personnel work under the arrangements for National Vocational Qualifications. Significantly, however, the IPM has yet to make CPD a mandatory requirement under its code of professional conduct; a decision about whether it should be included is not to be made until after a survey of members, beginning in July 1994. In practice, this means that the apprenticeship model of training remains dominant. In short, the IPM has not developed a hierarchy of qualifications, which would seem to be in keeping with the realities of the structure of the personnel function discussed in an earlier section.

In the words of its President (Farrance 1993: 61), the IPM has also taken significant initiatives to improve its standing as the 'authoritative voice on employment issues'. Two further developments, as well as the ITD merger and CPD initiatives, merit particular attention. One is an ongoing internal reorganization. Especially significant is the appointment of a Director General of stature who is capable of expressing the views of the membership. The position is currently occupied by Geoff Armstrong, who is not only a former personnel director of British Leyland, Metal Box and Standard Chartered Bank, but also chair of the Confederation of British Industry's Employment Policy Committee. The other is the commissioning of a major research programme to improve the quality of information and analysis available on personnel matters. Subjects have included a national minimum wage, performance pay, and participation and involvement, as well as the organization of the personnel function itself (IPM 1991).

Despite these initiatives, however, and despite its continued development of professional codes of conduct (e.g. dealing with recruitment, testing, continuous development, involvement and participation, and equal opportunities), the IPM has remained extremely cautious, so far as the major issues of the day are concerned. As well as the question of board-level representation, to which the final section returns, this is especially true of the role of the state in helping to fashion an appropriate human resource management regime to meet the demands of an increasingly global and competitive environment. The IPM seems to have chosen either to remain silent or to support the principle of voluntarism. This is perhaps understandable, in view of the concern of the bulk of the membership with the day-to-day issues of technique and the vigour with which the British government has promoted deregulation of the labour market. Sadly, however, it does mean that the 'cost minimization' approach has gone more or less unchallenged; the case for the 'asset management' approach has not been considered as seriously as it has in other countries. Policy-making, it can be argued, both at national and at company level, has suffered as a result.

CONCLUSIONS AND IMPLICATIONS

Remarkable as it may seem, HRM seems to have had little or no impact on the personnel function in the UK in the decade or so in which the thinking associated with it has been so pervasive. Hopes that HRM would lead to a more strategic approach to the management of human resources have been largely frustrated. There do not even appear to have been moves to adopt the new title. Critically, there appears to have been no increase in board-level representation, even in the very large companies.

Fears about a decline in the numbers and influence of personnel managers appear to have been equally groundless, however. Clearly there is evidence of line managers playing a more important role, above all where the 'contract manager' who negotiated with trade unions reigned supreme; but this type of personnel manager was probably a rarer breed than was assumed. Similarly it does not appear that personnel has turned into a peripheral function. There has been, it is true, greater fragmentation or 'balkanization' of the personnel function, but this is a very different matter and mirrors developments in management more generally.

Concerns about the implications of HRM for the values of the personnel profession also seem to have subsided. The Institute of Personnel Management continues to exhibit many of the hallmarks of the traditional profession. Membership grows from strength to strength, and the number of young people in particular who are prepared to submit themselves to the rigour of the IPM's examination scheme shows no sign of dropping.

One explanation for the relatively low impact is that, outside of a small number of mostly foreign-owned 'greenfield' workplaces, the UK has seen very little of HRM (Sisson, 1994). Certainly it has seen very little of the people-centred approach of the 'soft version'. Admittedly, there has been what Storey (1992: 28) has referred to as the 'remarkable take-up by large British companies of initiatives which are in the style of "human resource management" model'. Yet many of these initiatives, as Storey's study confirms, rarely add up to an integrated approach. Key ingredients such as single status and guarantees of employment security are noticeable by their absence. The managements introducing even some HRM initiatives have also been the exception. Paradoxically, as Millward and his colleagues (1992) confirm, these practices are much rarer in the majority of non-union workplaces.

It is even questionable whether there is much evidence of the 'hard' version of HRM. Certainly a great deal of what is going on, however it is labelled, is better understood in terms of the 'hard' rather than the 'soft' version. This is certainly true of many small and medium-sized enterprises, where the bulk of the evidence (see, for example, ACAS 1992, 1993; Millward *et al.* 1992: 364–5; Citizens' Advice Bureau 1993) suggests that the model of *Bleak House* is more appropriate than HRM. It is also probably true of most large mainstream organizations, where there is very considerable evidence of a shift from 'collectivism' to 'individualism' in management's approach. Yet, even in these cases, the notion of managers making strategic choices from a menu of options seems far removed from reality. They may be taking advantage of the political context to assert their control, but their use of it, and their response to business conditions, remains largely *ad hoc* and pragmatic.

Important though this first explanation is in terms of this volume as a whole, it is a second and related explanation which deserves attention here. As Storey's (1992) study so clearly shows, the HRM practices that have been introduced have largely been at the initiative of line managers. Also the introduction of these practices has been the corollary of fundamental changes in working arrangements, rather than any inherent belief in the HRM approach itself. In some cases the context has been set by the direct pressure of international competition, such as in the case of Rover, or the demands of customers, such as in the cases of the Japanese car manufacturers (Nissan, Honda and Toyota) in the motor components sector. In the public sector it has been the result of government pressure in the form of major reorganizations (e.g. the introduction of 'executive agencies' in the civil service and of 'trusts' in the NHS) or of reductions in expenditure. Very often personnel managers have not been involved in the initial stages of planning and development of the changes, and their role has been limited to dealing with the implications.

This is where the profile of personnel management presented earlier comes in. Not only do personnel managers in the UK comprise an extremely heterogeneous group in terms of their activities. It is difficult to avoid the conclusion that the great majority of personnel managers, above all in UK-owned organizations, are essentially 'clerks' or 'contract managers', rather than 'architects'. Their main activities involve relatively routine administration, which may be critical for the day-to-day operation of the business, but which are far removed from the grander notions of strategy, strategic choice and 'regime competition' which have become some of the defining characteristics of HRM.

The key question which this conclusion begs is whether it is possible to have anything but a very partial form of HRM with a personnel management profile such as exists in the UK. In particular, is it possible to have HRM if there is no board-level representation? Evidently, it is not a straightforward issue of cause and effect: appoint a personnel director to the board and assume the problems are solved. Such representation would seem to be a necessary, if not sufficient, condition for the strategic management of human resources, however. The evidence of CLIRS is that board-level representation is correlated with an array of personnel policies which, taken together, are to be seen as part and parcel of a general commitment to the management of human resources. Moreover, it is this commitment which seems to distinguish many foreign-owned companies from their UK counterparts.

As some personnel managers in UK-owned companies have pointed out to the author, they do not have the luxury of the strategic decision as to whether or not there should be board-level representation. The more thoughtful have also echoed Thurley's (1981) sentiment that, because of the corporate governance arrangements discussed earlier, personnel managers in the UK are 'working against the grain'. The key responsibility for change, they argue on the basis of this analysis, rests with senior managers and the Government.

Clearly, life would be a lot easier if these actors would take the initiative, but they are unlikely to do so. Even chief executives, as major proponents of the strategic HRM models of the 1980s have had to recognize (see, for example, Kochan and Dyer 1993), can become prisoners of their own strategies and structures. The Government remains committed to a policy of voluntarism, despite the growing body of evidence to suggest that, in Streeck's (1992: 20) words, 'a regime of free markets and private hierarchies is not enough to generate and support a pattern of . . . quality production'.

In these circumstances it is important that personnel managers and the IPM speak out if the rhetoric of 'asset management' is simply to be used as a mask for the reality of 'cost minimization'. The 'coping' strategy identified by Thurley (1981) more than a decade ago is surely no longer appropriate, i.e. using professionalism in an instrumental fashion to hide the mismatch between a pretentious and abstract model of what they should be doing, and the reality of a relatively fragmented and routine set of activities, and yet in reality conforming to local organizational (and governmental) norms. In particular, there is a need, as well as developing a hierarchy of qualifications much more in keeping with developments in personnel work than the existing apprenticeship model, to mount a major campaign for board-level representation in UK-owned companies. Such representation, as has already been pointed out, is not going to be sufficient to solve the problem of the mismanagement of human resources. One thing is very clear, however. If Cinderella does not even get to the ball, there can never be the prospect of a happy ending.

REFERENCES

Adams, K. (1991) 'Externalisation vs specialisation: what is happening to personnel?', *Human Resource Management Journal* 1(4): 40–54.

Advisory, Conciliation and Arbitration Service (1992) *Annual Report*, London: ACAS.

—— (1993) *Annual Report*, London: ACAS.

Armstrong, M. (1987) 'Human resource management: a case of the emperor's new clothes', *Personnel Management* August: 30–5.

Armstrong, P. (1984) 'Competition between the organisational professions and the evolution of management control strategies', in K. Thompson (ed.) *Work, Employment and Unemployment*, Milton Keynes: Open University Press.

Citizen's Advice Bureau (1993) *Job Insecurity*, London: Social Policy Section, Citizens' Advice Bureau.

Daniel, B. (1993) 'Who handles personnel issues in British Industry?', *Personnel Management* December: 25–7.

Drucker, P.F. (1961) *The Practice of Management*, London: Pan.

Farrance, R. (1993) 'Establishing standards of professional competence', *Personnel Management* October: 6.

Fowler, A. (1987) 'When chief executives discover human resource management', *Personnel Management* January: 3.

—— (1992) 'How to structure a personnel department', *Personnel Management Plus* January: 22–3.

Franks, J. and Mayer, C. (1992) 'Corporate control: a synthesis of international evidence', unpublished paper, London Business School/University of Warwick.

Hilton, P. (1993) 'Consultants get chance to tender for PO counters' personnel work', *Personnel Management Plus* July: 1.

Hunter, L. and Thom, G. (1991) 'External advisory services in labour management: a worm's eye view', *Human Resource Management Journal* 2(1): 22–41.

Institute of Personnel Management (1991) *IPM Research Prospectus*, London: IPM.

Kochan, T.A. and Dyer, L. (1993) 'Managing transformational change: the role of human resource professionals', proceedings of the Conference of the International Industrial Relations Association, Sydney, 1992, Geneva: International Industrial Relations Association.

Lawrence, S. (1993) 'Setback to new Institute plans', *Personnel Management Plus* October: 1–2.

Legge, K. (1987) 'Women in personnel management: uphill climb or downhill slide?', in A. Spence and D. Podmore (eds) *In a Man's World: Essays on Women in Male-Dominated Professions*, London: Tavistock Publications.

Long, P. (1984a) *The Personnel Specialists: A Comparative Study of Male and Female Careers*, London: IPM.

—— (1984b) 'Would you put your daughter in personnel?', *Personnel Management* April: 16–20.

Mackay, L. and Torrington, D. (1986) *The Changing Nature of Personnel Management*, London: IPM.

Marginson, P. and Sisson, K. (1994) 'The structure of capital in Europe: the emerging Euro-company and its implications for industrial relations', in A. Ferner and R. Hyman (eds) *The New Frontiers of Industrial Relations*, Oxford: Blackwell.

Marginson, P., Edwards, P.K., Armstrong, P. and Purcell, J. (1993a) 'Executive summary of findings. Second company level, industrial relations survey', Coventry: Industrial Relations Research Unit. Mimeo.

Marginson, P., Edwards, P.K., Armstrong, P., Purcell, J. and Hubbard, N. (1993b) 'Report of the initial findings from the second company-level industrial relations survey', *Warwick Papers in Industrial Relations*, No. 45, Coventry: University of Warwick.

Miller, K. (1975) *Psychological Testing*, Aldershot: Gower.

Millerson, G. (1964) *The Qualifying Associations*, London: Routledge & Kegan Paul.

Millward, N. and Stevens, M. (1986) *British Workplace Industrial Relations 1980–1984: the DE/PSI/ACAS Surveys*, Aldershot: Gower.

Millward, N., Stevens, M., Smart, D. and Hawes, W.R. (1992) *Workplace Industrial Relations in Transition: the ED/ESRC/PSI/ACAS Surveys*, Aldershot: Gower.

Recruitment and Development Report (1991) 'New ways of managing your human resources: a survey of top employers', *Industrial Relations Review* 15, March: 6–16.

Sisson, K. (1989) 'Personnel management in perspective', in K. Sisson (ed.) *Personnel Management in Britain*, Oxford: Blackwell.

—— (1994) 'Personnel management in Britain: paradigms, practice and prospects', in K. Sisson (ed.) *Personnel Management: A Comprehensive Guide to Theory and Practice in Britain*, Oxford: Blackwell.

Sisson, K. and Marginson, P. (1994) 'Management: systems, structures and strategy', in P.K. Edwards (ed.) *Industrial Relations in Britain*, 2nd edn, Oxford: Blackwell.

Storey, J. (1989) *New Perspectives on Human Resource Management*, London: Routledge.

—— (1992) *Developments in the Management of Human Resources*, Oxford: Blackwell.

Streeck, W. (1992) *Social Institutions and Economic Performance: Studies of Industrial Relations in Advanced Capitalist Economies*, London: Sage.

Thurley, K. (1981) 'Personnel management in the UK – a case for urgent treatment?', *Personnel Management* August: 24–8.

Torrington, D. (1989) 'Human resource management and the personnel function', in J. Storey (ed.) *New Perspectives on Human Resource Management*, London: Routledge.

Torrington, D. and Hall, L. (1987) *Personnel Management: A New Approach*, Hemel Hempstead: Prentice-Hall.

Tyson, S. (1979) 'Specialists in ambiguity: Personnel management as an occupation', PhD thesis, University of London.

—— (1987) 'The management of the personnel function', *Journal of Management Studies* 24, September: 523–32.

Tyson, S. and Fell, A. (1986) *Evaluating the Personnel Function*, London: Hutchinson.

Watson, T.J. (1977) *The Personnel Managers*, London: Routledge & Kegan Paul.

Chapter 5

Human resource management, trade unions and industrial relations

David E. Guest

INTRODUCTION

The rising interest in human resource management (HRM) throughout the 1980s coincided with a steady decline in the significance of industrial relations as a central feature of economic performance and policy. It also coincided with a decline in the membership and influence of trade unions – during the 1980s, trade union membership declined from 53 per cent to 33 per cent. Industrial conflict displayed a similar decline, so that in the early 1990s, strikes were at their lowest level for many decades.

It was tempting in the 1980s to seek an association between the apparent rise of HRM and the decline of trade unions and industrial relations. Part of the temptation lay in the knowledge that the early models of HRM were drawn mainly from successful American non-union firms. In the mid-1990s the emerging evidence paints a much more complex picture. To begin to understand it, we need to set both HRM and industrial relations within the wider economic and political system.

The central thrust of economic, industrial and legislative policy in the UK for well over a decade has been to create a market-driven economy. From an industrial relations perspective, the most telling feature of this policy has been the successive pieces of legislation designed to limit the role and rights of trade unions. This legislative programme has moved the unions in particular, and industrial relations in general, from the centre to the periphery of corporate concern. For many firms, industrial relations are no longer a contingent variable, helping to shape their business policy in the way they might have done ten or fifteen years earlier.

Organizations now have more choice about industrial relations. Do they also have a choice about HRM? If we follow the new market philosophy, then HRM should be driven by market factors. The dominant analyses provided by writers such as Porter (1980) and Miles and Snow (1978, 1984), and developed further with respect to HRM by Tichy *et al.* (1982) and Schuler and Jackson (1987) typically identify three main bases for competitive advantage. In broad terms these can be defined as market leadership based on innovation, on quality or on cost. These choices are explored more fully in other chapters. The point to emphasize here is that innovation, and more particularly, quality-based strategies, require for their success a workforce that is committed to the organization. To take a well-known example, an airline competing through quality must, at the point of customer contact, have staff with the autonomy and motivation to provide the kind of high-quality service that will 'delight' the customer. This will require enthusiasm and initiative on the part of the staff, and trust to permit autonomy on the part of the organization. This 'psychological contract' is a core element of the concept of organizational commitment. But if commitment is a central concept in an HR strategy for managing the workforce, where does this leave industrial relations? Commitment is an essentially unitarist concept. Is it possible to be committeed to both a company and a trade union, or is such dual commitment impossible? To understand the possible relationships between HRM and industrial relations and the role of trade unions in this market-driven economy, we must explore in more detail the concept of commitment and the feasibility of dual commitment.

The third strategy for competitive advantage, based on cost leadership, fits well with the political drive to present the UK as a cheap manufacturing base. The underlying assumptions are more pluralist in nature, to the extent that management will seek to minimize labour costs, while workers may well seek to maximize them. The context is therefore ripe for traditional industrial relations and apparently less suitable for the kind of HRM which has at its core the concept of organizational commitment. This certainly tends to be the conclusion of those writing from a strategic perspective. However, the legislation that has freed up the market has also extended the choice for employers. They may believe they can reduce costs more effectively without a trade union. The choice is therefore no longer HRM versus industrial relations; the new alternative is to have neither, and to get rid of all the expensive baggage with which each is associated. It follows that we need to incorporate this wider range of options in any review of trends in HRM and industrial relations.

Many of the strategic options available to management appear to challenge the role of trade unions and offer a potentially bleak view of their future. In some workplaces they may survive because they have always been there. Since they are built in to the system, they can be accommodated as long as they are not a drain on resources. But whenever a major strategic review occurs – for example, in the context of a takeover, or a rationalization programme – their role is likely to be challenged. The logic of a market-driven HRM strategy is that where high organizational commitment is sought, unions are irrelevant. Where cost advantage is the goal, unions and industrial relations systems appear to carry higher costs. If possible, it will be preferable to do without them. This scenario is one of continuing gradual decline in membership and influence, unless the unions can respond with new strategies of their own. Paradoxically, HRM, far from threatening the union role, may present one basis for a new union strategy.

Following the themes raised in this introduction, the chapter is divided into three main parts. The first examines organizational commitment and dual commitment as a basis for considering the interaction between HRM and trade unionism. The second examines the evidence on the choices being made by employers in the UK about the type of HRM and industrial relations they wish to pursue. The third part considers strategy from the trade union perspective and explores the possible agendas available to trade unions in an environment where HRM may be viewed as an opportunity as much as a major challenge.

COMMITMENT AND THE THEORY OF HUMAN RESOURCE MANAGEMENT AND INDUSTRIAL RELATIONS

Models of HRM (see, for example, Beer *et al.* 1985; Guest 1987) place organizational commitment at their core. Indeed it is the central feature that distinguishes HRM from traditional personnel management/industrial relations systems. Furthermore it has been suggested (Guest 1989) that if the four key HRM policy goals are strategic integration, quality, flexibility and commitment, then only commitment to the organization need present a direct challenge to trade unionism. It provides the basis for the contrasting values and assumptions underpinning normative views of HRM and industrial relations which have been presented by Walton (1985a), Guest (1987) and Storey (1992). The key constrasting dimensions are presented in Table 5.1.

Table 5.1 HRM's key dimensions

Dimension	*Industrial relations*	*Human resource management*
Psychological contract	Compliance	Commitment
Behaviour referent	Norms custom and practice	Values/mission
Relations	Low trust, pluralist, collective	High-trust, unitarist, individual
Organization and design	Formal roles, hierarchy, division of labour, managerial controls	Flexible roles, flat structure, teamwork/autonomy, self-control

This type of dichotomy reflects a 'soft' view of HRM as being concerned with the full utilization of human resources for the benefit of the organization. At the same time, however, there is an assumption that the best way to ensure the full utilization of human resources is to take care of what Herzberg (1966) would term the 'hygiene factors', such as job security and pay, through generous and fair provision, and to tap motivation by providing autonomy and challenge. To fill out the HRM model, the organization should invest in careful selection and extensive training to ensure the high quality of human resources. In many respects, this has always been the traditional means of managing and motivating managerial and professional staff. The new element within HRM is that this should be extended to all staff.

Organizational commitment is central to this approach for several reasons. First, by holding out the prospect that committed workers will be highly motivated and will go 'beyond contract', it promises higher performance. Second, committed workers can be expected to exercise responsible autonomy or self-monitoring and self-control, removing the need for supervisory and inspection staff and producing efficiency gains. Third, committed workers are more likely to stay with the organization, thereby ensuring a return on the investment in careful selection, training and development. Finally, but central to the discussion of HRM and industrial relations, it is assumed that a worker who is committed to the organization is unlikely to become involved in 'industrial relations' or any type of collective activity which might reduce the quality and quantity of their contribution to the organization. This is aided by moving away from the traditional psychological contract of 'a fair day's work for a fair day's pay', thereby reducing the potential for the effort bargain to operate as a potential focus for conflict and grievance. The commitment contract implies that, instead, the staff will go that extra mile for the company.

Placing organizational commitment at the core of the definition of HRM acknowledges the deliberate attempt to win the hearts and minds of the workforce. The traditional definition of organizational commitment (Mowday *et al.* 1982), and the one most relevant to this analysis, defines it as consisting of three components: an identification with the goals and values of the organization, a desire to belong to the organization, and a willingness to display effort on behalf of the organization. Union commitment can be defined in precisely the same way (Gordon *et al.* 1980). The key issue then becomes the compatibility of the goals and values of the company and the union. If they are compatible, then it is possible to display high commitment to both company and union. At the same time, it raises fundamental questions about the role of the union and the nature of the values for which it stands. Alternatively, we need to consider how far workers can live with the inherent conflict and ambiguity of identification with two potentially opposing sets of values. Research by Reichers (1985, 1986), for example, has suggested that workers can express commitment to potentially conflicting targets such as work group, career and company. These issues have stimulated research on dual commitment to company and union.

The choices about commitment to company and union can be presented in a simple matrix:

		Commitment to company	
		High	*Low*
Commitment to union	*High*	1	2
	Low	3	4

A matrix of this sort is a useful starting point for analysis of commitment to company and union. It is important to bear in mind that it is an over-simplification in two important respects. The first is that there may be intermediate levels of commitment to both company and union, reflecting, perhaps, a kind of conditional approval of both. The second, building on the work of Reichers and others, is that there are other potential focuses of commitment. These include a career, a profession and the family. Commitment to any of these may also conflict with commitment to either company and/or union.

There is a long tradition of research into dual commitment, stimulated initially by concern in the USA in the 1950s that the unions were becoming too powerful and were drawing commitment away from companies. More recently, the question has been one of whether unions can retain commitment in the face of the growing interest in HRM. Much of the research has been conducted in North America, with its rather different industrial relations systems, and this should be borne in mind.

One important strand of research has examined the antecedents of commitment to company and union. If the factors that shape commitment to each are different, then it should be possible for them to coexist, since a change on a factor affecting company commitment need not influence union commitment. On the other hand, if they are caused by the same factor, either they operate from the same end of a continuum and become indistinguishable, which may be the case with some Japanese 'in-house' unions, or they operate from competing ends of the same continuum and therefore are incompatible. The first case might include the quality of working conditions, the second might be the right to hold union mass meetings in working time. The underlying theories are concerned with cognitive dissonance and role conflict. From the limited number of studies of the antecedents, the view seems to be emerging (see, for example, Barling *et al.* 1990; Thaker *et al.* 1990) that union and company commitment, although psychologically similar constructs with similar classes of antecedent and outcome, are caused by different specific factors.

The key work is probably that reported by Angle and Perry (1986). In the study of dual commitment among bus company employees, they identified the industrial relations climate as a key mediating variable. Where there was a cooperative and conflict-free climate, dual commitment was feasible. However, where the climate was hostile, workers were forced to confront the competing commitment to company and union and make a choice, or alternatively to display commitment to neither. This implies that when conflict occurs, even though commitment to company and union may be caused by different factors, some choices among these factors have to be made. A longitudinal study by Fullager and Barling (1991) lends further weight to the importance of industrial relations climate, but was less successful in identifying predictors of dual commitment than specific commitment to company or union. Ironically, active participation in union activities among their sample of university employees seemed to result in disillusion with the union, leading to lower commitment to the union and higher commitment to the employer.

In one interesting study, Barling *et al.* (1990) had the opportunity to examine dual commitment in the aftermath of a strike. They found marked differences between those who viewed the industrial relations climate positively and negatively. In the former group, there was a correlation of .06 between commitment to a union and to the company but among those who perceived a poor industrial relations climate, the correlation was −.52. This takes us one step further in suggesting that it is not just the existence of conflict but the way it is perceived and interpreted that influences the feasibility of dual commitment.

There has only been a limited amount of research on this topic in the UK. Guest and Dewe (1991), in a study of workers in three organizations in the electronics industry, found little evidence of dual commitment, where commitment was defined in terms of identification with company and union. (It is also worth noting that levels of dual commitment in the Angle and Perry study were quite low.) Indeed, the predominant mode was commitment to neither company nor trade union. On the other hand, use of the same questions in other countries elicited evidence of higher levels of dual commitment in Sweden and West Germany, though, perhaps surprisingly, not in Japan (Guest and Dewe 1991). The European evidence does provide further indirect support for the importance of the industrial relations climate.

If we accept the tenor of this research, and with it the implication that dual commitment is possible within a positive industrial relations climate, we then need to know something about the characteristics of this climate. As a minimum, if it is an industrial relations climate (Dastmalchian *et al.*

1991), this implies the legitimacy of a pluralist perspective, in which both company and union have distinctive roles. There is choice about how far these are grounded in legislation, as is the case in most of Europe, and how far they rest on the voluntaristic assumptions of those in key positions on both sides. Whatever the context, the role of the unions can vary considerably.

At least three models for the union role in the context of dual commitment can be identified. In the first, typified by some Japanese organizations, the role of the union at the local level is very much that of another arm of the company. One important manifestation of this is that the head of the union may move into a senior management position. A second approach, typified by Germany and Sweden, integrates industrial relations with the political system, and is therefore enshrined in legislation. One important element in this is the distinction between the issues dealt with at plant and company level and those handled at national level. In these countries, the more contentious issues, particularly those concerning pay and working hours, have mostly been handled at the national level. At the local level the works council has dealt with more operational issues, often issues of mutual concern. The mode has been predominantly one that, in Walton and McKersie's (1965) terms, would be described as integrative bargaining, or problem-solving within a positive industrial relations climate, where dual commitment to company and union is possible. That cosy relationship may be breaking down in the face of the severe recession which has forced companies to lay off workers and to abandon the concept of labour as a largely fixed cost.

The third model is the voluntaristic UK approach, now reshaped by the new legislative framework. The tradition of bargaining at company or even plant level has reinforced a pluralist perspective. At the same time, it is important to recognize that relations in most workplaces are relatively harmonious and that the propensity for industrial action has always been low. However, the absence of legislative or cultural forces encouraging dual commitment makes its presence more fragile and more susceptible to the choices and actions of the key stakeholders. In practice, the stakeholder with the power to exercise choice is increasingly management. This raises the important question of what shapes managements' perceptions. It may be national fashions, personal experiences of dealing with unions, the personality of the key union officials, or simply inertia. The important point about this system is that it is inherently less stable and provides a less predictable basis for dual commitment.

During the 1980s, management in many UK organizations launched initiatives to win the hearts and minds of the workforce. Often, these fell under the broad umbrella of culture change programmes. One major initiative was the promotion of employee involvement as a mechanism, *inter alia*, to increase organizational commitment and reduce the sense of 'them and us'. Marchington *et al.* (1992) have shown that employee involvement programmes have had only a limited impact on organizational commitment. One reason for this is revealed in a longitudinal study (Guest and Peccei 1993), which found that an employee involvement exercise increased identification with the local work group, rather than with the organization as a whole.

Given the market imperatives which drive firms towards HRM, the evidence from reviews of the impact of employee involvement and performance management (IPM 1992) implies that managers have to work harder at their policies to generate commitment. In this context, they may confront the need for a union presence. At the same time, they may challenge the value of this 'soft', commitment-based approach to HRM, either abandoning it or complementing it with mechanisms of control and surveillance. One outcome may be the growth of a new 'hard' form of HRM. It acknowledges the need to make full use of employees if the organization is to succeed in a competitive market-place and to provide autonomy at the point of customer interface, because of the obvious gains in productivity that arise from resolving issues at their point of origin. But at the same time, it operates a range of controls, partly built around clearly specified goals, partly based on sophisticated monitoring of the performance of the workforce. This represents the 'glass prison' of the information technology age, noted by Zuboff (1988). It may also represent the kind of HRM emerging in those new factories where there has been careful recruitment of a young, compliant workforce. Certainly in the mid-1990s programmes of culture change and employee involvement, the 'soft' policies designed to generate organizational commitment, appear to have moved back-stage.

The evidence of limited dual commitment presents challenges for the unions. It would be unwise for unions to rely on one of the traditional bases of commitment to the union, namely a presumed belief in trade unionism (Guest and Dewe 1988). Unions must find a new basis for commitment. The apparent failure of many companies to generate enthusiastic commitment among their workforce suggests that opportunities for unions still exist. If management is tempted to pursue a 'hard' version of HRM, this might backfire, providing further scope for unions. These and other policy options for unions will be considered later in the chapter. First we analyse recent developments at the interface of HRM and industrial relations as a basis for understanding company policy and practice.

DEVELOPMENTS IN INDUSTRIAL RELATIONS AND HUMAN RESOURCE MANAGEMENT

If we extrapolate from the discussion of dual commitment, which is essentially concerned with the response at the individual level, to the analysis of policy options facing organizations, we can present the broad alternatives in a similar way:

		HRM priority	
		High	*Low*
Industrial relations priority	*High*	1	2
	Low	3	4

Option 1 gives priority to both industrial relations and HRM, implies that dual commitment is feasible and assumes a positive industrial relations climate. It might be termed 'the new realism' and is reflected, for example, in recent publications from the IPA (1992). Option 2 represents the stereotype of the traditional UK approach. It assumes that trade unions are well-established and that HRM has not figured significantly on the management agenda. This approach, a traditional collectivism, is probably most likely to be found in parts of the public sector. Option 3 represents the stereotype of individualized HRM, popularly associated with American electronics firms, where an individualistic philosophy assumes no need for trade unions or for any other type of collective activity. Option 4 reflects a view that cost advantage can best be achieved by avoiding both industrial relations and HRM. For those with a vested interest in industrial relations and HRM, and possibly for the workers affected by it, it represents a kind of 'black hole'. It is a neglected area of study which is just beginning to receive more attention. It is important because it helps to refocus a debate which can slip too easily into an analysis of the choice of either unions or HRM by suggesting the possibility of neither.

Within this framework we can analyse evidence on recent trends in industrial relations and HRM in the UK to determine developments in and between these options. Ideally, such evidence looks at industrial relations and HR trends together. This requires either sophisticated analysis of complex data sets or case studies. There are a number of both, although a lot of the evidence is more limited in scope. In this chapter we will emphasize developments in industrial relations, rather than in specific areas of HRM policy and practice, since these are covered in other chapters.

In any analysis of trends in industrial relations related directly or indirectly to HRM, we might wish to look at evidence such as:

- union recognition and derecognition
- developments in the 'new' industrial relations, such as single table bargaining and no-strike deals

- the role of unions in any changes affecting industrial relations
- the importance of industrial relations as an issue
- the outcomes of industrial relations, including levels of conduct activity, any union mark-up and productivity.

We will analyse developments as they apply to each of the four options/ quadrants in the model.

1: The new realism – a high emphasis on HRM and industrial relations

Kochan *et al.* (1986), proclaiming the transformation of American industrial relations, cited a limited number of cases illustrative of a collaborative joint endeavour to shape a new relationship between management and union. The cases appear to fit well with the rhetoric of the Harvard approach to HRM. Beer *et al.* (1985) discuss the coincidence of stakeholder interests and the importance of participation, power equalization, trust and commitment. Walton (1985b) emphasizes mutuality:

> The new HRM model is composed of policies that promote mutuality – mutual goals, mutual influence, mutual respect, mutual rewards, mutual responsibility. The theory is that policies of mutuality will elicit commitment, which in turn will yield both better economic performance and greater human development.

It would be dangerous to over-emphasize the importance of any new emergent pattern of industrial relations in the USA. However, it is this type of pattern that we might expect in those organizations in the UK where attempts are made by managers to pursue an approach that integrates HRM and industrial relations.

Evidence about a joint approach can best be gleaned from case studies. There are a number of cases which appear to fit this pattern. One of the best known is Nissan (Wickens 1987), although according to some commentators (Garrahan and Stewart 1992) it is a 'hard' version of HRM, in the sense that tight control and performance systems operate. Wickens (1993) has recently confronted this issue. He argues that the analysis developed initially by Walton (1985a), and presented earlier, which contrasts control/ compliance and commitment philosophies, presents a false dichotomy. In the car industry, he suggests, you need both. He further argues that, by and large, leading Japanese organizations in Japan, and Nissan in the UK, have achieved this. He accepts the need for a representative system for workers and the need to promote workers' interests, and in particular to ensure job security. But he further emphasizes that this must be based on cooperation rather than confrontation, and therefore he seems to develop his analysis within a predominantly unitarist perspective. Wickens deserves attention as one of the small band of senior managers who have tackled these issues at both the intellectual and operational levels, even if his emphasis on job security at Nissan has fallen victim to the effects of the recession on the car industry.

Many of the other examples of serious attempts at a joint approach – Rover being a case in point – come from the car industry, where the unions are very well entrenched but where market forces demand improvements in productivity and quality. Indeed the circumstances are similar to those in the cases cited by Kochan *et al.* (1986). In most organizations, managers start from a position where the unions are entrenched. The choice in new plants is more open. Therefore, taking some well-publicized cases, Toyota and Bosch recognized a single union, while Honda has decided to operate without any unions.

In new plants, one point at which high priority is given to both HRM and industrial relations is at the time of the so-called 'beauty contest', where unions have competed for recognition rights. From the union side, this constitutes a form of concession bargaining based on who promises an agreement closest to the management ideal. In some cases, such as the well-publicized ones of Toshiba (Trevor 1988) and Nissan (Wickens 1987) and the similar but less well known case of the Japanese/American joint venture IBC Vehicles, the positive initial relationship has continued. However, negotiations and all important representative meetings take place between management and a works council. The council represents all the workforce and union shop stewards have to stand for election alongside non-union workers. There is, therefore, a pluralist system, based on a management agenda and the principle of mutuality, but one where the role of the union is somewhat ambiguous. As a result it is not surprising that it has sometimes been difficult to recruit workers into the union. To date, union membership at Nissan in Sunderland has never exceeded 50 per cent of the workforce.

Another source of evidence about new collaborative arrangements comes from analysis of single-union and single-table bargaining. The third workplace industrial relations survey (WIRS3) (Millward *et al.* 1992) found no evidence of major growth in these areas. Nevertheless, a review of such arrangements (IRS 1993) concluded that they are almost always the result of employer initiatives, but that both employers and unions seem satisfied with them. They have facilitated greater flexibility, more multi-skilling, the removal of union demarcations and improvements in quality. From a union perspective they have produced extensions in consultation and moves towards single status.

The cases described by Storey (1992) provide some of the best information on recent trends, although again we must note that many of the cases are drawn from large companies which are household names, or at least industrial relations names. Storey concludes that there is little evidence of any frontal attack on unions, but equally little attempt to involve the unions in the planning and implementation of change. In most cases where unions have been well established in the past, the two systems of industrial relations and HRM operate side by side but with a tendency for management to give increasing weight to systems of employee involvement, and in particular communication, which tend to by-pass the union.

Storey's (1992) finding that the two systems can coexist and remain relatively compartmentalized is not in doubt; but it does raise interesting questions about the impact of the systems and more particularly the HRM system. If industrial relations remain healthy in the context of HRM, there are at least five possible explanations. First, the HRM may be so ineffective that it is having a minimal impact on values and commitment. Second, the 'hard' version is being used, and this leaves a level of anxiety such that workers continue to support the traditional industrial relations system and the trade union as a safeguard and safety net. Third, management, while supporting HRM, recognize the value of retaining collective arrangements because of their convenience, particularly in those establishments where large numbers are employed. Fourth, it is possible that the system of mutuality is viable and a mutually beneficial collaboration between management and unions can operate, resulting in the maintenance of both systems. Fifth, the industrial relations system may continue as a largely symbolic 'empty shell', insufficiently important for management to confront and eliminate, but retaining the outward appearance of health to the casual observer.

The cases described by Storey give some credence to the 'empty shell' hypothesis. Management sets the agenda, which is market-driven, while industrial relations issues are relatively low on the list of concerns. It may be misleading to suggest that the two systems co-exist. The evidence from both the cases and from WIRS3 suggests that the direct management channels are receiving increased attention, while the union channels are in decline. This applies to communication: WIRS3 reveals a growth in direct communication, alongside some decline in joint consultation. In a slightly different way, the growth and extension to the shop floor of individual performance-related pay schemes reinforces individual concerns at the possible expense of the collective union interest. Where it is badly handled – as, for example in the case of the tax inspectorate (Richardson and Marsden 1991) – this may backfire. However, as Marsden and Thompson (1990) observe, and Storey acknowledges, at some point, usually when flexibility requires significant changes in working practices which challenge union and skill demarcations, HRM and the industrial relations system are likely to come into conflict and some difficult choices have to be made.

There are very few well-documented cases of a robust trade unionism in the context of enthusiastic HRM policies. As Storey notes of Rover, the unions were invited to the party, but some declined the invitation. At Ford, the party was of a rather different sort – an attempt to form a new partnership, but with less HRM and more concern for quality of working life, including a range of health and education programmes. This fits the American model described by Kochan *et al.* (1986) and which included Ford in America as one of its cases. The policy choice for the unions, which we explore in a later section, is whether they should decline the invitation, sulk at home and be ignored, or have their own party.

The implication of Storey's analysis and of other available data is that there has been little attempt by management and unions to forge a new partnership which gives high priority to both HRM and industrial relations through some process of integration. Instead, managers have taken a lot of piecemeal HRM initiatives, and in so doing have ignored or by-passed the industrial relations system. It continues to exist, accepted by management as having a legitimate, sometimes useful, but limited role. On the surface, it may appear that HRM and industrial relations both receive a high priority. Often, in the case of both, it will be an illusion.

2: Traditional collectivism – priority to industrial relations without HRM

The second main policy choice is to retain the traditional pluralist industrial relations arrangements within an essentially unchanged industrial relations system. The evidence from WIRS3 (Millward *et al.* 1992) suggests that in many places where trade unions have been well established, the industrial relations system appears to continue to operate much as before. However, the empty-shell argument may apply with or without more vigorous HRM policies. Management may continue to use the industrial relations system, but accord it much less priority. Indeed it has been suggested (Smith and Morton 1993) that from a management perspective it is safer to marginalize the unions than formally to derecognize them and risk provoking a confrontation; better to let them wither on the vine than receive a reviving fertilizer.

An alternative management view may be that it is easier to continue to operate with a union, since it provides a useful, well-established channel for communication and for the handling of grievance, discipline and safety issues. In its absence, management would need to develop its own alternative, which could be both costly and difficult to operate effectively. The trade union and the shop stewards remain a useful lubricant.

There are a number of types of evidence which help us to reach a judgment about this. In a vigorous industrial relations system, management would take the unions and collective bargaining seriously, and this would be reflected in a range of processes and outcomes. The types of evidence include the role of the shop steward; the time spent informing and consulting with unions; the operation of the closed shop; the use of the industrial relations channel of the productivity bargain to obtain performance improvements, and the impact of any union mark-up on wages.

The anecdotal case evidence suggests that it is mainly in the public sector and some industries that have been removed from it, that traditional industrial relations continue to operate largely in the absence of HRM. British Coal, for example, still operates a traditional industrial relations system within a rapidly declining industry. Many of the productivity changes of the last decade have been achieved through a form of local productivity bargaining manifested in pit-level performance-related pay (Richardson and Wood 1989). In the privatized docks, the Transport and General Workers Union has negotiated new working arrangements including, in some cases, worker cooperatives (Turnbull and Weston 1993). However in some ports, derecognition has occurred and at Felixstowe the union members have conceded wage-cuts as part of a package to avoid derecognition. Large parts of the public sector, including the health service, the police service, local government and education, retain well-established industrial relations systems and, with a few exceptions, no real attempt to introduce HRM. The unions may play a less central role, but they are still significant players, as the response to a number of government initiatives in education and the police service has shown.

WIRS3 contains mixed news about the traditional institutional industrial relations. Brown (1993) estimates that on the basis of the WIRS3 data, only 47 per cent of the working population were covered by collective agreements in 1990, compared with 64 per cent in 1984 and 72 per cent in 1973. WIRS3 also shows some decline in the number of shop stewards, more especially in those plants with modest or low union density, increasing the risk that they are drifting towards derecognition. Furthermore it reveals a decline in the use of the union channel of communication and consultation and a marked decline in both the pre- and post-entry closed shop. Metcalf (1993) has reviewed the evidence on the union mark-up. Although it is hard to unravel, it does appear that the union mark-up – the extent to which a union presence results in higher wages, and therefore a major rationale for unions' existence – has declined. The picture on productivity bargaining is equally unclear. Based on his case studies, Storey reports that productivity bargaining has become much less frequently used, management preferring to obtain productivity increases through different methods. Against this, Gilbert (1993) uses evidence from the CBI data base to suggest that about one-third of settlements throughout the 1980s linked pay with productivity increases. Either way, management was more determined than in the past to ensure productivity gains. The evidence on productivity, at least in manufacturing, suggests that they were successful in this (Metcalf 1993).

The good news from WIRS3 for the trade unions is that in most workplaces where trade unions have in the past been well-established, trade union membership and organization has stood up well. Furthermore, any union presence was associated with positive benefits for the workforce. There was less wage inequality and less use of reward systems likely to engender greater inequality. There were more channels of communication, and more types of information were communicated. Workers in non-union plants were two and a half times as likely to be dismissed as those in unionized plants. Such evidence seriously challenges the empty-shell argument. Unions have been able to protect and promote workers' interests. Overall, WIRS3 reveals that at 32 per cent of establishments, managers reported constraints on their ability to organize work as they wished, but this rose to 46 per cent in unionized workplaces.

Taken together, and despite the evidence that in the declining proportion of organizations where they continue to exist, unions play a positive role, these findings again reveal a trend towards marginalization of unions and industrial relations. Brown (1993: 197), summarizing the picture revealed by WIRS3, suggests:

> It is now clear that in the course of the 1980s the coverage of collective bargaining has contracted substantially, that the scope of bargaining has narrowed, that the depth of union involvement has diminished, and that organizational security offered to unions by employers has deteriorated.

But as most observers note, the pattern is very uneven across industries and even within the same organization. A union presence is still associated with benefits to the workforce. However, in terms of the present analysis, the proportion of organizations giving a high priority to industrial relations but not HRM has declined and in the prevailing economic, political and legislative context, seems likely to continue to do so.

3: Individualized HRM – high priority to HRM with no industrial relations

One of the issues to address in considering the growth of HRM is whether companies are taking HRM seriously and, to the extent that they are, whether this includes operating without unions and an industrial relations system. We could debate what is meant by 'taking HRM seriously', but for many observers one criterion would be an attempt at strategic integration. However, a weaker test is to look at the way in which specific policy initiatives are implemented. A review of recent UK trends in selection, training and reward systems (Guest 1993) and reports on developments in employee involvement (Marchington *et al.* 1992) suggest that the approach is essentially piecemeal and opportunistic. At a more symbolic level, evidence from WIRS3 (Guest and Hoque 1993a) reveals that the 'human resource' title is used at less than 1 per cent of workplaces, although it is more common at company level. However, this does not stop managers from thinking that they are taking it seriously.

It is interesting to note that in the UK, our models of companies successfully practising HRM are all becoming somewhat dated. Few new names have emerged to add to those of the mid-1980s. Analysis of new establishments in the WIRS3 sample indicates that it is predominantly the North

American-owned firms that appear to promote a high HRM non-union approach. In other new establishments there is a low likelihood of union recognition, but also no particular emphasis on HRM (Guest and Hoque 1993b).

Several companies in the oil industry – a sector which has always had a high reputation for innovation in industrial relations and personnel management – have recently taken steps to derecognize trade unions. The reasoning behind this appears to be that unions are a constraint on the kind of flexibility that market conditions demand, namely functional flexibility to increase productivity, and numerical flexibility, reflected in the use of more contract labour and fixed-term contracts. Despite the market focus on cost advantage, this strategy contains elements of an integrated HRM approach which the companies apparently believe is easier to achieve with a significantly reduced union presence.

Recent attention in popular management writing appears to give more priority to quality and re-engineering than to HRM. Of course HRM may be a route to quality, but it is noticeable that the companies most associated with the 'soft' full-utilization form of HRM, the American electronics firm, have fallen on hard times. As those companies most associated with HRM become less attractive models of success, so it is possible that the image of HRM loses its lustre or transmutes into a 'harder' version.

4: The black hole – no HRM and no industrial relations

If HRM loses its attractions as a policy priority, or at best becomes no more than a set of piecemeal techniques, and there is no compelling reason to operate within a traditional industrial relations system, the alternative is to emphasize neither. In market terms this may imply a strategy based on cost advantage. Labour is viewed as a variable cost, perhaps resulting in increasing emphasis on short-term contracts.

There are several types of evidence which suggest that this option is becoming more prevalent. The first is the well-documented decline in trade union membership and trade union density. This decline continues to be partly structural, but is reinforced by two new factors. The first is a growth in partial or complete derecognition. The most convincing evidence for this comes from the recent company-level survey of industrial relations (Marginson *et al.* 1993), which shows that 19 per cent of the companies in the sample had partially or wholly derecognized unions at least at one site; this compares with 7 per cent where recognition had been extended. Derecognition is most likely to occur in privatized companies and in those with a decentralized system of bargaining. In both contexts, reasons for derecognition include diminishing union membership, the development of individual contracts, often in the context of privatization, and the move to single-union agreements. In many cases, initial derecognition applies to unions representing middle management. Gregg and Yates (1991) report a similar pattern for the 1980s, with 13 per cent of companies in their rather larger sample reporting at least one case of partial derecognition. Gall (1993) and others have noted high levels of derecognition in the provincial newspaper industry. Gall interprets this as a deliberate management strategy to remove any collective basis for opposition to corporate goals, especially in the light of changes in technology and work organization. There is some evidence that across industry, derecognition is gathering pace, opening up the possibility of a breakthrough in the credibility of this approach leading to a spiral of derecognition, membership decline and financial difficulties for unions.

The second type of evidence is the changing pattern of union recognition at new establishments. Disney *et al.* (1993), in their analysis of the workplace industrial relations surveys, have shown that the pattern of recognition at new plants has changed. They argue that the industrial relations climate at the time of the start-up is a crucial factor and that it was different in the 1980s compared with the previous decade. As a result, it was 28 per cent less likely, other things being equal, that a union would be recognized at a new establishment set up in the 1980s compared with one started in the 1970s. More specifically, WIRS3 reveals that in 1990, only 24 per cent of establishments less than ten years old recognized a union. This compares with 45 per cent of establishments less than ten years old in 1980. It appears (Disney *et al.* 1993) that the trend away from recognition began prior to 1980, and apart from a minor hiccup in the late 1980s, has continued to gather strength. If we look only at establishments employing more than fifty and where the traditional probability of a union presence is greater, the percentage recognizing a union in the 1980s was 41 per cent (Guest and Hoque 1993b). Marginson *et al.* (1993) reveal a similar pattern in their company-level survey. Fifty-nine per cent of the 140 companies in their sample that had opened a new site did not recognize a union at the site, including 38 per cent of otherwise unionized companies.

All the evidence suggests that when confronted with a decision about whether or not to recognize a trade union, companies are increasingly deciding not to do so. It is possible to conclude that this is now the dominant pattern in new establishments; indeed, it raises the question of why unions are recognized at all. The available evidence indicates that a union presence elsewhere in the company is a key positive influence on trade union recognition at new establishments. One interpretation of this is that management accepts, on the basis of experience, that unions have some value.

If a union is not recognized, there is little evidence that management replaces it with an HRM strategy to obtain full utilization of the workforce, by gaining its commitment to company goals and values. Millward (1993) has begun to paint a picture of policy and practice in non-union firms, based on the WIRS3 survey data. There are fewer procedures and fewer health and safety representatives. There are also fewer channels of information and consultation, less information from management and fewer personnel specialists. Although the workplace climate is described as better than in unionized establishments, there are more dismissals, more compulsory redundancies, more notices to quit and more low pay, alongside a greater dispersion of pay. Pay also appears to be both more often performance-related and more market-determined. For the workforce, this emerging non-union environment is bleak and insecure. Marginson *et al.* (1993) similarly found no support for a non-union HRM strategy. For example, non-union firms were no more likely to pursue employee involvement. The only possible exceptions were the very small number of cases where there had been a centrally agreed strategy to derecognize all unions and where some thought had been given to the strategic choices of what to put in their place.

In summary, employers seem to be following the government in slowly withdrawing support from institutional industrial relations. Despite the WIRS3 evidence which reports a continuing growth in the influence of personnel departments, from which a case might be made for the effective promotion of either industrial relations or HRM, it seems more likely, as Marginson *et al.* (1993) emphasize, that a financial controller model is dominating board thinking about how to manage the workforce. This does not fit comfortably with an HRM strategy in which labour is a relatively fixed cost, or with an industrial relations perspective which sees labour as a countervailing force, with the power to negotiate additional wage costs. Returning to the four options presented at the start of this section, the trend is away from the traditional collectivism of a representative industrial relations sytem, but the drift is towards the black hole of no industrial relations and no HRM, rather than towards individualized HRM or the new realism. More generally, management thinking seems to have moved on from HRM; it is no longer the current fashion. If we take the management press as a (unreliable) guide, it has been replaced by a greater concern for quality, which may provide a more specific focus for some dimensions of HRM, and more recently by a concern for process re-engineering, which challenges existing patterns of organization across both workgroups and functions. Unions, and even personnel departments, may have little place in the thinking of those promoting this approach.

TRADE UNIONS AND HUMAN RESOURCE MANAGEMENT

Most analyses consider HRM from a managerial and corporate perspective. Martinez Lucio and Weston (1992) provide one of the few attempts by academic writers to analyse potential union responses. The need for a positive union response is recognized by John Edmonds, who describes the union response to date as 'incoherent, tentative, anxious, befuddled and uncertain' (Storey *et al.* 1993: 64). Of course, the unions have been considering their response and Beaumont (1991), among others, has suggested that unions will become increasingly proactive with respect to HRM. However, his brief analysis of union responses to HRM in North America and the UK (Beaumont 1992) reinforces Edmonds' description. In this section we will develop a trade union perspective and set HRM within the wider context of strategies for union survival and revival. One feature of this is that HRM may shift from being perceived as a threat to becoming a possible opportunity.

A starting point for any analysis might consider what positive factors are operating in the unions' favour. Several can be readily identified. The first is that the unions are now more popular than they have been for many years (Waddington 1992). Part of the reason for this may be their lower profile, linked to the sharp reduction in strike activity. However, it is no longer possible to use them as a scapegoat for the industrial and employment problems of the UK. Surveys among members of the (British) Institute of Management in 1980 and 1990 (Poole and Mansfield 1992) found that in 1990 they perceived the unions as less powerful and less threatening, and saw little need for any change in the role of unions. Indeed the government is caught in something of a dilemma, since it claims to have 'solved' the problems of industrial relations through its legislative programme, yet continues with that programme. In the perception of some, this begins to take the form of overt anti-unionism and helps to generate sympathy for the union cause.

A second major argument in the unions' favour is that they appear to be associated with clear benefits for the workforce and no necessary costs to the company. The WIRS3 data reveal an association between a union presence and many of the practices most clearly linked to HRM. Much of the survey only touched indirectly on issues associated with HRM. However, if we look at the sample of establishments employing fifty or more staff, the presence of a recognized trade union was one of the best predictors of more channels of communication, with greater range of content. It was also associated with less use of individual performance-related pay, more welfare facilities and fewer redundancies and dismissals (Guest and Hoque 1993b). If we set this information alongside the evidence of the decline of the union mark-up and the evidence that where single-table bargaining has been established, any impact of trade unions on wages has been eliminated (Metcalf 1993), a case can be made to show that unions bring non-wage benefits to the workforce without costs to the company. Put another way, from a worker perspective, the alternative scenario presented in many of the new non-union plants is not an attractive one.

A third general point in the unions' favour is that British society in the 1980s and early 1990s has seen growing inequality and increased poverty.

The abolition of the wages councils is likely to exacerbate these problems and to provide new challenges for the unions. As we have just noted, there is less inequality in unionized workplaces; but in the wider society, in some respects the conditions are being recreated which led to the growth of trade unionism a century ago.

It was noted earlier that trade unions and industrial relations concerns more generally no longer shape the central management agenda. It seems likely that in the foreseeable future, short of a potentially self-destructive militancy, unions will only gain attention if they can set a new agenda. This agenda has to meet three objectives. The first is the need to attract new members while retaining their current members. The second is to persuade managers at new establishments that they should recognize a trade union. The third is to convince managers at existing plants that they wish to retain trade unions and continue to recognize them.

The 1993 Trade Union Reform and Employment Rights Act makes it easier for employers to remove the check-off system for the collection of union dues, providing an opportunity and a threat. As Willman *et al.* (1992) note, trade unions have come to depend for their survival on employers' goodwill. Such goodwill is increasingly in doubt. The new legislation is likely to alter the union role in retaining membership, from one of inertia-selling to a more purposive, activist voluntary organization. This requires new strategies.

In determining the strategy to pursue, unions should take account of evidence about why people join or belong to trade unions in the UK (Guest and Dewe 1988; Hartley 1992). The dominant influence, apart from the key initial issue of union availability, is instrumental; workers believe that the union can help them achieve certain outcomes. These may be both positive, such as increased pay, and negative, such as protection against arbitrary management action including dismissal. This acknowledges a pluralist perspective whereby workers perceive that their interests may from time to time diverge from those of management. Unions can promote those interests and provide a form of insurance. This recognizes the benefits of some form of collective representation and acknowledges some residual collective orientation (Gallie 1989; Waddington 1992).

There is little evidence that union solidarity – a commitment to the ideas of trade unionism, and therefore membership as an end in itself – is a strong influence on union membership and more particularly on union joining. Commitment to trade unions will therefore, for the most part, take the form of exchange commitment, instrumental upon the unions providing some sort of return. This will become even more the case as the removal of the union check-off system reduces the numbers who belong to unions through inertia. At the same time it will put more pressure on unions to sell their role to potential and actual members. How are they to do this?

An initial choice is whether to oppose all initiatives, whether at national, company or plant level, which threaten traditional collective bargaining. This would result in a refusal to cooperate with any management initiative falling under the broad umbrella of HRM and the new industrial relations. This strategy was at one point particularly associated with the Transport and General Workers Union. Such an approach may have seemed viable when the possibility existed of a Labour government being returned to office before change had gone too far. This is the approach of refusing to come to the party and has meant, for example, refusal to participate in single-union deals at new plants. Admittedly the party is on management territory, but if everyone else is going along, including the workforce, then nothing is gained by union obduracy. The TGWU has now modified its approach and displays guarded cooperation with companies which are pursuing HRM initiatives.

Once the decision has been taken to accept the need to work within the prevailing system, there is a choice of whether to do so on management's terms and to a management agenda, or to create a new and distinctive agenda. In the absence of any alternative, many unions have, by default, accepted the management agenda and as a result have often played a minor, largely defensive and reactive role.

It is more sensible, as the TUC and all leading unions now acknowledge, to create a new agenda which starts from, rather than denies, the new realities. Two leading American academics (Kochan and McKersie 1992), drawing on the experiences of the 1980s, and noting that the decline of union membership in the USA actually accelerated in the 1980s, argue strongly for a new union agenda which avoids the low-wage, low-cost, low-trust spiral, on the grounds that it is not in the interests of companies, workers or the country as a whole.

There appear to be three distinct but potentially overlapping strategies that unions could adopt at company and establishment levels. The first, and probably the most widely discussed, is to promote a high quality of working life campaign within the agenda of the European Social Chapter. This might appeal to existing union members. The second is to pursue the Friendly Society route, providing financial, legal and possibly social support to individual members. This might appeal to newcomers to organizations. Finally, unions might consider turning around the HRM agenda, one which managers might define as their own, and using it to promote workers' interests. This might appeal to companies, and may lead to dual commitment.

The quality of working life strategy

At the heart of the emerging strategy of the Conservative government in the UK within the context of the European Community is the promotion of a low-cost labour market. All the evidence suggests that this is also a low-investment, low-productivity environment. In particular there is a low investment in human resources through provision of training, safety and employment security. The alternative, which until recent years presented a highly attractive model of economic success, is reflected in the social and industrial relations policies traditionally pursued in countries like Germany and Sweden.

The core of the European Social Chapter is built upon assumptions of pluralism and of the value of partnership; in other words, the mutuality that Walton and others refer to as the basis for an integration of traditional industrial relations and HRM. The core issues which the Social Chapter addresses are by now familiar. Many of the Social Chapter provisions can be traced back to the quality of working life (QWL) movement, which came to the fore in the 1970s. Senior UK managers have expressed anxiety about the costs of some of the provisions, most notably those relating to working hours and employee participation. Despite senior management protestations, there is evidence to suggest that pursuit of such policies can be to the mutual benefit of employees and the organization. Unions in the UK were very sceptical about the potential benefits of QWL when it was first promoted in the 1970s. However, there is evidence from elsewhere that it can have benefits for the union. Traditional cases of such benefits are typically Scandinavian. More recent ones come from North America. Verma (1989) has provided evidence that participation in QWL activities enhances the union role. This is further reinforced by Fields and Thaker (1992), who report a longitudinal evaluation of a QWL programme. The QWL process as a whole enhanced commitment to the union. It only enhanced organizational commitment when the positive outcomes became readily apparent.

The Social Chapter has become an emotive issue in the UK. Unions may therefore strike a more positive response by using the language of QWL, capitalizing upon the generally positive attitude towards the concept of quality. The core of the union strategy then becomes the active promotion of a distinctive programme based on the mutual benefits to employees and company. This, in effect, is the approach adopted by the TUC in promoting its 'Quality Challenge' (TUC 1992). Although ostensibly directed at public services, and somewhat narrower than the concept of QWL, it has the potential for application in all sectors of employment.

There are a number of specific topics which can be promoted, monitored and reported at national, company and plant level, ranging from equal opportunity to health and safety. From the start of 1993, EC legislation has required action on six areas of health and safety. Given the cutbacks in the resources of the Health and Safety Executive, unions have an important role in promoting the measures. At the same time they should promote the advantages to organizations of a healthy workforce and of safe working, based on analysis of the costs of absence, disruptions to work and damage to public image as a consequence of a poor quality of service. Indeed, the TUC has called for joint safety committees to investigate, monitor and help to improve the health profile of the workforce. There is now widespread evidence of the benefits of good ergonomic design of workplaces, a point recently emphasized from an employer's perspective by Wickens (1993) and reinforced more generally by the potential costs to industry of repetitive strain injury.

A second major area of shared concern should be skill formation. One survey (ALBSU 1993) estimated the costs to industry of poor skills in reading and writing at £5 billion per annum. These costs result from lower efficiency, errors, rectification costs and damage to company image. Everyone gains from a more highly skilled workforce.

A third area of joint concern is job design. American organizations have traditionally favoured the more individualistic approach to job design reflected in job enrichment, but have recently shown much more interest in team-working. Europeans have preferred the more collective approach of team-working through autonomous work groups. The evidence (Wall and Martin 1987) shows that these can bring benefits to both company and workforce. One of the recent major surveys of the workforce (Gallie and White 1993) reveals a link between job design and organizational commitment. Increasing the autonomy of workers, particularly in tightly regulated and repetitive tasks, is likely to increase workers' well-being. Greater autonomy for workers also provides greater flexibility for the company.

A fourth potential topic of joint concern might be working hours. Unions in the UK have been rather schizoid about working hours. While sympathizing with attempts to regulate maximum working hours, they are aware of the need for their members to increase their earnings through overtime working. There is some scope for negotiating annual hours arrangements, possibly linked to longer-term guarantees of job security. Unions and management in some continental countries have explored innovative approaches to working hours in a much more imaginative way than their UK counterparts and they could provide challenging models of possible lines of progress. An additional reason for greater union interest in working hours is the difficulty they face in organizing part-time workers.

One of the attractions of QWL and many features of the Social Chapter is that it points to objective measures. The TUC has moved some way towards recognizing this through its 'Quality Work Assured Servicemark' (TUC 1992). Unions could go further in promoting standards, perhaps in collaboration with employers, perhaps through organizations such as the Industrial Society or the Involvement Participation Association.

Underpinning the whole approach is the presentation of an alternative route to economic success: a high-investment, high-productivity strategy based on high levels of functional flexibility, high involvement and high levels of dual commitment. The problem with some of the presentation of the Social Chapter is that it appears very one-sided in favour of workers' interests. For the unions, the challenge is to present it, perhaps under the guise of quality, as being of mutual benefit.

The Friendly Society strategy

A second strategy for unions is to emphasize their role in providing a range of services to their members. The withdrawal of the Welfare State and the growing trend among employers to offer short-term contracts with limited social and welfare benefits, creates an opportunity to fill the vacuum. One manifestation of the need for this type of role is provided by figures from the Citizens Advice Bureau for 1992, which reveal that it received over three-quarters of a million complaints against companies, with unfair dismissals to the fore. In most cases these came from people who were not union members, or who worked in organizations where a union was not recognized. Similarly, ACAS has a steadily increasing workload of individual grievances concerning unfair dismissal and discrimination.

The type of facilities that might be provided and which have been discussed at recent union conferences range from banking and insurance, legal advice and travel facilities to social welfare, educational and crèche facilities. Some unions already provide advice about individual contracts. The difficulty with this approach for the unions in the UK is that it will require higher union dues and a change of organization and role that they are not in a good position to provide.

One particularly challenging issue concerns union attitudes towards black workers. They are traditionally among the more likely to belong to a union, although membership has been declining. They may require special attention, not least because of the potentially greater problem of discrimination that they face.

Despite the difficulties, unions have gone some way along this route. One example is the type of education programme at Ford and Rover. It is also interesting to note that at several oil industry sites where unions have been derecognized for the purposes of collective bargaining, they retain representative rights for individuals on issues of grievance and discipline and in some cases on a collective basis for non-bargaining issues. There is little evidence on workers' reactions to union facilities and services, although one study by Lewis and Murphy (1991) looked at workers who retained union membership during unemployment. They found that benefits and services had little impact on the decision to retain union membership, although this was based on a low level of provision.

One test of union willingness to stand up and be counted on their service to members is to assess the quality of their work. MSF has decided to seek accreditation under BS5750. It may become necessary for unions to market themselves in the same way as many other service organizations, through some guarantee of quality of provision. It would certainly be a sign of TUC seriousness if they were to take a lead in promoting quality by having their own quality of service accredited.

The HRM strategy

Earlier it was suggested that a high HRM, high industrial relations strategy with dual commitment to both company and union was feasible in the right industrial relations climate. However, it is only being actively pursued in a few organizations, invariably at the initiative of management. Many more organizations have taken steps to introduce elements of HRM, often in a half-hearted and piecemeal way (Guest 1991) but have failed to develop a coherent strategy and therefore to have much impact. Unions may come to regret the failure of HRM initiatives if they are replaced by less palatable alternatives and may therefore be wiser to see HRM as an opportunity rather than a threat. Ironically, the inability of personnel and other managers to introduce effective HRM provides unions with an opportunity. Rather than oppose HRM, unions should champion it, becoming more enthusiastic than management.

If we dissect the policies inherent in a 'soft', high utilization approach to HRM, they include many to which unions could subscribe. For example, unions would approve of realistic job previews, of careful and fair selection, of extensive training which developed general as well as specific skills and left the workforce better qualified, of high basic pay, of high trust autonomous work groups, of clear targets, of open and extensive two way communication through a range of channels and of many more elements. Above all, unions should welcome single status and guarantees of job security.

Broadening the discussion from the specific issue of HRM, one of the challenges for unions is to discover a new and compelling ideology. For managers, HRM provided a compelling ideology in the 1980s, with an attractive metaphor for growth and progress. Unions may be understandably reluctant to embrace the manipulative connotations of HRM, but they can appropriate the substance and, when it suits them, use the language. In searching for a new but realistic ideology, unions might be wise to embrace HRM. As John Edmonds notes, 'It gives us a hand of high cards to play' (Storey *et al.* 1993: 65). It can be turned back on management, a potential rod, owned by management but appropriated by the unions, with which to beat them. However, the unions will wish to go further. Subsumed within HRM and associated debates are concepts which might form the basis for a distinctive approach. This is not the place to develop these, but one, which Dahrendorf (1982) among others has promoted, is the concept of community. Linked to this, but with distinctive features of its own, is the concept of corporate citizenship (Organ 1988). What begins to emerge is an alternative to the four 'C's – namely commitment, competence, congruence and cost-effectiveness. The new four 'C's of the union approach, using some phonetic license, would be cooperation, community, citizenship and quality. Rather stronger versions of cooperation might include co-determination or co-ownership. This new framework, preserving some of the elements of traditional solidarity, but expressed through community, presents a counter to the individualism of the American view of HRM.

Equally important, this new approach can blend with and grow out of HRM, using HRM as a legitimate basis for extending what has come to be known as the 'New Agenda'. As a first step, the unions have a vested interest in promoting a 'soft' full utilization version of HRM. They should be pushing, cajoling and negotiating with managers to promote HRM. They should be monitoring selection and training, encouraging the use of attitude surveys and systems of ethnic monitoring, insisting on extensive two-way channels of communication and promoting health and attendance programmes. They should turn management's HRM rhetoric back on them and transform it into reality.

Some unions have already taken tentative steps in this direction. The GMB, at a general policy level, have espoused elements of this approach in their document *A New Agenda: Bargaining for Prosperity in the 1990s* (GMB/UCW 1990). However, as Edmonds acknowledges (Storey *et al.* 1993), turning this into a practical workplace strategy is much more difficult. One notable success has been the agreement reached at Rover, with its guarantees of job security. Another of the more interesting proposals has been drawn up by the unions negotiating with BT. Known as the 'New Dialogue', it proposes among other things, that

> the company and its unions should work together on an Annual Quality Audit of human resource issues within BT. This audit should be founded on agreed quality benchmarks assessing BT's human resource management and the unions' delivery of their human resource responsibilities

Doing so, it is suggested

> will give BT the opportunity to be a 'Model of Excellence' in contemporary personnel practice – to set a standard for British companies in the 1990s and beyond.
>
> (BT Unions 1992)

Of course, the unions will face difficulties in promoting a union HRM perspective in non-union settings. Difficulties may also arise in the case of some American-owned organizations where the ideology of individualism results in no perceived benefits from worker representation. In contrast, many Japanese companies appear to welcome some form of representative system. UK-owned companies are still often open-minded about a union presence. The prospect of gaining competitive advantage through a well-integrated, flexible, committed and high-quality workforce, with the union sharing the task of promoting and monitoring high standards, may appeal to managements. It is recognized by those senior managers who support the activities of the Involvement and Participation Association by promoting partnership based on the foundations of job security and flexibility; and it sits comfortably with much of the ideology of the Institute of Personnel and Development. Such an approach appears to reflect the thinking of some trade union leaders and it can certainly fit the quality agenda of the TUC and the current fashion within union circles for 'partnership'.

One risk of half-hearted union compliance with HRM is that the union will remain on the margin, as appears to have happened at Toshiba and Nissan. However, both are also cases of how a collaborative approach can help the union, since both organizations have taken positive steps, particularly at the point of recruitment into the company, to encourage union membership. This implies the union has value for management. From the union perspective, an HRM-focused strategy implies that they operate as advocates and monitors. They encourage management to implement sound policy and practice and to assist in ensuring that this is the case. Their role increasingly becomes that of internal consultant, but part of a national network. This is closer to the role that has sometimes been adopted by Swedish unions. It has also emerged in a number of management buy-out cases in the UK. The viability of such an approach is reinforced by the trend, noted in WIRS3, for employers to give more emphasis to company-level bargaining and policy-setting. As Kelly and Henry (1989) have noted, unions face growing problems in resourcing organization of workplaces that tend to be diminishing in size. By seeking partnership at the company level, unions may work to their own strengths and influence policy at the level where the important issues still seem to be decided. HRM may provide unions with one of their best chances of survival. The alternative to a new role of this type, which promises to promote a number of worker objectives, may well be the black hole, with no role for the union.

In this section, we have examined three possible union responses to HRM and the 'new industrial relations'. The three strategies are distinctive in their starting points, QWL starting from a European semi-institutional framework, the Friendly Society from a welfare perspective and union HRM from an appropriation of management's own model. In the process of implementation they may well come together, especially the QWL and HRM approaches. In recognizing that the well-being of the enterprise depends more and more on collective effort and teamworking, employers might acknowledge the value of a constructive union voice. For unions, their distinctive voice as representative and promoter of workers' interests in a democratic society should be seen as being quite compatible with principled advocacy of HRM (Kessler 1993). Unions should also bear in mind that there should be much that is humane and stimulating for the workforce in HRM. People generally feel good working in a successful, positive, high-trust organization. A distinctively European approach to HRM and QWL, championed by unions, may provide one of the best chances of achieving this goal.

CONCLUSIONS

The debate on HRM and industrial relations has been dominated by the political and economic context. This is true of the past decade and seems unlikely to change. The Conservative government has continued its creeping attack on the unions through successive legislation. This may have reached a point of breakthrough where 'respectable' organizations – for example, in the oil industry, where unions have been long established – are starting to take derecognition seriously. They provide a more credible model for others to follow than Murdoch's International News.

The economic climate in which three million are unemployed provides a buyer's market where employers can find workers who will accept management terms, even when, as in the case of Timex at Dundee, they set themselves against union members who have been arbitrarily dismissed. Where companies are able to gain major increases in productivity through cost-cutting, the case for HRM becomes less attractive. Examples of companies such as Hoover expanding in the UK at the expense of France appear to vindicate the government's anti-Maastricht strategy, which is also in effect an argument for a low-cost, low-investment strategy. Although this approach has serious long-term limitations, in the short and medium term it works against both HRM and much that trade unions stand for.

Faced with these challenges, unions have a choice of either continuing their slow decline, or opting for radical change. The signs of turnaround are not promising. Admittedly the unions are no longer the ogres, the scapegoats for the British industrial malaise – they are no longer sufficiently important to justify this role. Despite the occasional twitch in the tail of the old carthorse of the trade union movement – at Timex or in the coal industry – the national view of the unions is an increasingly nostalgic one. The trade union is in danger of joining the Royal Family as a popular and largely historic relic; and like royalty it lives on in a somewhat anachronistic role, on the margins of the lives of most workers. The occasional burst into public consciousness, occasioned by a strike or some other 'misbehaviour' by a member of the trade union family, occurs mainly in those anachronisms – the mines, the railways and traditional manufacturing – which, like the unions, are rapidly disappearing from our industrial landscape. Approaching the twenty-first century, trade unions appear to have been a phenomenon of the twentieth century to which we prepare to say goodbye.

For those concerned with the growth of inequality, of insecurity and of arbitrary treatment which has accompanied the decline of trade unionism, their departure from any serious and significant role would be a tragedy. One purpose of this chapter has been to argue that too often they have not been replaced by an enlightened form of HRM of the sort which attracts the enthusiasm of workers. An effective union role is therefore as urgent as ever. But it must be a different role from the traditional one centred around adversarial collective bargaining. Some possibilities have been outlined. One conclusion is that unions should take an active role in promoting many of the more positive elements of HRM as managers turn to alternative approaches and pursue other interests in their search for competitive advantage.

REFERENCES

ALBSU (1993) *Basic Skills and Jobs*, London: ALBSU.

Angle, H. and Perry, J. (1986) 'Dual commitment and labor–management relationship climates', *Academy of Management Journal* 29(1): 31–50.

Barling, J., Wade, B. and Fullager, C. (1990) 'Predicting employee commitment to company and union: divergent models', *Journal of Occupational Psychology* 63(1): 49–61.

Beaumont, P. (1991) 'Trade unions and HRM', *Industrial Relations Journal* 22(4): 300–8.

—— (1992) 'Trade unions and human resource management', in B. Towers (ed.) *The Handbook of Human Resource Management*, Oxford: Blackwell.

Beer, M., Spector, B., Lawrence, P., Quinn Mills, D. and Walton, R. (1985) *Human Resource Management: A General Manager's Perspective*, Glencoe, IL: Free Press.

Brown, W. (1993) 'The contraction of collective bargaining in Britain', *British Journal of Industrial Relations* 31(2): 189–200.

BT Unions (1992) *The New Dialogue*, London: NCU.

Dahrendorf, R. (1982) *On Britain*, London: BBC.

Dastmalchian, A., Blyton, P. and Adamson, R. (1991) *The Climate of Workplace Relations*, London: Routledge.

Dickens, R., Gregg, P., Machin, S., Manning, A. and Wadsworth, J. (1993) 'Wages Councils: was there a case for abolition?', *British Journal of Industrial Relations* 31(4): 515–29.

Disney, R., Gosling, A. and Machin, S. (1993) 'What has happened to trade union recognition in Britain', CEP Discussion Paper No. 130, London: LSE.

Fields, M. and Thaker, J. (1992) 'Influence of quality of work life on company and union commitment', *Academy of Management Journal* 35(2): 439–50.

Fullager, C. and Barling, J. (1991) 'Predictors and outcomes of different patterns of organizational and union loyalty', *Journal of Occupational Psychology* 64(2): 129–43.

Gall, G. (1993) 'The employers' offensive in the provincial newspaper industry', *British Journal of Industrial Relations* 31(4): 615–24.

Gallie, D. (1989) 'Trade union allegiance and decline in British urban labour markets', Social Change and Economic Life Initiative Working Paper No. 9, Oxford: Nuffield College.

Gallie, D. and White, M. (1993) *Employment Commitment and the Skills Revolution*, London: PSI Publishing.

Garrahan, P. and Stewart, P. (1992) *The Nissan Enigma: Flexibility at Work in a Local Economy*, London: Mansell.
Gilbert, R. (1993) 'Workplace industrial relations 25 years after Donovan: an employer view', *British Journal of Industrial Relations* 31(2): 235–53.
GMB/UCW (1990) *A New Agenda: Bargaining for Prosperity in the 1990s*, London: GMB/UCW.
Gordon, M., Philpot, J., Burt, R., Thompson, C. and Spiller, W. (1980) 'Commitment to the union: development of a measure and an examination of its correlates', *Journal of Applied Psychology* 65: 479–99.
Gregg, P. and Yates, A. (1991) 'Changes in wage-setting arrangements and trade union presence in the 1980s', *British Journal of Industrial Relations* 29(3): 361–76.
Guest, D. (1987) 'Human resource management and industrial relations', *Journal of Management Studies* 24(5): 503–21.
—— (1989) 'Human resource management: its implications for industrial relations and trade unions', in J. Storey (ed.) *New Perspectives on Human Resource Management*, London: Routledge.
—— (1991) 'Personnel management: The end of orthodoxy?', *British Journal of Industrial Relations* 29(2): 149–75.
—— (1993) 'Current perspectives on human resource management in the United Kingdom', in C. Brewster (ed.) *Current Trends in Human Resource Management in Europe*, London: Kogan Page.
Guest, D. and Dewe, P. (1988) 'Why do workers belong to trade unions? A social-psychological study in the UK electronics industry', *British Journal of Industrial Relations* 29(1): 75–96.
—— and —— (1991) 'Company or trade union; which wins workers' allegiance? A study of commitment in the United Kingdom electronics industry', *British Journal of Industrial Relations* 29(1): 75–96.
Guest, D. and Hoque, K. (1993a) 'The mystery of the missing human resource manager', *Personnel Management* June: 40–1.
—— and —— (1993b) 'Are greenfield sites better at human resource management?', CEP Working Paper No. 435, London: LSE.
Guest, D. and Peccei, R. (1993) 'The impact of employee involvement on organisational commitment and "them" and "us" attitudes', *Industrial Relations Journal* 24(3): 191–200.
Hancke, B. (1993) 'Trade union membership in Europe 1960–90: rediscovering local unions', *British Journal of Industrial Relations* 31(4): 593–613.
Hartley, J. (1992) 'Joining a trade union', in J. Hartley and G. Stephenson (eds) *Employment Relations*, Oxford: Blackwell.
Herzberg, F. (1966) *Work and the Nature of Man*, London: Staples Press.
Institute of Personnel Management (1992) *Performance Management*, London: IPM.
Involvement and Participation Association (1992) *Towards Industrial Partnership: A New Approach to Management–Union Relations*, London: IPA.
IRS 1993.
Kelly, J. and Henry, E. (1989) 'Full-time officers and trade union recruitment', *British Journal of Industrial Relations* 27(2): 196–213.
Kessler, S. (1993) 'Is there still a future for the unions?', *Personnel Management* July: 24–30.
Kochan, T. and McKersie, R. (1992) 'Human resources, organizational governance, and public policy: lessons from a decade of experimentation', in T. Kochan and M. Useem (eds) *Transforming Organizations*, Oxford: Oxford University Press.

Kochan, T., Katz, H. and McKersie, R. (1986) *The Transformation of American Industrial Relations*, New York: Basic Books.

Lewis, P. and Murphy, L. (1991) 'A theory of trade union membership retention', *British Journal of Industrial Relations* 29(2): 277–93.

Marchington, M., Goodman, J., Wilkinson, A. and Ackers, P. (1992) *New Developments in Employee Involvement*, Research Series No. 2, London: Employment Department.

Marginson, P., Armstrong, P., Edwards, P. and Purcell, J. (1993) 'Decentralization, collectivism and individualism: evidence on industrial relations in transition from the 1992 company-level industrial relations survey', paper presented to the BUIRA Conference, York, July.

Marsden, D. and Thompson, M. (1990) 'Flexibility agreements and their significance in the increase in productivity in British manufacturing since 1980', *Work, Employment and Society* 4: 83–104.

Martinez Lucio, M. and Weston, S. (1992) 'Human resource management and trade union response: bringing the politics of the workplace back into the debate', in P. Blyton and P. Turbull (eds) *Reassessing Human Resource Management*, London: Sage.

Metcalf, D. (1993) 'Industrial relations and economic performance', *British Journal of Industrial Relations* 31(2): 255–83.

Miles, R. and Snow, C. (1978) *Organizational Strategy, Structure and Process*, New York: McGraw-Hill.

—— and —— (1984) 'Designing strategic human resource systems', *Organizational Dynamics* Summer: 36–52.

Millward, N. (1993) 'Industrial relations in transition: the findings of the third workplace industrial relations survey', paper presented to BUIRA, York, July.

Millward, N., Stevens, M., Smart, D. and Hawes, W. (1992) *Workplace Industrial Relations in Transition*, Aldershot: Dartmouth.

Mowday, R., Porter, L. and Steers, R. (1982) *Employee–Organization Linkages: The Psychology of Commitment, Absenteeism and Turnover*, London: Academic Press.

Organ, D. (1988) *Organizational Citizenship Behavior*, Lexington, MA: Heath.

Poole, M. and Mansfield, R. (1992) 'Patterns of continuity and change in managerial attitudes and behaviour in industrial relations 1980–1990', *British Journal of Industrial Relations* 31(1): 11–35.

Porter, M. (1980) *Competitive Strategy*, New York: Free Press.

Reichers, A. (1985) 'A review and reconceptualization of organizational commitment', *Academy of Management Review* 10: 465–76.

—— (1986) 'Conflict and organizational commitments', *Journal of Applied Psychology* 71: 508–14.

Richardson, R. and Marsden, D. (1991) 'Motivation and performance-related pay in the public sector: a case study of the Inland Revenue', CEP Discussion Paper No. 75, London: LSE.

Richardson, R. and Wood, S. (1989) 'Productivity change in the coal industry and the new industrial relations', *British Journal of Industrial Relations* 27(1): 33–55.

Schuler, R. and Jackson, S. (1987) 'Linking competitive strategies with human resource management practices', *Academy of Management Executive* 1(3): 207–19.

Smith, P. and Morton, G. (1993) 'Union exclusion and decollectivization of industrial relations in contemporary Britain', *British Journal of Industrial Relations* 31(1): 97–114.

Storey, J. (1992) *Developments in the Management of Human Resources*, Oxford: Blackwell.

Storey, J., Bacon, N., Edmonds, J. and Wyatt, P. (1993) 'The "New Agenda" and human resource management: A round table discussion with John Edmonds', *Human Resource Management Journal* 4(1): 63–70.
Thaker, J., Fields, M. and Barclay, L. (1990) 'Union commitment: an examination of antecedents and outcome factors', *Journal of Occupational Psychology* 63(1): 33–48.
Tichy, N., Fombrun, C. and Devanna, M. (1982) 'Strategic human resource management', *Sloan Management Review* 23(2) Winter: 47–61.
Trevor, M. (1988) *Toshiba's New British Company*, London: PSI.
TUC (1992) *The Quality Challenge*, London: TUC.
Turnbull, P. and Weston, S. (1993) 'Cooperation or control? Capital restructuring and labour relations on the docks', *British Journal of Industrial Relations* 31(1): 115–34.
Verma, A. (1989) 'Joint participation programs: Self-help or suicide for labor?', *Industrial Relations* 28: 401–10.
Waddington, J. (1992) 'Trade union membership in Britain, 1980–1987: unemployment and restructuring', *British Journal of Industrial Relations* 30(2): 287–324.
Wall, T. and Martin, R. (1987) 'Job and work design', in C. Cooper and I. Robertson (eds) *International Review of Industrial and Oganizational Psychology, 1987*, Chichester: Wiley.
Walton, R. (1985a) 'From control to commitment in the workplace', *Harvard Business Review* 63, March–April: 76–84.
—— (1985b) 'Toward a strategy for eliciting employee commitment based on policies of mutuality', in R. Walton and P. Lawrence (eds) *Human Resource Management, Trends and Challenges*, Boston, MA: Harvard Business School Press.
Walton, R. and McKersie, R. (1965) *A Behavioural Theory of Labor Negotiations*, New York: McGraw-Hill.
Wickens, P. (1987) *The Road to Nissan*, London: Macmillan.
—— (1993) 'Lean production and beyond: the system, the critics and the future', *Human Resource Management Journal* 3(4): 75–90.
Willman, P., Morris, T. and Aston, B. (1992) *Union Business: Trade Union Organization and Financial Reform in the Thatcher Years*, Cambridge: Cambridge University Press.
Zuboff, S. (1988) *In the Age of the Smart Machine: The Future of Work and Power*, New York: Basic Books.

Chapter 6

Accountancy and HRM

Peter Armstrong

INTRODUCTION

Over the past decade, writings on the personnel profession have been permeated by a sense of exclusion from the major management decisions. For example, Hunt (1987) reported that human assets are rarely considered in company acquisitions and that personnel managers are only involved in such peripheral aspects as the transfer of pension rights. Daniel (1986a) found that personnel managers play little part in the reorganizations which often follow the introduction of new technology, although they are sometimes involved in other forms of organizational change. Even here, Cowling (1985) found that personnel managers do not usually take an executive role.

At a more general level, recent major studies have revealed that corporate-level decisions rarely take account of personnel or industrial relations issues (Hill and Pickering 1986) and that at this level the personnel function amounts to no more than a 'fringe, lightweight, infrequently involved and infrequently influential player' (Hickson *et al.* 1986: 80; also quoted with masochistic gloom in Legge 1988: 25).

The obvious background to these alarms is the diminution of trade union bargaining power from the early 1980s onwards. Of this fact there can be no doubt. The third company-level industrial relations survey (WIRS3) shows marked declines in union density, employer recognition, coverage of the closed shop and indices of industrial action, compared to earlier surveys (Sisson 1993). Insofar as the traditional core expertise of the personnel profession lay in the area of collective bargaining, it is entirely explicable that a decline in the demand for this expertise should precipitate a general decline in the profession's influence.

Additional threats seem to be posed by the fashion for human resources management (HRM), where this is interpreted as a move to 'give personnel back to the line' (Guest 1986, 1987, 1989), and there have been parallel developments in what remains of the public sector, in which responsibility for budgetary performance and personnel issues have both been devolved to newly empowered line managers (Peat Marwick 1984). Rationalized as methods of integrating personnel considerations with business decision-making (or, more realistically, holding those who make personnel decisions responsible for their cost), such developments threaten to strip specialist personnel departments of their remaining functions.

When the foregoing trends are coupled with anecdotal evidence of the rundown of personnel departments (e.g. Purcell and Gray 1986), it is easy to see why recent writings on the profession have been characterized by endless ruminations on the meaning of human resource management and by a search for new 'models' (Tyson 1985) or 'paradigms' (Gowler and Legge 1986) of personnel management.

At first sight, this gloomy picture appears to be contradicted by a succession of survey findings, all of which report that the personnel function remains undepleted, both in numbers and in status, while the (self-rated) importance of its work has, if anything, increased (Batstone 1984; Torrington *et al.* 1985; Daniel 1986b; Sisson 1993). Even here, however, there is cause for concern in the fine print. In WIRS2, the most common reason given for an increase in the importance of the personnel function was financial stringency and the need for a peaceful negotiation of redundancies – scarcely a secure long-term base for the profession (Daniel 1986b; Legge 1988).

In terms of Tyson and Fell's (1986) typology, what appears to be happening is that the 'contracts manager' model of personnel management, centred on the 'old industrial relations game' is dying out with the diminution of trade union bargaining power. The hopes of the profession are personified by those few elite 'architects' of strategic human resources management who continue to make policy at the corporate headquarters level. Its nightmare is that the personnel manager will degenerate into a 'clerk of works', performing routine administrative work for a newly self-confident line management. Between these extremes, intermediate possibilities, such as the opportunist promotion of particular human resource management techniques (Monks' 1992 'innovative/professional' model), are endlessly debated.

The problem to which this chapter is addressed is that these debates have taken little account of the corporate context. More has happened to British companies since the late 1970s than a diminution of trade union influence. There has been a great deal of takeover and merger activity, in the course of which companies have become larger and more diversified. These developments have been accompanied by a continuing trend towards divisionalized forms of organization permeated by the performance targets, monitoring systems and cultural presuppositions of management accounting. For the personnel profession, two main consequences follow. First the functions which it proposes to perform must either make sense in the management accounting context, or they must constitute credible alternatives to it. Second, the prospects for the appropriation of these functions by personnel professionals will depend on the extent to which they overlap the work performed by other managers. After a brief sketch of the post-1970s development of accounting controls in British companies, the futures currently envisaged for the personnel profession will be discussed in the light of these two questions.

THE RECENT GROWTH OF ACCOUNTING CONTROLS IN BRITISH COMPANIES

The accounting profession and its general approach to management have long been prominent in British industry. For example, a 1965 survey by *The Director* revealed that about 15 per cent of directors of companies with a share capital exceeding £5m. were chartered accountants, far outnumbering all other professions. Despite this, the widespread use of management accounting techniques of any real sophistication is comparatively recent in Britain. Until the merger wave of the 1960s and the increasing adoption of multi-divisional forms of organization (Steer and Cable 1978), most large British firms were organized as holding companies in which headquarters control was largely limited to the periodical inspection of the accounts of constituent companies. Financial controls at lower levels were similarly undeveloped. As late as 1960, a noted authority (Parker 1969: 11) could comment on the rarity of standard costing systems in British firms. By 1980, however, Jones's survey indicated that over 90 per cent of companies were then using some form of budgetary control and financial performance indicators. Coates *et al.*'s (1983) survey of management accounting practice in multi-divisionals also revealed a very widespread use of accounting ratios as a key management control device. Over the past two decades, then, there has been a spectacular increase in the sophistication and prominence of accounting control in British companies.

The flow of variously qualified accountants into managerial positions is consistent with this picture of growing functional salience. Membership of the (now) Chartered Institute of Management Accountants, most of whom work in industry, increased from 15,837 to 29,422 between 1977 and 1990. The corresponding increase for the Institute of Chartered Accountants in England and Wales was from 63,494 to 94,938, and about 40 per cent of these are employed in industry. The current output of chartered accountants of all kinds is now over 5,000 per annum, which is roughly equivalent to the entire national output of business studies graduates.

Both of these trends are linked with the prevalence of merger and acquisition among British companies, and their consequent increasing diversification. The rival profit forecasts involved in takeover battles, for example, call for the expertise of the accountant. So does the framework of budgetary constraints and targets needed to control a diversified enterprise. In consequence, accountants have flooded into company head offices, while, at least in those companies in which a 'core' activity can no longer be identified, industrial relations and other personnel issues are devolved to operating subsidiaries (Hill and Pickering 1986; Sisson and Scullion 1985). While these trends have been good news for qualified accountants interested in managerial careers, they pose problems for those who believe that the personnel function has a part to play in the formulation of overall company strategy.

The growing decentralization of company structures, the diffusion of management accounting techniques, the tightening grip of accountants on senior management positions, and the treatment of personnel and industrial relations as issues to be dealt with at the operating subsidiary level – all of these are developments which broadly coincided with the diminution of trade union bargaining power during the 1980s. The notion that the personnel profession is faced with nothing more than a diminished demand for expertise in collective bargaining is far too simple. It must now make its way in a corporate world dominated by the control structures and culture of management accounting.

TRENDS IN COLLECTIVE BARGAINING AND THE ACCOUNTING ASCENDANCY

Recognition of the importance of accounting control systems for industrial relations – and, by implication, for the personnel profession – began with a prescient article of 1979 in which the late Eric Batstone explored the problems which they posed for the then current issue of workers' participation. Essentially, his argument was that management accountancy imposes a system of priorities and a 'vocabulary of motives' which makes it very difficult for workers' representatives to challenge any management action which is grounded in accounting logic. Subsequently this theme has been explored by many accounting writers, though not explicitly in an industrial relations context (e.g. Hopper and Powell 1985).

In fact Batstone's argument implied a fundamental incompatibility between accounting controls and all forms of pluralist industrial relations practice. Although unnoticed at the time, the implications for the personnel function were profound, since personnel professionals in the late 1970s were frequently the advocates, and sometimes the practitioners, of industrial relations reform on the 'constitutionalist' model. Batstone's article pointed towards a scenario in which this role would be much diminished. What Tyson and Fell (1986) subsequently characterized as the 'death of the old industrial relations' game might occur not so much by the starvation of recession as by strangulation at the hands of the management accountant.

On the whole, the literature of industrial relations has paid little attention to the overall context of corporate control. In consequence, the intersection of collective bargaining with the development of the management accounting framework during the 1970s is poorly documented. An exception is Brown's studies of non-negotiated local wage drift (1972, 1973). In ten case study factories Brown demonstrated that non-negotiated wage drift was accelerated in the absence of cost monitoring. Significantly, the only one of the factories which had a recognizable standard cost system was also the one with the lowest non-negotiated wage drift (1973: 164). Since wage drift was one of the policy issues which inspired the Donovan reforms, the message for those who cared to read it, was that cost accounting might achieve what pluralist industrial relations could not.

During the 1980s the role played by the management accounting framework became more visible, with the well-documented trend towards devolved bargaining in large, multi-plant companies (Brown 1988: 41, 1993). The first company-level industrial relations survey indicated that there is considerable establishment-level autonomy on such issues as local payments, overtime, shift-working, and the introduction of new technologies (Marginson *et al.* 1986: Tables 5.3, 6.1, 7.1) as well as discipline, short-time working and redundancies (Edwards 1987: 96). Despite the prevalence of company-wide job evaluation schemes by the early 1980s the establishment was the most important level of pay bargaining (Brown 1981; Daniel and Millward 1983; Edwards and Marginson 1988). The implication is that the autonomy of local managers is focused upon working methods, manning arrangements and wages – in other words, upon the substance of the work–wage bargain.

Within this establishment autonomy, there are indications that the industrial relations initiative now lies as much with line managers as with personnel specialists (Edwards 1987: 94). WIRS2 indicates that establishment managing directors think that their departmental line managers have more influence than local personnel managers on all industrial relations issues except the conduct of disputes not involving their own departments (Millward and Stevens 1986: 43–6). They also believe that the influence of departmental line managers is increasing, while that of personnel departments remains static (see also Mackay and Torrington 1987: 163; Storey 1987).

The trend, then, has been to push down management policy-making on the substantive conditions of employment to the establishment level, and, within that, towards a dominance of line management over the personnel/industrial relations function. While the personnel function may remain influential on procedural and policy basics, the implication is that management policy on substantive issues is now driven by the same pressures which drive local line management in general – those of financial target-setting and performance monitoring (Kinnie 1985). The bargaining autonomy of establishment-level line managers is therefore circumscribed by manpower budgets, and its financial consequences are monitored against such detailed targets as unit labour costs (Marginson 1988; Marginson *et al.* 1986) as well as overall profitability. There is also ample evidence that the material interests of establishment-level line managers are now linked to accounting indicators. In the case of companies which are organized as profit centres, the lowest level of profit centre is normally the operating establishment (Marginson *et al.* 1986; Marginson and Sisson 1988), and roughly 40 per cent of the managers of these are paid some form of performance-linked bonus (Coates *et al.* 1983).

These trends do not mean that the personnel function, either at headquarters or establishment level, is without influence. Local personnel managers are still consulted, and there is evidence that they act as the representatives of such headquarters industrial relations policy as exists. Millward and Stevens (1986: 31, 33) found that local personnel managers reported to personnel managers at divisional or headquarters level, rather than to local line managers, and that there was frequent consultation, on a range of industrial relations issues, between the different levels of personnel management.

Three recent case studies may illustrate how collective bargaining within the budgetary regime has developed. In two companies studied by Purcell and Gray (1986), the task of face-to-face bargaining with trade unions was wholly devolved to divisional personnel departments. However, it was the task of headquarters personnel management to ensure that the divisional office contained any settlement within the budgetary framework decided at head office. By these means, it was intended that the trade unions should continue to dissipate their energies in 'bargaining' at the devolved level, without challenging the budgetary process.

In a recent study of Coates Viyella by Leopold and Jackson (1990), the devolution of bargaining was aimed at securing local concessions on labour utilization and flexibility in return for the annual pay round. Aiming, as they put it, to institute the bargaining of 'something for something in place of something for nothing', the management withdrew from the bargaining arrangements of the Knitwear Industries Federation and began bargaining at sixteen profit centres. These had to prepare manpower budgets and get them approved by the divisional boards in advance of negotiation. Reaching any settlement in excess of these budgets 'would be a very difficult step for a managing director to take.'

This partial substitution of budgetary pressure on line management for industrial relations policy also appears to be occurring in the public sector. Pendleton's (1991) study of 1980s trends in British Rail revealed that reductions in the government grant had been transmitted to area managers as a tightening of budgetary controls. At the same time, senior management, impatient with the 'time-wasting' involved in local procedures, began to regard rigid adherence to these procedures as undesirable. At the local level, the result was a reduction in the time off given to union representatives for trade union activity and a tendency for area managers to break local agreements in their pursuit of reduced costs.

All of this means that, quite apart from the reduced incidence of collective bargaining, the position of industrial relations in the overall control system of many large companies has declined. During the 1970s, a plausible case could be made that industrial relations policy ought to be at the heart of corporate strategy in any unionized company. During the 1980s and 1990s, in contrast, industrial relations has tended to become a service, rather than a policy-making function. At the higher levels, it has become the executive arm of budgetary control, while, locally, it takes its bargaining agendas from line management. It is this trend, as well as the decline in collective bargaining, to which the personnel profession must respond.

PROJECTED FUTURES FOR THE PERSONNEL FUNCTION

In 1978, Legge produced an analysis of the forms of 'conformist' and 'deviant' innovation available to the personnel profession as means of increasing its influence in the face of the 'dominant utilitarian values and bureaucratic relationships' of the business organization (see also Tyson and Fell 1986; Guest 1990 and Monks 1992 for recycled versions of these categories). Though Legge's diagnosis of the problem made no explicit mention of accounting controls (the 1986 discussion by Gowler and Legge was more explicit in this respect) the clammy hand of the accountant was nevertheless visible, especially in the nature of the remedies proposed.

In the management accounting context, 'conformist innovation' implied the adaptation of personnel practice to the requirements of control and reporting systems, whereas 'deviant innovation' involves some form of challenge to the accounting frame of reference itself. Instances of 'conformist innovation' listed by Legge were the provision of 'hard' data by the personnel department for consumption by management accounting systems and attempts to justify personnel activity itself in cost terms. These have subsequently proved to be a fair guide to developments both at the intellectual and practitioner levels.

The 'hard data' option

A minimum level of 'conformist' adaptation is probably represented by a case reported by Tyson (1985) in which training costs were regularly reported to the accounting department and compared to predetermined budgets. Here, the personnel function had evidently done little more than respond to the demands of the accounting department for the kind of cost-control information typically extracted from operations units.

There are obvious dangers for the personnel function if the reaction is to be as passive as this. If the data provided are to be no more nor less than those demanded by the management accountant, what is to become of the distinctive personnel input to the management process? Even so, adaptation at this level may pose problems for some personnel departments. Given that much management information on absenteeism, time-loss analysis and the like is now electronically stored and processed, there is a danger that the apparent reluctance of the personnel profession to engage with computer technology (Torrington *et al.* 1985) may lead to managers in other functions (notably accountants) taking over the data-handling of this type.

Data currently being analysed from the second company-level industrial relations survey (Marginson *et al.* 1993) indicate that this possibility is only partially realized. Industrial relations data are more frequently collected by the personnel than accounting departments in Britain's large companies, though the incidence of the latter is by no means negligible. It is also noticeable that accounting departments more frequently collect those indicators of industrial relations performance which are also most relevant to financial performance (e.g. unit labour costs).

The justification of personnel work in accounting terms

Another form of conformist adaptation to the accounting ascendancy is evident in recent proposals that personnel activities should be justified in cost-effectiveness terms, though the extent to which practitioners have actually adopted this strategy is unknown. Cannon (1979) advocated the capital investment appraisal of programmes proposed by personnel departments, while Tyson and Fell (1986) suggested that the effectiveness of personnel management might be measured through indices of employee productivity. While quite logical in terms of Guest's (1982) observation that personnel activity is increasingly focused on, and must justify itself through, productivity improvements, such proposals displace the problem rather than solve it. Managers in other functions, to say nothing of employees, are unlikely to accept that real or projected productivity outcomes are measures only of the contribution of the personnel department (Legge 1978: 60–1).

The strategy has other pitfalls. First, it runs the risk of creating the expectation that all personnel department activity must be justified in cost-effectiveness terms – with implications that the profession would do well to ponder. Second, it voluntarily hands over the decision on whether or not to proceed with personnel department initiatives to managers outside the function. Storey (1992: 173) describes an example of this situation in British Rail. Following a reorganization into business units, line managers had become the 'purchasers' of personnel services and increasingly refused to fund any of these which they deemed not to be of value.

A further problem arises from the insensitivity of cost accounting systems to issues of quality, their tendency to sectionalize activities, and the 'make-or-buy' atmosphere of the 1980s and 1990s. Recruitment costs, for example, would probably be calculated on the basis of the staff time involved, plus advertising costs, plus some apportionment of general overhead. Such calculations encourage comparisons with the costs of external consultants or specialist in-house recruitment agencies. Questions of any value added by the broader experience of personnel managers might have a hard time gaining a hearing in this kind of debate. Adams's survey of ninety-eight large firms (1991) indicates that the costing of personnel work has been associated with moves to contract parts of it out. The reasons given were compulsory competitive tendering and changes to the financial reporting system.

Recently, there has been some debate on the implications of this tendency to 'balkanize' the personnel function (that is, to break it down into its component tasks and assign these to consultants or to other managerial functions). On the one hand, Torrington and Mackay (1986: 34–6) have argued that contracting out the more quantifiable aspects of personnel work makes it progressively more difficult to quantify the benefits of the remaining in-house activities. In other words, the strategy of justifying personnel work in accounting terms may be self-defeating. Against this, Clark and Clark (1991) have argued that the involvement of outside consultants actually strengthens the personnel function by enabling it to shed 'peripheral' activities. This does not ring true. It is hard to see executive recruitment and training (two of Adams's examples of contracted-out functions) as 'peripheral'. What is more likely to be at stake in the audit of personnel departments is illustrated in Burn and Thompson's (1993) case study of a local authority. There, the adopted measure of 'success' was the degree to which the personnel department was reduced in size as compared with similar organizations.

The 'hard' variant of human resource management (Storey 1992) might be regarded as a logical end-product of the strategy of justifying personnel management through accounting indices. If these are all that count, there seems little reason to retain a distinctive 'personnel' approach. In consequence, 'hard' human resource management tends to merge with the approach of the rest of the management team (ibid.: 168). While the case studies of Fox and McLeay (1992) indicate that the 'hard' HRM approach can out-perform the 'soft' variant, this might not be good news for personnel practitioners. In Fox and McLeay's companies, 'hard' HRM substituted recruitment by 'grapevine' for training and systematic staff selection. Improved results in acquired companies were achieved by staff cuts and by weeding out managers with the 'wrong' approach. Since none of this called for the particular expertise of human resource professionals, it was done without their assistance.

In sum, the strategy of justifying personnel work in accounting terms may backfire, and end up by diminishing the scope and security of the personnel function. As for the 'hard' variant of human resource management, this looks like a dead end for the profession.

Human resource accounting as deviant innovation?

Legge (1978) has discussed human resource accounting (HRA) as a form of *conformist*, rather than deviant innovation. From the perspective of human resource management, this may appear reasonable, since HRA proposed to admit accounting calculation into the practices of personnel management. From the accounting point of view, however, HRA looked like a highly confrontational form of deviant innovation. Its point of attack on current accounting conventions concerned the treatment of expenditures on training and staff development. Traditionally, the accounting principle of conservatism dictates that outgoings within an accounting period must be treated as expenses to be deducted from income, rather than additions to capital – unless some clearly specified return can be associated with the expenditures. Against this, HRA sought to find some way of treating expenditures on the development of human resources as capital investment, based on the intuitively appealing notion that a well-trained and well-motivated workforce represents a considerable business asset. If this could be achieved, HRA, according to one of its principal advocates (Flamholz 1974: 355) 'offers a way out of the limited role of the personnel function'. Perhaps for this reason, it has been the subject of a joint publication of the Institute of Personnel Management and the (then) Institute of Cost and Management Accountants (Giles and Robinson 1972), and it is now covered in approximately five hours of the IPM syllabus.

Unfortunately, the hopes placed in this initative as a means of coping with the accounting ascendancy do not yet appear to have been realized. The traditional accounting mind is proving inflexible on the question of whether formally free human beings can be regarded as assets in the same way as legally owned property (cf. Jauch and Skigen 1977). More important, the central and critical question from the point of view of conventional accounting systems – that of placing a monetary value on 'human assets' – has so far proved contentious. Whereas the advocates of HRA appear to be unable to advance beyond the measurement of inputs (analogous to the recording of conventional capital investment), the critics appear to demand some measurement of expected outputs (analogous to conventional capital investment appraisal). So matters stand. The institutional weight of accounting practice, which is prepared to swallow estimates of millions of pounds for trading 'goodwill', has so far refused to do the same for human assets.

In fact, the lack of success of HRA on this front may well tell us more about the deceptions of accounting exactitude as a means of assessing the real worth of a business than it does about the failings of HRA itself. Research by Hunt (1987) reveals that human asset values are rarely the subject of a professionally informed audit during takeover battles, yet they are often a source of disappointment once the dust has settled. Such a sequence of events makes little sense and it clearly indicates a place for some form of HRA in strategic decision-making. The uncertainty involved in valuing human assets is no reason at all for ignoring them, and is a very good reason for treating accounting numbers as only one of a number of inputs into managerial decision-making.

Strategic human resource management: an ecology

If HRA is the most confrontational form of 'deviant innovation' currently envisaged for the personnel profession, the most ambitious is strategic HRM. In effect, this involves bypassing the Maginot Line of accounting controls, and infiltrating the personnel function into company headquarters. Where the Donovan reforms once inspired the promotion of the company-level industrial relations policy (e.g. Cuthbert and Hawkins 1973), 'strategic HRM' is a slogan which now serves the same purpose (e.g. Guest 1987, 1990; Keenoy 1990). Despite the fact that the majority of present-day personnel managers are excluded from top-level decision-making (Guest 1991; Hickson *et al.* 1986; Hill and Pickering 1986), there are enough prominent counter-examples to lend the scenario a surface plausibility. These instances encourage the idea that it may be possible to persuade other companies of the competitive advantages to be gained by the enlightened practice of strategic HRM.

Whilst this may be so, it is possible to define the structural location of strategic human resource management in a way which argues against its easy generalizability. In a minority of large British companies, diversification has occurred around a recognizable 'core' of operational activities. In these companies, operations management and the personnel function retain a considerable headquarters presence. Sisson and Scullion (1985) argue that this has happened because the development of a workforce, management and working relationships appropriate to the core operation is a strategic contingency in such companies, and so warrants consideration at the highest policy-making level. Accordingly, it is mainly these 'critical function' companies which employ personnel executives operating at the level of corporate strategy and which approximate to Tyson and Fell's (1986) 'architectural' or Monks' (1992) 'innovative/sophisticated' model.

If this reasoning is correct, the important conclusion follows that unmodified 'architectural' models of personnel management cannot simply be transplanted into the typical highly diversified company. In these companies, projected futures for the personnel function which ignore the centrality of financial control systems or which seek to finesse them in some grandiose vision of company-level human resource policy-making are simply unrealistic.

Human resource management as an alternative to collective bargaining

Before looking at particular aspects of HRM as future activities for the personnel profession, a general comment is called for. It will be recalled that what is at issue is a search for alternatives to the profession's role in collective bargaining. If HRM is to offer a solution in this respect, it too needs to be, in some sense, an alternative to collective bargaining. At first sight, this seems to be the case. Originally an American import, and stigmatized in some quarters as 'industrial relations without trade unions', its focus on the individual employment relationship and on securing commitment in place of bargained cooperation appears promising. The recent WIRS3 survey will considerably dampen these hopes.

First, the adoption of human resource job titles by personnel practitioners has occurred in only a small minority of workplaces (and this finding is replicated in the second company-level industrial relations survey). While this coincides with the fairly widespread adoption of 'fragments' of the HRM approach, it nevertheless indicates that any change in the approach of personnel practitioners has been insufficiently marked to call for, or to be signalled by, a change in title. Second, the fragments of HRM are appearing in *unionized*, and not in non-unionized workplaces (again, a finding replicated in the second company-level industrial relations survey). In other words, insofar as HRM exists at all, it appears to be a response to collective bargaining, not an alternative to it (Sisson 1993).

In view of the hopes invested in HRM by the personnel profession, the implications are profound. Put crudely, HRM is not happening very much, and when it is, it is in the wrong place.

Management appraisal and development as core activities for the personnel profession

If a realistic future for the greater part of the personnel profession lies in the 'innovative/profession' promotion of the constituent techniques of HRM (cf. Monks 1992), rather than an insistence on its essential indivisibility (Tyson 1987), management appraisal and development are obvious candidates (Gowler and Legge 1986). The profession, after all, has historical roots in this area. During the 1960s, the levy-rebate system of industrial training required that training programmes had to be properly organized and available for inspection in order to qualify for rebates – a requirement which encouraged the recruitment of personnel managers. Today, however, the evolution of accounting controls has created a demand for accounting expertise in the design and operation of performance-linked management appraisal systems. The symptoms of this development are visible in the curriculum of the Chartered Institute of Management Accountants (CIMA).

While examination syllabuses are not infallible guides to professional practice, CIMA's are nevertheless a useful corrective to facile assumptions that management development will 'naturally' fall into the lap of the personnel practitioner. The syllabus comprises four stages. One quarter of stage 3 (approximately sixty hours of face-to-face study time) is entitled 'Management Development'. As it currently stands, the topics covered are 'Individuals', 'Groups', 'Organizations', 'Environment and management of change' and 'Human resource management and development'. Though this section is currently being revised and retitled, it seems unlikely that this will involve any substantive disengagement with the area.

It seems equally clear that if management appraisal and development is to be routinely regarded as a matter for personnel managers, they will have to demonstrate some competitive advantage in this area over management accountants, not to mention MBA-trained general managers. In the earlier version of this chapter (Armstrong 1989), it was proposed that this might be done on the basis of the considerable volume of critical research which has appeared on the operation of accounting control systems. This now appears unrealistic. The research in question is being performed by accounting academics and it is beginning to appear in accounting syllabuses, not those of the personnel profession and its associated behavioural sciences (see page 157 for an elaboration).

Pay determination within the accounting framework

Gowler and Legge (1986) envisaged a future for the personnel function in the development of reward systems designed to foster entrepreneurial values within the 'core' workforce. Such projections are evidently based on the 'received wisdom', noted by Smith (1992: 175), that a policy for wages and salaries cannot be designed unless it is based on a personnel policy. The fact is that it can: in a firm researched fifteen years ago by the writer, a sophisticated and influential personnel department had ceded the design of profit-related incentive schemes to the accounting department, one of whose efforts came close to provoking a walk-out of white-collar staff. The rationale for this takeover by the accounting department was that the data on profitability lay within their province, as did the 'expertise' of attributing responsibility for it.

This apparent oddity turns out to have been the wave of the future. Since then, the trend towards profit-related pay has been encouraged by the 1986 introduction of tax relief for that proportion of pay which varies with profit. Moreover, the terms of the tax relief make it virtually mandatory to involve professional accountants in the design of the schemes, since they must refer to identifiable 'employment units' for which independently audited profit-and-loss accounts are produced. Although Ogden (1993: 193) reports that the response up to 1990 was unenthusiastic, WIRS3 (Millward *et al.* 1992: 262–6) shows an increase in the proportion of private sector establishments with some form of profit-related pay, from 18 per cent to 43 per cent between 1984 and 1990. Similarly, preliminary analysis of data from the second company-level industrial relations survey shows that about 60 per cent of Britain's large companies have profit-related payment schemes, about half of which are cash-based. The data also indicate that the accounting and finance function plays a greater part in the overall pay-determination process in those companies with profit-related pay.

In fact there exists a sophisticated theoretical rationale in the form of agency theory for the involvement of accountants in incentive pay systems. Extremely prominent in the American academies, and increasingly so in the UK, agency theory assumes the rationality of 'economic man', and (in one version) purports to devise systems of monitoring and performance-related pay which ensure that self-interested agents (employees) act in the interests of principals (employers) – see Ashton (1991) for a summary. While there are question-marks against the practical relevance of this densely mathematical material (albeit not in the minds of its advocates), it is now taught on many advanced courses in management accounting. This can be construed as an expertise in the design of managerial evaluation and reward systems. It is one which is unlikely to be possessed by personnel managers.

Employee communication

In his search for symptoms of HRM in WIRS3, Sisson (1993) notes that there have been increases in a number of indices of employee communication, such as meetings of junior managers, newsletters, surveys and ballots. On the face of it, this kind of employee involvement seems tailor-made for the personnel function.

While this may be so, it needs to be recognized that the source of the substantive information to be communicated will not normally be the personnel function itself. This means that practitioners may have to 'invite themselves' into the process. Purdy's (1981) survey of twenty-eight companies indicates that, where financial information is concerned, there may be some way to go.

Not surprisingly, in all of the companies, the accounting function was involved in the preparation of financial reports for employees. By comparison, personnel and industrial relations managers were infrequently involved, even though there was a clear industrial relations rationale for presenting the information (the wish to discourage excessive wage demands and industrial action). Industrial relations managers were involved in only two of the companies, and the personnel function in only one.

Data currently being analysed from the second company-level industrial relations survey throws further light on the extent to which accountants are involved in employee communication. Accounting and finance managers prepared suitable financial information in 78 per cent of the companies and were physically involved in its communication in 67 per cent of them. In 43 per cent of the companies, it was accountants from UK headquarters itself who were directly involved in this fashion. While the survey does not contain comparative figures on the involvement of the personnel function in this particular area, the figures indicate clearly enough that there is little tendency to hand over the information to the personnel function once it has been prepared.

'People people' in a competitive world

If, at a non-strategic level, human resource management involves 'giving personnel back to the line', it is not immediately obvious that it offers any future at all for the specialist personnel function. According to Keenoy (1990), however, this is superficial thinking. Line managers, he argues, faced with the demands of 'neo-pluralist' practice will need to develop 'people skills', and it is in this area that he foresees a role for personnel managers as internal consultants.

Leaving aside the doubtful identification of any form of human resource management with pluralism, Keenoy's argument hinges on the credibility of the personnel manager as a purveyor of a distinctive people expertise. This idea is not, of course, new. It lurks, for example, in those hackneyed case studies in which a production manager blunders into people trouble so that he can be instructively rescued by the developing people skills of the (IPM) students. Logically speaking, a competitive advantage in people skills can only be the result of character, education or experience. Few who have encountered an IPM evening class will find it easy to swallow the notion that these are individuals possessed of superior insight and social competence. Nor is it obvious that the daily routine of the personnel manager is any more likely to develop people skills than that of the production engineer. As for education, Fowler (1985) has commented disparagingly on the 'handful of banal behavioural nostrums' offered by personnel managers as guidance in organizational restructuring. These, in any case, are taught to management accounting students, and, unlike the gobbets of behavioural 'science' taught to aspirant personnel managers, they are explicitly related to the management accounting framework within which the modern manager operates. The point is worth elaboration.

Although undergraduate and professional syllabuses by no means coincide with the store of formal and tacit knowledge at the command of the experienced practitioner, they nevertheless provide some indication of the knowledge-base upon which (s)he is expected to build. Undergraduates taking degrees in accounting are routinely offered optional courses in organizational behaviour, human resource management and the like. To the extent that they take these options, they will enter employment with just as much (or as little) grasp of the 'behavioural' aspects of management as the would-be personnel manager. Even when they do not, they will still get some grounding in behavioural science, some of it duplicating the material taught on personnel management courses, some more specifically adapted to the management accounting context. This can be illustrated from Wilson and Chua's widely-used text *Management Accounting: Method and Meaning* (1993).

The early chapters (1–3) make it clear that management accounting techniques are to be seen as part of an overall system of managerial control, in which human behaviour is a crucial link. On this rationale, the text covers the standard psycho-sociological material which is encountered in courses for personnel managers. Pages 264–76, for example, consider the behavioural aspects of budgeting, drawing on such heavily corroded sources as Maslow (1954), McGregor (1960) and Vroom (1964). In addition, however, the chapter discusses a number of themes indigenous to 'behavioural accounting', such as the effects of budgetary targets on performance (Stedry 1960; Hofstede 1967), the motivational effects of different usages of accounting data on the performance of subordinates (Hopwood 1973; Otley 1978), the tendency of subordinates to protect themselves by negotiating 'budgetary slack' (Schiff and Lewin 1970) and the intrusion of organizational politics into the budget-setting process (Wildavsky 1970). A later chapter (pp. 359–96) considers the evaluation of divisional performance within large companies. This involves consideration of a number of problems which involve both behavioural and accounting issues. For example, is it possible to devise indices of managerial performance, as distinct from indices of the performance of their divisions? What performance indicators will induce managers to maximize company performance, as opposed to that of their divisions? How can equitable transfer prices between divisions be determined? An understanding of these issues involves a grasp of the dysfunctional aspects of bureaucratic controls *and* the accounting mechanics of the controls in question. Courses taken by future personnel managers would include a general consideration of the problems of bureaucracy, but not their accounting manifestation.

To the extent that what is required in the modern corporate environment is not so much behavioural science itself, but its application to the accounting context, it may be the accounting student, not the aspirant personnel manager, who holds the competitive advantage.

CONCLUSIONS

The post-1970s decline in collective bargaining in Great Britain has precipitated a great deal of academic/prescriptive speculation on the future of the personnel profession. Missing from much of this work is an awareness of the overall context of corporate control within which that future will be worked out. An exception is Legge's (1978) discussion of 'conformist' and 'deviant' innovation, in which the relationship of personnel initiatives to their context is implicit. Since a core feature of the modern British corporation is its permeation with the characteristic performance targets, information flows and culture of management accounting, it is this which most importantly defines what is conformist and what is deviant.

Against this background, the variants of conformist innovation which have been proposed include the provision of 'hard' data for the accounting framework, and the evaluation of the outcomes of personnel activity in accounting terms. The logical end-point of this latter approach is the 'hard' variant of human resource management, in which personnel activity becomes exclusively directed towards quantifiable outcomes. In themselves, none of these options offers much future for the personnel function. They hand over the judgement of its effectiveness to managers in other functions. By encouraging cost comparisons, they encourage the contracting out of fragments of personnel work, and by prioritizing easily quantifiable outcomes, they undermine the case for a distinctive 'personnel' approach.

Judged against the accounting framework, the most radical forms of deviant innovation are the frontal assault of human resource accounting and the vaulting ambition of strategic human resource management. Quite correctly, the advocacy of human resource accounting is founded on a critique of accounting asset valuations which ignores the value of a trained workforce and smoothly functioning organization. So far, however, it has broken against the rock of entrenched accounting conservatism.

Strategic human resource management certainly exists, but it tends to be confined to companies which have a core activity for which the development of an appropriate workforce and management is a critical function for the company (roughly speaking, Goold and Campbell's (1987) 'strategic planners'). This argues against the possibility of its generalization to more diversified companies, in which these matters are typically devolved to subsidiaries and subordinated to the management accounting framework.

This leaves the opportunist adoption of particular fragments of 'soft' human resource management as a strategy for the profession. In general, this will require some promotional activity on the part of practitioners, because it presently appears that most British companies are only willing to adopt fragments of this approach under the pressure of collective bargaining.

The particular facets of soft human resource management considered in this chapter are management appraisal and development, reward systems, employee communication and behavioural science consultancy. What needs to be appreciated here is that, despite its historical stake in each of the areas, the professional has a natural monopoly in none of them. In each case the education of management accountants, and the associated research work constitute as plausible a warrant to practise as those of the personnel profession. The same may be true of other management specialisms.

This does not, of course, mean that there is no future for personnel practitioners in these areas. What it does mean is that there is no functional vacuum general to the modern corporation which awaits the arrival of refugees from the decline of collective bargaining. In this situation, talking of new areas of practice for the profession as a whole may mis-state the problem. What may be at issue is the ability of individual practitioners to spot particular opportunities for the expansion of the function in their own organizations. After two decades as a commentator on the future of the personnel profession, Guest (1991) now appears willing to write it off as a source of new ideas of this kind. This does not tally with what is known from published research. The astute promotion of new forms of behavioural remodelling and organizational development (for example) is nothing new for personnel practitioners (see, for example, Watson 1977; Pettigrew 1985). What has changed over the past two decades is that such initiatives must be adapted to the management accounting framework and promoted within a culture which takes for granted its operationalizations of company objectives and definitions of what is relevant to those objectives. A recent study by Jones *et al.* (1993) has shown how engineering managers are learning to promote their projects in these terms. There is no reason why personnel managers should not learn the same lesson. If, on the other hand, they remain incapable of speaking the language of management accountancy, they will remain unable to convince other managers of the relevance of their proposals.

REFERENCES

Adams, K. (1991) 'Externalisation vs. specialisation: what is happening to personnel?' *Human Resource Management Journal* 1(4): 40–54.

Armstrong, P. (1989) 'Human resource management in an age of management accountancy', in J. Storey (ed.) *New Perspectives on Human Resource Management*, London: Routledge.

Ashton, D. (1991) 'Agency theory and contracts of employment' in D. Ashton, T. Hopper and R.W. Scapens (eds) *Issues in Management Accounting*, Hemel Hempstead: Prentice-Hall.

Batstone, E. (1978) 'Systems of domination, accommodation and industrial democracy', in T. Burns (ed.) *Work and Power*, London: Sage.

—— (1984) *Working Order*, Oxford: Blackwell.

Brown, W.A. (1972) 'A consideration of custom and practice', *British Journal of Industrial Relations* 10: 42–61.

—— (1973) *Piecework Bargaining*, London: Heinemann Education.

—— (ed.) (1981) *The Changing Contours of British Industrial Relations*, Oxford: Blackwell.

—— (1988) *The Structure and Processes of Pay Determination in the Private Sector: 1979–1986*, London: Confederation of British Industry.

—— (1993) 'The contraction of collective bargaining in Britain', *British Journal of Industrial Relations* 31(2): 189–200.

Burn, D. and Thompson, L. (1993) 'When personnel calls in the auditors', *Personnel Management* January: 28–31.
Cannon, J. (1979) *Cost-Effective Personnel Decisions*, London: Institute of Personnel Management.
Clark, I. and Clark, T. (1991) 'Personnel management: defence, retrenchment, advance?', *Personnel Review* 20(1): 13–18.
Coates, J.B., Smith, J.E. and Stacey, R.J. (1983) 'Results of a preliminary survey into the structure of divisionalised companies, divisionalised performance appraisal and the associated role of management accountancy', in D. Cooper, R. Scapens and J. Arnold (eds) *Management Accounting Research and Practice*, London: Institute of Cost and Management Accountants.
Cowling, A. and Evans, A. (1985) 'Organization planning and the role of the personnel department', *Personnel Review* 14(4): 9–15.
Cuthbert, W.H. and Hawkins, K.H. (eds) (1973) *Company Industrial Relations Policies: the Management of Industrial Relations in the 1970s*, Harlow: Longman.
Daniel, W.W. (1986a) 'Four years of change for personnel', *Personnel Management* December.
—— (1986b) *Workplace Industrial Relations and Technical Change*, London: PSI.
Daniel, W.W. and Millward, N. (1983) *Workplace Industrial Relations in Britain*, London: Heinemann Educational.
Edwards, P.K. (1987) *Managing the Factory: a Survey of General Managers*, Oxford: Blackwell.
Edwards, P.K. and Marginson, P. (1988) 'Trade unions, pay bargaining and industrial action', in P. Marginson, P.K. Edwards, R. Martin, J. Purcell and K. Sisson (eds) *Beyond the Workplace: Managing Industrial Relations in Large Establishments*, Oxford: Blackwell.
Flamholz, E. (1974) *Human Resource Accounting*, Encino, CA: Dickenson Publishing Co.
Fowler, A. (1985) 'Getting into organisation restructuring', *Personnel Management* February: 24–7.
Fox, S. and McLeay, S. (1992) 'An approach to researching managerial labour markets: HRM, corporate strategy and financial performance in UK manufacturing', *International Journal for Human Resource Management* 3(3): 523–54.
Giles, W.J. and Robinson, D.F. (1972) *Human Asset Accounting*, London: Institute of Personnel Management and Institute of Cost and Management Accountants.
Goold, M. and Campbell, A. (1987) *Strategies and Styles: the Role of the Centre in Managing Diversified Companies*, Oxford: Blackwell.
Gowler, D. and Legge, K. (1986) 'Personnel and paradigms: four perspectives on the future', *Industrial Relations Journal* 17(3): 225–35.
Guest, D. (1982) 'Has the recession really hit personnel management?', *Personnel Management* 14(10): 36–9.
—— (1986) 'Human resource management', Manchester Business School conference on industrial relations strategy and management, 6–7 September.
—— (1987) 'Human resource management and industrial relations', *Journal of Management Studies* 24(5): 503–21.
—— (1989) 'Personnel management and human resource management', *Personnel Management* January: 48–51.
—— (1991) 'Personnel management: the end of orthodoxy', *British Journal of Industrial Relations* 29(2): 149–76.
Hickson, D.J., Butler, R.J., Gray, D., Mallory, G.R. and Wilson, D.C. (1986) *Top Decisions: Strategic Decision-Making in Organisations*, Oxford: Blackwell.

Hill, C.W.L. and Pickering, J.F. (1986) 'Divisionalisation, decentralisation and performance of large United Kingdom companies', *Journal of Management Studies* 23(1): 26–50.
Hofstede, G. (1967) *The Game of Budgetary Control*, London: Tavistock.
Hopper, T. and Powell, A. (1985) 'Making sense of research into the organisational and social aspects of management accounting: a review of its underlying assumptions', *Journal of Management Studies* 22(5): 429–65.
Hopwood, A.G. (1973) *An Accounting System and Managerial Behaviour*, Farnborough: Saxon House.
—— (1974) *Accounting and Human Behaviour*, London: Haymarket.
Hunt, J. (1987) 'Hidden extras: how people got overlooked in takeovers', *Personnel Management* July: 24–6.
Jauch, R. and Skigen, M. (1977) 'Human resource accounting: a critical evaluation', in G.J. Benston (ed.) *Contemporary Cost Accounting and Control*, Boston, MA: CBI Publishing Co.
Jones, C.J. (1980) *Financial Planning and Control: a Survey of Practices by UK Companies*, London: Institute of Cost and Management Accountants.
Jones, T.C., Currie, W.L. and Dugdale, D. (1993) 'Accounting and technology in Britain and Japan: learning from field research', *Management Accounting Research* 4(2): 109–38.
Keenoy, T. (1990) 'Human resource management: a case of the wolf in sheep's clothes', *Personnel Review* 19(2): 3–9.
Kinnie, N. (1985) 'Changing managerial strategies in industrial relations', *Industrial Relations Journal* 16(4): 17–24.
Legge, K. (1978) *Power, Innovation and Problem-Solving in Personnel Management*, Maidenhead: McGraw-Hill.
—— (1988) 'Personnel management in recession and recovery: a comparative analysis of what the surveys say', *Personnel Review* 17(2): 2–70.
Leopold, J. and Jackson, M. (1990) 'Decentralisation of collective bargaining: a case study', *Industrial Relations Journal* 21(3): 185–93.
McGregor, D. (1960) *The Human Side of Enterprise*, New York: McGraw-Hill.
Mackay, L. and Torrington, D. (1987) *The Changing Nature of Personnel Management*, London: Institute of Personnel Management.
Marginson, P. (1988) 'Centralised control or establishment autonomy?', in P. Marginson, P.K. Edwards, R. Martin, J. Purcell and K. Sisson (eds) *Beyond the Workplace: Managing Industrial Relations in Large Establishments*, Oxford: Blackwell.
Marginson, P. and Sisson, K. (1978) 'The management of employees' in P. Marginson *et al.* (eds) *Beyond the Workplace: Managing Industrial Relations in the Multi-Establishment Enterprise*, Oxford: Blackwell.
Marginson, P., Armstrong, P., Edwards, P.K. and Purcell, J. (1993) 'The control of industrial relations in large British companies', University of Warwick, working paper in Industrial Relations, No. 45.
Marginson, P., Edwards, P.K., Purcell, J. and Sisson, K. (1986) *The Workplace Industrial Relations Company Level Survey*, report for the Economic and Social Research Council, Industrial Relations Research Unit, University of Warwick.
Maslow, A.E. (1954) *Motivation and Personality*, New York: Harper & Row.
Millward, N. and Stevens, M. (1986) *British Workplace Industrial Relations 1980–1984*, Aldershot: Gower.
Millward, N., Stevens, M., Smart, D. and Hawes, W. (1992) *Workplace Industrial Relations in Transition*, London: Routledge.
Monks, K. (1992) 'Models of personnel management: a means of understanding the

diversity of personnel practice', *Human Resource Management Journal* 3(2): 29–41.
Ogden, S. (1993) 'The limitations of agency theory: the case of accounting-based profit sharing schemes', *Critical Perspectives on Accounting* 4(2): 179–206.
Otley, D. (1978) 'Budget use and managerial performance', *Journal of Accounting Research* 16(1): 122–149.
Parker, R.H. (1969) *Management Accounting: an Historical Perspective*, London: Macmillan.
Peat Marwick (1984) *Financial Management in the Public Sector: a Review 1979–84*, London: Peat Marwick.
Pendleton, A. (1991) 'Workplace industrial relations in British Rail: change and continuity in the 1980s', *Industrial Relations Journal* 22(3): 209–21.
Pettigrew, A.M. (1985) *The Awakening Giant: Continuity and Change in Imperial Chemical Industries*, Oxford: Blackwell.
Purcell, J. and Gray, A. (1986) 'Corporate personnel departments and the management of industrial relations: two case studies in ambiguity', *Journal of Management Studies* 23(2): 205–23.
Purdy, D. (1981) 'The provision of financial information to employees: a study of the reporting practices of some large public companies in the United Kingdom', *Accounting, Organisations and Society* 6(4): 327–38.
Schiff, M. and Lewin, A.Y. (1970) 'The impact of people on budgets', *The Accounting Review* 45(2): 259–68.
Sisson, K. (1993) 'In search of HRM', *British Journal of Industrial Relations* 31(2): 201–10.
Sisson, K. and Scullion, H. (1985) 'Putting the corporate personnel department in its place', *Personnel Management* December: 36–9.
Smith, I. (1992) 'Reward management and HRM', in P. Blyton and P. Turnbull (eds) *Reassessing Human Resource Management*, London: Sage.
Stedry, A.C. (1960) *Budget Control and Cost Behaviour*, Englewood Cliffs, NJ: Prentice-Hall.
Steer, P. and Cable, J. (1978) 'International organisation and profit: an empirical analysis of large UK companies', *Journal of Industrial Economics* 27: 13–30.
Storey, J. (1987) 'Developments in the management of human resources: an interim report', *Warwick Papers in Industrial Relations*, No. 17.
—— (1992) *Developments in the Management of Human Resources*, Oxford: Blackwell.
Torrington, D. and Hall, L. (1987) *Personnel Management: a New Approach*, Hemel Hempstead: Prentice-Hall.
Torrington, D. and Mackay, L. (1986) 'Will consultants take over the personnel function?', *Personnel Management* February: 34–7.
Torrington, D., Mackay, I. and Hall, L. (1985) 'The changing nature of personnel management', *Employee Relations* 7(5): 10–16.
Tyson, S. (1985) 'Is this the very model of a modern personnel manager?', *Personnel Management* April: 22–5.
—— (1987) 'Management of the personnel function', *Journal of Management Studies* 24(5): 523–32.
Tyson, S. and Fell, A. (1986) *Evaluating the Personnel Function*, London: Hutchinson.
Vroom, V.H. (1964) *Work and Motivation*, New York: Wiley.
Watson, A.J. (1977) *The Personnel Managers: a Study in the Sociology of Work and Employment*, London: Routledge.
Wildavsky, A. (1970) *The Politics of the Budgeting Process*, Boston, MA: Little Brown.

Wilson, R.M.S. and Chua, W.F. (1993) *Managerial Accounting: Method and Meaning* (2nd edn), London: Chapman & Hall.

Part III

Key practice areas of HRM

Chapter 7

Human resource planning

Sheila Rothwell

INTRODUCTION: HRM MODELS AND THE ROLE OF PLANNING

Human resource planning is usually seen as an essential feature of the ideal-type model of human resource management, even if it does not always appear to be given high priority in practice. It is a necessary condition of the 'business integration' and 'strategic' or forward-looking aspects of the model that appear to distinguish it from (traditional) *ad hoc* industrial relations or personnel administration. By implication, it is not the same as 'manpower planning' – a typical traditional function of the latter – although it may include some of the same techniques (Vickerstaff 1989).

An ideal-type feature of human resource management is the assumption of a 'developmental' approach to employees, which appears to imply some form of systematic management of the assessment and augmentation of their ability, in relation to business needs. Moreover, the other major feature or output of the human resource management model is the emphasis on commitment to the goals of the organization, in which techniques of reward and career development may play a significant part and for which human resource planning may be important.

The need for integration of all these aspects of human resource planning into business development should therefore ensure that human resource planning is seen as a 'line' responsibility, like other features of the 'new' model. Yet herein may lie part of the explanation of the gap between 'theory' and 'practice', given that line managers are arguably even less likely to undertake such activity than personnel managers, particularly in small, decentralized units where the emphasis on achieving financial targets is likely to predominate.

An illustration of a strategic human resource management (SHRM) model which is integrated with business strategy formulation, and not merely derived from it, has been developed by Butler *et al.* (1991). They show that combining human resource planning with strategic planning enables the firm to cope with contingencies such as mergers, international operations and corporate entrepreneurism – or others. They include provision for some of the unanticipated benefits that may also emerge from integration of the various planning processes, demonstrating the potential for a synergistic and dynamic approach to human resource planning.

Techniques of planning

Some awareness of the techniques available – and the range of options within them – is important for appropriate policy choices to be made. Figure 7.1 provides one framework for manpower planning which illustrates the classic approach to it: the attempt to forecast whether there is likely to be a mismatch between the supply of labour and the demand for it, and then to plan appropriate adjustment policies.

The external environment

Estimates of supply usually start from a scan of the external environment (see Figure 7.1) either to get a feel for the likely trends and changing patterns of skill availability for the established company, or to serve as a more precise guide for a start-up firm or one seeking a new location, or to recruit a particular type of employee, in which case more detailed information is needed. Details of education, skill and experience, though not always easy to acquire, are more straightforward than those of 'attitude' which may be more important in human resource terms. Information on this may derive largely from stereotyped hearsay, but can be more accurately assessed through appropriate recruitment techniques.

Internal supply

Data on the internal supply of labour are much more readily available, in terms of age, job history, pay and conditions, qualifications, sex, race, etc. (although company information systems do not always include prior work experience, or sufficient information on the range of an individual's skills, training and experience). Information on attendance, discipline and performance may also be available, where relevant, and as the result of other forms of assessment. From these data, predictions can be made of likely staffing levels and of retirement patterns by projecting forward current age profiles by three years, five years, or ten years, to see if they match a normal distribution curve, external population trends, or any other preferred pattern. This can also be done by division, occupational group, or grade level, and although it represents the simplest planning technique and can help to indicate likely forthcoming shortages, cost savings, or succession problems, such projections are neglected surprisingly often. Some professional bodies, e.g. in computing and paramedical functions, make projections of the relevant occupational labour markets.

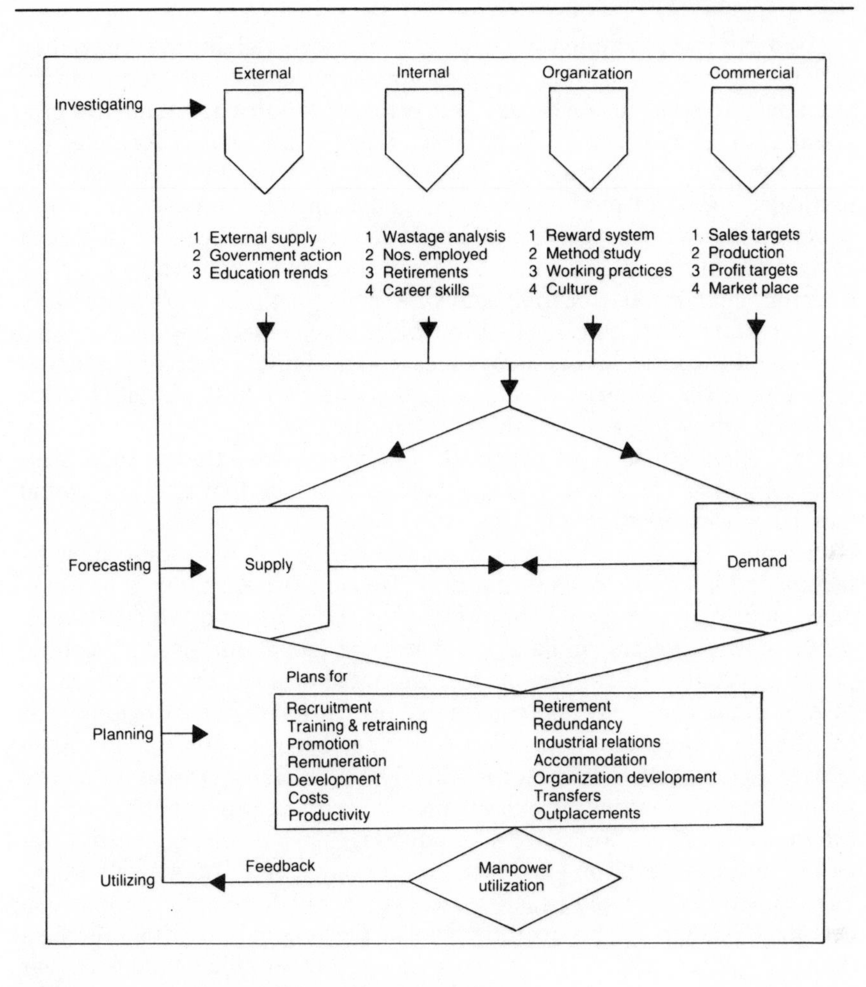

Figure 7.1 A framework for manpower planning
Source: Bramham (1989: 155)

The 'unknown' aspect of internal supply is of course the Achilles' heel of all 'human asset accounting' – the fact that people may choose to leave. The current rates of labour turnover or wastage can easily be estimated by dividing the numbers leaving in a period by the average number employed in the same period and multiplying by 100:

$$\text{e.g.}\ \frac{45}{500} \times 100 = 9\%.$$

This can be done by age group, grade, sex, occupation, department or division, but interpretation of the data and extrapolation of policy implications is much more problematic. If data are available over time, then patterns of 'normal' labour turnover for a particular population can be estimated. Average turnover may be 5 per cent, but that for computer programmers may typically be 20 per cent. Using mathematical formulae (or log-graph paper), predictions can be made of the likely staying-on rate of a particular cohort of graduate entrants, indicating that in order to ensure, for example, that ten people will move into senior management in fifteen years' time, it may be necessary to recruit thirteen to eighteen now.

Certain patterns are generally known – that young people are more likely to leave than older, and people in low-level rather than responsible jobs. New recruits tend to be very likely to leave in the initial period of 'induction crisis', which is followed by a testing-out phase of 'differential transit', following which a few more will go; after this there may be more stability and a 'settled connection' period. In operational and clerical jobs these phases may each last a few weeks; in professional ones they may last several months or even up to three years.

Increased levels of absenteeism may be a sign of impending dissatisfaction and intention to leave, but may also demonstrate patterns of workplace culture or managerial control systems (Edwards and Whitson 1989). While most managers would agree that some labour turnover is healthy, providing an opportunity for change, unwanted turnover can be influenced by improvements in pay and conditions, responsibility and recognition, or by better training, communication and supervision, as appropriate. Even those who are likely to leave for family, health, or transport reasons can be influenced by organization initiatives, unlike those who are 'pulled' by external attractions. Costing of alternatives is then possible, but needs to be done with care. Bennison (1991) cites one example of a firm with a particularly generous salary and benefits package, in which each policy had been cost-justified, but further investigation of the original proposals revealed that each policy ignored the existence of every other policy, and each was based on assumptions of reducing labour turnover by 10 per cent per annum (see also Fair 1992).

Since the 'tightness' of the external labour market is one of the single most influential factors in turnover, estimating supply in terms of workload planning, which normally requires incorporation of likely absence, holiday, and training time to give an accurate picture of person-hours available per week/month, also requires an awareness of the current phase in the economic cycle. At times of recession, when management might like voluntary turnover to increase, the opposite happens; whereas approaching the peak of a cyclical upturn, the reverse is true. The advent of a new firm as a competitor for particular skills is also likely to increase turnover. Labour market intelligence on this needs to be incorporated into external supply estimates.

Internal demand

Estimation of internal labour demand, although apparently easier, is frequently the more difficult aspect, in view of the many uncertainties of recession and the rapid changes which are taking place at the end of the twentieth century. Turbulence in the product or market environment may be the norm now, even for public sector organizations, which are increasingly subject to privatization and market-testing, as well as in many smaller businesses in what were once apparently stable markets. Predictions of both numbers and skills required are also more difficult to make, with changing technologies and new information systems. Thus even though manufacturing output is expected to expand as the economy improves, no great expansion in employment is predicted. The same is likely to be true of many middle management posts. Even in labour-intensive service industries, the emphasis is likely to remain on increasing productivity of existing staff, rather than increasing numbers employed, once market demand improves.

Techniques for obtaining estimates of demand may include extrapolations from budget, capital investment and business forecast plans, according to plus or minus a percentage of staff, or according to traditional ratios of customers: sales; field: in-house, direct: indirect, or supervisors: operators. This approach has tended to assume previous 'norms', however, and is seen as a recipe for high labour costs in many firms. Estimating demand has thus become subject to more rigid scrutiny, including requirements to detail the assumptions on which estimates are made, but strategic use of current ratios can be a useful planning tool as well as a convenient 'political' weapon. Restricting the making of estimates in terms of either cost limits and/or headcount limits is obviously likely to affect estimates of labour demand, but this will depend on how 'costs' are defined (e.g. wages only, or total cost; hourly or annual rates) or how 'headcount' is counted (e.g. actual numbers, or full-time equivalents). The politics of relationships between personnel and finance functions, or with line managers, may be a critical influence here. Other 'budget ploys' and the continuation (or otherwise) of incentives for senior managers to increase status by empire-building in terms of size of department will also affect the level of demand estimates. Scope and preferences vary between departments, thus simple aggregation of the data from sectional estimates may not provide accurate projections of organizational demand, whether for manual or computerized numerical 'matching'. Perhaps 'competence' estimates, or predictions only in relation to 'core' or 'key' skills, are all that is really needed.

Use of other qualitative techniques, ranging from informal conversations to more structured techniques, such as a Delphi survey whereby the views of influential people are surveyed and the results aggregated and then fed back (one or more times) with more probing questions, can give a more informed interpretation of likely trends.

Matching supply and demand

Matching estimates of supply and demand, whether in segmented or aggregated form, like the collection of data, can be done manually or by computer. Companies with sophisticated human resource information systems, especially those in which payroll and personnel records are combined, should find this easier.

The use of spreadsheets can enable calculations of projected costs and numbers to be made, and alternatives explored, using different estimates. Nevertheless, more sophisticated models may be needed to handle large sets of data. While a wide range of commercial packages are available for various specific record-keeping and administrative purposes (such as payroll, absenteeism, training, recruitment, and assessment), fewer incorporate planning processes. A widely used 'promotion' model, CAMPLAN, developed (from earlier models) by the Institute of Manpower Studies at Sussex, can enable quite large-scale modelling to be done, requiring fairly time-consuming company data input and the specification of assumptions about whether it is a 'pull' model' (promotions being driven by vacancies) or a 'push' model (upgradings being driven by time served, or some other criterion). Other models such as SUSSEX focus on the stimulation of manpower flows into and out of the organization by recruitment, wastage, transfer or promotion, either individually or collectively (Morgan *et al.* 1991). McBeath (1992) shows examples of planning for different groups using HR/View spreadsheet with requirements forecast data from the business plan and using data held in the Executive TRACK management development planning system to track flows of people through the organization as well as to plan their 'supply'. Other expert systems and decision-making models may also be utilized to assist in planning, or in estimating the feasibility of alternative matching solutions.

The production of 'career-curves' (see Figure 7.2), showing the normal length of time spent at a particular grade-level, according to age and ability or merit-level, may also be a useful way of obtaining data on existing patterns and what might be needed to be done to shift them so that more/fewer people are likely to reach a particular level at a particular time; or to discover what would be the effects and implications of the removal of a grade level.

The techniques available for adjusting mismatches are myriad and are traditionally grouped under those in which there is labour shortage or labour surplus, as shown in Figure 7.3.

Action-driven approaches

Action-driven human resource planning is likely to start with the current corporate strategic drive, or an existing business problem of high labour

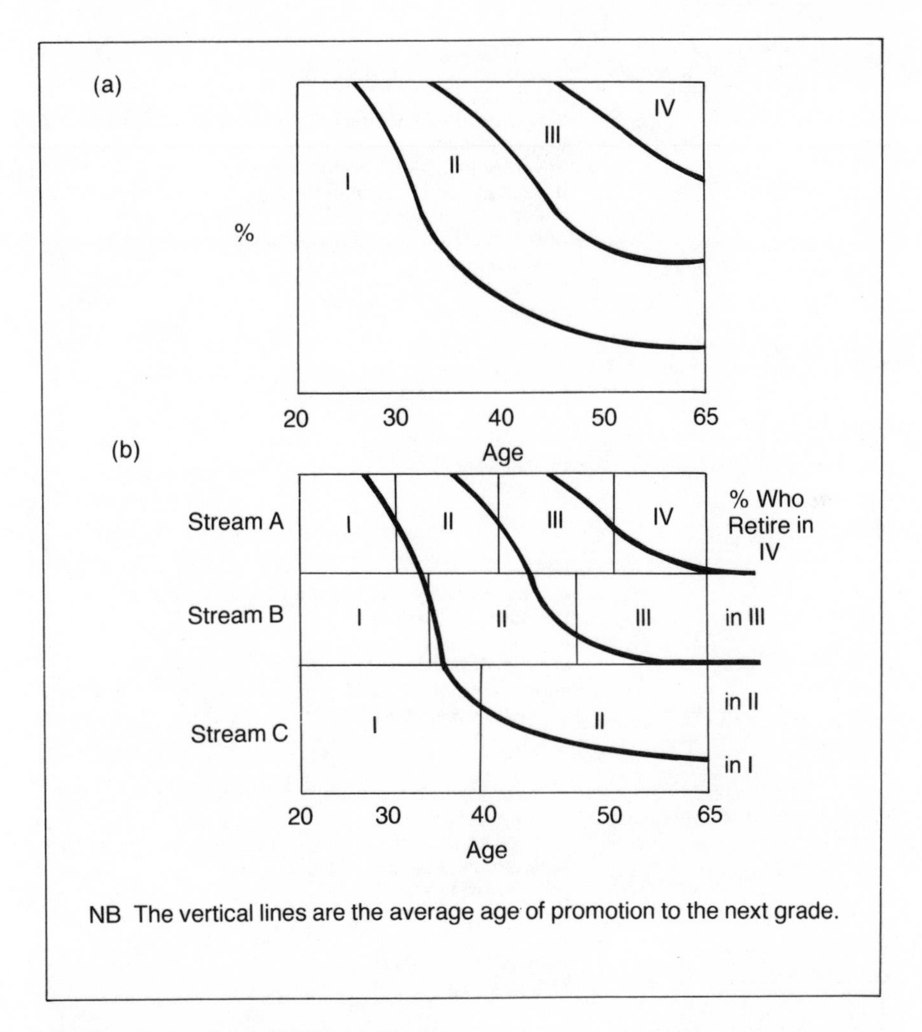

Figure 7.2 Career progression diagram
Source: Bramham (1989: 159)

costs, poor customer service, low quality products, or lack of innovation, and then to seek to address it by proposing possible solutions and sub-strategies. To be effective, however, such approaches need to be based on accurate diagnosis of the problem and analysis of alternative proposals. For this reason, quantitative techniques, in the sense of accurate data on numbers and costs, are still likely to be needed. For example, high labour costs (or any other of the above problems) might stem from:

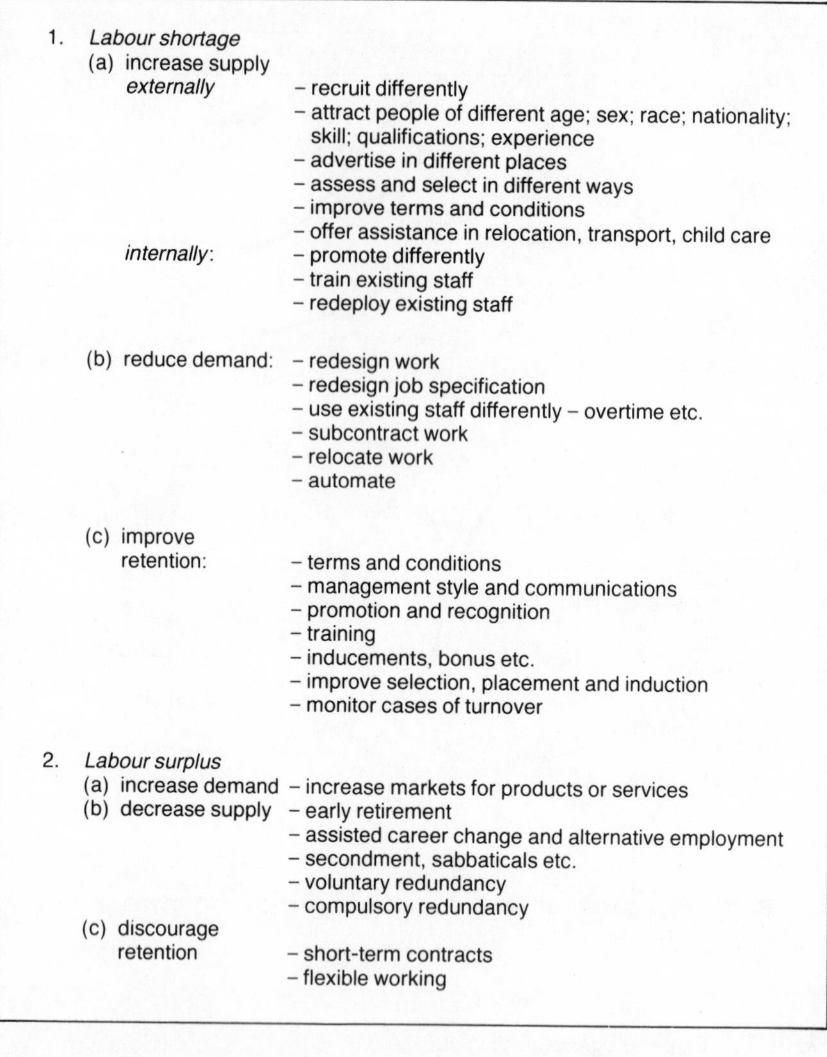

Figure 7.3 Options for matching supply and demand

- expensive/poor recruitment techniques leading to high turnover or poor quality employees
- high absenteeism
- ineffective utilization of skills or of working time
- inappropriate rewards.

Changes in any of these might be more effective in reducing costs – albeit more slowly – than a redundancy programme. The use of 'annualized hours' techniques to replace overtime and achieve more effective utilization of people and plant has proved highly efficient in much of manufacturing industry, but requires close coordination of human resource and production and market planning in order to predict and match peaks and troughs in demand.

'Action-driven' planning may be able to focus more accurately on particular sectional or skill-needs of parts of the organization rather than on producing large numerical calculations for the whole. For example, if a building society becomes a bank and introduces new financial services (or vice versa), planning for the people needed to do that may be a higher priority than planning for traditional services, although the implications and possible synergies should not be overlooked. On the other hand, an over-segmented approach might not only fail to take account of an organization's overall mission and values approach, but might also ignore tensions between an employer's needs for flexibility, control of costs and development of employee loyalty, and the need to develop firm-specific skills and for an integrated, committed workforce.

One example of a broad-brush approach to manpower planning/career planning for a high-tech organization in the UK in the 1980s, with a highly developed professional internal labour market (but aiming at an 80:20 insider:outsider ratio of managers) was that of ICL (see Figure 7.4). The model was 'essentially a corporate planning tool to help management assess our "stock" of high potential people against our annual requirements' (Beattie and Tampoe 1990). Detailed audits of functions or sections could be done separately and matched with the ratios of upwardly and laterally mobile staff, and individual needs. Assessments of potential were made on recruitment, two to three years in, and at the eight to ten year stage. The diagram represents a four-stream approach, taking account of potential, direction and speed of promotion.

THE EXTENT OF PLANNING: THE GAP BETWEEN THEORY AND PRACTICE

The need for more effective planning for people had been identified long before the advent of human resource management (Ministry of Labour and National Service 1958; Manpower Services Commission/National Economic Development Office 1978) yet, apart from isolated examples, there has been little research evidence of its increased use or of its success. It is not clear, despite all the textbooks and the policy encouragement, why this has been so, or whether the situation is now changing.

Empirical, survey-based research illustrates the issue. If one takes policy-making as part of the planning process, then certain data from Marginson *et al.* (1988) illustrate the size of the gap. They found 84 per cent of UK managers claiming they had an overall employee policy; 50 per cent had a

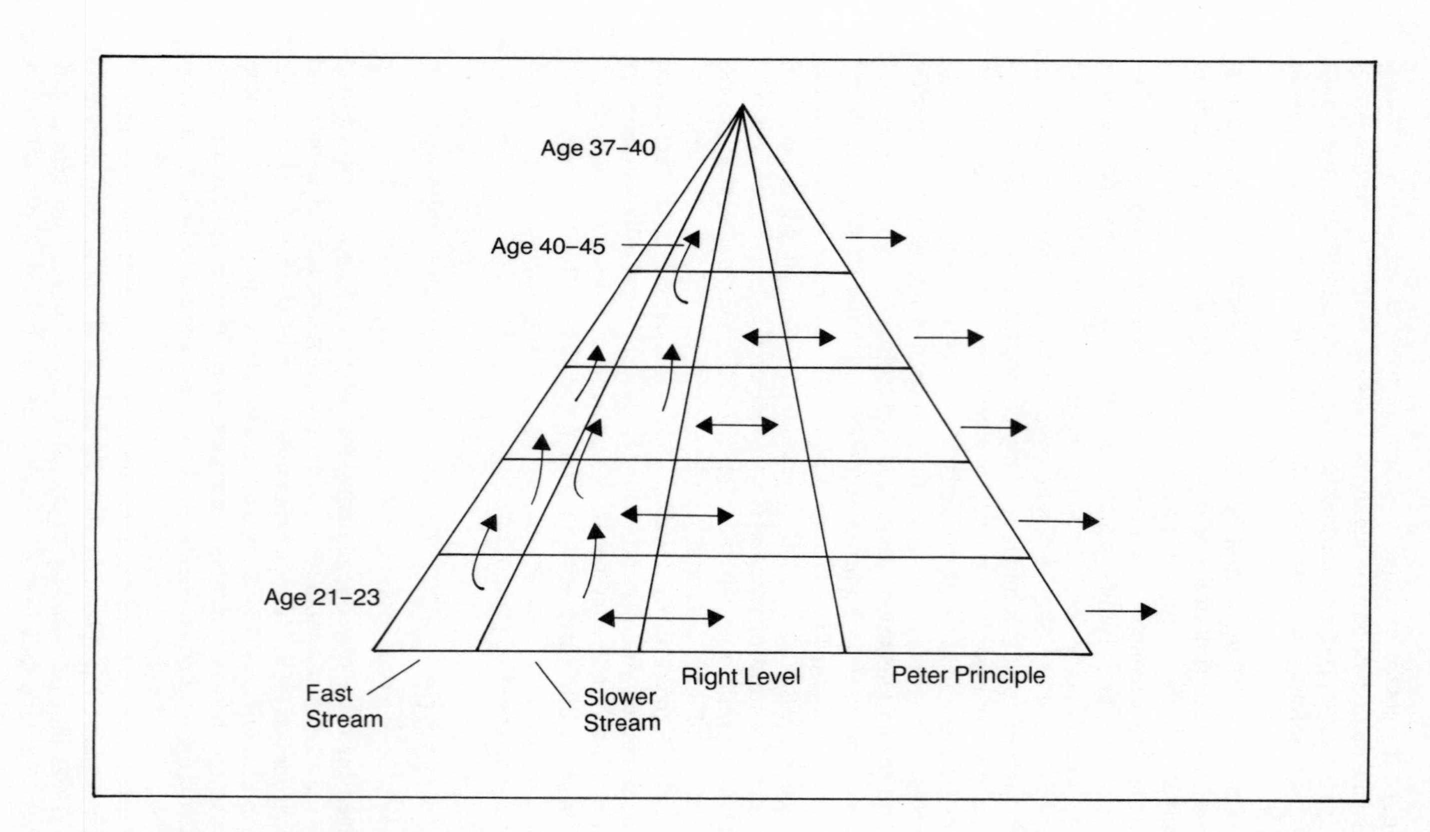

Figure 7.4 Providing different career patterns
Source: Beattie and Tampoe (1990: 21)

written policy; and 23 per cent said they gave a copy to employees. However, most could not describe the strategy in any detail. The Cranfield/ Price Waterhouse comparative European study found that the proportion of all managers claiming to have a written human resource strategy ranged from 74 per cent in Norway to 20 per cent in Denmark (and 45 per cent in the UK). Even fewer were likely to translate them into operational programmes, but were more likely to do so in relation to management development (Brewster and Hegewisch 1993).

US researchers found similar results. For example, a 1981 survey found 54 per cent of a sample of Fortune 500 companies did some human resource planning, but only 15 per cent did so in the comprehensive way suggested in their literature. Those that did so were more likely to apply it to management succession and development than to any other personnel activity (Nkomo 1986). Lengnick-Hall and Lengnick-Hall (1988) also found widespread research evidence of the gap between corporate and personnel policies and their application in practice.

The 1975 Institute of Personnel Management survey (Institute of Personnel Management 1975, cited by Timperley and Sisson 1989) found widespread claims but very 'partial' activity – the likelihood of demand/supply forecasts being made decreasing by grade – and relatively limited evidence of the uses to which it was put. Mackay and Torrington (1986) also found little use, even with the advent of computerization. Henley research into the introduction of new technology (Rothwell 1983, 1985) also found the personnel role generally restricted to operational assistance to the department affected in terms of redundancy or training, with little evidence of proactive or corporate-wide planning; more recent surveys of personnel directors attending workshops found the majority claiming a strategic planning approach, but discussions revealed little evidence of planning in practice. Storey (1992) observed that in the (mainly manufacturing) companies in his sample, most would have 'ticked' survey questions about human resource planning, but a substantial number did not do it. Bennison and Casson (1984) quote Purkiss (then Director of the Institute of Manpower Studies) on the traditional view of manpower planning as 'a tedious mathematical technique, largely ignored'.

Goold and Campbell's sixteen companies showed a wide range of planning practices, although only six engaged in the formal process of strategic planning at the centre (Goold and Campbell 1989). Peters and Waterman (1982), and writers on Japanese companies, continuously point to the scope for achieving competitive advantage through people, and the Schein model (Schein 1977) is cited as a popular approach to career planning and matching organization and individual needs. NEDO and MSC promoted this idea of matching through a series of case study booklets showing how ten different low-tech and high-tech, new and old established firms took a strategic approach to developing people (Manpower Services Commission/ National Economic Development Office 1987), but still only a relatively small number seemed to have an integrated strategic planning approach, and those attending the workshops were largely self-selected.

On the other hand the 1990 Workplace Industrial Relations Survey (WIRS) found 41 per cent of all managers claiming to be involved in staffing/manpower planning, one of the highest of all employee relations activities. Fifty-five per cent regarded it as a matter for consultation at higher levels, but the amount of consultation or information on it given to trade union or employee representatives was low, and was the only such activity which had fallen compared with previous years (Millward *et al.* 1992: Tables 2.7 and 5.6). To some extent these examples are using the terms 'strategy' and 'planning' almost interchangeably, but this is also illustrated in the Employers Labour Use Surveys, following up in greater depth the WIRS survey of establishments. Thus the ELUS1 survey concluded that one-third of employers had a (flexible) labour use strategy, while two-thirds operated on an opportunistic basis (McGregor and Sproull 1991). The follow-on case-study research (ELUS2) found similar evidence, but concluded that there was little practical difference between the two groups, with both showing a predominantly *ad hoc* rather than a strategic or planned response to labour or product market pressures, resulting in a variety of solutions (Hunter and MacInnes 1991).

Explanations of the gap

Explanations for the apparent lack of human resource planning in the development and implementation of human resource strategy fall under four main headings. First, the extent of change impinging on organizations externally, or generated by them in terms of changing patterns of world trade and increasing competition, new forms of foreign or domestic government policies or regulations, or through new technologies, may mean that planning becomes so problematic as to be useless, despite the growing need for it. The need for planning may be in inverse proportion to its feasibility. This could be one explanation of why, even if planning takes place, it is rarely implemented.

Second and related to it, are the 'realities' of organizations and the shifting kaleidoscope of policy priorities and strategies which depend on the policies of the powerful interest groups involved (Watson 1986). Thus planning will need to take account of these, but by virtue of doing so may become overtaken in turn, or become merely a presentational 'gloss' on a rather different reality. Human resource planning may be particularly prone to these pressures, especially at a time of economic recession, by virtue of the weak power-base of the human resource function, which either precludes the allocation of adequate resources to planning, or, more often, detracts from the ability to ensure implementation (Legge 1978; Collinson *et al.* 1990).

A third and similar group of factors relates to the nature of management and the skills and abilities of managers, who, in the UK particularly, have a preference for pragmatic adaptation over conceptualization, and a distrust of theory or planning. Lack of data, lack of line management understanding, and lack of a corporate plan, were the main reasons given by personnel managers in the IPM survey. This may vary, however, according to the values, culture or strategy of different divisions, companies, or industries, and could be susceptible to research investigation, possibly along the lines of some current research into managerial labour markets (Fox and McLeay 1992). There are also issues of the multiple (and often conflicting) nature of organization goals, with pressures for consistency and for flexibility; for prediction and for planning, but also for speed and for response. Presumptions of 'fit' between HR and business strategy may be misplaced, although widely researched and advocated (e.g. Schuler and Walker 1990; Butler *et al.* 1991; Wright and McMahan 1992).

Fourth, explanations must therefore also be sought in the way research is done on HRP. Have some approaches to 'successful' human resource management been over-prescriptive and idealistic? On the other hand, have some academic approaches to testing been over-theoretical, taking insufficient account of the realities of organizations and the ways in which managers operate in response to specific problems, so that the form and extent of planning used in practice have not been adequately explored?

For example, while the findings from fifteen large case studies (Storey 1992) tended to show that their human resource planning was essentially *ad hoc*, 'it would be wrong to conclude from this that no strategic thinking about resourcing was occurring'; the introduction of annualized hours at Golden Wonder Crisps provided an illustrative example of this. Similarly, Hendry *et al.* (1991), in their study of human resource development in small and medium-sized firms, found much activity that was fragmented and *ad hoc*, but concluded that planning did take place and found that seven types of skill supply strategy could be identified that were appropriate to the market contexts of these firms. Analysis of team-building in an insurance company found that top–down vertical approaches largely failed, while bottom–up horizontal ones were effective and rationalized *post hoc* by senior management as successful strategy implementation. Research interpretations could diverge: but Kerfoot and Knights (1992: 655) argue that 'the practices in a company may be "ahead" of the policies which are supposed to guide them'. Thus 'the discrepancy between policy and practice may also work in the opposite direction to that implied by the phrase', suggesting that 'HRM can be seen as a product of the knowledge and rationalizations surrounding management policies and practices, and of the "expertise" of those consultants and academics who write about them' (p. 652).

Perhaps the difficulties of research interpretation have arisen because the research categories (or the responses) have been too aggregated to be able to explore differences? For example, studies of the existence of strategic human resource management have often conflated many of its aspects, including the distinctions between the formulation and implementation of strategy; between different vertical levels of management or workforce; between individual, group or organization; and between content and process. Is case-study research, rather than survey research, likely to throw more light on the interplay of organizational issues and to be more appropriate to the micro-level 'decentralized' model of employee relations represented by human resource management? However, predictive theories based upon patterns of findings are still needed and at present much of the applied case literature depends on practitioner accounts of 'successful' achievements. Understanding of planning is particularly vulnerable to the polarization between theoretical interpretations of either what 'is' in terms of a model of 'the new human resources' or of the 'control/de-skilling' debate, on the one hand, and normative advice to practitioners on the other.

Many of the above explanations reflect the speed and scope of change in the modern world and the difficulties this presents for those trying to manage businesses or to research and interpret them. The need for analysis of changing scenarios is therefore an integral part of the human resource planning process.

CHANGING SCENARIOS

The first step in human resource planning is usually the 'environmental' scan: if this review has not already been carried out in some depth as part of the formulation of corporate strategy, consideration of critical trends may be a major contribution which the HRM function can make to the organization (Institute of Personnel Management 1992). Use of simplified techniques of scenario planning may be a useful approach to dealing with future uncertainties and their possible implications (Skills and Enterprise Network 1991). If this is already done by other specialist functions such as corporate planners or marketing, then HRM people can concentrate on those issues which are likely to be most relevant to the labour markets within which they operate. Either way, this 'social research' contribution of the HRM function to the organization may become more important in future, if the more 'proactive' and externally oriented model of the function is adopted.

International

The growing internationalization of business in the face of changing patterns of world trade and the emergence of new competitors and new markets in Asia, America, the Middle East or Africa, in addition to changes in the older industrialized countries as well as in Eastern and Western Europe (and the EC), all have some impact on the labour markets of even the smallest firm trading in a national market. This is because, at the very least, its supply of skills is likely to be affected by such factors, and also its demand for skills, if sales of its products fall as a result of inroads by new competitors, particularly in a more open EC market.

Most larger and medium-sized companies are, however, likely to be trading internationally in some way and will need to understand the labour markets in those countries, if they are to recruit staff abroad or if they expect to send their own staff to work there. The whole issue of international management development has major implications for strategic planning – is the business to be global, European, or local; ethnocentric, etc. – and for human resource forecasting and implementation. Evidence so far suggests there are many inadequacies in both the planning and implementation of management mobility, and that there is a widespread reliance on *ad hoc* use of expatriate managers (see Chapter 14 of this volume). Guidance on access to international data on HRM issues is only gradually becoming more readily available (Ferner and Hyman 1992; Bamber and Whitehouse 1992).

Political

International and political issues are clearly closely linked – the move towards greater European unity, the unification of East and West Germany, the opening up of Eastern Europe, the fighting in former Yugoslavia, and the Gulf War, are just a few recent examples of events with implications for business planning. The so-called 'peace-dividend' means the shift of large numbers of ex-military personnel on to civilian labour markets, as well as a decline in all the manufacturing and service activities associated with defence industries in very many countries (Lovering 1991).

The political complexion of a government tends to affect the type of economic policy in place, the attitude to full employment, trade union and employee rights, as well as the level of support for private or public sector enterprises. External political factors, and especially the broader social and regulatory legacies of industrial relations, provide a socio-political context in which managerial strategies have had to develop and by which they have been conditioned (Lucio and Simpson 1992). At a time of economic recession in particular, the costs of worker protection policies may be seen as unacceptably high, as France and Germany have shown recently. Government policies affect the extent to which the gap between a nation's rich and poor increases or diminishes. Much of the change in employment patterns in Britain – particularly the increased subcontracting of public sector services – has resulted directly from the 'Thatcherite' policies of increasing the influence of market forces (cf. Rubery 1993). Examples, however, of large organizations which were making major changes to their human resources policies in response to future demographic trends include British Steel and the Alliance and Leicester Building Society (Industrial Relations Service 1990; Fairchild 1989).

Demographic

An awareness of population trends is critical in understanding labour markets, and national population statistics are readily available, even if disaggregation to regional and local level may be slightly more difficult to obtain in some areas. Planning to take account of demographic trends is not often done early enough: for example, several regions of the British National Health Service did little advance planning to shift from their traditional reliance on recruiting as nurses eighteen-year-old girls (with a certain level of educational qualifications), even though the decline in size from the mid-1980s by almost 30 per cent of this age group had been known for eighteen years. A lack of advance planning tends to increase labour costs, as firms have to increase wages and salaries in order to retain staff or poach them from other firms. This tended to be the most widely adopted approach of UK firms experiencing skill shortages in the late 1980s (National Economic Development Office/Training Agency 1989; Parsons 1990).

Analysis of population trends shows that the number of 45–59 year-olds in the British population will marginally exceed those aged 16–24 from 1995, although in 1985 the younger age group had exceeded the older by over three million. But just as more people are living longer, healthier lives, so early retirement is becoming more common (Rajan and Bevan 1990).

Most of Western Europe has an ageing workforce, but in the USA, with a high immigrant population, there is a considerable number of young people: the problem there is that they tend to have low educational qualifications, whereas the demand in the future is likely to be for 'knowledge workers' in the information society. Young British people, too, seem to be worse educated than their counterparts in many other European countries (National Institute for Economic Research 1993), although since 1990, despite a fall in the eighteen-year-old population, more have been entering higher education.

Awareness of population patterns elsewhere may be important – for example, in the later 1980s, British firms with a shortage of computer skills recruited from Ireland, which has a young population, many of whom had been trained in those skills to meet the needs of inward-investing computer companies, which withdrew from Ireland when markets shrank or subsidies ended. Very many third-world companies have exploding young populations and low labour costs and, depending on skill levels, are being seen as sources of cheap labour, particularly for subcontracted software, data processing or assembly operations, by multi-national companies.

Labour market information by age, sex and ethnic origin is readily available from official statistics on a regional basis, but only disaggregated by broad occupational bands in most instances; but earnings data are available under a wider range of categories. Traditional patterns of occupational segregation as between men's and women's jobs and between earnings of men and women (now 75 per cent of men's, on average) have only shifted slightly since the Sex Discrimination Act came into force in 1975. Women have increased their proportion of the labour force to 42 per cent and constituted 48 per cent of those in employment in 1992, having taken most of the new roles created in the economy in the previous decade. Nevertheless, the significance of this may be queried since many of these jobs were low-level, part-time ones (Hakim 1993; Jonung and Persson 1993). But if workforce diversity comes to be valued, then there are implications for more than recruitment aspects of planning, if the careers of white males and traditional family patterns (such as the breadwinner father and the non-working mother of babies and school-age children) are not taken as the planning norm (Sinclair and Ewing 1992/3). Patterns of working time, of training, of promotion and of benefits may all need to be changed.

Skills

If HRM is driven by demand for labour, rather than by its supply, awareness of shifting patterns of skills is critical. In the UK, all the forecasts show a decline in firms' demand for the low-skilled (and skilled manual) occupations, and an increase in managerial, professional (especially) and technical jobs, together with those in personal, protective and leisure services (Institute for Employment Research 1993; Rajan 1992; Skills and Enterprise Network 1993b).

There is a regional element to the pattern of UK demand for labour, but this is constantly shifting. Thus sales and secretarial skills are still in fairly high demand nationally, and pockets of particular skill shortages (including some of the 'declining' engineering craft skills) can be found locally. In the South East, and particularly in the Thames Valley area, during the 1990s recession the pattern of labour demand fell off abruptly to the same level as that of Northern and Midland areas, whereas in previous recessions the South East had remained much more buoyant.

While information on local skills availability in the UK is still not easy to obtain, other than by contact with individual colleges, training bodies, or employers, recent development of regional Training and Enterprise Councils (TECs), new Labour Force Quarterly publications, and regional information produced by the Employment Service is helpful. Data on employment and unemployment, unfilled vacancies, skill shortages and numbers trained are available regionally. On-line information on local labour markets under travel to work areas is available to subscribers from NOMIS (at University of Durham).

Public policy emphasis on training, the coordination of a plethora of national vocational qualifications, and the setting of national education training targets (e.g. that 50 per cent of young people and of the workforce as a whole should be qualified up to NVQ level III by the year 2000), all mean that some aspects of estimating external skill supply will be improved. Data on graduate qualifications are readily available, but interpreting likely trends in supply and demand is complex (Pike *et al.* 1992). For example, if student costs continue to rise and employer demand falls, as in the early 1990s, is the supply also likely to decrease to be replaced by another mismatch when the economy picks up? Accounting and technical qualifications are likely to be most in demand, but courses in these areas are not necessarily the most attractive to students. Data on the activities of graduates after qualifying are usually available on an annual basis, so trends can be observed, but the data are not necessarily sufficiently up-to-date for employers' needs, other than in identifying trends (Skills and Enterprise Network 1993a).

Demand-side factors stem mainly from the business strategy, but need to take account of other skills that may be needed – for example in physical environmental awareness and the implications for products or processes and energy use; or in marketing, in concepts of relational marketing, customer education and general supply chain management. If mergers or acquisitions are expected, is new expertise needed to handle that? Or if organization structures are changing to create flatter organizations or new internationalized business market divisions, are there skills available in managing networks, managing projects or managing cross-culturally? Firms that use 'competence-mapping' techniques may be able to provide data relevant to human resource planning, but where these activities are done by different people and/or at different locations, such linkage cannot be made. The creative or entrepreneurial skills often included in 'competence' listing are not necessarily addressed in human resource planning (Mitrani *et al.* 1992). In some cases, perhaps the scale of operations is too great for this synergistic planning to be readily feasible without overbureaucratizing the whole process and absorbing more staff time and energy than it is worth. Computerized modelling processes, however, may enable a better grasp to be taken.

The external labour market environment is also to some extent shaped by firms' business strategies. Thus scans of labour market statistics do not always sufficiently reveal the changing patterns of employment taking place, as has been shown by research into local labour markets in South Wales (Rees 1993). They might not show that many of the employees involved in career jobs, and moving through relatively secure internal labour markets have largely firm-specific skills, while those in the external labour market are either already possessors of skills that are in short supply and able to demand very high rates of pay, or else are at the opposite end of the spectrum, with low pay and low skills, but are readily available, even on a short-term basis.

Technological

While the implications of new technology have been the object of intensive academic and policy debates for the last twenty years, the speed of recent change has been such that the applications of computerized technology in products and processes are now driving and facilitating much of the market, organizational, and communication changes that are taking place. The impact of new materials in manufacturing could be equally as great. The need for human resource planning would therefore seem to be greatest in high-tech firms, but a study of twenty electronics firms in the labour market of Central Southern England in 1988–90 and their approach to the recruitment and retention of technicians, found some elements of a long-term approach (with 'systematic' planning in seven of the twenty firms) but concluded that a variety of *ad hoc* responses predominated, arising from funding mechanisms and the nature of the labour market (Causer and Jones 1992/3).

The scope for substitution of labour by capital, and the need for more creative and more 'relational' uses of human skills, particularly those involving interpersonal relationships and the ability to relate ideas laterally, are growing considerably in most countries, industries and companies. The implications for numbers, skills, location (teleworking) and design of jobs and employment contracts are therefore more significant than is currently realized by many HR managers, who are often too busy coping with the cost-cutting redundancies arising from what appear to be largely cyclical economic effects, but which may also be caused by real structural changes now taking place in employment. Changing patterns of employment in financial services in the 1990s are largely following trends predicted by researchers in the 1980s (Cressey and Scott 1992). The wider use of electronic data interchange (EDI) techniques could have a widespread impact on employment in many industries within a few years and the need for 'empowerment' of people may arise as much from the so-called 'technological imperative' as from other drivers of change.

Employee attitudes

Consumer attitudes tend to be surveyed more regularly than those of employees (unless the organization is one of those few which undertakes regular employee surveys), but shifts in employee preferences are perceptible, often on a generational basis. In the USA, the attitudes of recruits from the 'baby-bust' generation are observed to be very different from those of the 'baby-boomers' (who were more grateful for having a job), in that they are more independent in outlook, expect more autonomy, and divide their priorities between work and family. In the UK, where regular information is available from the British Social Attitudes Survey, the demographic time-lag has been slower, but nevertheless employees are seen, like consumers, as having become more individualistic, less likely to accept authority, expecting to have a say and be given a choice, and also to be putting more emphasis on quality of leisure and family life. They choose to live in the country towns rather than inner city areas, where possible. The priority perks for those in work are those related to health and to education and training. Employees are also less likely to expect to remain with one employer.

While these attitudes are found particularly among 'knowledge-workers', and may have been modified by experience of recession and widespread white-collar unemployment, they can also be observed to some extent at other levels. Social polarization – between the haves and have-nots – both between those in and out of employment, and within firms between different grades or 'core' and 'periphery' workers, does, however, appear to have been increasing, with potentially disruptive future implications, particularly if social protection policies decrease.

If a major difference between HRM planning and manpower planning lies in its emphasis on motivating people (Bramham 1989), understanding the starting point and changing the direction of employee attitudes could become more important. In the UK, many of the large utilities which were public corporations and have now been privatized, have experienced some of the tensions of both 'hard' and 'soft' HRM policies in the reduction in numbers employed and in attempts to 'change the culture' towards a more commercial, achievement-oriented ethos (Ferner and Colling 1991). The incorporation of both 'individual' and 'organization' needs is therefore the major challenge for human resource planners and should be reflected in the application of the planning processes to the ways in which people are employed.

POTENTIAL USES OF HUMAN RESOURCE PLANNING

The uses to which planning techniques are to be put should be the starting point for the activity – the lack of a clear rationale at the outset may be one reason why little use appears to be made of it in some organizations. More likely, however, is that the multiple – and sometimes even contradictory – purposes which it is expected to serve, confound the methods and approaches adopted. Moreover, the more account that is taken of individual needs, and the more use that is made of qualitative judgement as against numerical calculations, the more scope there is for 'political' or 'interest group' influence, through subjective interpretation. What may be of interest to researchers is when, and in whose interests, different approaches are taken. Practitioners, meanwhile, may be more interested in how their own influence may be strengthened: whether in justifying adherence to or departure from numerical indicators, or in reinforcing their (in)applicability.

Recruitment and redundancy

Identification of likely mismatch between 'supply' and 'demand', and adjustment through recruitment or redundancy, has formerly been seen as the rationale for traditional manpower planning. However, the characteristics of human resources are that they have individual interests, needs and skills, which means they cannot be treated simply as interchangeable numbers. Broad band groupings, such as manual, clerical and administration, technical/professional, functional management, and general management, often need to be subdivided by department and division or location, for planning purposes. These groupings may become even smaller in future, as individuals with specialized combinations of skills or competencies need to be identified.

Nevertheless, minimal planning techniques, particularly if assumptions have been systematically specified, should give indicators of the likely need for 'more' or 'less', where and when. 'Competency' profiling of individuals or jobs or analysis in terms of knowledge, skills, attitudes and experience required, can allow quantitative techniques to be complemented by more systematic use of subjective judgement about recruitment requirements, or in deciding on redundancy (where legal interpretations have set some requirements for objectivity and consistency in use of redundancy selection processes which depart from 'last in, first out' principles).

One organization that claims to have moved from the concepts of jobs to roles and to individual competency profiling is the National and Provincial Building Society. The new approach is used in recruitment, succession planning and development: 'Manpower planners are no longer counting heads. What they are after is a good fit' (Falconer 1991).

HRM planning could thus be of an indicative nature and give a broad, forward-looking insight into not just the numbers but also the type – the skills and attributes – of the people that will be needed to deliver the innovative products or high-quality service on which the business strategy focuses. Yet, even when detailed competency profiling has been undertaken, recruitment and selection mechanisms do not necessarily take it into account: the terms of the job advertisement, or the assumptions of the interviewer, may still be traditional. Specifications of 'leadership' and 'creativity' in plans and advertisements may not be particularly welcome to senior managers who prefer to appoint those who will not 'rock the boat'. Moreover, cost-cutting pressures are likely to mean heavy loading of requirements onto more lowly paid jobs. This may appear feasible at times of recession, but could lead to high turnover later.

All too often, organizations are laying off people in one section while recruiting them in another: this may be justifiable in terms of different skill requirements, but opportunities for redeployment could be revealed by more comprehensive planning and a greater will to retrain and develop. Unionized firms might be more susceptible to pressures to protect employees' interests, but often tend to be particularly 'sectional' and traditional in approach. The larger computer firms, and some of the Japanese ones, may be more willing to transfer and retrain more frequently.

The replacement of job-security assumptions by redundancy planning as part of long-term structural change can often be phased over a five-year period, and use made of natural wastage and voluntary methods. Continued technological change and reduction of numbers employed can be so gradual that shop stewards themselves are barely aware of it. Nevertheless, large-scale lay-offs like those of British Telecom and other large firms in manufacturing, computing and financial services in the early 1990s have resulted from a combination of structural change and cyclical falls in demand. The majority of redundancies have been made in response to an urgent need to cut costs, with apparently very little advance planning having taken place, other than in financial terms. But in many cases, managers who have been made redundant are then re-employed as consultants, or on other temporary contracts. Some flexible employment contracts may cost more than the use of permanent employees. Whether the chief executive demands redundancies of 10 per cent, 15 per cent or 20 per cent may depend as much on fashion or 'feel', as on objective measurement or costing of alternatives, even when sheer survival is not necessarily at stake.

Surveys of the personalities of redundant executives have tended to show that a greater proportion of creative people, independent thinkers, or more critical and abrasive personalities lose their jobs, rather than the loyal team-workers. The ending of the psychological contract of most white-collar workers of implied job security in return for loyal service is likely to be permanently altered by the experience of redundancy. But even for those who remain, expectations of steady promotion and advancement through the organization are also being damaged by the restructuring of organizations and the disappearance of traditional career patterns.

Succession planning

This is often seen by chief executives as the major rationale for any form of human resource planning, and while in some organizations it may be focused mainly on only the few top positions, the need to consider at least a five-year period (and even fifteen to twenty years, if that is the time taken for a graduate recruit to reach the top) can mean that it becomes a more significant operation, and eventually drives a whole management recruitment and development programme. Systematic succession planning can also be a starting point for discussions about organization style, value and culture as a whole. Even if top appointments are still largely made on 'feel' and are under the patronage of the chief executive or board, the pool of candidates, whether internal or external, could be more 'objectively' identified and should be of high quality. Succession planning usually includes identification of up to three candidates for each senior post:

1 ready now, in the event of emergency
2 ready in two to three years time
3 ready in five years time.

An example of a typical succession chart for the top management positions of a company, summarizing the data available on each post and likely person can be found in McBeath (1992).

Planning techniques include 'back of the envelope' guestimating by one senior manager; systematic annual review of the positions and the pool by a senior management committee or HR manager (and continued down through the organization at different levels); and sophisticated computer analysis and/or competency-profile matching. A combination of several of these is likely. The complexity and sheer numbers involved in this sort of exercise means that some computerised calculations and 'what-if' modelling is essential; in the past, months of work could be nullified by one key person leaving unexpectedly and upsetting the whole plan. Even now, more effort may go into the preparation of such plans than their use can justify, although senior managers may see their chief value as in highlighting likely weaknesses in the quality of their managers or of the development system, and thus as revealing the need to make other changes.

Career planning

This is now seen as a more fashionable term to use than succession planning, and ostensibly is more individually focused. Like succession planning broadly interpreted, it requires an understanding of processes that can integrate an individual's characteristics and preferences with the implications of:

- organization culture, values and style
- business strategy and direction
- organization structure and change
- reward systems
- training and development system
- appraisal and promotion systems.

In some organizations, much more emphasis is now put on an individual's responsibility for her/his own career development. 'Mentoring' systems, whether formal or informal, may be introduced to assist in this.

One example of the elements of career planning is given by Mayo (1991), who presents details of how to integrate the various elements in a way that is mutually beneficial, although no empirical survey evidence of individual attitudes to it is presented. The variety of processes – organizational, individual and joint planning opportunities – which relate to the management of careers is shown in the top half of Figure 7.5. The lower half illustrates a framework for building up an individual's personal growth profile and plan, and then for matching this to the 'person-specification' or 'competences' required of particular general or specialist positions, whether now or in the future.

1 Possible elements in a career management framework

Individual career planning processes	Joint career planning processes	Organisational processes
Occupational choice assessment/counselling Career planning workshops Self-development plans/activities Pre-retirement courses Career resource centres Careers seminars Use of computerised career planning Writing CVs and 'personal growth profile'	Appraisal and development reviews Potential assessment centres Career guidance/ development centres Mentoring Career counselling/career planning Outplacement Career breaks and alternative methods of employment	Appointment processes Career structures High flier schemes Organisation/grade structures Succession planning Creating opportunities for experience Manpower planning Expatriate policies Defining person specifications for jobs

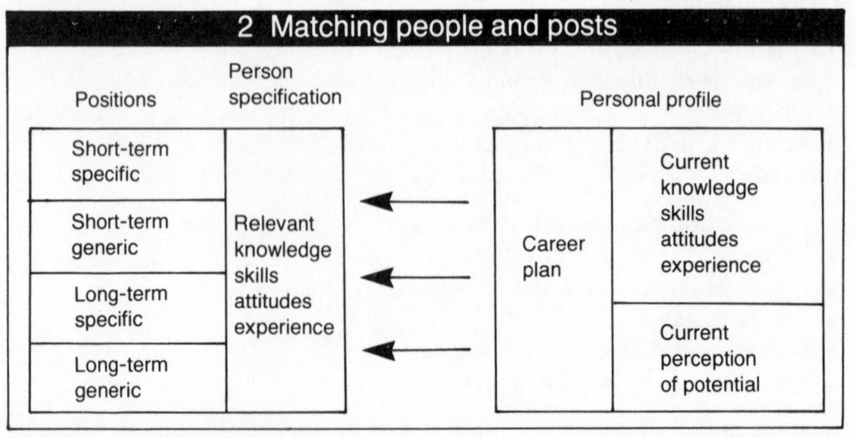

Figure 7.5 Career planning
Source: Mayo (1992: 38)

Common problems are related to key people leaving, or to managers' lack of broad experience. The requirements of different types of organizations (static; fast-growing; international, etc.) for detailed planning clearly vary. The need for creating 'bridges' between different occupations and for the identification of 'development positions' are both significant techniques in career planning. The Nationwide Building Society claims that use of its 'career analysis' model successfully integrates organizational and individual ('hard' and 'soft' analysis) career development needs (Jacobs and Bolton 1992).

Nevertheless, the predominant influence is that of the organization's needs, as mediated and interpreted by particular managers, at certain phases of its development. What is said about career planning may be interpreted very differently by those who experience it. But the 'myths' of the organization in this sense may also be significant: those who decode them appropriately are those who obtain advancement.

Studies of individual career experiences in the UK by Nicholson and West (1988) and others in the 1980s found that a career was experienced largely as a 'series of encampments among the foothills', rather than a climb up a single mountain peak. In the 1990s, with even more emphasis on careers consisting of horizontal development rather than vertical progression for the majority, the discrepancies for individuals between established expectations of increases in reward and status and actual experience, makes even more critical the responsibilities of those people in organizations who have to manage the changes. Selection and development of the very few who will be needed at the top is even more difficult. Decentralization into smaller units and the use of project and task-force management techniques raise both opportunities and challenges. Multi-functional development concepts overturn many previous assumptions of specialized functional career paths – but at the same time, the need for very specialized expertise may become even greater in some organizations. Whether 'dual' career ladders will proliferate, or whether the chances of high reward will become even more restricted to a few senior managers, rather than including specialists, remains to be seen. The health service is likely to see further conflict over this issue, between administrators, professionals and those who perform dual functions.

Concepts of empowerment imply greater responsibility for those at lower levels, but the chances of this leading to opportunities of promotion, already weakened by graduate entry level to most management positions, are even lower in the 'flatter' or 'shamrock' organization (Handy 1989), in which services or functions, previously performed internally, have become hived-off or subcontracted externally (Rees 1993). Those who find themselves, voluntarily or involuntarily, as 'entrepreneurs' running small businesses (e.g. in housing maintenance, as contractor to a district council or housing association) are likely to remain subject to the pressures of that world, rather than moving into the management hierarchies of larger firms again.

Concepts of careers for manual workers, while gaining some credence as appraisal systems and personal training and development plans become more widely introduced, will create new challenges to traditional approaches to planning. But just as planners' projections are often unknown to plant personnel managers, let alone the line managers who handle most of the appraisal and career discussions, so the reverse is true. The lack of organizational integration between succession planning, promotion processes and career pathing found in recent research into the management of job mobility may be reflective of many of the problems of human resource planning (Forster 1991).

A strategic approach to planning for training is a key aspect of any approach to strategy (and is dealt with in Chapter 9). The contrast between what is feasible in large firms, and the difficulties of small and medium-sized ones, is particularly significant in this respect, given their closeness to the market, the likely scarcity of internal training expertise and the difficulty of sending people on external courses. The comment of one manager interviewed in a case-study (Hendry *et al.* 1991) exemplifies this:

> 'We've made training plans over the years, but they get blown away. I've come to the conclusion that training is reactive. For example, twelve months ago, marketing said there would be no sales for three months, because BT had put a block on. We saw it as an opportunity to do training for the longer term (and it would have been enthusiastically supported by management). But then they came back with some European sales, and the training was put on ice' (personnel director, Fibres).

Flexibility and core–periphery approaches

The model of the 'flexible firm' (Atkinson 1985), introduced as an attempt to bring together a variety of current trends and the implications of new business directions, has been criticized from all sides – on the grounds that it was conflating a variety of trends in employment patterns, some temporary and some long-standing, which had often been adopted for very differing reasons (Pollert 1988); that there was little empirical evidence of its existence as a whole or that managers were implementing it strategically; and that where it was found, it represented tactical moves to serve a variety of *ad hoc* purposes, such as cost reduction or to cover for temporary shortages of labour or peaks in market demand (Hunter and MacInnes 1991). Debate over interpretations of empirical research have also become part of the 'flexible specialization' and 'de-skilling' labour process debate.

Nevertheless, it is possible that just as researchers have demolished the concept, managers have started to adopt flexible contracts more strategically. In planning terms, the need both to reduce costs and to meet customer service needs at particular times of the day, week, or year, appears logically to imply adjustment of the traditional full-time eight-hour day, five-day week or forty-eight week year, and to give scope for temporary, part-time working hours, or other 'flexible' working. As already mentioned, however, the downside problems of lower commitment, a divided workforce, less chance of training for those outside the core, and problems of managing such diversity, may all act as restraints on planning logic. There is some evidence, too, of complex interplay between supply-side and demand-side influences: some women with children are only willing to work during school hours; most managers only offer part-time twilight shift or some forms of temporary work to female and not male employees, or only reorganize work in this way for those workers.

Initiatives include those where certain employees, such as those at Oxfordshire County Council and British Telecom (Industrial Relations Services 1992b), have been given the option of working partly or mainly from home. Another development is signalled by Glaxo, which has subcontracted all of its head office clerical work to a secretarial agency operating on site.

More sophisticated models of primary and secondary labour markets, and of internal and external labour markets, have been developed by academics to explain the variety of patterns found (e.g. Hakim 1990; Loveridge 1983; Crompton and Sanderson 1990; Rubery and Horrell 1992/3; Piore and Sabel 1984; Osterman 1987; Williamson 1981). Yet most of these are unknown to human resource planners or other managers who are seeking to make sense of a variety of external competitive pressures as well as the internal cost, cultural and other constraints under which they find themselves (Rubery 1993). Whether they also choose to accommodate (some) individual employee preferences, and also whether the form of flexibility is functional, contractual, financial, or numerical therefore depends on a variety of circumstances. The most 'strategic' description of policy, found by Hunter and MacInnes (1991) was:

> To keep the permanent levels as low as possible and use temporary workers to meet production demands for specific projects and to increase the range of work done by permanent employees. To enable a better control of manpower costs against production as you can release temporary employees.
>
> (Ibid.: 31)

Many managers, however, when questioned, admitted that 'Almost anything we could do to improve the margins by reducing over-commitment to costs would be accepted'.

The extent to which flexible firms are feasible and efficient depends also on government policies – both fiscal, labour market and other. Although across the EC, about one-third of the labour force is in atypical work, patterns vary considerably. In France, for example, part-time work among women is low partly because infant schooling is available from age three, but also because employers pay the same social insurance tax regardless of hours worked by an employee, whereas in the UK considerable advantages can derive from hours-related assessment of social security contributions by both employer and employee (depending on his/her preferences). Temporary work is restricted by law in France. Attempts to relax restrictions, even by a socialist government, were ended when evidence of increasing exploitation of staff was found.

Most EC countries, with the exception of Britain, have statutory regulations on daily and weekly working hours, holidays and night work, so that some of the UK's strongest opposition to implementation of the Social Charter has focused on the Working Time Directive – arguments about 'flexibility' and jobs are set against those based on protection of standards of living and the 'level playing field'. Most multinational firms appear to be able to plan effectively for different national legal requirements, but the continued British 'exception' may in future make their planning more complex, and thus minimize some cost advantages.

Cost-competitiveness pressures are likely to make greater requirements of managers in future to justify the effectiveness – or lack of it – of their planning processes, in anticipating and making provision for changes in organizations and individuals, whether at global or local level. Appropriate techniques of evaluation are therefore likely to be needed.

EVALUATION OF HUMAN RESOURCE PLANNING

Purposes

Whether the function of HR planning in the 'hard' sense is to serve as an indicator of the likely match or mismatch of the supply and demand for the right number of people with appropriate skills, or in the 'soft' sense is to alert the organization to the implications of business strategy for people development, culture and attitudes as well as numbers and skills, then some form of audit or review is necessary. Only then is it possible to see if planning is either achieving results or has been overturned by other changes in the organization's policy or environment, requiring adjustments to HRM policies or those of the organization.

Over the last ten years there have been significant changes in the graduate labour market. In the late 1980s, high employer demands led to a concern over the possible shortage of new graduates in the future. The recent economic climate of recession has dramatically reduced immediate

> demand while, over the next three years, there is an expected 20 per cent increase in the number of new graduates entering the labour market.
> (Skills and Enterprise Network, 1993a: 1)

Graduate recruitment is an obvious example of the need for adaptive forecasting in the light of changing trends in labour markets and in business policy, as the annual IMS reviews have shown. In this way the planning process becomes part of a practical process of projection, implementation, review and adjustment. While this may take place annually in most firms, in accordance with the business planning cycle, it may need to be more frequent in those operating in rapidly changing markets such as food and fashion retailing. Whether it takes place at all as a discrete process, may be even more open to question than the use of HR planning in the first place, since many managers are reluctant to 'waste time' looking back to analyse, explain and learn from the past. It may, however, take place in conjunction with other auditing, planning or strategic review processes, as was the case at ICL (Beattie and Tampoe 1990):

> Manpower planning is not a precise science. It can clearly only be a best view at a point in time. But if manpower planning is a regular and integral part of the business planning and review cycle, as it is in ICL, then the shifts in skills implicit in our business plans can be detected and plans formulated to respond to those requirements. The manpower planning system in ICL is an important supporting process to the review of organization and manpower issues through the OMR.
> (Ibid.: 24)

Emphasis on outputs and performance achievement, rather than on input, was a feature of organization change in both the public and private sectors in the late 1980s which seems likely to continue throughout the 1990s, so that techniques of 'outcomes' evaluation are also likely to be of increasing importance.

Techniques

Techniques may include the following:

- Simple audits of whether targets were met in terms of numbers reduced or increased, vacancies filled, numbers trained or costs reduced. The level of audit – organization-wide, business unit, or section – will depend on the purpose and on the extent to which analysis of the reasons for deviation or success takes place.
- Evaluation as part of other organization review procedures in standard use:
  - 'Total quality' procedures, several of which make rigorous

monitoring demands and can draw attention to human resource inadequacies.
- 'Investors in People' procedures, which similarly require monitoring of training outcomes against training needs analysis of all employees on a continuing basis. While evaluation of training outcomes has long been a difficult area, that of planning and input is easier. 'Competency-based' human resource systems tend to lend themselves to audit, since desired outcomes are part of the specification of these standards of competence.
- In parallel with reviews of work subcontracted outside the organization or under consideration. The requirements for subjecting an increasing range of public sector services to external competitive tendering is encouraging a more analytical approach to the utilization of human resources and to the monitoring of outcomes.

• Evaluation as part of a general communications audit or employee attitude survey: if HR planning is aiming to change the culture or improve the quality of working life, then mapping of changes in employee attitudes is essential.
• Inclusion as part of a wider audit or review of the HR function:
  - To see to what extent it 'added value' to the organization, for example in developing people or reducing labour turnover; although examples of uses of highly quantified 'human asset' accounting and auditing techniques seem rare outside academia and consultancy.
  - In meeting the targets that the HR department or function set itself: one example of this might be the 'milestones' set out by County Natwest in 1990 (Riley 1991) or the example provided by North Western Regional Health Authority in 1991–2 (Industrial Relations Services 1992a). This advised managers on means of measuring outputs in HRM, and encouraged them to develop their own, whether in terms of cost, quantity, quality or time.
  - In monitoring achievements of 'equal opportunity targets' in terms of gender or race. While continuous surveys of statistics can simply become an excuse to avoid taking any positive action, evaluation of any policy changes and their impact is important in triggering understanding of outcomes.
  - As part of some form of internal or external bench-marking comparison of HR planning uses and outcomes in other parts of the same organization, or in different ones. Increasing use of this technique in industry under the influence of TQM procedures is now spreading more widely to HR functions in so-called 'leading-edge' organizations. Firms 'select' others whom they regard as being in the same league, whether or not they are competitors, and exchange information to a greater or lesser degree of detail on various policy approaches. Large consultancy firms also do this, some maintaining

their own data bases of comparative practices. Newer ones are also developing to meet a growing need for techniques of audit and comparison, such as that used by Berkshire County Council's Personnel Department (Burn and Thompson 1993).

- Individual appraisal reviews, whereby the HR director, HR planner, or line managers may have either 'hard' or 'soft' targets to meet in terms of HR planning and may be expected to discuss the extent to which they were achieved, are probably the most widespread form of evaluation (Institute of Personnel Management 1992).

Criteria

Apart from straightforward matching of numerical targets, which few would expect to achieve in the 'people' field other than within fairly broad parameters, managerial criteria of achievement are more likely to relate to other organization aims and also to be more politically sensitive to the objectives of the evaluator or of other powerful groups in the organization. Redundancies, downsizing and de-layering, are the obvious examples and may represent an achievement of cost-saving from one perspective, but may also be a loss of skill, experience and of future potential for the organization, or of managerial status in terms of size of department, quite apart from the impact on individuals' welfare. Achievement of cross-functional career moves may similarly be viewed differently by planning departments, by 'parent' and by 'receiving' departments, as well as by the individual concerned.

At the very least, some mutuality of satisfaction in meeting employee as well as employer needs would seem to be a necessary criterion of evaluation. This could imply greater scope for employee – or trade union – involvement in the planning and implementation process. Lack of knowledge and understanding of such HR planning as has taken place also suggests that personnel managers need to involve the line managers both in the processes of doing it and of selling it more effectively.

CONCLUSIONS

Human resource planning is a complex subject, particularly at a time of rapid global business change which increases the tensions between the greater need for planning and the greater difficulties of prediction, whether of organizational requirements or of individual expectations. Traditional quantitative manpower planning techniques may still have a role to play through more accessible computerized modelling systems, but are likely to become more closely integrated with strategic business planning systems and to be qualitatively driven by line managers' views of the core competences which are required by the business, if changing customer needs are to be understood and met flexibly.

The challenge to academics of researching such 'ad hocracy' (Mintzberg 1983) becomes correspondingly greater, as the relationships between 'practice' and 'policy' continually shift, and the difficulties of either building theoretical models or of deriving effective 'prescriptions' increase. Many researchers have tended to assume a model of 'rational people operating within efficient technical systems' (Lee and Piper 1987) and yet continue to criticize managers both for being overly ratio/technical and also too tactical and responsive. Greater sensitivity to the variety of 'political' and 'functional' interests found and the interplay between them may be needed to shape the more focused empirical research into human resource planning processes which is still required. Yet the problems of interpretation of the subtle and often paradoxical processes thus revealed are likely to increase, given the lack of general agreement on definitions of 'strategic' and of 'planning', or of criteria of effectiveness. Perhaps the real criterion of evaluation should concern the learning outcomes of the planning process for whoever is involved.

REFERENCES

Atkinson, J. (1985) *Flexibility, Uncertainty and Manpower Management*, IMS Report No. 189, Brighton: Institute of Manpower Studies.

Bamber, G. and Whitehouse, G. (1992) 'International data on economic, employment and human resource issues', *International Journal of Human Resource Management* 3(2), September.

Beattie, D.F. and Tampoe, F.M.K. (1990) 'Human resource planning for ICL', *Long Range Planning* 23(1).

Bennison, M. (1991) 'Controlling manpower costs', *Personnel Management* November.

Bennison, M. and Casson, J. (1984) *The Manpower Planning Handbook*, Maidenhead: McGraw-Hill.

Bramham, J. (1989) *Human Resource Planning*, London: IPM.

Brewster, C. and Hegewisch, A. (1993) 'A continent of diversity', *Personnel Management* January.

Burn, D. and Thompson, L. (1993) 'When personnel calls in the auditors', *Personnel Management* January.

Butler, J., Ferris, G. and Napier, N. (1991) *Strategy and Human Resources Management*, Cincinnati, OH: Southwestern Publishing Company.

Causer, G. and Jones, C. (1992/3) 'Responding to skill shortages: recruitment and retention in a high technology labour market', *Human Resource Management Journal* 3(3).

Collinson, D., Knights, D. and Collinson, M. (1990) *Managing to Discriminate*, London: Routledge.

Cressey, P. and Scott, P. (1992) 'Employment, technology and industrial relations in UK clearing banks', *New Technology, Work and Employment* 7(2), Autumn.

Crompton, R. and Sanderson, K. (1990) *Gendered Jobs and Social Change*, London: Unwin Hyman.

Edwards, P.K. and Whitson, C. (1989) 'Industrial discipline, the control of attendance and the subordination of labour: towards an integrated analysis', *Work, Employment and Society* 3(1), March.

Fair, H. (1992) *Personnel and Profit*, London: IPM.

Fairchild, P. (1989) 'A planned response to demographic change', *Personnel Management* September.

Falconer, H. (1991) 'Number games', *Personnel Today* 18 October.

Ferner, A. and Colling, T. (1991) 'Privatisation, regulation and industrial relations', *British Journal of Industrial Relations* 29(3), September.

Ferner, A. and Hyman, R. (eds) *Industrial Relations in the New Europe*, Oxford: Blackwell.

Forster, N. (1991) 'Developing the role of the personnel function in the management of job mobility', *Human Resource Management Journal* 2(1), Autumn.

Fox, S. and McLeay, S. (1992) 'An approach to researching managerial labour markets: HRM, corporate strategy and financial performance in manufacturing', *International Journal of Human Resource Management* 3(3), December.

Goold, M. and Campbell, A. (1989) *Strategies and Styles – the Role of the Centre in Managing Diversified Corporations*, Oxford: Blackwell.

Hakim, C. (1990) 'Core and periphery in employers' workforce strategies: evidence from the ELUS survey', *Work, Employment and Society* 4(2).

—— (1993) 'The myth of rising female employment', *Work, Employment and Society* 7(1), March.

Handy, C. (1989) *The Age of Unreason*, London: Business.

Hendry, C., Jones, A., Arthur, M. and Pettigrew, C. (1991) *Human Resource Development in Small to Medium Sized Enterprises*, DE Research Paper No. 88, London: Employment Department Group.

Hunter, L.C. and MacInnes, J. (1991, reprinted 1993) *Employers' Labour Use Strategies – Case Studies*, DE Research Paper No. 87, London: Employment Department Group.

Industrial Relations Services (1990) 'British steel confronts demographic change', *Industrial Relations Review and Report*, No. 455, January.

—— (1992a) 'Auditing the management of human resources in the NHS', *Industrial Relations Review and Report*, No. 510, April.

—— (1992b) 'Introducing the flexible workplace at Oxfordshire County Council', *Industrial Relations Review and Report*, No. 517, August.

Institute for Employment Research (1993) *Review of the Economy and Employment, Occupational Studies*, Warwick: IER.

Institute of Personnel Management (1975) *Manpower Planning in Action*, London: IPM.

—— (1992a) *Statement on Human Resource Planning*, London: IPM.

—— (1992b) *Performance Management in the UK: An Analysis of the Issues*, London: IPM.

Jacobs, R. and Bolton, R. (1992) 'Career analysis: the missing link in managerial assessment and development', *Human Resource Management Journal* 3(3).

Jonung, C. and Persson, I. (1993) 'Women and market work: the misleading tale of participation rates in international comparisons', *Work, Employment and Society* 7(2), June.

Kerfoot, D. and Knights, D. (1992) 'Planning for personnel? – human resource management reconsidered', *Journal of Management Studies* 29(5), September.

Lee, R.A. and Piper, J.A. (1987) 'Towards a conceptual framework for analysing managerial promotion processes', Loughborough University, Department of Management Studies, mimeo.

Legge, K. (1978) *Power, Innovation and Problem Solving in Personnel Management*, Maidenhead: McGraw-Hill.

Lengnick-Hall, C.A. and Lengnick-Hall, M.L. (1988) 'Strategic HRM – a review of the literature and a proposed typology', *Academy of Management Review* 13(3).

Loveridge, R. (1983) 'Labour market segmentation and the firm', in J. Edwards *et al.* (eds) *Manpower Planning, Strategy and Techniques in Organizational Context*, Chichester: J. Wiley.

Lovering, J. (1991) 'The British defence industry in the 1990s: a labour market perspective', *Industrial Relations Journal* 22(2), Summer.

Lucio, M.M. and Simpson, D. (1992) 'Discontinuity and change in industrial relations: the struggles over its social dimensions and the rise of human resource management', *International Journal of Human Resource Management* 3(2), September.

McBeath, G. (1992) *The Handbook of Human Resource Planning*, Oxford: Blackwell

McGregor, H. and Sproull, A. (1991) *Employers' Labour Use Strategies: Analysis of a National Survey*, DE Research Paper No. 83, London: Employment Department Group.

Mackay, L. and Torrington, D. (1986) *The Changing Nature of Personnel Management*, London: IPM.

Manpower Services Commission/National Economic Development Office (1978) *Case Studies in Company Manpower Planning*, London: NEDO.

—— (1987) *People: The Key to Success*, London: NEDO.

Marginson, P., Edwards, P.K., Martin, R., Sisson, K. and Purcell, J. (1988) *Beyond the Workplace*, Oxford: Blackwell.

Mayo, A. (1991) *Managing Careers: Strategies for Organizations*, London: IPM.

—— (1992) 'A framework for career management', *Personnel Management*, February.

Millward, N., Stevens, M., Smart, D. and Hawes, W.R. (1992) *Workplace Industrial Relations in Transition: The ED/ESRC/PSI/ACAS Surveys*, Aldershot: Dartmouth Publishing.

Ministry of Labour and National Service (1958) *Positive Employment Policies*, London: HMSO.

Mintzberg, H. (1983) *Structures in Fives: Designing Effective Organizations*, Englewood Cliffs, NJ: Prentice-Hall.

Mitrani, A., Dalziel, M. and Fitt, D. (eds) (1992) *Competency Based Human Resource Management*, London: Hay Group Kogan Page.

Morgan, I., Seccombe, I. and Such, J. (1991) *Career Models for the 1990s: a Technical Review Paper*, IMS Paper No. 16, Brighton: Institute of Manpower Studies.

National Economic Development Office/Training Agency (1989) *Defusing the Demographic Time Bomb*, London: NEDO.

National Institute for Economic Research (1993) *Educational Provision, Educational Attainment and the Needs of Industry: A Review of Research for Germany, France, Japan, the US and Britain*, London: NIESR.

Nicholson, N.A. and West, M.A. (1988) *Managerial Job Change*, London: Cambridge University Press.

Nkomo, S. (1986) 'The theory and practice of HR planning', *Personnel Administrator* August: 71–84.

Osterman, P. (1987) 'Choice of employment systems in internal labour markets', *Industrial Relations* 26(1), Winter.

Parsons, D. (1990) 'Winning workers', *Employment Gazette* February.

Peters, T. and Waterman, R.H. (1982) *In Search of Excellence*, New York: Harper & Row.
Pike, G., Gower, H. and Jagger, N. (1992) *IMS Graduate Review, 1992*, IMS Report No. 232, Brighton: Institute of Manpower Studies.
Piore, M. and Sabel, C. (1984) *The Second Industrial Divide*, New York: Basic Books.
Pollert, A. (1988) 'The flexible firm: fixation or fact', *Work, Employment and Society* 2(2): 281–316.
Rajan, A. (1992) *1990s: Where the New Jobs Will Be*, Tunbridge Wells: Centre for Research in Employment and Technology in Europe (CREATE).
Rajan, A. and Bevan, S. (eds) (1900) *British Socio-Economic Trends to 1995, and Their Employment Implications*, IMS Report No. 189, Brighton: Institute of Manpower Services.
Rees, G. (1993) 'Labour markets and training regimes', paper prepared for presentation at Employers Labour Market Behaviour Seminar, Employment Department.
Riley, K. (1991) 'Milestones for the personnel department', *Personnel Management* August.
Rothwell, S.G. (1983) 'Company employment policies and new technology in manufacturing and service sectors', in M. Warner (ed.) *Microprocessors, Manpower and Society*, Aldershot: Gower.
—— (1985) 'Company employment policies and new technology', *Industrial Relations Journal* 16(3).
Rubery, J. (1993) 'Internal and external labour markets: towards an integrated analysis', paper presented at Employers Labour Market Behaviour Seminar, Employment Department.
Rubery, J. and Horrell, S. (1992/3) 'The new competition and working time', *Human Resource Management Journal* 3(2), Winter.
Schein, E. (1977) 'Increasing organizational effectiveness through better HR planning and development', *Sloan Management Review* 19(1), Fall: 1–20.
Schuler, R. and Walker, J.W. (1990) 'HR strategy: focussing on issues and actions', *Organizational Dynamics*, Summer.
Scullion, H. (1992) 'Strategic requirement and the development of the international manager: some European considerations', *Human Resource Management Journal* 3(1), Autumn.
Sinclair, A. and Ewing, J. (1992/3) 'What women managers want: customising human resource management practices', *Human Resource Management Journal* 3(2), Winter.
Skills and Enterprise Network (1991) 'Scenarios: planning for improbable events', SEN Briefing No. 59, Employment Department Group, November.
—— (1993a) 'Evaluating the graduate labour market', SEN Briefing No. 142, London: Employment Department Group, March.
—— (1993b) 'Where will the new jobs be?', SEN Briefing No. 155, London: Employment Department Group, May.
Storey, J. (1992) *Developments in the Management of Human Resources*, Oxford: Blackwell.
Timperley, S. and Sisson, K. (1989) 'From manpower planning to HR planning', in K. Sisson (ed.) *Personnel Management in Britain*, Oxford: Blackwell.
Vickerstaff, S. (1989) 'Human resource planning', in C. Molander (ed.) *Human Resource Management*, Bromley: Chartwell-Bratt.
Watson, T.J. (1986) *Management, Organization and Employment Strategy*, London: Routledge & Kegan Paul.

Williamson, O. (1981) 'The economics of organization: the transaction cost approach', *American Journal of Sociology* 87(3), November.

Wright, P.M. and McMahan, G.C. (1992) 'Theoretical perspectives for strategic human resource management', *Journal of Management* 18(3).

Chapter 8

Recruitment, selection and assessment

*Paul Iles and Graeme Salaman**

INTRODUCTION

For too long the study of processes of selection and assessment has been left to the industrial psychologist and the personnel specialist and has (with certain exceptions – Rose 1988; Holloway 1991; Silverman and Jones 1976; Salaman and Thompson 1976; Townley 1989; Windholf and Wood 1988) been insufficiently considered by the organization theorist and organizational sociologist. This is unfortunate, particularly at a time when selection and assessment are increasingly seen as being critical to large-scale processes of organizational change. Beaumont (1993), for example, when arguing the 'enhanced potential importance' of the selection process, notes the role of strategic selection, wherein 'the design of a selection system . . . supports the overall organisation strategy, the monitoring of the internal flow of personnel . . . matches emerging business strategies, and [there is] a need to match key executives to business strategies' (ibid.: 57). Yet despite the need for a fuller understanding of these processes, the bulk of existing social science and human resource strategy (HRS) literature is concerned primarily and solely with assessing the efficiency of these processes. Indeed, Beaumont's own chapter is itself mainly concerned to assess the efficiency of current selection processes.

Yet such a concern does not exhaust the possible implications of these key organizational processes. They have a far wider significance, one of which is their role as the embodiment and operationalization of a form of psychometrically based expertise which critically defines the skills, values and qualities (or 'competences' – see below) required by modern forms of organization. Thus they reveal and represent the form and direction of current forms of organizational change – the working out, the play of power within organizations. In principle, and also in effect, contemporary processes of selection and assessment represent the moment when organizational

* Graeme Salaman would like to acknowledge the support of the ESRC through grant number R000234869 for a research project entitled 'Making Up Managers' which he is conducting with Paul du Gay.

restructuring meets and impacts on individuals, either as putative or actual employees, and in so doing, defines, understands, and assesses them in terms of organizationally defined critical qualities, and is the site of individual entry into – or rejection from – newly defined organizational roles. The issue, therefore, is not simply or primarily one of efficiency or rationality, but one of power: the capacity of, and the forms of knowledge and associated technologies through which organizations identify and define and assess individuals against structures of necessary competences.

Townley (1989) has usefully noted that current interest in more rigorous processes of selection can be seen not simply as being related to a concern for more efficient selection, but as being

> integral to what has been identified as HRM. The latter is understood as being characterised by an increasing emphasis placed on the attitudinal and behavioural characteristics of employees, factors which readily lend themselves to monitoring through selection and performance review.
>
> (Ibid.: 92)

At a time when programmes of HRS-inspired change encourage a focus on the 'organizational change lever' of selection and assessment – arguing the strategic significance of identifying and assessing key managerial and other competences to support structural change – it is imperative not only to know what is happening in this area, but to understand its significance. As we shall argue in the final section, it is also important to get inside the structure of interrelated ideas, techniques and assumptions which comprise current models of selection and the qualities these schemes typically seek to identify, and to understand how they work to define the new manager and his/her necessary qualities.

More than this, the limitation of the psychological and personnel-driven approaches to selection is that they are entirely, if understandably, concerned with improving the efficiency of the processes, and not with understanding their wider provenance and significance. They focus on degrees of, and deviations from, scientific rationality; but they do not address the nature or implications of that rationality. Indeed, they are themselves part of the very discourse they describe, accepting the assumptions of the selection process, supplying technological improvements and evaluations. As Miller and Rose (1993) point out, this concern with efficiency itself is an aspect of a particular conception of, and approach to, the 'government' of organizations:

> Evaluation, . . . is something internal to the phenomenon . . . this imperative to evaluate needs to be viewed as itself a key component of . . . forms of political thought . . .: how authorities and administrators make judgements, the conclusions that they draw from them, the rectifications

they propose and the impetus that 'failure' provides for the preparation of new programmes of government.

(Ibid.: 78)

Such an assumption is based, these authors note, on 'an eternal optimism', that aspects of society could always be better administered, known, organized or measured; that reality is ultimately programmable.

In the case of the subject matter of this chapter – assessment and selection – this process of evaluation occurs at a number of levels. First, it is of course absolutely fundamental to the processes of selection and assessment themselves. Second, it is a key feature of the recent emphasis to identify and assess competences, which are seen as a superior basis for managerial selection. Third, the appraisal of evaluation (selection and assessment) – that is, the assessment of the validity of the process, constitutes a major focus of much of the literature in the area.

The subject matter in this chapter is the process whereby modern organizations seek to recruit and select staff in order to support the achievement of strategic objectives. The chapter has two purposes: to describe and explain developments and tendencies in assessment and selection, and to relate these to prevalent directions of organization change and to address the ways in which these processes have been treated within the literature. The chapter does this by describing some major approaches to the understanding of these processes, from the psychometric to the sociological. Although recruitment and selection processes constitute our prime focus, the chapter seeks to do more than merely offer an overview of current practice and issues in the field of assessment. The chapter is as concerned with the ways in which these processes are understood and described, as with how they are conducted. And crucially, we are interested in the interconnections between the techniques of selection and assessment, and the models which inform and explain these practices.

We shall argue first, that recent changes in organizational systems and structures (of a sort often associated with the human resource strategies approach to organizational change) are commonly associated with the search for recruits from within the organization, or outside it, with new attitudes, skills and experiences (or competences) as organizations make significant changes in their key competences. Current organizational emphasis on the systematic search – often by means of psychometric techniques – for individuals who display evidence of those competences identified as critical to the newly defined performance of key managerial roles in furtherance of newly structured and focused organizations, reveals the nature of organizational change and the degree to which, and the manner in which, this change is centred around newly defined organizational employees.

This discussion constitutes the first section. In the second section we present and discuss some current trends in selection methods and practices. In the third section we focus attention on the methods of identification and assessment of management competences, since this represents a major development in the constitution of the new manager and a major element in efforts to discover individuals with the required managerial qualities. This section includes a discussion of job analysis as a process which underlies the identification of competences. In the fifth section we consider a number of models of selection and assessment; the first of these – the psychometric model – is fundamental to any understanding of the design of selection systems, selection methods and selection criteria, for it supplies their basic rationale. This is the approach which underpins 'scientific selection' (Holloway 1991; Rose 1985). The 'social process' model differs slightly, in focusing less on the individual as a set of stable qualities; this approach views selection as a process, wherein the individual him or herself is constructed. For example, one explanation of the high degree of validity of the assessment centre approach to identifying promotion potential may be that superior assessments are based on a recognition of the various qualities (not all formal, or job-related) that are required for success in an organization; or post-assessment centre judgements may be coloured by knowledge of the individual's performance in the assessment centre.

One form of this social process approach simply notes the interplay between selection events, candidates' feelings and responses, and organizational outcomes, emphasizing the mutual adjustments and 'negotiations' that occur. But a more interesting and more radical form sees the candidate and the selection decision as in various ways constructed by the process of selection and measurement. Thus assessment centres could be seen not as *discovering* potential, but as defining and constructing it.

We conclude the chapter with some consideration of a radically different approach to the understanding of the selection process. The earlier models are in some way centred on a conception of the selection process in terms of its efficiency. The third approach eschews all concern with the relevance or effectiveness of the identified competences and those procedures which are designed to identify them, and offers instead a conception of these activities as part of a form of discourse of HRS which supports the process of government of the enterprise.

THE STRATEGIC ROLE OF RECRUITMENT AND SELECTION PROCESSES

In the 1980s, as part of the move towards human resource strategies, many organizations in North America and Europe began thinking of their recruitment and selection processes as major levers to support strategic and cultural change. In part this was due to a growing conceptualization of strategic management as involving more than a search for product market-based competitive advantages. Underlying the development of specific products with their limited life-cycles was the acquisition and development of strategic skill pools. With the rise of skill-based competition (Klein *et al.* 1990), competitive advantage was increasingly seen as being based on exploiting and developing the 'core competences' of the organization (Pralahad and Hamel 1990). Alongside this increased awareness of skill, capability and competence as keys to competitive advantage has been an appreciation of the increased demands now being placed on managers and other key staff as a result of current organizational changes. Facing an increasingly difficult and demanding environment with increasing competitive pressures, many UK organizations have taken up a variety of HRM initiatives in order to encourage employee initiative, proactivity and entrepreneurialism (Storey and Sissons 1993).

A variety of 'key HRM levers' have been employed but chief among them has been viewing recruitment and selection activities as 'integrated key tasks' for organizations. As one way of delivering behaviours seen as necessary to support organizational strategies, recruitment and selection initiatives have become increasingly important alongside training and development and large-scale cultural change and total quality management initiatives. A particular focus has been on management as the key to organizational effectiveness, as it is the competence of managers that will influence the return that an organization will secure from its investment in both human and material capital (Mangham and Silver 1990: 2). This concern has been most often expressed in the increasing emphasis given to managerial competences, and to the need to identify the key managerial skills that underlie or underpin effective management performance. Once these underlying competences have been identified, recruitment and selection processes can be installed to ensure that managers with the requisite skills and qualities are successfully attracted to the organization, assessed, placed in appropriate jobs or roles, and appraised, developed and rewarded against appropriate competency criteria (e.g. Boyatzis 1982; Bethell-Fox 1992; MCI 1990).

The particular approach to recruitment and selection processes will be considered in some detail later. At this point it is worth noting a number of examples of how UK organizations in the 1980s and 1990s have revamped their recruitment, assessment and selection strategies following strategic realignments and the redefinition of organizational mission and culture. New skills and competences required for managing in the new organization have often been specified, with people identified externally and internally who seem to display such qualities. Recruitment, selection and placement activities have then been undertaken to match competence profiles with job demands and requirements. For example, in the UK computer supply industry, immediate competitive pressures in the 1980s led many companies to neglect the long-term planning of recruitment and selection activities.

With IT becoming a key to competitive advantage and with greater sophistication among purchasers demanding more specialized software, the strategic relationship between user and supplier grew in importance. This focus on 'total service', consultancy support and software applications, led to a need to acquire and develop staff with new managerial skills, not just in IT but in communication, leadership, process, project management and entrepreneurship. This increased focus on business solutions and customer relationships ran alongside skills shortages. High attrition rates often led to greater use of cross-functional development and more focused recruitment, with greater use of contract staff, networking, and the recruitment of younger, less-skilled engineers to maintain the high-volume end of the market. Graduate recruitment has been of continuing importance, but companies have widened their recruitment net through trying to recruit from a wider range of disciplines, targeting more female graduates, and initiating international graduate recruitment activities. Psychometric assessment techniques such as tests of cognitive ability have also grown in importance as ways of identifying potential (Sparrow and Pettigrew 1988; Sparrow *et al.* 1989).

Similarly in the personal financial services industry, increasing competition for personal deposits, money transmission and lending and investment services has led to shifts in managerial roles from lenders and administrators to marketeers, sellers and entrepreneurs responsible for a wider range of products and services. Managerial jobs have become more outward-looking, market-focused and team-oriented. While technical competence remains important, new commercial and managerial skills have become more central, requiring that such skills and qualities be more effectively identified and more sophisticated techniques introduced to bring about improved linkages between business strategy and appraisal, staff development and recruitment and selection (Higgs 1988). In contrast to the former assumption that, for males at least, every entry job gave access to a single career path to the top, many organizations in this sector have introduced 'tiered' recruitment strategies. Some companies now recruit for specific basic entry-level technical jobs, and career paths are often more closely aligned with different business and product life-cycle needs. One major clearing bank, for example, recruiting at various levels, has developed a range of assessment procedures to identify, track and develop potential at all stages of an individual's career. In order to identify high-potential staff earlier, push them forward faster, and retain talented people, it developed a strategy which 'tiered' employees at various points in their careers, drawing from a large pool of potential recruits (Gratton 1989; Robertson *et al.* 1991). Many banks have also begun to make extensive use of part-time and temporary staff in a search for both financial and numerical flexibility (Atkinson 1988), as well as instituting cultural and structural change programmes. These have attempted to transform bureaucratic organizations, stratified by grade and work role and hierarchically structured with narrow job tasks in cultures emphasizing deference, caution and loyalty to a paternalist employer, into profit-centred, performance-oriented enterprises (see e.g. Cressey and Jones 1992). Since such a model 'demands quite different staff, with different qualities and outlooks' (ibid.: 70–1), it is hardly surprising that recruitment and selection activities, including the assessment of internal staff for promotion, placement, transfer and development, loom large in many HRM initiatives. For example, many banks have introduced large-scale assessment programmes involving biodata, psychometric testing and assessment centres (Robertson *et al.* 1991).

The recruitment and selection 'lever' has also been extensively employed by the building societies. In addition to intensified competition and rapid technological change, specific legislation such as the Financial Services Act (1987) and the Building Societies Act (1986), as well as general legislation like the Social Security Act (1986) promoted private pensions which has shaped the rules and regulations under which building societies operate, regulating what they can and cannot do. In particular, the external environment has become more competitive, with less differentiation between organizations and products, an increased, more rapidly changing product range, shorter product life cycles, and ventures into new areas (not always successful, such as the move into estate agencies in the 1980s). There has also been a growth in the number of mergers, acquisitions, and joint ventures (such as the proposed union between the Leeds and the National Provincial in 1993 and that between Abbey National and Scottish Mutual).

In 1990, the National and Provincial Building Society took the view that the new competitive environment called for a new corporate culture demanding accountability, enterprise, customer care and success. The value of enterprise in particular was seen as a radical break with a paternalistic culture valuing sobriety, caution, loyalty, respectability, thrift and stability. The Society wished to have staff in place with the skills and abilities to work effectively in the new culture and in the new job roles created by such a strategy. It attempted to identify 'key post competences', profiling key posts in terms of their present and future competence requirements and assessing present and potential job-holders in terms of how they matched up to these requirements. Recruitment, selection and appraisal were conducted against such competency criteria, and selected individuals were given the opportunity of being assessed in a development centre generating a personal development plan for each participant. These assessment activities were conducted at business unit level, but an annual HRD review was held to review key post-holders, agree successors, agree personal development plans and review any recruitment issues arising (Smith 1990; Mabey and Iles 1993).

Recruitment and selection has become a key strategic lever in other sectors too, and not just for managerial staff. For example, in British

Aerospace, restructuring – in particular, the move to cellular working – led the organization to identify the skills and qualities required to implement the new strategy, through intensive job analysis. More rigorous assessment techniques such as assessment centres were introduced to select appropriate candidates for such positions as team leader and manufacturing centre manager.

In this company and in many other manufacturing organizations, restructuring and job redesign have often demanded financial flexibility and greater emphasis on multi-skilled teams working in flatter, delayered organizations. There has been a shift to employee autonomy, self-monitoring and devolved decision-making in a less stable, more uncertain and more dynamic environment. This has led to greater emphasis on such skills and qualities as teamwork, openness, adaptability, broader vision, tolerance of ambiguity, self-confidence, a positive orientation to change, an ability to see multiple perspectives, a desire to improve, develop, and take on responsibility, and a wish to seek out and act on performance feedback. This has led to the greater use of structured interviews, work sample tests, self-assessment, assessment centres, and psychometric tests (Pearn and Kandola 1988).

In the National Health Service the introduction of General Management in 1984 stimulated interest in ensuring a supply of appropriately qualified people through a three-stage accelerated General Management Training Scheme, to prepare people for board-level posts. Methods were devised which could aid selection decisions, identify high-potential employees, and assist self-development, with many health authorities using assessment centres to identify candidates. This was felt to be particularly important in establishing a common language of managerial competence and a common methodology in a sector where the presence of different professional groups made it difficult to make judgements and comparisons (Alimo-Metcalfe 1989). The 1991 NHS Act has dramatically altered the organization, administration and funding of the NHS by introducing an internal market and a split between purchasers and providers and the creation of NHS trusts with relative commercial and managerial autonomy in such matters as pay, conditions, pricing and contracts. In response, the Oxford Regional Health Authority has instituted programmes of cultural change to help its units make the transition from being bureaucratic and responsive organizations to becoming more entrepreneurial, proactive and autonomous organizations and to help its managers cope with the new demands. Competency models for top and senior managers were devised in order to inform and direct recruitment, selection and development activities, involving psychometric tests, interviews and development centres (Iles and Forster 1993, 1994).

Having outlined some of the ways in which British organizations have attempted to respond to rapid environmental change by specifying the skills, qualities and competences required by employees and by introducing more sophisticated assessment and selection procedures to assess such qualities, we will go on to review some recent trends in recruitment and selection practice before critically examining three models of assessment and selection processes.

RECRUITMENT STRATEGIES

Little systematic research has been done into the ways organizations go about actually attracting candidates to apply for jobs. A useful analysis of the options which are open to organizations attempting to enhance their recruitment efforts is presented by Rynes and Barber (1990) – organizations can attempt to change their recruitment practices, change the inducements or incentives offered to applicants, or widen their recruitment net to target 'non-traditional' sources of applicants such as ethnic minorities, women returners and people with disabilities. In this section we will examine changes in recruitment practices and in particular 'targeted recruitment' in more depth, though it must be acknowledged that recruits are very sensitive to such incentives as job titles, salaries, and bonuses, especially when considering whether to accept a job offer. However, the actual channels or vehicles used to attract candidates also seem to influence whether the right kinds of applicants are encouraged to apply, and to persist in their application. The recruitment stage is the first phase of a process in which both applicant and organization send out signals, check if expectations have been met, make decisions on whether to go to the next stage, and negotiate both legal and psychological contracts. Both parties to the relationship will attempt to influence each other's expectations through a process of mutual exchange and negotiation (Herriot 1989). The kinds of recruitment literature sent out by organizations do seem to influence applicants' intentions to apply, but informal sources of job information such as 'word of mouth' and referrals are generally seen as more specific and accurate sources of information than formal advertisements. These sources seem to attract employees who show longer tenure and lower turnover. This seems due to such applicants having lower (and more realistic?) expectations, and displaying less 'reality shock' when actually appointed (Iles and Robertson 1994). As a result, informal word-of-mouth recruiting is attractive to many employers, in addition to being seen as cheap and as fostering an image of a 'family firm'. Recruits may also be more amenable to social control, due to the obligations felt to sponsors (Jenkins 1986). However, such informal recruiting practices may reduce diversity and encourage the recruiting of 'like by like', perhaps inhibiting creativity, as well as ensuring that sections of the community which are currently under-represented in an organization's workforce remain so, lacking access to the informal networks maintained by employees' families and friends (Iles and Auluck 1991).

If organizations are to recruit more people from currently under-represented groups, passive adherence to formal procedures apparently accessible to all may not be enough. More targeted recruitment practices aimed at particular sections of the community may be necessary, given the substantial evidence for continuing discrimination against women and black people in particular, on grounds unrelated to job performance. Such applicants may not, despite the prejudices of many employers, be less qualified or competent. Women managers, for example, often seem to be more highly qualified than equivalent male managers (Alimo-Metcalfe 1993). In order to pursue such targeted recruitment initiatives, a variety of changes to recruitment practices may be needed. These include statements of equal opportunity intent and of welcoming all applicants, representing diverse employees in photographs, representations, videos, and pen-portraits; advertising vacancies in a wider range of sources and languages; making contacts with a wider range of potential sources of applicants; re-examining personnel specifications to check that they do not discriminate indirectly against particular groups or do include references to such job-relevant attributes as knowledge of community languages or market preferences; and training recruiters so as not to engage in off-putting and perhaps discriminatory questions, messages and signals (Iles and Auluck 1991; Paddison 1990). It appears that such targeted recruitment initiatives can be effective in stimulating applications from the targeted group without deterring applicants from more traditional groups. However, such initiatives often require careful planning and attention to possible legal pitfalls, though the Sex Discrimination Act of 1975 and the Race Relations Act of 1976 do allow 'positive action' in recruitment to encourage applications from under-represented categories. Considerable changes in other HRM areas such as induction, training and development, work practices and organizational culture may also be needed if organizations are not just to recruit but to retain and develop such employees. However, these changes may well improve the effectiveness of HRM generally, not just enhance its impact on under-represented groups.

The recruitment message itself seems likely to affect applicant attraction. Glossy positive images may attract applicants, but may lead to greater disillusionment and higher turnover later, while more 'realistic' job previews, conveying less uniformly favourable messages, may attract fewer applicants but recruit more committed employees as a result. Assessment centres and work samples may also provide such realistic job previews by giving applicants a 'taste' of the job in question, allowing self-selection to take place if this does not match applicants' expectations. Site visits and opportunities to talk to potential colleagues may help in this respect also. Different messages may have different impacts on different groups: subsidized childcare may attract parents, flexible schedules, retired people.

The actual behaviour of recruiters also appears to affect applicants. Women, for example, may be put off from pursuing their application by 'offensive' questioning and comments; the presence of women recruiters and managers on site visits and on interview panels may create more positive impressions. Applicants respond well to recruiters who are seen as competent, informed credible and interpersonally skilled. Especially at the early stages of recruitment, these positive impressions of recruiters seem to influence applicants' willingness to take up job offers (Iles and Robertson 1994). 'Unprofessional' practices and long delays in response seem to put off applicants, who appear to take these signals as an indication of how they will be treated if they should take up a job offer. Applicants also seem to respond more positively towards recruiters who are demographically similar to themselves – an important factor if the organization wishes to engage in 'targeted recruitment'.

Many organizations have increasingly 'externalised' their recruitment activities, especially executive recruitment (Torrington and Mackay 1986). Recruitment consultancies in this area have grown rapidly in recent years, both for executive search (identifying candidates through direct personal contact) and for executive selection (identifying candidates through advertising and shortlisting). In both cases, the consultancy acts as an intermediary between the employer and the candidate. It seems as if companies use executive recruitment consultancies when they feel they lack in-house capabilities, when there is an advantage to having an outside opinion, when confidentiality is crucial, and when speed of recruitment is a priority. Executive recruitment consultancies do not appear to use more sophisticated techniques than references and interviews, though they may subcontract psychological testing (Clark and Clark 1990; Clark 1993).

The recruitment strategies used by organizations appear to interact with other HRM activities. Existing HRM practices, for example, may put a brake on innovative recruitment practices. An emphasis on internal pay equity may reduce the scope for innovative incentive strategies. Centralized HRM procedures may make localized recruitment policies less likely. Changes in recruitment practices may not be effective unless there are changes in other HRM policy areas. Targeting under-represented groups in recruitment, for example, may not be effective if selection criteria and practices remain unchanged, or if appraisal practices are left untouched, or if organizational cultures fail to value positively diversity and differences. Without such changes, such employees may feel marginalized or even harassed, and may leave early. Similarly, recruiting high-level, more qualified applicants may not work unless jobs are redesigned to give greater autonomy, significance and identity.

It is interesting to note that, typically, organizations tend to evaluate the success of their recruitment initiatives in immediate short-term ways, such as whether vacancies are filled with minimally qualified people at acceptable cost, or whether recruitment efforts produce a rise in the number of applicants. However, the quality of the applications and of the acceptances

– measures of effectiveness – are not often assessed. Measures of efficiency, such as cost per period of time taken, acceptance-to-offer ratios, or time lapses between various stages of the process, are also often not taken (Cascio 1987). The ripple effects of recruitment practices on other HRM areas, such as negative or positive impressions gained by applicants transferring to potential applicants or affecting the company image in general, or the effects of salary incentives offered to one group of recruits having a knock-on effect on salary claims of existing staff, or the effects of going outside to recruit staff on the aspirations and commitment of existing staff, are also often not considered.

ASSESSING AND IDENTIFYING OCCUPATIONAL AND MANAGERIAL COMPETENCES

A major issue in recruitment and selection in recent years has concerned the process of identifying relevant qualities in existing staff and potential applicants that will enable an appropriate match to occur between person and job. These qualities have been variously described as skills, knowledge and other attributes (e.g. personality traits) and are increasingly termed 'competences' (UK) or 'competencies' (US) – concepts which we will examine in more detail shortly.

The tool traditionally used to identify relevant attributes has been job analysis, regarded as a critical initial stage in the recruitment and selection process. Job analysis can be categorized into task-oriented and person-oriented methodologies. Task-oriented methodologies generate a list of the activities or tasks required of the job-holder, as derived from observations, diary studies, interviews and surveys. Such tasks are often rated in terms of their importance and frequency. Task-oriented analyses are often specific to a particular job and give little information on the skills or qualities needed to do the job adequately; these need to be inferred. Indeed, increasingly, many staff, such as graduates, are taken on not to do a specific job but to develop a career involving frequent job changes. And recent developments in HRM practice such as flexibility, teamwork and multi-skilling also limit the usefulness of such task-oriented approaches. As a consequence, person-oriented approaches, such as the critical incident technique, and repertory grid and behavioural event interviews have grown in importance as a way of generating more directly the skills and behaviours needed to perform a job (e.g. 'interpersonal skills', as compared to 'chairing meetings').

A principal aim of the job analysis is to generate a job description (the job context, its associated tasks, responsibilities and duties) and the person specification (the skills, characteristics and other attributes deemed necessary to do the job). Conventional job analysis tends to assume that there is such a target as 'the job', defined in terms of a stable collection of discrete tasks, and that the knowledge, skills and abilities identified as required for performance are for a job that currently exists. However, in the face of the variety of changes currently experienced by organizations (technological change, restructuring, globalization, the growth in a diverse workforce, mergers and acquisitions) such assumptions are unlikely to hold. In addition many jobs are newly created, with no precedents to fall back on.

Conventional job analysis procedures may therefore be historic and backward-looking, rather than forward-looking and strategic. One alternative is to carry out a strategic job analysis, where workshops are held with key employees and other experts to identify future trends and their implications for future skills, involving such techniques as looking at best practice, examining other sectors, and scenario planning (Schneider and Konz 1989). For example, one UK-based accountancy firm which wished to move towards becoming a more entrepreneurial, market-oriented 'managed business' attempted to identify the skills and qualities required by partners in the future as well as in the present. These included identifying selling opportunities, commercial awareness, and persuasiveness. It then held development centres to assess partners against such competences (Shackleton 1992).

Recent attempts to identify and assess the key skills and attributes needed by managers and other employees in making selection and placement decisions, have focused on the concept of 'occupational competences'. This is characteristic of both American and British approaches, though there are some significant differences as well as similarities between the two approaches. Job competency in the American tradition has been defined as 'an underlying characteristic of a person which results in effective and/or superior performance in a job' (Klemp 1980), and such competences are derived through a person-oriented job analysis known as a 'behavioural event interview'. The aim has been to identify those characteristics that distinguish superior managerial performance, regarded as generic though receiving different emphases depending on managerial level or sector. This research (Boyatzis 1982) has distinguished between 'threshold' competences, necessary as minimal requirements to do the job at all, and 'differentiators', seen as bringing about superior performance. In addition to behavioural event interviews, projective tests of motivation such as the picture story exercise and learning styles inventories have also been used. This 'motivational' emphasis seems to be a product of the long-standing interest of David McClelland, the head of the McBer consultancy which carried out work on behalf of the American Management Association in the late 1970s, in motivation and the notion of a basic 'drive for competence', mastery or effectiveness, held to characterize all human beings. One British example of an organization using the Boyatzis generic competency model for senior managers is Manchester Airport (Jackson 1989).

The UK approach to occupational and managerial competences, as embodied in the work of the National Council for Vocational Qualifications and the Management Charter Initiative, is somewhat different, being more geared to job performance in specific functions and to developing national standards of performance expressed in terms of outputs rather than inputs. Occupational competence is defined as the ability to perform the activities within an occupation to the standards expected in employment. These standards are described in terms of elements of competence which identify a required function, performance criteria which identify acceptable performance in the function, and range statements which indicate the contexts in which the standards are to be met. The job analysis technique used – functional analysis – contrasts with the American approach in being task-oriented, identifying necessary roles, tasks and duties of the *occupation*, rather than the skills exhibited by successful role *incumbents*. There is, however, a parallel 'personal competence' model based on a person-oriented critical incident and repertory grid technique and resembling Boyatzis (1982) very closely. The UK emphasis is much more on minimal standards of performance as exhibited by experienced managers, rather than the characteristics associated with effective or superior managers as in Boyatzis (1982).

Four main types of criticisms have been made of such generic competence models:

1 One line of criticism concerns the conceptual ambiguity underlying the term, since it sometimes seems to refer to behaviours or actions, sometimes to the abilities or characteristics underlying behaviour, and sometimes to the outcomes or results of actions. Interestingly, the distinction between 'performance' and 'competence' was popularized in American behavioural science by Chomsky (1957) in linguistics; the British use of the term seems to make competence synonymous with performance. Sparrow and Bognanno (1993), for example, distinguish between 'competences' – identified through functional analysis and indicating 'areas of competence' and used to generate standards (typified by the MCI approach) – and 'competencies', behavioural repertoires brought to a role by effective or excellent performers (typified by Boyatzis (1982)) and the organization-specific competency models discussed below. However, it is not the competency labels that are crucial, but the specific behavioural indicators.
2 A second line of criticism has been to focus on the generic 'off-the-shelf' nature of existing competency models, arguing that particular sectors, industries, and organizational cultures require much more organization-specific sets of competences, in part to ensure that employees can identify with the language of the model used, and to generate greater commitment and ownership. For example, Cadbury-Schweppes has sought to focus even more closely on competence, as restructuring and de-layering have highlighted the importance of managerial skills. It has attempted to define a 'language of competence' in order to 'find better ways of describing

managers' and to help managers gain 'behavioural literacy' (Glaze 1989: 44). In the late 1980s BP was also undergoing a series of changes, involving increased internationalization, greater emphasis on corporate and national cultures, a move towards enhanced entrepreneurialism and market orientation and devolved accountability. It sought to identify key behaviours associated with effective management performance as a way of tapping into the corporate culture, involving key players and using the language of the organization (Greatorex and Phillips 1989). In attempting to implement the corporate strategy around an organization-specific corporate-wide competency-based model, BP had problems in transferring this Anglo-American model across a variety of national cultures. BP regarded the competencies as generally capable of cross-cultural implementation and as accurately stating the shifts required in management behaviour. The behavioural anchors used to describe specific competencies, however, were sometimes seen as 'culturally provocative' (Sparrow and Bognanno 1993: 55), so different countries were encouraged to offer their own illustrations of how they might change behaviour within the context of the broad competency framework.

3 A third criticism of many existing competency models is that they are often present- or past-focused, drawing on what has made for successful performance in the past, rather than what will make for successful performance in the future. Whether generic or specific, competency models tend to be historic and retrospective in nature, rather than strategic and prospective. A variety of responses has been made to the challenge that, if the essence of the HRM approach is to respond to organizational change and the implications of that change for employees' roles and skills, then competence models based on empirical studies of what present managers do and have done will describe the requirements of the past rather than the future. One response has been to identify 'competences for changing conditions', which are more suitable for dynamic, turbulent environments than for bureaucratic, stable environments. For example, in the USA Schroder (1989), on the basis of complex team simulations, attempted to identify eleven 'high performance competencies', or observable skills resulting in high levels of performance in changing environments. Arguing that the financial services sector is now operating in just such a turbulent environment, Cockerill (1989) contends that such competences can be reliably assessed by behavioural observations in the workplace as well as under simulated assessment centre conditions. The approach taken by BP was similar, in that it attempts to identify competences which 'enabled change to happen', whatever that change might prove to be (Sparrow and Bognanno 1993). Again Morgan (1988) on the basis of workshops with a small number of Canadian managers, attempted to describe managerial competences for a turbulent world', that is behaviours that will enable change to happen and enable managers

to 'ride the waves of change'. The danger of such a list is that such competences are often described in very abstract, generalized terms, remote from observable behaviour, making it very difficult for assessors to discern how managers are expected to do these things well. Sparrow and Boam (1992) and Sparrow and Bognanno (1993) argue that in many cases, organizations will want more specific, focused sets of strategic, future-oriented competences – not so much 'competences for change' as 'changing competences', that is, competences which are specific to particular organizational contexts, situations and environments. The relevance of particular competences to the organization as a whole or to a particular job or career stream will shift; so competences may well exhibit 'life cycles'. Some may be 'emerging', not particularly relevant at present but of growing importance in the future. Others may be 'mature', becoming of less importance in the future due to strategic shifts, technological change or organizational restructuring. Others may be transitional, relevant to an early stage, such as a new venture, but perhaps less so as the organization matures. Still others may be 'core', of enduring importance and underlying effective performance, whatever strategic direction is taken by the organization. In consequence, competence profiles will have a 'shelf life', though 'the more forward-looking the profile the longer is its shelf life' (Sparrow and Bognanno 1993: 56).

4 The fourth criticism of existing competence models is that they give insufficient emphasis to key managerial activities and skills like creativity, impact or sensitivity (termed 'soft' competences by Jacobs (1989)) which are hard to measure in any circumstances (though they are the kinds of qualities psychometric personality inventories are specifically designed to assess).

However, despite these criticisms, it remains the case that competence approaches can help achieve a more strategically focused HRM, described by Sparrow and Bognanno (1993) as exhibiting 'vertical integration' with business strategy and 'horizontal integration' across all the HRM policy and practice areas. Mabey and Iles (1993), using the terms 'internal' and 'external' integration, argue that competence approaches, by being couched in terms of actual behaviour and being sensitive to the language used by line managers, can help achieve the external integration of HRM and business strategies by specifying individual behaviours that can clearly exemplify the direction taken by the new strategy or culture. They can give opportunities for people to identify with and commit themselves to such changes. By using a common competence language across all the HRM 'levers' such as recruitment, selection, appraisal and development, coherence and consistency can be given to HRM policy and practice. This can help ensure that internal integration is achieved through 'competency architectures' (Mabey and Iles 1993).

MODELS OF SELECTION AND ASSESSMENT

The psychometric/objective model of selection and assessment

Selection and assessment research and practice in the UK have been heavily influenced by what might be termed the 'psychometric' model, a model which has been most fully developed in the United States. This model, in a variety of forms, is represented in most textbooks of HRM personnel management and organizational psychology as good professional practice, if not fully represented in actual practice.

The model has its roots in nineteenth- and early twentieth-century British work on individual differences and in the development of sophisticated psychometric and statistical techniques. Its paradigm status in work psychology and personnel management owes much to its application to mass vocational selection in the USA during both World Wars. Its principal focus is the 'job', conceived of as a set of discrete tasks. In this model, performance criteria are selected and individual attributes of various kinds (knowledge, skills, abilities, etc.) are chosen as predictors of job performance. The attributes selected are then measured through a variety of procedures (tests, interviews, biodata, etc.) and the assessment process validated, primarily in terms of criteria-related predictive validity (how well the predictor actually predicts job performance), usually expressed as a correlation coefficient. Other validity dimensions (e.g. construct, content validity) are also sometimes considered.

This model appears to value individualism (individual attributes are taken to predict individual performance), managerialism (the major criterion of performance is the achievement of organizational goals as defined by top management) and utility (cost-benefit analysis of the monetary benefits conferred on organizations in using different selection procedures), though other concerns such as bias or adverse impact on women and minorities are also taken into account. Recent developments in utility theory in assessing the benefits of investing in good selection practice have been often attempted to give psychologists a say in the 'language of business' equal to that of other business professionals (Herriot 1993).

However, this model rests on a number of assumptions that are open to challenge. One is that, by and large people do not change much – the characteristics they display before assessment remain quite stable, which is why prediction of job performance is possible. It also assumes that objective assessment of individual attributes is possible, and that this can be used to predict job performance. In addition the assumption seems to be that job content also does not change much, and that it consists primarily of specific sets of tasks which can be identified through job analysis. It also makes the assumption that job performance is measurable, though 'objective' assessments of job performance are often hard to come by and supervisors' evaluations of performance are often used instead. Finally, the central assumption made is that the key purpose of assessment is the prediction of job performance.

Clearly this model has a number of considerable strengths. Individual differences in performance do contribute significantly to differences in organizational performance, a contention underlying much of the growth in HRM in recent years. However, many other factors also affect organizational performance, and it does seem that people change as a result of job experiences. The kinds of attributes assessed by psychologists – for example, locus of control, self-direction, intellectual flexibility – do seem to be affected by such work experiences as occupational success, racial discrimination, and the kinds of jobs one performs (e.g. Kohn and Schooler 1982; Iles and Robertson 1994).

A variety of factors are causing many researchers and practitioners, especially in Western Europe, to question fundamental aspects of this model. As organizations change, decentralize, restructure, get flatter, and devolve accountability, the conception of the 'job' as a stable collection of discrete tasks has come under pressure (e.g. Atkinson 1984). Multi-skilling, flexible specialization and self-directed work teams have made this notion of a 'job' rather outdated, and these and other changes such as downsizing and the growth of 'portfolio careers' have changed our concepts of career success and career development. Knowledge and skill-based reward systems have also undermined the use of job evaluation and the role of the 'job' as the basis for reward systems (e.g. Armstrong 1993; Luthans and Fox 1989). Self-directed work teams, matrix structures and notions of empowerment have challenged the traditional role of the supervisor and the role of supervisors' evaluations, and the increasingly diverse nature of the workforce has challenged some of our assumptions about evaluation and the validity of assessment instruments. In addition, in Western Europe, assessment has come to play a more strategic role in facilitating individual development and cultural and organizational change, rather than in selection alone (Iles 1992; Mabey and Iles 1993). Many of these changes have led to the rise of a more 'process' model of assessment in Western Europe, a model rooted in social psychology rather than in the psychology of individual differences.

A more long-standing challenge to this paradigm of assessment has come from political and legal challenges to the fairness and validity of assessment and selection procedures. In the US in particular, such challenges have arisen over groups with 'visible differences', such as race, age and gender. Similar concerns, especially with regard to gender but less markedly with regard to age and race, have been manifest in recent years in Europe. With the rise of the civil rights movement and feminism, equal employment opportunity and the avoidance of unfair discrimination have become important social values.

Assessment instruments have increasingly been seen as exhibiting unfair and illegal discriminatory features, and the criterion of 'bias' or 'adverse impact', defined as the degree to which a technique or procedure rejects or accepts a disproportionate number of applicants from one social group, or screens out groups' members unfairly in a way that cannot be justified in terms of their ability to do the job, has become an increasingly important evaluative standard against which to judge selection procedures. In part, this situation led to a fall in the use of psychometric tests in the 1970s; in part it also stimulated research into 'validity generalization', to show that tests *were* in fact valid across situations. It also stimulated research into creating selection procedures which were as valid, if not more so, as psychometric tests but which generated less adverse impact. Work samples, assessment centres and structured, criteria-related interviews seemed to fit the bill in this respect. All of these procedures display a concern with thorough job analysis to identify the criteria or competences held to constitute effective job performance and a concern to sample job content directly in the selection procedure itself, in the form of simulations of some kind. This in itself marks an interesting departure from the traditional psychometric paradigm, with its concern to assess rather abstract and general 'signs' as predictors. Traditionally, the predictor signs (rather abstract personality traits or intellectual abilities) are quite remote from actual measures of job performance (Wernimont and Campbell 1968). In the 'sample' approach, predictor and criteria measures become as close as possible, both representing job performance in some way. Such procedures not only seem less biased than psychometric tests or traditional unstructured interviews; they also seem to be of similar or even greater validity (Robertson and Iles 1988).

This whole area shows that the agenda for the psychometric-objective model has not in fact been set by neutral, scientific interests, but by political, social and legal pressures. More sophisticated critical adherents to the model (e.g. Hesketh and Robertson 1993) have called for a clearer conceptual appreciation of the relationships between and among predictors and criteria, and for a better understanding of measurement issues in selection. This position acknowledges that

> the selection literature has been atheoretical, with a primary focus on identifying approaches and techniques that have practical utility. Comparatively little emphasis has been placed on the development of conceptual frameworks for selection or on trying to understand why some procedures work and others do not.
>
> (Ibid.: 3)

Their call is for developing a process model of selection that places it in a broader theoretical perspective of human abilities, personality, motivation and skill acquisition. Such a model also requires an examination of the task demands of environments and their interaction with individual psychological variables (ibid.). Hesketh and Robertson point out that research findings on the assessment centre challenge the construct validity of what is being assessed,

> with studies showing that ratings tend to cluster according to exercises rather than in terms of the dimensions being assessed. This question of what is being measured by these attempts to assess job competences is unresolved and the basis of the validity of such methods is uncertain.
>
> (Ibid.)

This focus on measurement issues leads to a discussion of an interactionist social process model of assessment and selection, one much more influenced by a European social and political agenda and one much more rooted in social rather than in differential psychology. Its concerns are less with measurement, prediction and job performance than with relationships, attitudes, interaction, negotiation, identities and self-perceptions – distinctly social psychological concerns.

Towards an emerging social process model?

In one form, this approach focuses on impact and process and considers the selection process as a social process (e.g. Herriot 1989), as well as the impact of selection and assessment processes on candidates (e.g. Iles and Robertson 1989; Iles *et al.* 1989; Robertson *et al.* 1991; Fletcher 1991; de Witte *et al.* 1992). Iles and Robertson (1989, 1994), for example, have presented a theoretical model of the impact of selection and assessment processes on individuals, arguing that both the selection decision and candidates' attitudes to the selection process are likely to have effects on a variety of psychological processes, including organizational and career attitudes, self-efficacy, self-esteem and other psychological states, and that these are likely to lead to such behaviours as job and career withdrawal.

The impact of such processes is likely to be moderated by a variety of factors such as candidates' individual differences, prior information and explanation, features of the assessment process such as the quality, quantity and timing of any feedback, and contextual variables such as the amount of organizational and social support provided to candidates. Partial support was provided for this model by empirical studies of development centres and assessment procedures in UK financial services organizations. Participants in a UK clearing bank's fast-track management development programme perceived the fairness, accuracy and adequacy of the assessment techniques used in the programme (biodata, situational interviews and assessment centres) very differently, and their perceptions were influenced by whether they were judged to have passed or failed the procedure.

In general, participants viewed assessment centres more positively, and were more likely to react positively to procedures if selected by them. In early career stages candidates' post-assessment commitment to their organization was related primarily to the perceived career impact of the procedure. In later career stages, commitment was more related to the perceived adequacy of the procedure (Robertson *et al.* 1991). Other British studies have shown that assessment centre failure may lead to lower self-esteem and a need for achievement (Fletcher 1991) and that development centre participation can affect career plans and attitudes (Iles *et al.* 1989).

This 'social process' model of assessment makes several assumptions which contrast with those underlying the US psychometric model. One is that people do change constantly in the course of their career in organizations. This assumption underlies much of the British work on career transitions and work-role transitions (Nicholson 1984), as well as providing much of the impetus to the European training and development work, which often make extensive use of action learning and work-based learning. Another assumption, in contrast to the US model, is that subjective self-perceptions are critical to people's work motivation and performance, and that these are influenced by assessment and selection procedures. The jobs people do increasingly involve interaction, negotiation and mutual influence, often taking place in multi-skilled, flexible, self-directed work teams. This emphasis on negotiation, interaction and mutual influence is perhaps one reason why European organizations continue to rely on the interview as the main selection method, as it opens up opportunities for a bilateral exchange of views, mutual decision-making, and mutual negotiation. In addition the recognition that assessment processes are social processes is particularly appropriate to the role of assessment in facilitating development, whether it be individual or organizational development.

Some recent American research into the impact of selection and assessment techniques, perhaps stimulated by the European research, has also looked to social psychology to examine assessment processes. One stream of research has examined the interview as a process of interaction, looking at the role of such variables as non-verbal behaviour, age, disability, appearance, gender, race and physical attractiveness on interviewers' ratings, though often in acontextual, ahistorical ways and often employing students as 'interviewers' and using 'paper people' consisting of CVs, photographs, or brief taped transcripts of interviewers (e.g. Herriot 1987; Powell 1990; Heilman 1985). British research in this tradition has been more likely to employ field studies, examining line managers' ratings and actual assessment centre results (e.g. Iles 1991). In this particular study a bank's assessment centre ratings were in general not related to ratings of appearance, physical attractiveness, or gender, in contrast to the results obtained in many American laboratory interview studies.

Other forms of this social process approach stress how actual selection processes deviate from the prescribed, idealized psychometric model. In some cases researchers simply stress this divergence:

> recruitment practices are not as sophisticated as the professional model implies: that job descriptions are not widely used; that no explicit evaluation of methods is used . . . [but] . . . Firms do have institutionalized methods of recruitment . . . however these recruitment procedures are normally a product of custom and practice.
>
> (Windholf and Wood 1988: 1)

In other cases, the researcher seeks to explain this discrepancy in terms of key organizational processes. Here the focus is less on accounting for the gap between reality and rhetoric, and more on understanding how the rhetoric is used to justify a decision made on grounds other than those allowed for by the formal rules. Salaman and Thompson (1978), for example, argued that the selection of British army officers reveals the use, in practice, of a set of values, understandings and assumptions among selecting officers, shared among them as part of their officer culture, which determine the outcome of selection choices, but which are masked by the deployment of, and by reference to, the formal procedures: 'These factors ensure that an inevitable residue of flexible *ad hoc* practices within the otherwise scientific selection process undermines the scientificity (objectivity and universalism) of the evaluations, while maintaining the "scientific" character' (ibid.: 303).

Another form of a social process perspective is far more radical. Unlike the psychometric approach, this focuses not on the rational properties of actions but on the processes whereby selection systems and decisions are presented as rational at all – how a decision is formulated so that it complies with and thus supports the impression of reasonableness. Thus the conventional approach to selection which seeks to assess the scientificity and systematic status of a process or decision is replaced by an approach which looks at how selectors and others demonstrate to themselves and others, that the process and decision were reasonable (Silverman and Jones 1973, 1976).

Selection, knowledge and power

Selection and assessment can be seen not in terms of their efficiency or reasonableness, or even in terms of the ways in which reasonableness is constructed and displayed, but in terms of the relationships between these processes and the expertise on which they are based, and the practice of power within organizations. So far, the models of selection discussed take efficiency as their primary concern, focus on ways of improving the efficiency of the processes, or seek to explain current developments in selection procedures and criteria in terms of changes in the nature of work organization – in particular, as Townley (1989) argues, in terms of 'the importance attached to increased individual discretion, and the implications this has for the administration of work' (ibid.: 102).

Thus selection, and current developments in the identification of competences, may be regarded as elements in the 'government' of organizations.

This approach addresses the ways in which power, knowledge and practice mutually support and reproduce each other. This is not simply to argue that practices and knowledge support power in an ideological or legitimating manner; it is instead to argue that power is that

> which traverses *all* practices – from the 'macro' to the 'micro' – through which persons are ruled, mastered, held in check, administered, steered, guided, by means of which they are led by others or have come to direct or regulate their own actions.
>
> (Rose 1990)

Power is thus not located merely in the actions of the State, or, within the enterprise, in the actions of senior managers; it is present in all knowledge and practice that regulate individuals, including of course their own. Thus this approach allows us to look for the exercise or practice of power in activities which initially may seem far removed from established centres of power, or removed through the nature and exercise of scientific expertise from the interests and values of the powerful. The process of selection is an obvious example of the exercise of power within the detached and scientific process of competence-based assessment (Hollway 1991).

Power is inherent in knowledge itself, and in the techniques which that knowledge informs and justifies; for knowledge, as the analysis of competences and the assessment processes reveals, plays a major role in constructing the individual manager as someone calculable, discussible and someone who is capable of being comprehended in the process of, and as the subject of, senior managerial interventions and decisions: the process of selection and assessment. The definition of competences may be based on psychometrically informed structures of competence and the process of assessment may be based on psychometrically scrupulous testing instruments, but these expertises are not simply the servants of power; they *are* power itself, having crucial significance for key decisions about selection, promotion, rejection, and for the characteristics which are defined – and accepted (by all parties) – as necessary and properly constituting the new manager. Nor is this their only significance. What is also central to the importance of competence-based assessment is that it defines key selection qualities, and maintains the necessity and neutrality of these dimensions.

As Hollway (1991) has noted, the expertise surrounding the assessment process should be regarded as being produced rather than discovered (ibid.: 1). Similarly, the search for managerial competences has been produced as a key feature of the process of HRS change.

Miller and Rose (1993) have made the point that, following Foucault, the term 'government' can usefully be employed to focus on

> the shifting ambitions and concerns of all those social authorities that have sought to administer the lives of individuals and associations, focusing our attention on the diverse mechanisms through which the actions and judgement of persons and organisations have been linked to political objectives.
>
> (Ibid.: 75–6)

These authors argue that this project will be greatly enhanced by a further concept – that of 'governmentality' – which is used to draw attention to the diverse and various processes and techniques. They quote Foucault: 'an ensemble formed by the institutions, procedures, analyses, and reflections, the calculations and tactics, that allow the exercise of this very specific albeit complex form of power' (Foucault 1979: 20, quoted in Miller and Rose 1993: 76).

The processes of selection and assessment offer a striking example of a major way in which selectors' actions and judgements on candidates (internal in assessment, external in selection) which are critical for organizational restructuring and for individual experience, are structured and made rational in terms of expert-derived systems and criteria of selection. For example, during 1991–2, within the Post Office a process of staff assessment was conducted wherein 17,000 staff were assessed against the identified competences required for their current job. The process of assessment varied in intensity, but for many involved attendance at a two-day assessment centre. The process of assessment was geared to the identified competences, which were themselves geared to the new styles of leadership seen as required for the new-style Post Office; it resulted in the loss of 3,500 members of staff.

Processes of assessment and selection reveal the interrelationships between knowledge and power, demonstrate the ubiquity of power/knowledge practices, and show the role of a form of organizational governmentality which allow the exercise of power through calculation, assessment and knowledge. Processes of selection and assessment, wherein individuals and employees are 'known' in terms of a set of qualities (competences), measured against these, and processed in terms of this assessment, are as revealing of organizations as they are of individuals.

To see the processes of selection and assessment as elements of a discourse of HRS means regarding selection and assessment as an element of governmentality. Miller and Rose (1993) define discourse as

> a technology of thought, requiring attention to the particular technical devices of writing, listing, numbering and computing that render a realm into discourse as a knowable, calculable and administrable object. 'Knowing' an object in such a way that it can be governed is more than a purely speculative activity: it requires the invention of procedures of

> notation, ways of collecting and presenting statistics, the transportation of these to centres where calculations and judgements can be made.
>
> (Ibid.: 79)

This is a major focus of our conception of the selection process. We note the ways in which the identification of management competences occurs; the technology of the assessment of these competences represents a remarkable instance of the 'knowing' and constituting of individuals and managers and individuals as managers. The discourse discussed here consists of a complex of intellectual, science-based conceptual frameworks (units of competence identified and distinguished through an elaborate research process involving the opinions of managers themselves, then formulated into discrete 'real' and relevant elements of human action) being allied to a psychologically and psychometrically based technology for the identification and assessment and, crucially, measurement of individuals against the selected competences.

The 'knowing' and measurement of individuals in terms of frameworks of managerial competences is clearly an example of the exercise of organizational power – specifically the power of HRS changes, and their impact on and requirements of individuals, as candidates or employees.

Keenoy and Anthony (1993) have argued that one of the implications of the approach to organizational change known as human resources management or strategy is that it allows a

> distancing of managerial responsibility from the outcomes of HR policies . . . [this] is also reflected in the particular practices which have come to be associated with HRM. In general what they seek to do is incorporate responsibility for outcomes into the performance of the individual employee.
>
> (Ibid.: 245)

This analysis also holds for the assessment of competences. Townley (1989), for example, argues that recent changes in selection processes and criteria, of the sort described earlier in this chapter, are associated with the emphasis, within HRS/M-style change, on

> the increased emphasis on 'flexibility' or the requirement for greater exercise of discretion. . . . The changes which have been associated with the introduction of selection and HRM generally, have been primarily associated with moves towards 'Japanisation' or 'flexibility' and the commitment to move away from 'bureaucratised' procedures.
>
> (Ibid.: 106)

However, the approach suggested here differs somewhat in emphasis from that of Townley. Townley seeks to make connections between structural (HRM) changes and developments within the selection process, arguing that developments in selection methods reflect and channel the organizational priorities or processes of HRS change. In a sense, her analysis therefore focuses on the rationality of these selection developments, albeit a rationality that is defined in terms of new organizational forms for new forms and dimensions of control. Here, however, we wish to draw attention not to the ways in which developments in selection processes support structural changes, in practice, but to the ways in which processes of organizational change and developments in selection criteria and systems cohere and support each other as a set of related and mutually supportive ideas, a discourse of HRS which certainly impacts on employees and candidates, and demonstrates the practices of power, but the effectiveness of which is defined by the discourse itself.

A further and closely related feature of such discourses is that they attend to, and define and constitute, the self – the subject – in this case, the manager, composed of measured quantities of identified competences. And it is precisely by constituting, rather than opposing, the subjectivity of individuals that the power of organization, and indeed of human resource strategies, is exercised. The HRS discourse which defines managers and managerial competences, and which is represented in the human technology of the assessment centre, creates and shapes individuals as subjects – in this case in terms of the constituent competences of the 'new' managers as 'required' by prevalent forms and directions of organizational change. Furthermore the discourse of HRS also constructs a necessary and closed loop of causation: a conception of the environment which requires that organizations develop certain forms of business strategy, which in turn needs the support of certain organizational structures, cultures and personnel systems. These in turn require the new, competence-based manager. Thus we witness how, as Rose (1990) remarks, power works, not against, or in opposition to, the subject (the individual versus the State, private versus public, the organization against the employee, etc.) but through the construction, measurement, analysis and treatment of subjectivity – through the ways in which 'subjectivity has become an essential object and target for certain strategies, tactics and procedures of regulation' (ibid.: 15).

The frameworks and associated assessment procedures discussed in this chapter can be seen as offering a striking instance of the expert constitution of the self. Competences themselves, as we have seen, are presented as real and deep underlying features of humans, *qua* managers. Further organizational progress (the 'career') is based upon evidence that an individual is able to offer that s/he has such competences. Frequently, disappointed and rejected candidates from the assessment process will be offered counselling or training in order to support them through the trauma of discovery not simply that they had failed a test, but that they had revealed a lack of key deep qualities. The focus of the discourse therefore is the topic on which, as argued here, it centres – the subjectivity of the individual, defined in terms of qualities and competences, assessed against these, and offered support to develop, or compensation and counselling for lacking these qualities. We maintain not only that efforts to define and measure managerial competences represent a paradigmatic example of a discourse within an organizational content, but also that to regard these processes in this way helps to illuminate aspects and implications overlooked by more traditional discussions of the topic.

The majority of studies focusing on the government of organizations have chosen to address the nature and impact of 'enterprise' as a significant theme (see Rose 1990). Such a focus is understandable and valuable. It has found echo in the earlier discussions (see above on the relationship between developments in selection and restructuring towards more devolved, decentralized, less bureaucratic forms). However, the focus here is slightly different: while the notion of enterprise undoubtedly serves as a major element of the process under discussion, not least because it serves as a powerful relay allowing and defining critical connections between notions of 'environment', organization and organizational change (in certain directions which liberate employees' creativity and commitment) and the individual, in our analysis we also wish to include another meta narrative – that of human resource strategies (HRS) which, while it is significantly infused with enterprise, also carries other elements which deserve attention. While HRS certainly depends upon notions of enterprise as a quality which is necessary for survival within a market economy it also introduces a package of elements focusing on such key ideas as the importance of 'integration', of achieving a strong culture, of quality, flexibility, etc., all of which relate to conceptions of the key competences and responsibilities of management. Also one of the features of HRS is that while on the one hand it accords a special status to enterprise (and associated values such as 'ownership' of individuals' work responsibilities, devolution of authority to the lowest level, etc.) at all levels of analysis (environmental, organizational, individual), it is also forced to recognize the possibility of conflict between some key HRS themes and market forces.

In the context of this chapter the most important element of HRS is that is serves as an overarching set of assumptions, techniques, data, frameworks, models and assessments which make sense of, and guide, the restructuring of organizations and management, within which the development and assessment of management competences occurs, contributes and makes sense.

REFERENCES

Alimo-Metcalfe, B.C. (1989) *The Use of Assessment Centres in the NHS*, Leeds: NHS Training Authority, University of Leeds.

—— (1993) 'Women in management: organizational socialization and assessment practices that prevent career advancement', *International Journal of Selection and Assessment* 1(2): 68–83.

Armstrong, M. (1993) *Managing*, Buckingham: Open University Press.

Atkinson, J. (1984) 'Managing strategies for flexible organizations', *Personnel Management*: 28–31.

Beaumont, P. (1993) *Human Resource Management: Key Concepts and Skills*, London: Sage.

Bethell-Fox, C. (1992) *Identifying and Assessing Managerial Competences*, Milton Keynes: Open University.

Boam, R. and Sparrow, P. (1992) *Focusing on Human Resources: a Competency-Based Approach*, Maidenhead: McGraw-Hill.

Boyatzis, R.E. (1982) *The Competent Manager: a Model for Effective Performance*, New York: John Wiley.

Cascio, W.F. (1987) *Applied Psychology in Personnel Selection* (2nd edn), Englewood Cliffs, NJ: Prentice-Hall.

Chomsky, N. (1957) *Syntactic Structures*, The Hague: Moufflon.

Clark, I. and Clark, T. (1990) 'Personnel management and the use of executive recruitment consultancies', *Human Resource Management Journal* 1(1): 46–62.

Clark, T. (1993) 'Selection methods used by executive search consultancies in four European countries: a survey and critique', *International Journal of Selection and Assessment* 1(1), January.

Cockerill, A.C. (1989) 'The kind of competence for rapid change', *Personnel Management* 21(9), September.

Cressey, J. and Jones, B. (1992) *Banks and Cars in European Perspective*, Milton Keynes: Open University.

de Witte, K., van Laere, B. and Vervaecke, P. (1992) 'Assessment techniques: towards a new perspective?', paper presented to the workshop on Psychological aspects of Employment, Sofia, September.

Fletcher, C. (1991) 'Candidates' reactions to assessment centres and their outcomes: a longitudinal study', *Journal of Occupational Psychology* 64: 117–27.

Glaze, A. (1989) 'Cadbury's dictionary of competence', *Personnel Management*, July: 44–8.

Gratton, L. (1989) 'Work of the manager', in P. Herriot (ed.) *Assessment and Selection in Organizations*, Chichester: John Wiley & Sons.

Greatorex, T. and Phillips, P. (1989) 'Oiling the wheels of competence', *Personnel Management* August: 36–9.

Heilman and Stopek, M.H. (1985) 'Attractiveness and corporate success: different causal attributions for males and females', *Journal of Applied Psychology* 70: 379–88.

Herriot, P. (1987) 'The selection interview', in P.B. Warr (ed.), *Psychology at Work* (3rd edn), Harmondsworth: Penguin.

—— (1989a) *Recruitment in the 1990s*, London: Institute of Personnel Management.

—— (1989b) 'Selection as a social process', in J.M. Smith and I.T. Robertson (eds) *Advances in Selection and Assessment*, Chichester: John Wiley & Sons.

—— (1993) 'A paradigm bursting at the seams', *Journal of Organisational Behaviour* 5: 23–6.

Hesketh, B. and Robertson, I. (1993) 'Validating personnel selection: a process model for research practice', *International Journal of Selection and Assessment* 1(1): 41–9.

Higgs, M. (1988) *Management Development Strategy in the Financial Sector*, London: Macmillan.

Hollway, W. (1991) *Work Psychology and Organisational Behaviour*, London: Sage.

Iles, P.A. (1991) 'Using assessment and development centres to facilitate equal opportunity in selection and career development', *Equal Opportunities International* 8(5): 1–26.

—— (1992) 'Centres of excellence? Assessment and development centres, managerial competences and human resources strategies', *British Journal of Management* 3(2): 79–90.

Iles, P.A. and Auluck, R.K. (1991) 'The experience of black workers', in M. Davidson and J. Earnshaw (eds) *Vulnerable Workers: Psychological and Legal Issues*, Chichester: John Wiley.

Iles, P.A. and Forster, A. (1993) 'Collaborative development centres, approaches to increasing change in European organizations', paper presented to American Society for Training and Development Conference, Atlanta, May.

—— and —— (1994) 'Collaborative development centres: the social process model in action?', *International Journal of Selection and Assessment* 1: 59–64.

Iles, P.A. and Mabey, C. (1993) 'Managerial career development techniques effectiveness, acceptability and availability', *British Journal of Management* 4: 103–18.

Iles, P.A. and Robertson, I.T. (1989) 'The impact of selection procedures in candidates', in P. Herriot (ed.) *Assessment and Selection in Organisations*, Chichester: John Wiley & Sons.

—— and —— (1994) 'The impacts of personnel selection techniques in candidates', in A. Anderson and P. Heriot (eds) *Handbook of Assessment and Selection in Organizations*, Chichester: John Wiley & Sons.

Iles, P.A., Mabey, C. and Robertson, I.T. (1990) 'HRM practices and employee commitment: possibilities, pitfalls and paradoxes', *British Journal of Management* 1: 147–57.

Iles, P.A., Robertson, I.T. and Rout, U. (1989) 'Assessment-based development centres', *Journal of Managerial Psychology* 4(3): 11–16.

Jackson, L. (1989) 'Turning airport managers into high-fliers', *Personnel Management* October: 80–5.

Jacobs, R. (1989) 'Getting the measure of management competence', *Personnel Management* June: 32–7.

Jenkins, R. (1986) *Racism and Recruitment: Managers, Organizations and Equal Opportunity in the Labour Market*, Cambridge: Cambridge University Press.

Keenoy, T. and Anthony, P. (1993) 'HRM: metaphor, meaning and morality', in P. Blyton and P. Turnbull (eds) *Reassessing Human Resource Management*, London: Sage.

Klein, J.A., Edge, G.M. and Kass, T. (1991) 'Skill-based competition', *Journal of General Management* 16(4): 1–15.

Klemp, O. (1980) 'The assessment of occupational competence', report to the National Institute of Education, Washington DC.

Kohn, M.L. and Schooler, C.C. (1982) 'Job conditions and personality: a longitudinal assessment of their reciprocal effects', *American Journal of Sociology* 87: 1257–86.

Luthans, F. and Fox, M.L. (1989) 'Update on skill based pay', *Personnel*: 26–31.

Mabey, C. and Iles, P.A. (1991) 'HRM from the other side of the fence', *Personnel Management*, February: 50–3.
—— and —— (1993) 'The strategic integration of assessment and development practices: succession planning and new manager development', *Human Resource Management Journal*.
Management Charter Initiative (1990) 'Consultative document on the proposed national framework for management development', *Journal for Management Education and Development*.
Mangham, I. and Silver, M. (1986) 'Management training, context and practice', ESRC Pilot Survey on Management Training.
Miller, P. and Rose, N. (1993) 'Governing economic life', in M. Gane and T. Johnson (eds) *Foucault's New Domains*, London: Routledge.
Morgan, G. (1988) *Riding the Waves of Change: Developing Managerial Competencies for a Turbulent World*, Oxford: Jossey Bass.
Nicholson, N. (1984) 'A theory of work-role transitions', *Administrative Science Quarterly* 29: 172–91.
Paddison, L. (1990) 'The targeted approach to recruitment', *Personnel Management* November: 55–8.
Pearn, M. and Kandola, R.C. (1988) *Job Analysis*, London: Institute of Personnel Management.
Powell, G.N. (1990) *Women and Men in Management* (2nd edn), Newbury Park: Sage.
Prahalad, K.K. and Hamel, G. (1990) 'The core competencies of the corporation', *Harvard Business Review* May–June: 79–91.
Robertson, I.T. and Iles, P.A. (1988) 'Approaches to management selection', in C.L. Cooper and I. Robertson (eds) *International Review of Industrial and Organisational Psychology*, Chichester: John Wiley & Sons Ltd.
Robertson, I.T., Iles, P.A., Gratton, L. and Sharpley, D. (1991) 'The psychological impact of selection procedures on candidates', *Human Relations* 44(9): 963–82.
Rose, M. (1988) *Industrial Behaviour*, Harmondsworth: Penguin Books.
Rose, N. (1985) *The Psychological Complex*, London: Routledge & Kegan Paul.
—— (1990) 'Governing the soul', paper presented at conference on The Values of the Enterprise Culture, University of Lancaster, 1989.
Rynes, S.L. and Barber, A.E. (1990) 'Applicant attraction strategies: an organizational perspective', *Academy of Management Review* 15(2): 286–310.
Salaman, G. and Thompson, K. (1978) 'Class culture and the persistence of an elite: the case of army officer selection', *The Sociological Review* 26(2): 283–304.
Schackleton, V. (1992) 'Using a competency approach in a business change setting', in R. Boam and P. Sparrow (eds) *Focusing on Human Resources: a Competency-Based Approach*, London: McGraw-Hill.
Schneider, B. and Konz, A. (1989) 'Strategic job analysis', *Human Resource Management* 28: 5–62.
Schroder, H.M. (1989) *Managerial Competence*, Iowa: Kendall/Hunt.
Silverman, D. and Jones, J. (1973) 'Getting in: the managed accomplishment of "correct" selection outcomes', in J. Child (ed.) *Man and Organisation*, London: Allen & Unwin.
—— and —— (1976) *Organisational Work*, London: Collier Macmillan.
Smith, E.J. (1990) 'Developing business men and women in financial services', *BSI Journal* 198(344): 4–7.
Sparrow, P.R. and Boam, R. (1992) 'Where do we go from here?', in R. Boam and P. Sparrow (eds) *Focusing on Human Resources: a Competency-Based Approach*, London: McGraw-Hill.

Sparrow, P.R. and Bognanno, M. (1993) 'Competency requirement forecasting: issues for international selection and assessment', *International Journal of Selection and Assessment* 1(1): 50–8.

Sparrow, P.R. and Pettigrew, A. (1988) 'Strategic human resource management in the UK computer supplier industry', *Journal of Occupational Psychology* 61(1): 25–42.

Sparrow, P.R., Gratton, L. and McMullan, J. (1989) *Human Resource Issues in Information Technology*, a survey conducted by PA Consulting Group and co-sponsored by British Telecom, February.

Storey, J. and Sisson, K. (1993) *Managing Human Resources and Industrial Relations*, Milton Keynes: Open University Press.

Torrington, D. and McKay, L. (1986) 'Will consultants take over the personnel function?', *Personnel Management* February 4: 34–7.

Townley, B. (1989) 'Selection and appraisal: reconstituting social relations', in J. Storey (ed.) *New Perspectives on Human Resource Management*, London: Routledge.

Wernimont, P.F. and Campbell, J.P. (1968) 'Signs, samples and criteria', *Journal of Applied Psychology* 52: 372–6.

Windholf, P. and Wood, S. (1988) *Recruitment and Selection in the Labour Market*, Aldershot: Avebury.

Chapter 9

Training and development

David Ashton and Alan Felstead

INTRODUCTION

There is widespread consensus among commentators and politicians alike that training should be encouraged, since it has a desirable effect on productivity and improves national economic performance. Much of this evidence comes from research conducted by the National Institute for Economic and Social Research, and is widely quoted in the press and in policy-making circles (Daly *et al.* 1985; Prais and Steedman 1986; Prais and Wagner 1988; Prais *et al.* 1989; Steedman and Wagner 1987, 1989; Steedman 1988).

Far less consensus has been apparent, however, over attempts to put a figure on the amount British employers actually spend on training their workforces. An estimate of £14.4bn. a year, made in 1986–7 (Training Agency 1989a), has been hotly disputed – the accuracy of this figure itself has been questioned, and in any case, it has been cited by some as evidence of employers' already hefty commitment to training and by others as proof that employers' commitment is inadequate (Training Agency 1989a: 29; Ryan 1990; Finegold 1991). The water is muddied still further when international comparisons of training expenditure are made. For example, while it is generally accepted that Japanese companies have a higher commitment to training than the British, comparing training expenditures tells a contrary story – Japanese companies actually spend less than their British counterparts (Dore and Sako 1987). This paradox is explained by Japanese companies' greater reliance on the internal labour market and on-the-job training for the process of skill formation. Here the emphasis is on demonstration, learning by doing and imitating the teacher. This is best done within the firm and cannot be acquired from instructors in the classroom or in training facilities geared up to provide training to several companies. The fact that expenditures incurred in on-the-job training are not easily identifiable makes it difficult to cost, and it is therefore not adequately represented in training expenditure comparisons (Koike and Inoki 1990; McCormick 1991). Assessments of training must embrace the labour market regimes which impact upon training policies and practices, thereby giving a more complete picture of the role of company training.

The role of training and development in the 'human resource management revolution' has brought many of these issues to the fore with renewed vigour. Will those companies which do not take on the mantle of HRM wither away? How committed are British employers to investing in their workforces, and has this commitment hardened? Are British companies looking more inwardly – training and developing existing employees, rather than buying in appropriately qualified and experienced workers when necessary? If there really has been an HRM 'revolution', then the answers to all these questions should be in the affirmative. Despite the conceptual debate about what HRM is and whether or not it is something new (Noon 1992; Storey 1989, 1992; Legge 1989), there is apparently widespread agreement on these points. We can therefore take the level of commitment a company shows towards investing in the skills of its workforce as a litmus test of whether or not British employers are changing the way they manage labour. A company which fails to train will find itself dependent on the external labour market, and hence in a position in which it is unable to regard labour as anything but a cost. On the other hand, a company which does train is more likely to protect its investment by offering promising career prospects for those who do well, as well as seniority payments and wages higher than those that would be available on the open market. It is also likely to take employee selection and appraisal more seriously.

In *New Perspectives on Human Resource Management*, Keep (1989) identified a number of strands which run through the practices of those companies, such as Jaguar Cars, Lucas Industries, ICL, IBM, Marks and Spencer and British Steel, which are widely acknowledged to be at the forefront of the HRM movement. To this list we may now add the Japanese multi-nationals, such as Nissan, which inward investment has brought to Britain. All of the companies that Keep identified were seen to be integrating training and development into their wider business planning, instituting manpower planning, increasing the use of formal performance and training needs appraisal procedures and enhancing their training activities at all levels within the organization. However, while it is widely acknowledged that an effective HRM policy can contribute to financial success, the fact that some of the companies which Keep identified in 1989 as prominent in the field of HRM – such as IBM – faced major financial crises in the early 1990s suggests that there is no guarantee that investment in human resources necessarily pays off in financial terms. Moreover, it is far from clear that training is *the* crucial determinant of a company's financial performance – there is more than one route to company success, when production for profit is the goal of private capital and companies remain able to accumulate capital through low-skill, labour-intensive forms of production (Cutler 1992; Green 1992).

This chapter attempts to assess whether company training policies and practices have changed or are moving towards HRM principles. The growing body of evidence on this topic points to a relatively complex set of changes taking place in company training practices, but contrary to the hype surrounding the HRM debate, company attitudes to training have changed very little. What change there has been suggests that some employers are being constrained by external pressures to undertake more training, while others cut back, but there is little evidence of any sudden growth in commitment to HRM principles. This is hardly surprising, given the institutional structures and the global market-place in which British companies operate. HRM practices require the formation of internal labour market structures and quality, rather than price, competition. At present, neither exists in Britain, nor have they historically (Glynn and Gospel 1993; Gospel 1992). This point is further reinforced by comparing Britain with countries such as Japan, Germany and Singapore. The chapter concludes that the adoption of HRM will require far more than change at the company level; widespread changes will also be called for if HRM is to be used by more than a narrow band of British employers.

BRITAIN'S NATIONAL TRAINING INFRASTRUCTURE

The national training infrastructure provides more than just a backdrop within which employers' training practices are located. Comparative research (Ashton and Green 1994) illustrates how national training infrastructures can influence both the level and amount of training undertaken by companies. In Britain the story has been one of a minimalist training infrastructure emerging in the nineteenth century; the employers who pioneered the process of industrialization were able to compete successfully in national and international markets with a relatively low-skilled labour force. This was a society which industrialized without a national system of compulsory education to ensure minimal levels of literacy and numeracy, in which it was left to employers, workers' organizations and individuals to provide the requisite skills.

The fragmented educational system of the nineteenth century supplied leadership skills through the private (public) schools for a small elite, but for the masses – insofar as they attended schools – the main function of education was one of securing literacy and social control (Gardner 1984). Employers who expected to provide their own supply of skilled labour looked to techniques such as on-the-job training, often organized through a system of subcontracting (Littler 1982). In some trades, such as construction, furniture-making, engineering and printing, employers used the remnants of the old medieval apprenticeship system to form a system of occupational labour markets. This provided a pool of skilled labour in the localities from which new employers could draw their labour force.

These occupational labour markets enabled the individuals who entered them to acquire skills over which they had a sense of ownership and which were transferable between employers. Access to these skills was controlled in some cases by employers, in others by unions, or alternatively was jointly controlled. The costs of acquiring such skills were shared between the employer and the employee, while apprenticeship papers provided a nationally recognized form of skill certification. The result was a system of training which combined reliance on occupational labour markets with a minimal amount of firm-specific on-the-job training. This produced a system of skill formation which was front-end loaded, in that the training provided on entry to the labour market was expected to last for the rest of a person's working life. For a minority, apprenticeship training provided access to the lower levels of management. However, because the skilled workers monopolized a wide range of tasks, the majority of lesser skilled workers were denied the chance of obtaining a skill through on-the-job learning.

During the twentieth century, and especially after the Second World War, occupational labour markets were gradually undermined as the basis of skill acquisition, for two reasons. First, the introduction of US management systems and (mass) production techniques gave management greater control over the production process at the expense of the skilled worker (Littler 1982). Second, the economic base of skilled work shrank with the decline of the manufacturing sector, while the growth occupations in the service sector were outside the control of unions. In the service sector, the absence of a strong union influence meant that management could exercise greater control over the skill-formation process. The result was that companies came to exercise greater control over the amount and level of training activity. In a few cases they provided a substantial investment in training. However, many others chose to minimize such activity and to buy in such skills as they needed. British employers who have been accustomed to producing low value-added goods, chose to compete on price rather than quality (Lazonick 1979, 1981; Elbaum *et al.* 1979; Zeitlin 1979).

In the aftermath of the Second World War, fear of falling behind foreign competitors did give rise to anxieties among politicians and some business leaders about the wisdom of relying exclusively on employers to achieve an adequate level of skill for the nation as a whole. Previous government initiatives in the provision of training had been primarily directed at the unemployed. There was now an attempt to put pressure on recalcitrant employers to enhance the level of training they provided and thereby to share the costs of training more equitably between employers. This took the form of the 1964 Training Act, which signalled a significant shift from a voluntaristic to an interventionist strategy. Intervention in the process of training took the form of Industrial Training Boards (ITBs) (Sheldrake and Vickerstaff 1987). These consisted of representatives of employers and unions and were charged with the task of monitoring the level and quality of training in the industry, and, through the imposition of a levy on employers, equalizing the cost of training among employers, while improving the quality. In many respects the ITBs were based on the concept of an occupational labour market, in which it is assumed that skills are transferable between firms and therefore all should carry an equal share in the costs of training. Nevertheless, they represented the first attempt on a national scale to close the low-skills route.

The ITBs lasted for twenty years, in one form or another, but were eventually disbanded for a combination of reasons. These included objections from many employers, and ideological objections among government politicians to state intervention. Also they were disbanded because the changes identified above – namely, the growth of mass production and later the decline of manufacturing industry – were undermining the use of occupational labour markets as a basis for skill formation (Sheldrake and Vickerstaff 1987). In the 1970s the industry-by-industry approach to encouraging training activities was replaced by the more highly centralized and direct strategy of the Manpower Services Commission. Established in the 1970s as a quasi-governmental corporatist body under the direction of employers, unions and the State, the MSC sought to establish a national system of vocational education and training, partially funded from the public purse (Ainley and Corney 1990). Some progress was made, but the attempt by the MSC to use its programmes as a basis for a national system of training failed, primarily because the Thatcher government insisted on reverting to the traditional strategy of using training programmes to provide a cheap 'solution' to the problem of unemployment. Employers were being left to determine their own level of training activity, and as the government started to look to the market to provide the solution to Britain's training problem, the MSC was dismantled, paving the way for current government policy.

The period following the end of the Second World War also witnessed attempts to extend secondary education to the masses, through the introduction of first the tripartite system, and in the 1960s comprehensive schools. However, in spite of these and subsequent changes, the majority of young people continued to reject the watered-down academic curriculum on offer and chose to leave school at the earliest date. Apart from an influx of young people into the more 'adult' atmosphere of the colleges of further education in the 1970s and 1980s, this situation did not change significantly until the 1990s. However, as the apprenticeship system collapsed with the demise of occupational labour markets, and with the availability of unskilled jobs declining in a context of high levels of unemployment, there was mounting pressure on young people to continue within the educational system in the hope of securing the credentials which would enable them to enter higher-level employment (Ashton *et al.* 1990). Moreover, the expansion of educational opportunity following the Second World War meant that a larger proportion of the parents of children in the late 1980s had further education, thereby increasing the level of motivation among young people to stay on at school. The result has been a significant increase in the educational participation rates of sixteen- and seventeen-year-olds during the late 1980s and early 1990s. However, the participation rate of sixteen-year-olds in full-time post-compulsory education remains much lower than is found among most competitor nations. For example, the UK figure for 1989 of 53 per cent compares with figures of between 80 and 95 per cent in most other industrialized economies (see Table 9.1). Even if we take into account the recent increase which has brought the participation rate to 66 per cent in 1992, the UK rate still lags behind those of its major competitors (Robson 1993). This is the source of the low levels of management and worker education that Keep (1989) identified as one of the major factors inhibiting the take-up of HRM practices by UK employers. Moreover, once they are in the labour market, empirical studies highlight the fact that training is skewed towards those with the highest qualifications, higher incomes and in better jobs (OECD 1991). It is in this context, that of a relatively low but slowly improving level of education and training among the labour force, that we turn to an examination of current government policy on the provision of a training infrastructure.

There are two main strands to current government policy. The first is to

Table 9.1 Post-compulsory education participation rates: international comparisons*

Country		*Minimum leaving age*	*Full-time education at 16 years (% of cohort)*
Australia		15	73
Belgium		14	92
Canada		16/17	92
Denmark		16	89
France		16	80
Germany, Federal Republic		15	71
Italy		14	54
Japan		15	92
Netherlands		16	93
Spain		16	65
Sweden		16	91
United Kingdom	(1987)	16	50
	(1989)	16	53
United States		16–18	95

Source: *Training Statistics 1993*, London: Employment Department (1993b: 125)

Note: * Unless otherwise stated, the figures given here refer to 1989.

create a training market. For example, 'training credits', 'career development loans', 'gateways to learning' and 'skills choice', all aim to provide individuals with the purchasing power and information with which to demand and purchase training to meet their own needs (see Table 9.2). The Youth Training Scheme which, as Keep recorded in 1989, was introduced in order to upgrade the quality of the workforce, is to be phased out and replaced by training credits. The second strand of the government's policy is to place employers in control of the delivery of training at the local level, in order that the market meets local needs – hence the introduction of Training and Enterprise Councils to spearhead the training effort under the control of employers. These are locally based and, in theory, have the ability to ensure that the training delivered is tailored to local demand. Moreover, it is assumed that individuals, through the various government programmes, will be empowered to respond to employers' needs. Having created a market, the assumption is that the market will then match the needs of employers with those of individual employees, thereby providing the solution to the training problem.

Table 9.2 Training market initiatives

Government training market initiatives	*Outline of initiatives*
Career Development Loans	Allows individuals to borrow 80 per cent of the cost of vocational training courses with three months' interest-free holiday.
Gateways to Learning	Guidance vouchers issued to targeted adults (the unemployed, women returners, recent redundant workers) to spend at approved guidance providers.
Skill Choice	Extension of Gateways to Learning beyond 'target' groups.
Training Credits	Designed to replace Youth Training by 1996. All 16- and 17-year-olds leaving full-time education given a training voucher to cash with an approved training provider of their choice.

Source: Felstead (1993a)

We argue that this premise represents a fundamental misunderstanding of the source of the British training problem. If employers are demanding only low-level skills, then placing them in control of the delivery of government training programmes and encouraging individuals to respond to employers' demands is merely to reproduce the low skills base of the UK economy (Ashton and Green 1992). This policy therefore increases the supply of skills for low-level (semi-skilled) jobs (NVQ levels one and two). If we compare Britain with other countries, such as Germany and Japan, where the skill level is acknowledged to be higher, it is evident that the heart of the British training problem is the failure of employers to demand higher-level skills. In order to sustain their competitive advantage in product markets German and Japanese employers demand a higher level of skill from their entrants and then organize their workforces in such a way as to enhance the skills of their workers (Streeck 1989; Koike and Inoki 1990).

This problem has not been totally ignored, in that programmes such as 'Investors in People' (IiP) do attempt to enhance the level of training undertaken, by linking employers' training strategies to their business objectives. If employers are more aware of the link between effective business performance and higher skill levels among their workers, this should enhance their demand for skills, thereby forging a connection central to the establishment of strategic HRM. However, while this appears on the surface to be a more imaginative solution, its implementation has remained within the voluntarist framework. There are no sanctions against non-take-up; reliance has been placed on exhortation, and consequently take-up has been slow – only around 250 companies have so far been recognized as Investors in People (*Guardian*, 15 June 1993).

In many respects IiP can be seen as part of the more widespread advocacy of HRM as a solution to the training problem, the argument being that if only employers would see the link between effective HRM policies and the production of better-quality, higher value added goods and services, this would go a long way toward enhancing the competitiveness of British industry. Yet while HRM is very much a buzz-word in management circles (Guest and Hoque 1993), whether anything of practical significance has changed in the workplace is less well known. The following section will look at the evidence.

BRITAIN'S COMPANY TRAINING AND DEVELOPMENT POLICIES AND PRACTICES

So much for Britain's national training infrastructure; how are employers actually using training and development in their own organizations, and is it changing? To begin to answer these questions we have to draw on disparate debates and data often collected for quite different purposes. Needless to say, dedicated research data on the role of training and development in the management of human resources is most pressing and ripe for future enquiry, as this section will show. Two quite separate debates in the literature stand out in terms of their implications for training and development. One is the upskilling/de-skilling debate, the other is the debate surrounding the 'flexible firm'. In this section we will consider both of these, before more explicitly reviewing the company-level data on training and development.

Upskilling/de-skilling, training and development, and HRM

The debate surrounding the long-term trajectory of skills – downward or upward – has raged for decades. On the one hand, there are those who argue that technological change has raised the complexity of work tasks and the skills required to carry them out (Kerr *et al.* 1960; Blauner 1964). This has implications for work organization – greater emphasis is placed on nurturing employee initiative and the provision of greater discretion at work. Failure to do so will put the organization at a competitive disadvantage and it may eventually be driven out of business. Evidence of upskilling could therefore provide fertile ground for the development of HRM practices.

However, there are a number of writers who hold a very different view of the trajectory of skill development (Braverman 1974; Zeitlin 1979; Elbaum *et al.* 1979). For them, technological change is used by employers to remove employee discretion from work, to routinize jobs, and to make it easier to substitute one employee for another. The underlying motivation of these changes is the desire to tighten the grip on the work process, thereby raising productivity and profit. The 'de-skilling' senario emphasizes labour as a cost and certainly not as a resource, as the 'HRM revolution' would suggest.

Between the 'upskillers' and the 'de-skillers' there is a third position which combines elements of the two. Rather than arguing for one general tendency or another, this position recognizes that each tendency might hold greater sway in one occupational sector but not in another. Some occupations might be better placed to benefit from the upskilling tendency, whereas others might be more prone to de-skilling. Conceptually the labour market can be divided in two: a primary labour market catering for the highly skilled, with greater reliance on worker discretion and autonomy; and a secondary labour market, in which management makes little effort to maintain and enhance skills through training, but relies on intensifying work through de-skilling and direct control (Edwards 1979; Friedman 1977). By looking at product-market positions, some writers have attempted to identify which labour market regime applies to which companies. In short, large firms catering for near monopolistic product markets are seen as primary labour market users, whereas smaller companies in competitive product markets are equated with secondary labour markets (Doeringer and Piore 1971). For simplicity we can refer to this as the polarization thesis.

Much of this debate has been conducted by means of case study investigation, and has focused on particular industries such as printing (Zeitlin 1979) and engineering (Jones 1982; Wilson 1988), and sometimes on particular occupational areas such as clerical and secretarial work (Wainwright and Francis 1984; Webster 1986).

One particular investigation, the Social Change and Economic Life Initiative (SCELI), has produced the first systematic survey data with which to assess the nature of skill change in Britain (Gallie 1991). The data are based on interviews conducted in 1986 with over 6,000 individuals in six different localities. Respondents were asked to compare their current job with what they were doing five years earlier, in terms of the level of skill and responsibility required. Over the five-year period, 52 per cent experienced an increase in the skills required, compared to only 9 per cent who saw their skills decline (ibid.: Table 3). In other words, the commonest experience had been that of upskilling. This was true for all occupational categories – from top to bottom. However, those already in highly skilled occupations were more likely to have experienced upskilling than those working in lower skilled occupations. Hence, 'the argument that is best supported is that of a polarisation of skill experiences between the classes' (ibid.: 349).

According to the Employment in Britain survey, these trends appear to have continued well into the 1990s. Like the SCELI survey, the Employment in Britain survey collected data from individuals aged between twenty and sixty. This time, however, 3,855 individuals were interviewed across Britain, between May and September 1992 (Gallie and White 1993: vii). According to this evidence, higher-level qualifications are now required for the jobs respondents currently do compared to what was required in 1986 – the proportion of jobs where no qualifications were required was 6 per cent lower in 1992, whereas the proportion of jobs requiring at least one A level had increased by the same amount (ibid.: Table 2.1). Furthermore, the overall proportion of respondents who had experienced an increase in their skills over the previous five years leapt from 52 per cent in 1986 to 63 per cent in 1992 (ibid.: 22). The proportion who had experienced a decline in their skills remained unchanged, at 9 per cent. The polarization of skills also continued, with professional groups reporting the greatest proportion of individuals experiencing upskilling, and semi/non-skilled manual workers reporting the lowest (ibid.: Table 2.2).

In addition to the evidence that jobs have become more skilled in the 1990s, as seen by people in those jobs, the Employment in Britain survey provides a further basis for believing that there is fertile ground for HRM. For instance, it suggests that more people are now being trained, more want to be trained and more are willing to pay for it themselves. For example, the Training in Britain survey found that 32 per cent of employed people aged 19–59 had received training in the past three years (Training Agency 1989b: 49). For employees aged 20–60, this had risen to 54 per cent by 1992, and training spells had also lengthened. Similarly, the proportion of people paying for their own training rose from 9 per cent in 1986–7 to 13 per cent in 1992. Furthermore, 38 per cent said that they saw good training as being more important than they did five years ago (Gallie and White 1993: 29–31).

This discussion, then, provides seemingly optimistic evidence for the development of HRM policies and practices among British employers. However, two notes of caution must be entered. First, the data are based on individual, not corporate responses. As has been shown elsewhere (Burchell *et al.* 1993; Burchell and Rubery 1993), employees' and employers' perceptions can often differ considerably. For example, a company which pays its employees above what it sees as the 'going rate', to protect its investment in employee training, may not be successful in reducing employee turnover and other productivity-reducing behaviour. Employees may not know that they are being paid premium rates of pay, or alternatively their points of comparison may be so fragmentary and incomplete as to make the premium rates necessary prohibitively expensive. Also, the evidence does not make the link between the alleged change in the management of human resources and individual experiences. Indeed, the upskilling/de-skilling debate is couched in terms of the effect of technological change, rather than management change on the skill composition of the workforce, although technological change and the process of management interact. We are therefore still left with the question: has an HRM revolution taken root in British companies, as reflected in their treatment of training and development?

The 'flexible firm', training and development, and HRM

The debate surrounding the now familiar construct of the 'flexible firm' returns us squarely to alleged changes in employer strategy (Atkinson 1984; Atkinson and Meager 1986). In short, the argument is that 'flexible firms' divide their workforces into 'core' and 'peripheral' groupings (see Rothwell, this volume). This two-tier employment structure separates full-time workers from those who work under a range of non-conventional employment contracts, such as part-time work, homeworking and temporary work, on the one hand, and the 'displacement of employment contracts by commercial contracts' (Atkinson and Meager 1986: 9), as exemplified by subcontracting, self-employment, agency working and franchising (Felstead 1993b), on the other.

The 'flexible firm' has assumed an important place in academic and policy-making circles; yet it is not without its critics (Pollert 1988a, 1988b, 1991; MacInnes 1987a: 113–24, 1987b; Marginson 1989). Doubts have been expressed as to how extensive a phenomenon it really is, and whether it represents a strategic rather than an *ad hoc* response to fluctuations in work activity. Nevertheless, it is undeniable that non-standard forms of employment have grown rapidly during the last decade. It is among these workers that the training incidence is lowest and that the emphasis on labour as a cost to be minimized is greatest. Moreover, British employers have historically preferred to rely on the external market for labour – recruiting and laying off workers as demand changes, filling higher positions with external as well as internal candidates, and fixing wages in accordance with external market pressures. This is a far cry from HRM techniques which internalize the employment relationship by more systematically screening and recruiting workers, by making every effort to make them permanent employees, by developing internal job ladders and using internal promotion wherever possible, by fixing wages in accordance with internal administrative principles rather than market forces, and by developing more extensive fringe benefits, often based on seniority within the firm (Gospel 1992). HRM may fail to touch this growing army of 'peripheral' workers; if HRM is to be found anywhere, it will be among a narrow band of 'core' workers.

Company-level data, training and development, and HRM

One might reasonably assume that a good place to look for evidence on the development of HRM would be the Workplace Industrial Relations survey (WIRS). However, the latest WIRS, conducted in 1990 and published in 1992 (Millward *et al.* 1992) is bound, in large part, by its predecessor surveys (Daniel and Millward 1983; Millward and Stevens 1986). It is wedded to an institutionalized, rules-and-regulations view of industrial relations. Many of the issues raised in this book – selection, manpower planning, appraisal, and training and development – are not investigated. Indeed, as Sisson has pointed out, there are only three references to HRM in the latest WIRS source book (Sisson 1993: 201). However, a parallel survey of Employers' Manpower and Skill Practices was also conducted in 1990, but it has yet to be published. This will contain much-needed information on how training and development is being used by British employers. Until then, we will have to rely on fragmented evidence.

For example, there has been a substantial fall in the number of designated personnel specialists who regard themselves as responsible for training – down from 78 per cent in 1984 to 67 per cent in 1990 (Millward *et al.* 1992: 39). It is impossible to say whether this represents a shift in emphasis towards the line manager acting as trainer, or the contracting out of the training function. Similarly, around 63 per cent of firms questioned for the Skill Needs in Britain survey in 1993 reported the existence of a training plan, and 47 per cent of those who had funded or arranged off-the-job training over the previous twelve months had someone at board level responsible for training (IFF 1993: 90–5). However, comparing these figures, albeit over a short time horizon, with those collected in 1990 reveals little change. There are other snippets, such as the finding that among 134 manufacturing plants surveyed, there was an 89 per cent increase between

1986 and 1990 in the number which had a training budget with at least a two-year time horizon (Wood 1993: Table 1). However, to really substantiate the role played by training and development in company thinking, many more questions need to be answered, both at the level of the large-scale survey and, perhaps more importantly, at the level of the case study.

An attempt to begin this process has already been made by Felstead and Green (1993, 1994a and 1994b). The research combined large-scale survey evidence on training with employer interviews. The first part of the research was to compare, like-with-like, the results from the Labour Force Survey (LFS) for spring 1990 with the results for spring 1992. The LFS is a nationally representative sample survey of around 60,000 households in the UK, conducted on behalf of the Employment Department. It asks individuals several questions about their work-related education and training. The second angle was to reinterview, in late 1992, a sample of 157 employers about their training policies and practices and compare their answers to those they had given in late 1990. This enabled an assessment to be made of how and why training fared in the recession of the early 1990s, thereby indicating whether HRM techniques had not taken root to the point of determining the level of training and development activity.

The LFS component of the research drew on the responses individuals gave to the question: 'Over [the last four weeks] have you taken part in any education or training connected with your job, or a job you might be able to do in the future?', as well as a number of associated questions. The figure derived for training incidence showed a marked increase in the number and proportion of workers receiving job-related training throughout the 1980s; the number almost doubled and the proportion rose from 9.2 per cent in 1984 to 15.4 per cent in 1990. However, training incidence has fallen back since then to 14.5 per cent in 1992 (it was 14.7 per cent in 1993 (Employment Department 1993a: Table 8)).

At first sight, this appears to suggest that employers' training practices have changed significantly in recent years. If we are to put this down to the adoption of HRM techniques, then the factors behind the upward trend in training incidence and the factors holding it up in recessionary times must be the internal desire to develop the human resource. Examining what has happened to Britain's training effort during the early 1990s recession gives little support to this hypothesis. Analysis revealed that the fall in training incidence was not spread evenly across the employed population. On the contrary, the biggest falls were among those whose training incidence was highest, and vice versa. So, those in 'intermediate occupations', for example, saw the likelihood of their receiving job-related training in the four weeks prior to interview fall by three percentage points. At the other end of the scale, unskilled workers saw their training incidence rise from 3.5 per cent to 5.4 per cent. However, despite the narrowing of the gap between the social classes in terms of training incidence, the differences remained pronounced; workers in professional occupations were almost five times as likely to receive job-related training as their unskilled counterparts in 1992 (compared to about eight times as likely in 1990).

The two-year period also saw a shift towards shorter courses among those who received job-related training. For example, courses lasting less than one month made up about 45 per cent of all job-related courses in 1992, compared to 40 per cent in 1990. The shift was even greater for courses lasting less than one week – rising from 34 per cent in 1990 to 40 per cent in 1992. The rise in short courses was most pronounced among the unskilled.

The second part of the research was a set of re-interviews with 157 training managers, who were first interviewed in autumn 1990 before the full effects of the recession had been felt. There was a target sample of 202 employers in four localities. While the sample was representative of the British economy in terms of industry and size, a high proportion were users of work-related further education programmes, suggesting a predominance of firms with some form of active training policy. Nevertheless, the interviews did reveal evidence of the main determinants of employers' training decisions and, in particular, how those decisions were influenced by the recession, HRM techniques or other factors.

Not unexpectedly, there was evidence of the full range of increases, decreases and stability in training activities among the sample. One of the key questions asked of respondents was the following: 'How has the overall amount of training given to employees (both existing and new recruits) changed over the last two years (as measured by hours of training)?' Of the 157 responding firms, sixty-eight (43 per cent) claimed to have increased their training activities over the last two years, forty-five (27 per cent) reported no change in their overall training commitment, and thirty-nine (25 per cent) reported cutbacks in training. Given the nature of the sample, these figures cannot be taken as indicative of national trends. However, the explanations they gave for the swings in their training activity do shed considerable light on the extent to which HRM is now influencing employers' training and development policies and practices. Having said this, the results of the study show that while there is substantial training activity in Britain, it is not closely linked to any widespread adoption of HRM strategies.

While training did indeed remain buoyant in many areas during the recession of the early 1990s, this was largely due to factors external to the firm. The main determinant of company training appears to have been 'push' factors such as BS5750, health and safety requirements and occupational regulations, rather than the 'pull' of HRM techniques. Evidence that companies are increasingly looking inwardly to invest in their human resources is lacking. This should come as no surprise. British employers have historically relied on external forces and institutions to manage industrial relations, work relations and employment relations (Gospel

1992). It is difficult to envisage moves towards internalization as taking place in anything other than a slow and hesitant manner.

CONCLUSION

In conclusion, we can see that while at the individual level there has been an increase in the proportion of people who experience upskilling and who attach greater value to training, at the company level the situation is far less rosy. The incidence of training has increased over the last decade, but whether that just means more but shorter spells of training is an open question. On its own, such evidence tells us little about the volume of training employers have undertaken. Companies have maintained training levels during the recession, but only because they have been pushed by external factors. There is certainly no systematic evidence to suggest that there has been a conversion to human resource management which is producing a transformation of training activity at the company level.

Attempts have been made to improve management education, such as the introduction by the Thatcher government of the Management Charter Initiative, but as yet there is no evidence to suggest that such initiatives have raised the qualification levels of UK management. Similarly, attempts to upgrade the skill level of the workforce, for example through the introduction of NVQs, have been driven by government initiatives rather than being employer-led. Moreover, comparison with other countries suggests that even among Britain's most successful competitors, it has not been a conversion to HRM practices that has driven the commitment to high levels of training, but a combination of external pressures and a high level of skill among young adults entering the labour market.

In the case of Germany, the medieval apprenticeship system was built on, not destroyed as in the UK, and used as a basis to develop a national system of training. This has provided a high level of intermediate-level skills training for the majority of German youth and has helped ensure that all young people were kept in some form of vocational education and training until the age of eighteen, much of it work-based. For their part, German employers cooperated in providing an appropriate work-based context for learning. The German apprenticeship system had invoked a long-standing commitment to skills training among German employers, but this in itself was not sufficient to provide a high level of skill-formation. The system was reinforced by external constraints, in the form of legal requirements and pressures from the Chambers of Commerce and the *Länder* to ensure that they fulfilled their obligation to train young people (Blossfeld 1993).

Similarly in the case of Japan, the State provided an educational system which kept the majority of young people in education until the age of eighteen, reaching relatively high levels of educational attainment. This ensured a high level of basic skills among the population flowing into the labour market. Like the Germans, the larger Japanese employers exhibited a commitment to training, but this was also bolstered by a series of external constraints. There, a series of such factors, including pressures from the Ministry of International Trade and Industry for the production of high-quality, high value added goods and a system of business finance which reinforced the commitment to lifetime employment also played a part in encouraging employers to invest in human resource development (McCormick 1991). Thus, not only do Japanese employers start from a higher base level of skills among their labour force, they are also subject to pressures which ensure that they facilitate learning at work.

These lessons have not been missed by the new arrivals among Britain's industrial competitors in South East Asia. In Singapore, the State has played an even greater role through its industrial trade policy directed at ensuring the production of high value added goods. Like the Japanese, the Singaporean government has pursued a policy of investing heavily in the education and training of young people, to ensure a high level of skill among young people entering the labour market (Castells 1992). The government cannot rely on the goodwill of multi-national companies to build on this and deliver a high level of skill formation in the workplace: faced with this, the response has been to use all the resources available to the State to ensure that the economy has the higher-level skills necessary to ensure success in the international market-place. Government training programmes have been used to enhance the base-line skills of the older workers, joint government/employer training ventures have been set up to provide selected high-level skills, and government funds have been used to entice employers into providing enhanced training for their employees. Outside the field of training policy, other measures have been used to ensure that employers do not opt for the low-skills route: for example there is a tax on companies employing low-paid labour.

Against this background, the outlook for skills training in the UK does not look promising. We have seen the collapse of the old regulatory system based on occupational labour markets. As this has occurred there has not been any attempt to provide an alternative regulatory framework of the kind established in those countries which are characterized by high levels of skill formation. On the contrary, employers are increasingly left to their own devices to decide what level of training they invest in. As we have seen, the pace of technological change has resulted in individuals experiencing a sense of upskilling, but there is no evidence that this has been driven by the training policies of employers. Since Keep wrote on these issues in 1989, the only major change that has taken place has been the rapid increase in the staying-on rate of young people in education, but that still leaves young people in the UK leaving education earlier than their counterparts in competitor nations. Employers' training activities have remained at the same level – the incidence of management and professional training has declined, while that of the unskilled and semi-skilled has increased. Some of the larger and better-known companies identified by Keep continue to fly the HRM flag, but for the majority all we appear to be witnessing is a series of externally-imposed incremental changes. Meanwhile, rather than reinforcing these external constraints on employers to increase the level of work-based learning, government policy, is doing precisely the opposite. By leaving the market to determine the level of investment in training and human development, the government have placed employers in the driving seat of their training policy.

The evidence from the most successful of the competitor nations suggests that what we regard as full-blown HRM requires a supportive institutional structure at the national level, so that employers' room for manoeuvre is restricted to investing in people. Simply relying on the market to provide fertile ground for HRM will not produce the results. The available evidence, institutionally and in practice, suggests that HRM policies and practices associated with training have taken root in only a few British companies – falling far short of that which would be required in order to fuel an HRM revolution.

REFERENCES

Ainley, P. and Corney, M. (1990) *Training for the Future: The Rise and Fall of the Manpower Services Commission*, London: Cassell.

Ashton, D. and Green, F. (1992) 'Skill shortage and skill deficiency: a critique', *Work, Employment and Society* 6(2), June: 413–35.

—— and —— (1994) *Training in the World Economy*, Aldershot: Edward Elgar.

Ashton, D., Maguire, M. and Spilsbury, M. (1990) *Restructuring the Labour Market: The Implications for Youth*, London: Macmillan.

Atkinson, J. (1984) 'Manpower strategies for flexible organisations', *Personnel Management* 16(8), August: 28–31.

Atkinson, J. and Meager, N. (1986) *Changing Working Patterns: How Companies Achieve Flexibility to Meet New Needs*, London: National Economic Development Office.

Blauner, R. (1964) *Alienation and Freedom*, Chicago, IL: University of Chicago Press.

Blossfeld, H. (1993) 'The German dual system in cross-national comparison', paper prepared for the first international meeting of the European Research Network on Transition in Youth, Barcelona, 20 September.

Braverman, H. (1974) *Labor and Monopoly Capital*, New York: Monthly Review Press.

Burchell, B. and Rubery, J. (1993) 'Internal labour markets from managers' and employees' perspectives', in J. Rubery (ed.) *Employers and the Labour Market*, Oxford: Oxford University Press.

Burchell, B., Elliot, B., Rubery, J. and Wilkinson, F. (1993) 'Management and employee perceptions of skill', in R. Penn, M. Rose and J. Rubery (eds) *Occupations and Skill*, Oxford: Oxford University Press.

Castells, M. (1992) 'Four Asian tigers with a dragon head: a comparative analysis of the State, economy and society in the Asian Pacific rim', in R.P. Applebaum and

J. Henderson (eds) *States and Development in the Asian Pacific Rim*, London: Sage.
Cutler, T. (1992) 'Vocational training and British economic performance: a further instalment of the "British labour problem" ', *Work, Employment and Society* 6(2), June: 161–83.
Daly, A., Hitchins, D. and Wagner, K. (1985) 'Productivity, machinery and skills in a sample of British and German manufacturing plants', *National Institute Economic Review* 111, February: 48–61.
Daniel, W.W. and Millward, N. (1983) *Workplace Industrial Relations in Britain: the DE/PSI/SSRC Survey*, London: Heinemann.
Doeringer, P. and Piore, M.J. (1971) *Internal Labor Markets and Manpower Analysis*, Lexington, MA: Heath & Co.
Dore, R.P. and Sako, M. (1987) *Vocational Education and Training in Japan*, London: Centre for Japanese and Comparative Industrial Studies, Imperial College.
Edwards, R.C. (1979) *Contested Terrain: The Transformation of the Workplace in the Twentieth Century*, New York: Basic Books.
Elbaum, B. and Wilkinson, F. (1979) 'Industrial relations and uneven development: a comparative study of the American and British steel industries', *Cambridge Journal of Economics* 3(3): 275–303.
Elbaum, B., Lazonick, W., Wilkinson, F. and Zeitlin, J. (1979) 'The labour process, market structure and Marxist theory', *Cambridge Journal of Economics* 3(3), September: 227–30.
Employment Department (1993a) *Quarterly Bulletin – Labour Force Survey*, London: Employment Department.
—— (1993b) *Training Statistics 1993*, London: Employment Department.
Felstead, A. (1993a) 'Putting individuals in charge, leaving skills behind? UK training policy in the 1990s', *Discussion Papers in Sociology*, No. S93/7, September, Leicester: University of Leicester.
—— (1993b) *The Corporate Paradox: Power and Control in the Business Franchise*, London: Routledge.
Felstead, A. and Green, F. (1993) 'Cycles of training? Evidence from the British recession of the early 1990s', *Discussion Papers in Economics*, Leicester: University of Leicester.
—— and —— (1994a) 'Cycles of training? Evidence from the British recession of the early 1990s', in A. Booth and D. Snower (eds) *The Skills Gap and Economic Activity*, Cambridge: Cambridge University Press, forthcoming.
—— and —— (1994b) 'Training during the recession', *Work, Employment and Society*, forthcoming.
Finegold, D. (1991) 'The implications of training in Britain for the analysis of Britain's skill problem: how much do employers spend on training?' *Human Resource Management Journal* 2(1), autumn: 110–15.
Friedman, A. (1977) *Labour and Industry*, Basingstoke: Macmillan.
Gallie, D. (1991) 'Patterns of skill change: upskilling, deskilling or the polarisation of skills?' *Work, Employment and Society*, 5(3), September: 319–51.
Gallie, D. and White, M. (1993) *Employee Commitment and the Skills Revolution*, London: PSI Publishing.
Gardner, P. (1984) *The Lost Elementary Schools of Victorian England*, London: Croom Helm.
Glynn, S. and Gospel, H. (1993) 'Britain's low skill equilibrium: a problem of demand?', *Industrial Relations Journal* 24(2), June: 112–25.
Gospel, H. (1992) *Markets, Firms, and the Management of Labour in Britain*,

Cambridge: Cambridge University Press.
Green, F. (1992) 'On the political economy of skill in the advanced industrial nations', *Review of Political Economy*, 4(4): 413–35.
Guest, D. and Hoque, K. (1993) 'The mystery of the missing human resource manager', *Personnel Management*, June: 40–1.
IFF Research (1993) *Skill Needs in Britain – 1992*, London: IFF Research.
Jones, B. (1982) 'Destruction or redistribution of engineering skills: the case of numerical control', in S. Wood (ed.) *Degradation of Work: Skill, Deskilling and the Labour Process*, London: Hutchinson.
Keep, E. (1989) 'Corporate training strategies: the vital component?', in J. Storey (ed.) *New Perspectives on Human Resource Management*, London: Routledge.
Kerr, C., Dunlop, J.T., Harbison, F.H. and Myers, C.A. (1962) *Industrialism and Industrial Man*, Boston, MA: Harvard University Press.
Koike, K. and Inoki, T. (1990) *Skill Formation in Japan and South East Asia*, Tokyo: University of Tokyo Press.
Lazonick, W. (1979) 'Industrial relations and technical change: the case of the self-acting rule', *Cambridge Journal of Economics* 3(3): 231–62.
—— (1981) 'Production relations, labor productivity and choice of technique: British and US cotton spinning', *Journal of Economic History* 41(3): 491–516.
Legge, K. (1989) 'Human resource management: a critical analysis', in J. Storey (ed.) *New Perspectives on Human Resource Management*, London: Routledge.
Littler, C. (1982) *The Development of the Labour Process in Capitalist Societies*, London: Heinemann.
McCormick, K. (1991) 'Japanese engineers, lifetime employment and in-company training: continuity and change in the management of engineering manpower resources', in P. Ryan (ed.) *International Comparisons of Vocational Education and Training for Intermediate Skills*, Lewes: Falmer.
MacInnes, J. (1987a) *Thatcherism at Work: Industrial Relations and Economic Change*, Milton Keynes: Open University Press.
—— (1987b) 'The question of flexibility', Research Paper No. 5, Department of Social and Economic Research, University of Glasgow, August.
Marginson, P. (1989) 'Employment flexibility in large companies: change and continuity', *Industrial Relations Journal* 20(2), summer: 101–9.
Millward, N. and Stevens, M. (1986) *British Workplace Industrial Relations 1980–1984*, Aldershot: Gower.
Millward, N., Stevens, M., Smart, D. and Hawes, D.R. (1992) *Workplace Industrial Relations in Transition: the ED/ESRC/PSI/ACAS Surveys*, Aldershot: Dartmouth.
Noon, M. (1992) 'HRM: map, model or theory', in P. Blyton and P. Turnbull (eds) *Reassessing Human Resource Management*, London: Sage.
Organisation for Economic Cooperation and Development (1991) 'Enterprise-related training', *OECD Employment Outlook*, Paris: OECD.
Pollert, A. (1988a) 'Dismantling flexibility', *Capital and Class* 34, spring: 42–75.
—— (1988b) 'The "flexible firm": fixation or fact?', *Work, Employment and Society* 2(3), September: 281–316.
—— (ed.) (1991) *Farewell to Flexibility?*, Oxford: Blackwell.
Prais, S. and Steedman, H. (1986) 'Vocational training in France and Britain', *National Institute Economic Review* 116, May: 45–56.
Prais, S. and Wagner, K. (1988) 'Productivity and management: the training of foremen in Britain and Germany', *National Institute Economic Review* 123: 34–47.
Prais, S., Jarvis, V. and Wagner, K. (1989) 'Productivity and vocational skills in

services in Britain and Germany: hotels', *National Institute Economic Review* 130, November: 52–74.

Rigg, M. (1987) *Training in Britain: A Study of Funding, Activity and Attitudes – Individuals' Perspectives*, Sheffield: Training Agency.

Robson, J. (1993) 'Changes over time, or who is staying on in full-time education using Youth Cohort Study data', paper presented to the Delivery of Effective Training seminars, 14 October, Sheffield.

Ryan, P. (1990) 'How much do employers spend on training? An assessment of the Training in Britain estimates', *Human Resource Management Journal* 1(4), autumn: 55–76.

Sheldrake, J. and Vickerstaff, S. (1987) *The History of Industrial Training in Britain*, London: Gower.

Sisson, K. (1993) 'In search of HRM', *British Journal of Industrial Relations* 31(2), June: 201–10.

Steedman, H. (1988) 'Vocational training in France and Britain: mechanical and electrical craftsmen', *National Institute Economic Review* 126, November: 57–71.

Steedman, H. and Wagner, K. (1987) 'A second look at productivity, machinery and skills in Britain and Germany', *National Institute Economic Review* 122, November: 84–95.

—— and —— (1989) 'Productivity, machinery and skills: clothing manufacture in Britain and Germany', *National Institute Economic Review* 128, May: 40–58.

Storey, J. (1989) 'Introduction: from personnel management to human resource management', in Storey, J. (ed.) *New Perspectives on Human Resource Management*, London: Routledge.

—— (1992) *Developments in the Management of Human Resources*, Oxford: Blackwell.

Streeck, W. (1989) 'Skills and the limits of Neo-Liberalism: the enterprise of the future as a place of learning', *Work, Employment and Society* 3(1): 89–104.

Training Agency (1989a) *Training in Britain: A Study of Funding, Activity and Attitudes – Employers' Activities*, Sheffield: Training Agency.

—— (1989b) *Training in Britain: A Study of Funding, Activity and Attitudes – The Main Report*, Sheffield: Training Agency.

Wainwright, J. and Francis, A. (1984) *Office Automation, Organisation and the Nature of Word*, London: Gower.

Webster, J. (1986) 'Work processing and the secretarial labour process', in K. Purcell, S. Wood, A. Watson and S. Allen (eds) *The Changing Experience of Employment*, London: Macmillan.

Wilson, F. (1988) 'Computer numerical control and constraints', in D. Knights and H. Willmott (eds) *New Technology and the Labour Process*, London: Macmillan.

Wood, S. (1993) 'Explaining the developing human resource management on the shop floor', paper presented to the Employers' Labour Market Behaviour seminar, 14 May, London.

Zeitlin, J. (1979) 'Craft control and the division of labour: engineers and compositors in Britain 1890–1930', *Cambridge Journal of Economics* 3(3), September: 263–74.

Chapter 10

Reward systems

Ian Kessler

The way in which employees are rewarded is central to the regulation of the employment relationship. It is not surprising, therefore, that the recent emphasis placed upon the workforce as a source of competitive advantage has encouraged a strong interest in methods of reward among practitioners, policy-makers, academics and other commentators. This has manifested itself at the level of prescription, description and conceptual analysis (Storey 1992). Key opinion leaders have placed particular emphasis on the use of specific types of reward system as a means of pursuing organizational efficiency and effectiveness; considerable attention has been devoted to looking at changing practice in remuneration policies and practices; and rewards have invariably held a central place in conceptual models of human resource management.

It is equally apparent, however, that the picture at all three of these levels is highly complex. For example, the importance attached to a direct link between pay and individual performance by key opinion leaders has varied. The support for this concept by the government (Citizen's Charter 1991) and the Confederation of British Industry (1988) can be set against the highly critical comments expressed by a number of management gurus including Deming (1982), Peters (1988) and Moss Kanter (1989) on this form of pay system.

Commentators have also differed in their opinions on the extent of change in the coverage and operation of reward systems. The suggestion that there have been 'unprecedented' (Curnow 1986) and 'revolutionary' (Murliss and Wright 1993) changes in approaches to reward can be contrasted with the observations of others that the traditional 'ad hocery' of British management in the field of reward systems is still very much to the fore (Smith 1992) and that any innovation in this sphere has by-passed whole swathes of workers, especially at the shopfloor level (Smith 1989).

Moreover, while reward systems and policies have been integral to influential conceptual HRM models, the normative assumptions informing their use have been markedly different. For instance, Beer *et al.* (1984), in highlighting the difficulties associated with using rewards to pursue human resource goals, suggest that they should play a strictly supportive role in relation to other, less problematic techniques. Yet Fombrun *et al.* (1984) pinpoint rewards as the 'most underutilized tool for *driving* organizational performance' (emphasis added).

It is pertinent to ask whether any sense can be made of these recent competing conceptions and perceptions of developments and trends in reward policy and practice in Britain. The primary objective of the chapter is to address this question, focusing, in particular, upon pay as a reward, rather than upon rewards in a broader sense. Intrinsic and non-monetary extrinsic benefits are not therefore dealt with in detail.

The chapter is divided into three parts: the first outlines the major types of payment system as a prelude to briefly reviewing trends in their use over the years; the second assesses the treatment of reward systems in the human resource management literature and evaluates current trends in reward policies in the light of past practice; the final section focuses more sharply on what are perceived to be the distinctive features of current reward policy and practice.

It will be argued that in the post-1945 period, pay systems have broadly been been used in an *ad hoc* manner to address specific managerial problems or goals generated by particular social, economic and political pressures. More recent trends conform in important respects with this pattern, in that reward systems have been mobilized to deal with a given set of managerial concerns derived from a timebound configuration of circumstances and needs. Nonetheless, it will be suggested that the use of reward systems to encourage and reinforce the broader process of organizational transformation is new and constitutes a distinctive feature of current reward policy and practice.

PAYMENT SYSTEMS AND THE EXERCISE OF CHOICE

Managerial perceptions of an 'appropriate' or 'viable' payment systems have been subject to considerable change and fluctuation over time. Indeed, the pursuit of the 'perfect' pay system has assumed something akin to the search for the Holy Grail and has often been reflected in pay fads, fashions or cycles. This section describes the different types of payment system available for use and then proceeds to consider the manner in which choice was exercised in the years after 1945 and up until the 1980s.

Types of payment system

The founding principles of a pay system are simple and enduring. Such systems have been based upon time or upon performance. In structural and administrative terms, payment by time is relatively straightforward. Employees are paid to work for stipulated periods of time and their pay is expressed on the basis of these time periods as an hourly rate, weekly wage or annual salary.

The notion of pay for performance, in contrast, embraces a wide range of pay systems. These vary according to the unit of performance – whether it is the individual or the collective – and the nature of the performance measures – whether they are in the form of particular inputs or outputs. These two dimensions provide the basis for Table 10.1, which sets out the main types of performance pay system. The individual-output systems tend to link pay to relatively tangible and quantifiable measures of employee performance – in the case of piecework, the unit of production or time saved, and with commission, the sales achieved. In addition, performance-related pay has been narrowly defined for the purpose of this typology to identify a pay system which relates pay to concrete individual targets or objectives. It is distinguished from merit pay, the major individual-input scheme, which bases pay upon behavioural traits such as flexibility, cooperation or punctuality, which employees may bring with them to the job. Skill-based pay can be seen in similar terms, rewarding employees for coming to their posts with certain physical and mental capacities or capabilities.

Table 10.1 Types of performance-based pay systems

Type of performance	*Unit of performance*	
	Individual	*Collective*
Output	Piecework Commission Individual bonus Individual performance-related pay	Measured daywork Team bonus Profit sharing Gain sharing
Input	Skill-based pay Merit pay	Employee share ownership schemes

Source: Purcell 1993, unpublished

In general, collective-output schemes rely upon a geared relationship between pay and the performance of the collective, whether this be the work group, the plant or the company. In other words, a stipulated level of performance, defined as a predetermined level of group output, profit, sales or added value, leads automatically to a pay out-turn. In contrast to many of the individual schemes, these schemes do not require an appraisal of employee performance or the extensive use of managerial discretion and judgement. Employee share ownership schemes can perhaps be related more closely to questions of ownership and participation than to the issue of pay. The operation of such schemes is dependent upon capital being brought to the company, usually in the form of a bank loan, which is then used to buy shares for the employees. These employee shares and the subsequent dividends represent the pay out-turn for the workers.

Selecting a payment system

In distinguishing the variety of payment systems available to organizations, two sets of issues arise: the first relate to the factors influencing the choices made, and the second to trends in the use of such systems across space and time.

The most systematic attempt to deal with the range of factors influencing the selection of payment systems has been undertaken through the application of a contingency approach (Lupton and Gowler 1969). This approach, presented both as a normative and an analytical framework, suggests that the choice of a payment system could and should be based upon a recognition of the goals managers are pursuing and upon an appreciation of the internal and external organizational circumstances within which the system is to function.

Extensive lists of goals to be pursued through pay systems have long been available. They include not only the traditional objectives of recruitment, retention and motivation, but also others such as the maintenance of quality, increased output, greater employee commitment and enhanced employee flexibility (Bowey *et al.* 1982: 32). Moreover, in highlighting contextual factors, particular importance has been attached to work characteristics and technology, as well as to labour and product markets (Lupton and Gowler 1969: 11–15; Mahoney 1992: 343: Bowey *et al.* 1982: 16).

The contingency approach has been influential in policy terms, implicitly informing the prescriptions and recommendations made by a succession of state-sponsored bodies with a direct and indirect interest in the reform of pay determination in the post-1945 years (see National Board for Prices and Incomes 1971: 7; Commission on Industrial Relations 1974: 14). The current advisory booklet on payment systems published by ACAS, for example, is structured around a consideration of the 'appropriateness' of various payment systems in different organizational circumstances, and notes that 'a payment system has a better chance of success if it is carefully selected and shaped to meet the specific needs of the organization and work group in which it is to apply' (ACAS undated: 4).

The contingency approach is also a useful analytical device for tracing pay developments over recent decades. Thus, it is possible to characterize changes in terms of general managerial responses to changing perceptions of problems and needs generated by shifting internal and external circumstances. The increasing coverage of piecework schemes in the years following the Second World War, for instance, can be seen as being stimulated by a particular combination of labour and product market pressures.

At the time, piecework was a system particularly well suited to encouraging high-volume, low-cost production in the face of increased foreign competition (Behrend 1955: 137). Similarly, the different phases of productivity bargaining from the early 1960s to the mid-1980s were a response to different contingent circumstances and needs. Initially, productivity agreements were a means of creating greater craft flexibility and job enlargement; then as a direct response to successive government incomes policies, especially as a means of generating self-financing pay increases; and finally as an instrument for the restructuring of work and demanning as a way of coping with recessionary pressures (Ahlstrand 1990).

A wide variety of different payment systems have long been available, therefore, for management to choose from. Choice, in turn, has been linked in part to the goals management are seeking to pursue through the payment system, with the implication that different systems are better suited to the pursuit of particular goals. In addition, the internal and external circumstances facing an organization have also been important in the selection of a payment system. Thus, the appropriateness of a payment system has been related to the technology used, as well as the labour and product market within which the company operates. Historically, and in general terms, shifting managerial goals and organizational circumstances have stimulated certain changes in payment systems. The question central to this chapter is whether more recent developments in reward systems can be presented in similar terms.

CURRENT PRACTICE: SHUFFLING THE PACK?

Debate on reward systems within the human resource management literature has borrowed heavily from contingency theory. In essence, conceptual HRM models have highlighted the importance of pursuing a specific set of organizational goals as a means of addressing intensive competitive pressures and have suggested that reward is a key policy-making area or lever to be used in their achievement. These goals have been presented in slightly different forms (Beer *et al.* 1984; Fombrun *et al.* 1984; Storey 1992) but have generally coalesced around those distinguished by Guest (1987) as commitment, flexibility, quality and strategic integration.

The preceding analysis has indicated that the linkage between reward and these goals is far from new. It is clear, however, that a concern with strategic integration is founded upon a precise and particular view of the managerial decision-making process. Thus, strategic integration in this context implies that the management process is governed by some underlying rationale leading to the selection of a reward system which is sensitive to the organization's circumstances and needs, underpins broader business plans and supports other human resource management techniques. It is a 'tight' view of managerial decision-making, which can be distinguished from the 'looser' view outlined in the preceding section which suggested that historically, management responses to changing contingent circumstances have been much more *ad hoc*, reactive and opportunistic.

This 'tighter' approach is confirmed by a number of recent attempts which have been made to relate the selection of specific types of reward system to particular contextual factors. For example, it has been suggested that the choice of payment might be influenced by an organization's diversification strategies (Salter 1973; Norburn and Miller 1981; Kerr 1985), by the product life cycle and by the company's structure (Balkin and Gomez-Mezia 1987).

It is clear that organizations have been changing their approaches to pay (Casey *et al.* 1992; Cannell and Long 1991). An ACAS survey (1988), for example, found that almost 40 per cent of the companies covered had altered their pay systems within the past three years. These changes have primarily been designed to create a closer link between pay and performance. In part, this has been reflected in a strengthening in the relationship between pay and company performance. By the end of 1992, there were well over 4,000 approved profit-related pay schemes, covering almost a million employees; while the number of approved employee share ownership schemes stood at over 2,000, with around three million workers covered.

More significant, perhaps, has been the spread of individual performance-related or merit-based pay schemes. A recent Policy Studies Institute survey (Casey *et al.* 1992: 457) highlighted the spread of such schemes in two regional markets, concluding that 'an individualization of pay has indeed taken place'. Moreover, these schemes are extending across the public and private sector, as well as filtering down the organizational hierarchy. The Workplace Industrial Relations survey for 1990 (Millward *et al.* 1992) found that although merit pay was more prevalent at senior managerial levels, it was still in evidence for clerical and administrative staff in around a third of the establishments covered, and for skilled manual workers in a quarter of the cases.

Can these changes simply be dismissed as another 'shuffling of the pack', or do they constitute a qualitative change from past approaches? More specifically, can the increased use of pay systems tied to performance be seen as a further variation on the theme by which management choose a new approach to pay as a means of responding in a relatively *ad hoc* manner to a new set of timebound problems, or is there now a more strategic approach which suggests some forethought and consideration are being given to the selection of pay systems?

The remainder of this section assesses the way in which pay has been related to the three substantive HRM goals of commitment, flexibility and quality. It explores the way in which these goals have been related to contextual features, and at the same time examines the potential tensions in these linkages which in the past have often provided a dynamic for change in pay systems.

Reward and commitment

The relationship between rewards and employee commitment, particularly as a means of stimulating motivation and improved job performance, has been subject to long-standing research and comment. From a managerial perspective, however, the perception that employees may be committed to various interests beyond and especially within the workplace has consistently encouraged attempts to use rewards as a means of strengthening identification with and loyalty to the organization and the job (Guest 1987). This approach has often gone hand-in-hand with attempts to weaken commitment to what are seen as competing interests, particularly those organized on a collective basis – mainly trade unions – which serve to dilute and check the exercise of managerial prerogatives. Recent attempts to use rewards to strengthen employee commitment to the organization can be seen as part of this ongoing process, with the prevailing economic, social and political conditions combining to lend weight to managerial endeavours.

The search for greater employee commitment to the organization has explicitly informed the more recent use of various long-established systems linking pay to indicators of company performance, and has been similarly important in the introduction of other forms of financial participation, such as employee share-ownership (Schuller 1989; Duncan 1988). Such a goal has clearly underpinned the statutory support provided over the last decade for employee share-ownership and profit-sharing schemes. As the Green Paper on profit related pay stated, 'PRP schemes should lead to a closer identification of employees with the companies in which they work' (1986: para 9). This goal similarly seems to underlie the increasing use of these schemes by employers. A survey of over 1,000 companies in 1985 found that the most commonly-cited reasons for introducing the various Inland Revenue approved schemes was 'to make employees feel they are part of the company' and 'to increase employees' sense of commitment to the company' (Smith 1986; Poole 1988). These finding were generally confirmed in a more recent survey covering a similar number of companies (Smith 1993).

There is less agreement about the effectiveness of such schemes. One body of research has focused specifically upon the relationship between financial participation and employee attitudes towards the company. While some of this work suggests that schemes may have some positive impact upon commitment (Bell and Hanson 1984), research under controlled conditions has cast some doubt on this finding (Dunn *et al.* 1991). Another group of researchers has assessed the effectiveness of financial participation by looking beyond the specific human resource management goal of commitment to the broader company aim of improved organizational performance.

Using various indicators of company performance, there appears to be a greater degree of consensus on the positive impact of these schemes (Richardson and Nejad 1986; Blinder 1990). It clearly remains difficult, however, to isolate the specific effect of financial participation on corporate performance from other management policies and practices. Thus, it appears that there is often a relationship between the introduction of financial participation and the use of other techniques to involve employees in the decision-making process. Reviewing American evidence, for instance, Blinder concludes: 'It appears that changing the way workers are treated may boost productivity more than changing the way they are paid' (ibid.: 13).

Certainly, some of the older forms of financial participation – for instance, the Rucker and Scanlon Plans, which linked pay to added value and sales value respectively, were as much about employee involvement as they were about reward. These schemes were originally conceived as being based upon accompanying consultative machinery allowing employees to feel that they had some impact upon the decisions affecting company performance.

The use of profit-sharing and employee share ownership schemes to strengthen worker commitment to the organization at the expense of the union appears to have informed these schemes to some degree – it is noteworthy, for example, that schemes are usually introduced at management's initiative, with the unions rarely involved in their design or implementation (Smith 1986: 383). Indeed, some union concern at the way in which these schemes might undermine their role is reflected in findings from the Workplace Industrial Relations survey in 1984 which indicated that share-ownership and profit-sharing schemes were less in evidence where unions were strong (Gregg and Machin 1988).

A more fundamental assault upon collective employment relations through the encouragement of individual commitment to the organizations has been reflected in the increased use of individual performance-related pay. The search for commitment has often been a stated reason for the introduction of such pay schemes (Kinnie and Lowe 1990; ACAS 1990; *IRRR* 1987a). The ways in which the individual performance-related pay systems have sought to generate employee commitment are more varied and perhaps more sophisticated than those associated with company-based schemes (Kessler and Purcell 1992).

First, assessed pay criteria are often derived from corporate plans or missions. Cascading goals and values are translated into individualized performance targets or behavioural traits, and have the effect of 'locking' the individual into the organization in a highly visible and meaningful way.

Second, the process of appraisal for pay purposes usually forces direct communication between employee and immediate line manager in determining the formalities of the effort–reward bargain, without the intervention of a third party. The process of setting performance criteria and assessing whether they have been met generates a dialogue between subordinate and superordinate, creating a direct bond between them.

The third and most explicit attempt to use individual performance-related pay as a means of undermining collective employment relations can be seen in the bypassing and, in certain cases, the de-recognition of unions for pay-bargaining purposes on the introduction of such schemes. At British Rail, for example, the Transport Salaried Staff Association was de-recognized following the implementation of such a scheme for 10,000 middle and junior managers (*Involvement and Participation* 1990). More typically, the introduction of performance pay linked to the establishment of individual contracts at more senior management levels has led to union de-recognition at, for instance, Thames Water, Amersham International and British Telecom (Petch 1990).

This attempt to undermine the collective approach to pay determination through merit pay accounts for the general hostility of many unions to such pay systems. A number of unions, including NALGO, AUT, TSSA and NATFHE, have national policies of outright opposition to the principle of merit pay, while there are many instances of unions balloting for industrial action against the introduction of such schemes. The MSF, for example, conducted such a ballot among members at an insurance company Trade Indemnity in 1988 (*Financial Times*, 3 March 1988) and the NUT has balloted for action against appraisal on the grounds that it may well be linked to performance-related incremental points recommended by the teachers' review body (*The Independent*, 14 April 1993). This hostility may account for the fact that merit pay schemes are less likely to be found in unionized than non-unionized workplaces (Millward *et al.* 1992: 261–2).

Despite their concerns, unions have sometimes been flexible in their approach to merit pay, seeking influence over aspects of its operation where they lack the power to resist the principle. Unions have been involved in the design of schemes through, for example, agreeing performance criteria, retaining a role in negotiating the size of the pay pot as opposed to its distribution, representing members appealing against appraisals or pay judgements, seeking disclosure of information on occasion, through recourse to the Central Arbitration Committee, as a means of monitoring the 'fairness' of the system. This monitoring, specifically as a means of guarding against possible discrimination in the operation of merit pay schemes, has assumed particular importance in the light of evidence suggesting that such discrimination can take place (Bevan and Thompson 1992), the Danfoss decision at the European Court dealing with sexual discrimination, and a domestic legal settlement based upon racial discrimination in the operation of performance pay at London Underground (*The Guardian*, 4 April 1993).

The pursuit of employee commitment through pay schemes linked to individual, company and, to a lesser extent, group performance, can create problems for management; in particular, their use raises questions about the compatibility of these different schemes. For example, criticism has been levelled at individual performance-related pay schemes which, in rewarding the achievement of narrow and short-term personal goals, may undermine work group cooperation and the longer-term perspective necessary for the future well-being of the organization (Hammer 1975; Lawler 1990).

It is also apparent that in practice, the financial constraints under which these schemes operate may *weaken* rather than strengthen employee commitment. Where a company's financial performance prevents profit-sharing pay-outs or the allocation of significant sums to reward 'high fliers', disappointment in the context of raised expectations is likely to be a source of disaffection with the company, rather than increased commitment. More generally, the use of performance pay as a means of greater financial control over the paybill, allowing the abandonment of across-the-board, cost-of-living increases and the introduction of more targeted awards, may serve to undermine commitment to the company throughout the workforce.

In addition, disaffection with the company rather than commitment, may arise where perceived procedural injustices arise. One of the most commonly-cited criticisms of merit pay is the scope for subjectivity and inconsistency in managerial judgements (Kessler and Purcell 1992; Cannell and Wood 1992). A survey by Wyatts, a firm of consultants, found that in 60 per cent of the 600 companies covered, inconsistency was a major problem, while in well over half the cases subjectivity was seen in a similar light (*Personnel Today* 1990b).

Finally, individual performance pay can be seen as a technique more in tune with the 'harder' approach to human resource management. The employee appraisal under such a pay system is, after all, a judgemental process, with potential penalties as well as benefits derived from a failure to meet standards. In this sense, performance pay can be seen as being at odds with a 'softer' developmental approach seeking commitment through a recognition of the employee's future career interest and needs (Bevan and Thompson 1991).

Reward and flexibility

The search for employee flexibility, reflected in the performance of a range of workplace tasks or duties, has been a perennial managerial concern. This search has, however, been constrained in a number of respects. Employees have exercised countervailing pressures to ensure that the utilization of labour is structured and informed by a consideration of their interests and needs, while managers in their own right have recognized the importance for some overriding framework to provide a rational distribution of work and to ensure the degree of flexibility accords with organizational requirements.

Traditionally, this balance between flexibility in the performance of tasks and some framework for the structuring of duties has been enshrined within job-evaluated grading structures. An internally consistent set of job rates has been established depending upon the size of the job, rather than upon the individual filling it. Where individual performance has merited increased reward, promotion has been available to a higher grade or a 'bigger job' with a more demanding but equally rigid set of associated tasks and duties.

In recent years the pursuit of employee flexibility has intensified; this partly reflects the re-emergence of certain traditional pressures. Founded upon the principle of ensuring internal equity by systematically measuring very different types of jobs within the same organization, job-evaluated grading structures have always lacked a sensitivity to external market pressures. Over the last few years, differentiated pressures within an increasingly fragmented labour market have increased the significance of this drawback. In the late 1980s many organizations – for example, the Civil Service and various local authorities – were forced to pay market supplements to specific occupational or regional groups of employees within broader grades as a response to particular labour market needs (Kessler 1990; LACSAB 1990).

Moreover, established grading structures and demarcations have invariably had to contend with job redesign, technological change and the emergence of new production methods. Moves towards team or cellular working represent the most recent challenge in this respect, necessitating more flexibility across skills and tasks, particularly at the shopfloor level (Grayson 1982).

In addition to these more traditional pressures, job-evaluated grading structures have also had to confront newer pressures related to the changing character of organizations. The collapse of organizational hierarchies, and the emergence of organic structures responsive to fluctuating circumstances, place a premium upon employee performance beyond the constraints of rigid job descriptions. In short, employee adaptiveness to shifting needs becomes more important than the shape of a job ossified within job-evaluated grades. Lawler (1990) captures this point well when he notes that:

> In today's rapidly changing and highly competitive environment, a message that says grow, develop and perform well seems to be more on target than one that says you will be rewarded for outgrowing your job and getting promoted. In organizations whose key assets are its human resources, a system that focuses on people rather than on jobs would seem to be a better fit.
>
> (Ibid.: 142)

Nonetheless, despite these intense pressures and the perceived need to encourage greater employee flexibility and adaptiveness, it is noteworthy that organizations have not generally abandoned job evaluation. The Workplace Industrial Relations survey in 1990 indicated that the percentage of workplaces with job-evaluation schemes had actually risen from 21 per cent to 26 per cent over the decade (Millward *et al.* 1992: 268). This is partly explained by countervailing pressures, particularly generated by equal pay legislation, for the maintenance of evaluated structures. As indicated, it also reflects the ongoing need for such frameworks as a means of responding to broader organizational needs. Moreover, it is apparent that job-evaluated grading structures are not incompatible with the operation of individual performance-related pay – an increasing number of employers have introduced such structures for this very reason (Spencer 1989). The operation of job-evaluated grading structures has, however, been modified in important respects.

First, grading structures have been created on the basis of generic job descriptions and broader bands allowing for flexibility of task performance at given levels within the organization. Furthermore, there are examples of companies which have moved away from grades with fixed increments, to pay ranges which merely set a minimum and a maximum, providing greater scope for pay variation in response to the individuals's performance.

Second, there have been attempts to establish what can be called 'growth structures' (Murliss and Fitt 1991). These seek to balance reward for individual performance with a formal structure defining a clear career path governed by tangible criteria. They are usually applied to professional job families, such as scientists or engineers. At Rolls-Royce's plant at Derby, for instance, such structures have been established for technologists. The structure comprises a number of levels founded upon generic job categories. Movement through these levels is based upon the achievement of stipulated professional qualifications and standards, rather than solely through a promotion which in the past might have taken place only when vacancies arose at more senior levels.

Third, flexibility has been encouraged through the development of grading structures which integrate both manual and white-collar workers. Often associated with the more general move to harmonized terms and conditions, these have been introduced, for instance, at Johnson and Johnson (*IRRR* 1986b) and at the BP Chemicals factory in Wales (*IRRR* 1986a).

Finally, some grading structures have been adapted to ensure that progression is dependent upon the acquisition of skills or competencies. Some companies in the service sector have introduced such schemes. British Home Stores, for example, is prepared to make pay enhancements to employees who successfully attain National Retail Council qualifications (*Pay and Benefits Bulletin*, 7 June 1991). At the Material Division of Courtaulds Aerospace, attempts have been made to link the pay of administrative and managerial staff to National Vocational Qualifications. Nonetheless, skills acquisition pay systems are more typically applied to craft workers. At Amersham International, for instance, attempts were made to develop multi-skilled workers as a means of reducing reliance on contractors (IDS 1990). On greenfield sites at Pilkington Glass, Venture Pressing and Pirelli Cable the application of this type of pay system was perceived as a way of encouraging more flexible working on new technologies (IDS 1992; Yeandle and Clarke 1989).

The pursuit of flexibility in these ways has, however, given rise to managerial problems. These problems revolve around heightened employee expectations which sometimes cannot be fulfilled. The promise of increased pay for flexible performance which is associated with broadened and extended grades, growth structures and skills acquisition systems may be difficult to fulfil given clear limits on the level of skills and flexibility required within any given organization. Payment for skills which are unwanted is naturally perceived as costly and wasteful. When such limits are reached, management is forced to modify and restrict the rules governing the operation of its own schemes. At Pirelli Cable's new plant in Abderdare, for example, management overestimated the need for flexibility, particularly across the blue and white-collar divide. This miscalculation was compounded by the fact that with a slackening in the local labour market conditions, fewer multi-skilled employees actually left the company and needed to be replaced. In combination, these factors led to a suspension of the skills acquisition scheme earlier than expected, and at the cost of considerable employee disappointment.

Further managerial difficulties can arise from the fact that certain types of performance pay inhibit rather than encourage flexibility. Individual performance pay which involves setting personalized targets can encourage a rigid approach to work, with the employee focusing narrowly upon the achievement of specific short-term objectives, to the neglect of other aspects of the job. This was one of the major drawbacks to the scheme established and later abandoned by Coventry City Council. As a personnel manager in the authority noted: 'When the scheme was running staff were less concerned with their daily tasks than with their target sheets' (*Personnel Today* 1990a: 23).

Pearce (1987) makes a similar point, noting that such pay plans place the employee in the position of a 'labour contractor', with performance solely being judged in relation to the 'contract measures', and less account being taken of performance outside of the established criteria, future performance or potential. He also stresses that if business and individual performance requirements are uncertain, the writing of a fixed pay contract actually restricts, rather than enhances, the scope for flexibility and discretion.

Reward and quality

The search for a balance between quantity and quality in production through the use of different reward systems has already been presented as a well-established managerial concern. Recent changes in internal and external contextual factors have nudged the pendulum towards an emphasis on quality. Confronted with an intensification in competition in many product markets, organizations have increasingly been forced to compete on grounds of quality, rather than cost or volume. Moreover, moves to 'leaner' production systems have placed a premium upon combining speed with the maintenance of quality, spawning such initiatives as 'total quality management'.

This repackaging of the quality issue has raised a number of new questions about the structure and administration of reward systems. Although the prescriptive quality literature has remained relatively quiet on these questions (Bowen and Lawler 1992), a review of practice indicates the kind of changes which have been taking place in response. For example, attention has been drawn to the way in which a concern with quality has implications for the character of the reward process. Schonberger (1992) states that: 'Once reward and recognition were reducible to little more than two monetary numbers, wages and benefits. . . . Since TQM is a continuous push for improvement, the management system must itself continuously shift, prod, encourage, praise and reward' (ibid.: 21). This has implications for the range of rewards available and the frequency of their application. In a prescriptive vein, Schonberger uses this rationale to argue for the use of three different rewards for each employee: individual monetary, group monetary and non-monetary.

This need to reward continually has more fundamental implications for management skills. If managers are now being asked to reward in a continuous fashion and on the basis of the way staff perform, rather than simply on the basis of how much they produce, this necessitates the development and application of a considerable range of new management skills: the establishment of valid and viable performance criteria; judgement on whether they have been met; consideration of the relationship between assessed performance and rewards; as well as a host of interpersonal skills such as coaching, counselling and interviewing.

Some of the traditional payment systems, particularly piecework, were used in lieu of managerial competence and skill (McKersie 1963). The establishment of a simple, direct and mechanistic link between pay and output was often seen as being enough to stimulate the requisite level of employee motivation and productivity. While a substantial body of literature describing the way in which piecework schemes could degenerate suggests that such a view may have been somewhat misconceived (NBPI 1968; Brown 1973), it is easy to overlook other evidence indicating that in certain circumstances there was indeed a positive link between PBR and productivity levels (Yetton 1979; Richardson and Wood 1989; Whipp 1992).

There have been suggestions that some of the new, more sophisticated performance-related payment systems are similarly being used as a substitute for 'good' management. The implication in some schemes, that all managers need to do to ensure high performance is assess an employee for pay purposes once a year, has prompted 'a performance management backlash', with its emphasis on the need for a closer, ongoing management–employee relationship (Armstrong and Murliss 1991). Nonetheless, a distinctive feature of many new pay schemes is the way in which the procedures and processes associated with them are being used to encourage the development of management skills.

There are a number of examples of the way in which new pay systems have been used to develop and enhance the role of the line managers (IDS 1990; Swabbe 1989) but it is reflected particularly well in Goodswen's (1988) account of performance-related pay at the National Westminster Bank:

> NatWest's culture had entered a new phase and the climate was favourable for a shift in emphasis from management by control to management by leadership. It is essential that leaders make sure that the broad picture is known, understood and reflected in measurable personal objectives for those in their management team. They must provide individual members of those teams with personal job satisfaction through feedback on performance against objectives. Management leadership also requires the ability to discriminate in the reward given to the exceptional, compared with the standard performance.
>
> (Ibid.: 62)

A similar point is put more succinctly by the leader of Kent County Council:

> Our experience is that Performance Related Pay focuses attention on action plans and targets; *it brings home to line managers their accountability for people*; and it sends clear messages on the importance of performance standards in providing *good quality service*.
>
> (*Financial Times*, 24 July 1992; emphasis added)

Kessler and Purcell (1992) have also pointed to pharmaceutical and engineering companies where performance-related pay systems have been used to develop the managerial skills among those who were promoted to management position because they were 'good' scientists or engineers, rather than because they were 'good' managers.

This approach to the use of payment systems does, however, present organizations with a dilemma. If managers do not initially have the skills which the system seeks to develop, how can they be expected to operate effectively performance-related pay schemes at the outset? There is a very real danger that in the absence of the requisite skills, the payment system may become discredited in the eyes of the workforce, before it can have the desired effect on management behaviour. Personnel departments within organizations have often responded by providing strong guidance to line managers on how to operate these schemes, in the form of tight definitions of performance objectives, assessed performance levels and on the distribution of markings. But this, in turn, has only served to stimulate line management resentment at the intrusiveness of the personnel specialist.

The use of rewards to reinforce the pursuit of quality has, in addition, taken a number of more tangible forms. First, there are examples of companies which have sought to encourage senior managers to take quality more seriously by setting them quality-related targets. In certain cases, this kind of pay–quality link has assumed an almost symbolic significance, indicating to both staff and customers that the quality issue is being taken seriously. Hill (1991), for instance, cites the case of a US automotive company where:

> Following an internal survey which showed many employees were not convinced of the company's commitment to quality as its first priority, it was decided that managers should be required to develop group improvement activities as an integral part of their job and these were not optional activities. As a result, senior department managers were set numerical targets for the involvement of their subordinates in group activities which carried financial bonuses. The upshot was the group activities . . . were worth getting right.
>
> (Ibid.: 559)

Similarly, in Rank Xerox, the performance of European executives is reviewed partly on the basis of targets linked to customer satisfaction and customer loyalty, with a bonus of up to 30 per cent of salary payable for meeting these targets (IDS 1991c).

Second, attempts have been made to link pay to behavioural traits which relate to quality. Central to the drive for quality has been the way in which internal and external consumers are treated. There are instances where pay has been tied to behaviours which satisfy consumer needs. Thornburn (1992), for example, summarizes a Hay Consultancy model in which:

> individuals are evaluated for base pay on such variables as ability to communicate, customer focus and ability to work on a team. Managers are rated on employee development, group productivity and leadership. Variable pay for both is based on what is accomplished. Because customer focus is a critical part of the TQM effort, a three category rating system that involves not meeting customer expectations, meeting them or far exceeding them is easy to implement.
>
> (Ibid.: 59)

The final approach is an extension of the preceding two, in that a number of organizations have sought to devise broader, company-wide indicators of quality performance which can be linked to a bonus payment for the workforce as a whole. At Elida Gibbs, for instance, a scheme covering all non-management employees pays a bonus which is related to the achievement of company-wide sales turnover and customer service targets. Similar schemes have been introduced using such quality measures at Scottish Widows, British Steel, 3M, Companies House and Bull UK (IDS 1991a).

While noting examples of attempts to establish a pay–quality link, few organizations have ventured down this path (IDS 1991a). This may well be because it is difficult to establish viable quality measures. It may also reflect the fact that it is an extremely resource-intensive process to administer a quality link. The application of customer questionnaires, the main means of establishing customer satisfaction, can prove to be highly time-consuming.

A review of recent developments suggests that the relationship between reward policy and practice and the goals commonly cited within the human resource management literature can comfortably be accommodated within the 'looser' contingency model. From a well-established list of pay options, many organizations have selected systems which related pay more closely to various indicators of individual, group or company performance. These are being used as the means for pursuing the equally long-standing managerial goals of commitment, flexibility and quality which have presented themselves in particular ways within the context of certain time-bound internal and external pressures. The remaining question to address is whether the response of organizations conforms to the historical pattern outlined in being *ad hoc* and reactive, or whether the response is more considered, proactive and, consequently, strategic.

REWARDS AND STRATEGIC INTEGRATION: A DISTINCTIVE APPROACH?

There are strong grounds for contesting the suggestion that rewards systems in Britain have been selected on the basis of a systematic assessment by managers of business plans, other human resource management policies and the range of internal and external contingent factors. Smith (1992), for example, notes that in contrast to the United States, the British debate on reward has simply not been informed by notions of 'fit' and 'integration'. Rather, it has been driven by relatively crude and unplanned attempts to relate pay to performance in a manner detached from a consideration of contextual factors.

This view finds strong support from a number of sources. Crowe (1992), as a management consultant in this field, notes that 'I am often involved in a review of one particular aspect of an organization's reward systems but I am very rarely asked to consider the reward system as a whole' (ibid.: 116).

Others have drawn attention to the absence of a considered approach in the selection of reward systems. ACAS (1991), for example, in referring to the introduction of individual performance-related pay states that: 'In some instances at least, it was clear that the circumstances in which such schemes are to operate, the method of their introduction and the design accompanying schemes had not always been adequately considered' (ibid.: 23). Another commentator, considering the same type of pay system, stresses that: 'Many organizations were vague and uncertain about what they were doing; some were swept away by the mood of the times' (*IDS Focus* 1991: 6).

Moreover, it is clear that some of the changes in reward policy and practices have been driven by short-term cost considerations and the need to respond to the immediate labour market pressures in specific regions and for particular occupations. A survey of local authorities, for example, found that the need to address recruitment and retention difficulties was one of the primary reasons for introducing performance-related pay (LACSAB 1990). While the PSI pay survey (1992) concluded that 'the resurgence of "flexible" payment systems in recent years may be as much a symptom of tightening labour markets as a principled attempt to tie pay more closely to individual performance' (ibid.: 29).

Any discussion of the strategic intent of British managers should however, be treated with some care. The assumption that the selection of a reward system can ever be governed by some rationale leading to the systematic evaluation of pay alternatives may be oversimplified, given the attention drawn to the complexities and 'irrationalities' of the managerial decision-making process (see, for example, Behrend 1959; Shimmin 1959; Pettigrew 1973; Ahlstrand 1990). There is also a marked absence of research tracing the evolution of rewards systems and the related decision-making processes. This restricts the possibility of generalization on whether or not strategic considerations are taken into account. Most significantly, however, there is a danger that in moving to the very end of the 'tight' spectrum and applying too demanding a definition of strategic integration, many important developments in reward systems.

There is some evidence to suggest that reward systems are being used in a considered way to facilitate organizational transformation and culture change. In part, this evidence comes in the form of an increasing number of case study reports. These are often produced by the practitioners involved in the changes, who may be inclined to provide some *post hoc* rationalization and justification for change, down-playing the operational difficulties and exaggerating subsequent benefits. It cannot be denied, however, that these accounts do at least indicate *attempts* to use reward systems in a considered way and as a means of supporting broader organizational change. Moreover, these accounts have also found some support in academic studies which suggest that new payment systems are being used as a means of changing employee attitudes, values and assumptions (Kessler and Purcell 1992; Thompson 1992) in response to the pressures faced by organizations.

A review of the evidence highlights the different circumstances in which reward systems have been used in this way. First, there are instances where reward systems have been an integral part of organizational responses to shifts in product market conditions and an intensification of competition. In the finance sector, for example (Swabbe 1989; Goodswen 1988; Mumford and Bailey 1988; *IRRR* 1987b; Snape *et al.* 1993) increased competition between banks and building societies forced companies to extend the range of services provided, to market products more aggressively and to innovate in terms of product development. The successful implementation of these changes was seen to be crucially dependent upon changing employee attitudes and values; rewards were perceived as being central to this process. Ottley (1992), referring to a clearing bank, highlights the importance of individual performance-related pay in this respect:

> Bankings' changing environment necessitated new strategies and business objectives. . . . It was then logical to set targets at all levels in the organization to communicate these strategies to managers and to motivate them to achieve these goals. United Bank chose to introduce a link between achievement of targets and payment of monetary reward. This decision seems so radical within the traditional banking environment that it indicates how important it was to produce a significant shift in the bank's managerial culture.
>
> (Ibid.: 99)

A similar picture is presented at Abbey National:

> We needed a set of human resource strategies which would change the culture of the society into a more dynamic, commercially oriented, market and customer led and profit conscious organization. A sea change was required of which the keystone would be leadership and management style. There were a number of strategies involved. . . . It was considered essential to have reward systems in place which reinforced the performance and results oriented culture we wished to evolve.
>
> (Murphy 1989: 41)

These instances are not restricted to the finance sector. Pottinger (1989) recounts the case of a traditional engineering company, Cummins Engines, where increased competition, the introduction of new technology and the consequent need to redesign work also necessitated a change in organizational culture. A new pay system was again central: 'The organization was not simply trying to negotiate the introduction of a revised remuneration package, it was attempting cultural change and a redesign of the traditional concept of work' (ibid.: 74).

Second, a number of the changes in reward systems, again in the finance sector, can be related not only to changes in the external context but also to changes in organizational structure and corporate identity. It is noteworthy that the wave of mergers between building societies in the 1980s was accompanied by changes in pay systems, partly as a means of devising a new and distinctive organizational culture. For instance, at the Alliance and Leicester: 'The merit system was adopted and adapted for the new organization as the vehicle for change' (*IRRR* 1987b: 6).

Third, attention has been drawn to the careful consideration given to the use of payment systems by organizations moving to greenfield sites and often setting up new technological systems. Whitaker (1986) and Yeandle and Clarke (1989) note very similar developments in the establishment of greenfield sites by Cadbury and Pirelli. Both companies set up working parties to devise future human resource management policies, with pay figuring prominently – indeed, pay systems were developed at both new sites which were distinctive within the broader corporate context, and specifically designed to be sensitive to the new geographical and technological environment. As Whitaker states:

> The project team paid considerable attention to the issue of which payments system was appropriate and concluded that a measured daywork system offered most in terms of overall aims for the plant. Once again this represented deliberate rejection of existing practices within Cadbury. (Ibid.: 667)

Finally, examples are at hand of public utilities using pay systems to change existing organizational culture, sometimes as part of the privatization process. Batstone *et al.* (1984) drew attention to the importance of individual performance-related pay as part of a management strategy designed to break down the Post Office ideology of corporate paternalism and bureaucratic centralism, while Kessler and Purcell (1992) refer to the adoption of a similar type of pay system at a water company following privatization as a means of communicating changed values and operational principles.

These examples suggest that some organizations are systematically considering contextual factors in the design and implementation of reward systems. Moreover, while the list of cases is not extensive, it is broad enough to allow two distinctions to be made in the approaches being adopted. First, there are differences of degree in the importance attached to rewards as a means of change: are rewards a lead technique in driving these changes, or do they play a much more supportive role in relation to other practices? While many of the cases cited place great weight on the use of rewards as an engine for change, the dangers of over-reliance have also been stressed. Beer *et al.* (1984), for example, note:

> The design and management of reward systems constitute one of the most difficult human resource management tasks for the general manager. Of [all] the policy areas in human resource management, this is

where we find the greatest contradiction between the promise of theory and the reality of implementation.

(Ibid.: 113)

Second, a contrast can be drawn between approaches which develop reward systems compatible with organizational culture and those which use reward systems to change company attitudes and values. One of the most noteworthy features of recent use of reward systems is the extent to which they have been mobilized to transform the organization – in other words, to change the internal context, rather than being sensitive or reactive to it. However, the 'correct' balance between change and sensitivity can be difficult for organizations to manage. While there are a number of self-proclaimed successes in the use of rewards as a means of generating change, counter-examples are readily available of where the introduction of reward running against 'the organizational grain' has led to conflict and employee resistance. For example, in the Civil Service (Kessler 1990) and the university sector (*Times Higher Educational Supplement*, 14 May 1993) there are instances of employees protesting against merit pay by pooling their individual performance awards on a departmental or school basis.

SUMMARY AND CONCLUSIONS

This chapter has argued that the presentation of rewards as a key lever in the pursuit of commitment, flexibility and quality in the human resource management literature is far from new and in many respects can simply be seen as another 'shuffling of the pack'. In other words, a review of many of the recent developments in pay policies and practices indicates that organizations are selecting yet another set of well-established pay options, revolving around a closer link between pay and performance variously defined, to deal with a new configuration of long-standing managerial problems. However, it has also been suggested that the use of reward systems, sometimes in combination with other human resource management techniques, to facilitate or support the process of organizational transformation and culture change is an important departure from past practice. There are examples of rewards being used in qualitatively different ways to restructure and develop certain attitudes, values and skills. This has a number of implications for existing analytical models and for the practical evaluation of recent developments.

In analytical terms, it is apparent that the contingency approach needs to be refined. In part, this involves an expansion of the model's analytical parameters. Thus among the goals that management might seek to pursue in choosing an 'appropriate' payment system may be some attempt to change organizational culture, a goal rarely presented by contingency theorists. However, at a more fundamental level this may also involve some shift in direction of causation. For while contingency approaches have normally been founded upon the assumption that organizations develop policies and practices sensitive to their internal and external circumstances, the analysis presented here indicates that reward systems may actually be used to change internal and external contextual factors.

At a practical level, this discussion also raises a number of important questions revolving around the issue of effectiveness. In general, very little work has been conducted into the effectiveness of recent pay schemes, particularly through the establishment of a direct and quantifiable link between pay schemes and individual or organizational performance (National Research Council 1991). This is especially the case with individual performance- or merit-based pay schemes, and reflects the difficulty of isolating the impact of a single variable – a reward system – upon performance. Accepting these limitations, it is nonetheless clear that any assessment of effectiveness must be located within the context of the broader process of organizational transformation. Seen as an integral part of the process for change, employers are likely to be less concerned with the immediate, direct and tangible impact of new reward systems upon individual and organizational performance and more interested in their longer-term impact upon employee values, attitudes and skills.

Finally, the evaluation of effectiveness in these terms may have implications for the future dynamic of change in the use of pay systems. In the past, it was noted that this dynamic was founded in large part upon the short-term managerial need to address tangible problems arising from the degeneration of the prevailing pay system. It has been noted that recent attempts to use pay as a means of pursuing the goals of commitment, flexibility and quality may indeed give rise to certain concrete, short-term problems and tensions. Placed within the context of long-term, fundamental organizational change and the use of pay systems to restructure employee perceptions, these dysfunctional consequences may be viewed by management in a more tolerant light and within a longer time-frame. As a consequence, many of the new developments in reward systems outlined in this chapter can less readily be dismissed as passing fads or fashions.

REFERENCES

ACAS (1988) 'Developments in payment systems', Occasional Paper No. 45, London: ACAS.

—— (1990) *Appraisal Related Pay*, Advisory Booklet No. 14, London: ACAS.

—— (1991) *Annual Report*, London: HMSO.

—— (undated) *Introduction to Payment Systems*, London: ACAS.

Ahlstrand, B. (1990) *The Quest for Productivity*, Cambridge: Cambridge University Press.

Armstrong, M. and Murliss, H. (1991) *Reward Management*, London: Kogan Page.

Balkin, D. and Gomez-Mezia, L. (eds) (1987) *New Perspectives on Compensation*, Englewood Cliffs, NJ: Prentice Hall.

Batstone, E., Ferner, A. and Terry, M. (1984) *Consent and Efficiency*, Oxford: Blackwell.

Beer, M., Spector, B., Lawrence, P., Mills, D. and Walton, R. (1984) *Managing Human Assets*, New York: Free Press.

Behrend, H. (1955) 'Financial incentives as the expression of a system of beliefs', *British Journal of Sociology* 10(2): 137–47.

Bell, D. and Hanson, D. (1982) *Profit Sharing and Employee Shareholding Attitude Survey*, London: Industrial Participation Association.

Bevan, S. and Thompson, M. (1991) 'Performance management at the crossroads', *Personnel Management* November.

—— and —— (1992) *Merit Pay, Performance Appraisal and Attitudes to Women's Work*, University of Sussex: IMS.

Blinder, A. (ed.) (1990) *Paying for Productivity*, Washington, DC: Brooking Institution.

Bowen, D. and Lawler III, E. (1992) 'Total quality oriented human resource management', *Organizational Dynamics* 20(4): 29–41.

Bowey, A., Thorpe, R., Mitchell, F., Nicholl, G., Gornold, D., Savery, L. and Hellier, P. (1982) *Effects of Incentive Payment Systems*, Department of Employment Research Paper No. 36, London: DE.

Brown, W. (1973) *Piecework Bargaining*, London: Heinemann Educational Books.

Cannell, M. and Long, P. (1991) 'What's changed about incentive pay?', *Personnel Management* October: 58–63.

Cannell, M. and Wood, S. (1992) *Incentive Pay*, London: IPM.

Casey, B., Lakey, J. and White, M. (1992) *Payment Systems: A Look at Current Practice*, London: Department of Employment.

Citizen's Charter (1991) Cmnd. 1599, London: HMSO.

Commission on Industrial Relations (1974) *Final Report*, London: HMSO.

Confederation of British Industry (1988) *People at the Cutting Edge*, London: CBI.

Crowe, D. (1992) 'A new approach to reward management', in M. Armstrong (ed.) *Strategies for HRM: A Total Business Approach*, London: Kogan Page.

Curnow, B. (1986) 'The creative approach to pay', *Personnel Management* October: 70–5.

Deming, W. (1982) *Out of Crisis*, Cambridge: Cambridge University Press.

Devanna, M., Fombrun, C. and Tichy, N. (1984) 'A framework for strategic human resource management', in C. Fombrun *et al.* (eds) *Strategic Human Resource Management*, New York: John Wiley.

Duncan, C. (1988) 'Why profit related pay will fail', *Industrial Relations Journal* 19(3): 186–99.

Dunn, S., Richardson, R. and Dewe, P. (1991) 'The impact of employee share ownership on worker attitudes: a longitudinal case study', *Human Resource Management Journal* 1(3): 1–17.

Fombrun, C., Tichy, N. and Devanna, M. (1984) *Strategic Human Resource Management*, New York: John Wiley & Sons.

Goodswen, M. (1988) 'Retention and reward of the high achiever', *Personnel Management* October: 61–4.

Grayson, D. (1982) *Job Evaluation and Changing Technology*, London: Work Research Unit.

Gregg, P. and Machin, S. (1988) 'Unions and the incidence of performance linked pay schemes in Britain', *Industrial Journal of Organizations* 6: 99–107.

Grint, K. (1991) *Sociology of Work*, Cambridge: Polity Press.

Guest, D. (1987) 'Human resource management and industrial relations', *Journal of Management Studies* 24(5).

Hammer, W. (1975) 'How to ruin motivation with pay', *Compensation Review* 7(3): 17–27.
Hill, S. (1991) 'Why quality circles failed but total quality management might succeed', *British Journal of Industrial Relations* 29(4).
Howell, P. (1951) 'Incentives in action', *Journal of Institute of Personnel Management* XXXIII(37): 215–25.
IDS (1989) Top Pay Unit, Review 104.
—— (1990) Top Pay Unit, Review 110.
—— (1991a) *Bonus Schemes, Part 1*, study no. 488.
—— (1991b) *Bonus Schemes, Part 2*, study no. 492.
—— (1991c) *Bonus Schemes, Part 3*, study no. 494.
—— (1992) *Skills Based Pay*, study no. 500.
IDS Focus (1988) No. 49, December.
—— (1991) No. 61, December.
Industrial Relations Review and Report (IRRR) (1986a) 'BP Chemicals Barry: a move to staff status', 362, February: 9–11.
—— (1986b) 'Johnson and Johnson: integrated payment structure', 378, October: 3–9.
—— (1987a) 'Abbey National', 390, April: 2–5.
—— (1987b) 'Alliance and Leicester', December: 2–8.
Involvement and Participation (1990) 'BR take the PRP line', Autumn: 12–13.
Kerr, J. (1985) 'Diversification strategies and managerial rewards: an empirical study', *Academy of Management Journal* 28(1): 155–79.
Kessler, I. (1990) 'Flexibility and comparability in pay determination for professional civil servants', *Industrial Relations Journal* 21(3): 194–208.
Kessler, I. and Purcell, J. (1992) 'Performance related pay – objectives and application', *Human Resource Management Journal* 2(3): 34–59.
Kinnie, N. and Lowe, D. (1990) 'Performance related pay on the shopfloor', *Personnel Management* November: 45–9.
LACSAB (1990) *Performance Related Pay in Practice*, London: LACSAB.
Lawler III, E. (1990) *Strategic Pay*, San Francisco, CA: Jossey Bass.
Lupton, T. and Gowler, D. (1969) 'Selecting a wage payment system', research paper III, London: EEF.
McKersie, R. (1963) 'Wage methods of the future', *British Journal of Industrial Relations* 1(2): 191–212.
Mahoney, T. (1992) 'Multiple pay contingencies: strategic design of compensation', in G. Salaman (ed.) *Human Resource Strategies*, London: Sage.
Millward, N., Stevens, M., Smart, D. and Hawes, W. (1992) *Workplace Industrial Relations in Transition*, Aldershot: Dartmouth.
Moss Kanter, R. (1989) *When Giants Learn to Dance*, London: Simon & Schuster.
Mumford, J. and Bailey, T. (1988) 'Rewarding behavioural skills as part of performance', *Personnel Management* December.
Murliss, H. and Fitt, D. (1991) 'Job evaluation in a changing world', *Personnel Management*, May.
Murliss, H. and Wright, V. (1993) 'Decentralizing pay decisions: empowerment or abdication', *Personnel Management* March: 28–33.
Murphy, T. (1989) 'Pay for performance: an instrument for strategy', *Long Range Planning* 22(4): 40–5.
National Research Council (1991) *Pay for Performance*, Washington, DC: National Academic Press.
NBPI (1968) *Payment by Result Systems*, Report No. 65, Cmnd. 3627, London: HMSO.

—— (1971) *Fifth and Final General Report*, London: HMSO.
Norburn, D. and Miller, P. (1981) 'Strategy and executive reward: the mis-match in the strategic process', *Journal of General Management* 6(4): 17–27.
Ottley, D. (1992) 'United bank: a case study on the implication of a performance related reward scheme', in W. Bruns (ed.) *Performance Measurement, Evaluation and Incentive*, Boston, MA: Harvard Business School Press,
Pearce, J. (1987) 'Why merit pay doesn't work', in D. Balkin and L. Gomez-Mejia (eds) *New Perspectives on Compensation*, Englewood Cliffs, NJ: Prentice Hall.
Petch, S. (1990) 'Performance related pay – problems for the trade unions', paper to TUC seminar on PRP, 21 January.
Peters, T. (1988) *Thriving on Chaos*, London: Macmillan.
Pettigrew, A. (1973) *The Politics of Organizational Decision Making*, London: Tavistock.
Personnel Today (1990a) 'Failing the test', August: 22–8.
—— (1990b) 'Do you play the rating game?', October: 28–31.
Philips, M. (1962) 'Merit rating for skilled and semi-skilled workers', *Personnel Management* XLIV(360): 120–9.
Poole, M. (1988) 'Factors affecting the development of employee financial participation in contemporary Britain', *British Journal of Industrial Relations* 26(1).
Pottinger, J. (1989) 'Engineering change through pay', *Personnel Management* October: 73–4.
Profit Related Pay – A Consultative Document (1986) Cmnd. 9835, London: HMSO.
Richardson, R. and Marsden, D. (1991) *Does Performance Pay Motivate?*, London: LSE.
Richardson, R. and Nejad, A. (1986) 'Employee share ownership schemes in the UK – an evaluation', *British Journal of Industrial Relations* 24(2): 233–50.
Richardson, R. and Wood, S. (1989) 'Productivity change in the coal industry and new industrial relations', *British Journal of Industrial Relations* 27(1): 33–56.
Salter, M. (1973) 'Tailoring incentive compensation to strategy', *Harvard Business Review*, March–April: 94–102.
Schonberger, R. (1992) 'TQM cuts a broad swathe through manufacturing and beyond', *Organizational Dynamics* 20(4): 16–28.
Schuller, T. (1989) 'Financial participation', in J. Storey (ed.) *New Perspectives on Human Resource Management*, London: Routledge.
Shimmin, S. (1959) *Payment By Results*, London: Staples Press.
Smith, G. (1986) 'Profit sharing and employee share ownership in Britain', *Employment Gazette*, September.
—— (1993) 'Employee share schemes: the result of a survey', *DE Gazette* 101(4): 149–53.
Smith, I. (1989) *People and Profits*, London: Croner.
—— (1992) 'Reward management and HRM', in P. Blyton and P. Turnbull (eds) *Reassessing Human Resource Management*, London: Sage.
Snape, E., Redman, T. and Wilkinson, A. (1993) 'Human resource management in building societies: making the transformation', *Human Resource Management Journal* 3(3): 43–60.
Spencer, S. (1989) 'Devolving job evaluation', *Personnel Management* January: 48–50.
Stewart, A. (1952) 'Merit pay incentive schemes', *International Labour Review* LXV(4): 442–61.
Storey, J. (1992) *Developments in the Management of Human Resources*, Oxford: Blackwell.

Swabbe, A. (1989) 'Performance related pay: a case study', *Employee Relations* 11(2): 17–23.
Swanson, L. and Corbin, D. (1969) 'Employee motivation programmes: a change in philosophy', *Personnel Journal* 48(11): 895–8.
Thompson, M. (1992) *Performance Pay: The Employer Experience*, Brighton: IMS.
Thornburn, L. (1992) 'Pay for performance: what you should know (part 1)', *HR Magazine* 7(6): 58–61.
Thierry, H. (1992) 'Pay and payment systems', in J. Hartley and G. Stephenson (eds) *Employment Relations*, Oxford: Blackwell.
Walton, R. (1985) 'From control to commitment in the workplace', *Harvard Business Review* 63(2): 77–84.
Whipp, R. (1992) 'HRM, competition and strategy', in P. Blyton and P. Turnbull (eds) *Reassessing Human Resource Management*, London: Sage.
Whitaker, R. (1986) 'Managerial strategy and industrial relations: a case study of plant relocation', *Journal of Management Studies* 23(6): 657–74.
Yeandle, D. and Clarke, J. (1989) 'Personnel strategy for an automated plant', *Personnel Management* June: 51–5.
Yetton, P. (1979) 'The efficiency of piecework incentive payment systems', *Journal of Management Studies* 16(3): 253–69.

Chapter 11

Involvement and participation

Mick Marchington

INTRODUCTION

For many observers, notions of employee involvement (EI) and participation are central to any consideration of human resource management (HRM). Terms such as 'empowerment', 'teamworking', 'autonomy' and 'communications' are peppered throughout the management literature which publicizes and celebrates the latest initiatives in HRM. Similarly, the concepts of involvement and participation form part of many academic discussions of HRM, either as explicit elements of its policy and practice, or implicitly as a potential contributor to the achievement of higher levels of employee commitment.

It will be apparent from earlier chapters in this book, however, as well as from several other collections of readings on the subject (see, for example, Storey 1989; Blyton and Turnbull 1992; Towers 1992), that much depends on the version of HRM under consideration. If HRM is conceived in terms of its 'hard' variant, where the major issue is how well the management of human resources is integrated with other elements of corporate strategy, then the place of EI is far from assured. In some of these situations, EI may not be seen as important by senior managers, given an emphasis on tight cost control, de-skilled jobs, and a lack of investment in training. In others, EI may be little more than one-way communications channels, designed merely to convey the latest news to employees and indicate to them the merits of management's decision. In these cases, if EI is practised, it is likely to take a rather diluted and marginal form.

In contrast, if HRM is defined in terms of its 'soft' variant, the emphasis shifts – at least in theory – to the management of 'resourceful' humans, and to assumptions that employees represent an important asset to the organization and a potential source of competitive advantage. In these situations, which are often characterized by employers whose products are marketed on the basis of quality rather than price, EI may take a variety of forms, including regular communications, problem-solving techniques, consultation, and financial involvement (see, for example, Schuler and Jackson

1987; Marchington 1992a). The analysis of EI which follows in subsequent sections of this chapter is based around the concept of 'soft' HRM to a much greater extent than its 'hard' version, although in reality, of course, shades of both may exist in parallel at the same organization and in relation to the same employees.

Even where 'soft' HRM is espoused as a policy goal by senior management and in the public relations literature of their organizations, this will not guarantee that EI will be practised at the workplace, or that it will make any impact whatsoever. As with other aspects of management and human resource strategy, there is often a sizeable gap between the espoused policy and the concrete practices at establishment level or below (Brewster *et al.* 1983; Marchington and Parker 1990; Storey 1992). In addition, even though there are claims that EI will have a positive effect on the organization, it is difficult to determine its precise impact, if any, on employee and management attitudes, or the relationship between EI and performance.

While it may be commonplace to argue in certain circles (for example, Department of Employment 1989: 4) that direct EI is connected with high levels of commitment and organizational performance, this is predicated upon a series of assumptions, none of which can be taken for granted: the assumptions that line managers are committed to EI and are able to make it operate effectively in the workplace; that EI has a positive effect on employee attitudes, which leads to changes in work behaviour that feed through to higher levels of productivity and effectiveness; and that the role of workplace trade unionism will also be adjusted so that employee representatives and union members acquiesce with management plans and policies, or indeed are further marginalized or removed altogether. If none or only some of these are achieved, the impact of EI – and with it, one key element of HRM – is much reduced. In short, rather than assuming that EI will operate automatically as part of a 'soft' human resource strategy, it is argued here that the translation of EI from broad management policy to specific workplace practice, let alone employee commitment and performance, is problematic. This is the central theme of this chapter.

There are five main sections to the chapter. First, there is a short analysis of the nature and extensiveness of EI, a description of its principal forms, and mention of the major differences between EI and industrial democracy. Second, we analyse the depth of line-management support for EI, and the degree to which managers and supervisors are sufficiently well-trained and rewarded to make it work in practice. Third, there is an evaluation of the impact of EI upon employee attitudes and performance, and some consideration of the major methodological problems connected with assessing this. Fourth, we move on to analyse the relationship between EI and workplace trade unionism, and in particular address the question of whether unions are being marginalized by EI, either by design or as a consequence of new initiatives. Finally, a few general conclusions are drawn.

THE NATURE AND EXTENT OF EMPLOYEE INVOLVEMENT IN BRITAIN

EI is a relatively new term which entered into the vocabulary both of practitioners and academics during the 1980s, not just in Britain but also elsewhere (see, for example, Marchington 1989, 1992b; Cotton 1993). It appears to represent the most recent attempt by employers to find participative ways in which to manage their staff, and to some extent – with the support of government and employers' organizations – it has for the moment replaced earlier variants, such as workers' participation and industrial democracy.

EI is a phrase which is redolent of employer initiatives. The decision about whether or not to 'involve' employees rests with management, who are able to define and limit the terms under which EI can take place, and gear their operation to strengthen the individualization of employment relations (Sisson 1993). It is established very much at management's discretion, resting almost exclusively upon a voluntary as opposed to a statutory base. This has led to EI being extolled by various Conservative governments of the 1980s and 1990s in preference to European-wide initiatives emerging out of the Social Charter. The only legal obligation is on public limited companies which employ more than 250 people. These employers are required to include a statement in their annual report indicating what action has been taken over the previous year to introduce, maintain or develop employees involvement. Four categories of EI are specified: the provision of systematic information, consultation, the encouragement of financial involvement, and practices designed to promote a common economic and financial awareness among employees. However, it should be recognized that the legal pressures on employers via this route are negligible (see Marchington 1992a: 35–8).

Industrial democracy, on the other hand, commences from the standpoint that employees ought to have the opportunity to become involved in decision-making at work, in much the same way as political democracy refers to their rights as citizens (see, for example, Blumberg 1968; Brannen 1983; Pateman 1970; Poole 1986; Schuller 1985). It is an explicit form of power-sharing between employers and employees, usually via worker/union representatives, which is practised throughout much of mainland Europe through worker director and works council arrangements (Gold and Hall 1992; Hall 1992). Perhaps the difference is most easily captured by the point that EI starts from the assumption that managers might see the advantage of *allowing* employees to become involved, whereas industrial democracy has its source in the *right* of the governed to exercise some control over those in authority. As suggested in the previous section, EI is the term which fits more easily with HRM, given its managerialist and neo-unitarist underpinnings, and its ethos of common and shared interests (Marchington 1992a: 23–30).

The extensiveness of EI can be estimated by consulting, among other sources, the Workplace Industrial Relations surveys of 1980, 1984 and 1990 (Daniel and Millward 1983; Millward and Stevens 1986; Millward *et al.* 1992) and the case study research on twenty-five organizations conducted for the Employment Department in 1989–91 (Marchington *et al.* 1992). In broad terms, according to the 1990 survey (Millward *et al.* 1992), EI appears to have grown considerably since the early 1980s, to the extent that it is now part of the common parlance of most senior managers. This picture is reinforced by anecdotal and case study evidence. It takes a wide range of forms in practice, but for simplicity these can be categorized into five groups.

Downward communications

The first category is downward communications from managers to employees, the principal purpose of which is to inform and 'educate' staff so that they accept management plans. Used in this sense, it can be seen as a euphemism for leadership (MacInnes 1987: 131). This includes briefing groups/team briefing and other regular structured techniques for information-passing, informal and non-routinized communications between managers/supervisors and their staff, formal written media such as employee reports, house journals or company newpapers, and videos which are used to convey standard messages to employees about the organization's annual financial performance or to publicize some new managerial initiative.

Most studies seem to indicate that these forms of EI are among the most popular in Britain in the early 1990s – in particular, team briefings and regular meetings between senior managers and their staff (Millward *et al.* 1992: 175–6).

Upward problem-solving

Secondly, there is the category of upward problem-solving, which is designed to tap into employee knowledge and opinion, either at an individual level or through small groups. These techniques have several objectives, such as to increase the stock of ideas within an organization, to encourage cooperative relations at work, and to legitimize change. The best-known of these are quality circles, suggestions schemes, attitude surveys, and (possibly) total quality management/customer care committees. Of these, Marginson and his colleagues (1988) noted that 'quality circles appear to be part of a wider strategy for winning the hearts and minds in heavily-unionized workplaces' (ibid.: 111).

Although TQM is now well-established as one of the most recent and extensive innovations in management practice, and many of its proponents utilize the language of EI, the degree to which this is promoted in practice is much more open to question (Wilkinson *et al.* 1992). Of the others, suggestions schemes are still relatively popular, although quality circles and attitude surveys are used in only a minority of establishments (Millward *et al.* 1992: 167; Gallie and White 1993: 39).

Task participation

The third set of EI initiatives is task participation and job redesign, in which employees are encouraged or expected to extend the range and type of tasks undertaken at work. As with the previous two categories, these are also a form of direct EI which relates to the individual employee, although it is important to note that these are not new inventions of the last decade; see, for example, the quality of working life experiments in the 1960s and 1970s (Kelly 1982; Knights *et al.* 1985). Among the forms which this takes in practice are horizontal job redesign (a wider range of jobs undertaken at the same level), job enrichment and vertical role integration (taking greater responsibility for supervisory duties), and teamworking (where the work-group organizes the job as a whole).

Once put forward as a counter to alienation at work, methods of task-based participation are now sometimes viewed as making an important contribution to the achievement of competitive advantage (Walton 1985). After years of being informed that higher productivity was only feasible with increased de-skilling, managers are now being confronted with the argument that expanded jobs, team-working and empowerment are the keys to organizational success. Despite many quoted examples of job redesign (Walton 1985; Buchanan 1986; Wood 1986; Berggren 1989; Oliver and Wilkinson 1992), it is difficult to estimate the extent of these practices, given the lack of representative data.

Consultation and representative participation

Fourth is consultation/representative participation. This differs from each of the previous categories outlined above in that employees are involved through representatives drawn from among their number – in a slight majority of cases, on the basis of union membership. In a sense, this represents the most formal and potentially most influential form of EI discussed in this chapter, and it is probably the closest that we get in Britain to models of representative participation practised throughout the rest of Europe (Marchington 1992a: 149–50). One of its major objectives, according to managers, is to act as a safety valve – an alternative to formal disputes – by means of which more deep-seated employee grievances can be addressed. In other situations, there are suggestions that joint consultation is being used to hinder the recognition of trade unions or to undermine their activities in highly unionized workplaces (Marchington 1992a: 136–41).

There has been a decline in the extensiveness of formal consultation over the course of the last decade, and it is now estimated that joint consultative committees exist in less than 30 per cent of all workplaces with twenty-five or more employees (compared to 34 per cent in 1980). According to Millward *et al.* (1992: 154), this decline was due principally to a fall in the number of larger workplaces in Britain.

Financial involvement

The final category is financial involvement, encompassing schemes designed to link part (or occasionally all) of an individual's rewards to the success of the unit or enterprise as a whole. These take a variety of forms in practice, ranging from simple profit-sharing schemes and employee share ownership systems, which have been assisted by legislation in Britain (Smith 1986; Poole 1989; Schuller 1989). ESOPs (employee share ownership plans) are growing in Britain (see Pendleton 1992; Wilkinson *et al.* 1994), but are much more extensive in the USA (see Cotton 1993: 200–30 for a review of the American data). Although the rationale for financial involvement is similar in many respects to those already discussed (e.g. educating employees about the performance of the organization and its commercial environment), there is also an assumption that employees with a financial stake in the overall success of the unit/enterprise are more likely to work harder for its ultimate success. Of course, much depends upon whether employees also identify such a link, and how much control they have over the performance of the unit concerned. In the case of employee share ownership arrangements, the most popular of these schemes, this is negligible in financial terms (Baddon *et al.* 1989).

It is apparent, therefore, that a range of schemes exists for promoting EI, and that even in formal terms these can vary quite markedly. Some are based upon the direct involvement of employees, while others are predicated upon the principle that representatives (unionized or not) act for individual employees. Some are concerned primarily with downward communications, whereas others are based upon employees contributing ideas and helping to solve work-related problems. Some are holistic, relating to extensions to the individual's job or new methods of organizing work, while others are more tangential and only require 'involvement' for brief periods on a regular or infrequent basis. Some schemes are designed to link directly part or all of an individual's pay to the performance of a unit or enterprise, whereas the majority do not. On the other hand, despite the differences, other features are common to all forms of EI: managers have been the prime instigators of new initiatives; employees are assumed to be keen on greater involvement, whatever form it takes; a unity of purpose or common interest between managers and non-managerial employees is thought to be achievable at the workplace; and increased levels of employee commitment to the organization and improvements in performance or/productivity are anticipated.

MANAGERS AND EMPLOYEE INVOLVEMENT

Managers at all levels in the organizational hierarchy are expected to play a crucial role in the development and maintenance of EI, whichever form it takes in practice. There are, however, a number of critical points at which managerial actions or inactions can reduce the impact of schemes or cause them to function in ways which were not intended by their architects. For example, there may be incomplete coverage of a particular form of EI across an organization, which means that sizeable numbers of employees fail to be 'involved' in the manner prescribed by specialists at corporate headquarters. Equally, different EI techniques may contradict and conflict with one another (or with aspects of human resource/management policy), rather than being integrated and working in conjunction, a problem especially if there has been a tendency to adopt a faddish and fashion-oriented approach to new initiatives. Moreover, supervisors and first-line managers may not share the commitment of their senior colleagues to EI, and be dubious about its benefits for the organization or for themselves. Finally, supervisors and first-line managers may lack the skills and attributes needed to operate EI, perhaps because they feel uncomfortable in such situations or have never been adequately trained by their organizations. Each of these is now addressed in turn.

Incomplete coverage

Some of the case study evidence makes it clear that there are often significant gaps between formal policy statements and senior management beliefs on the one hand, and the reality of EI at workplace level. A cursory examination of any company's statement on employee involvement contained in their annual report might suggest a hive of activity, an assessment which can seem unrecognizable to the participants themselves. Perhaps this is best illustrated by examples relating to quality circle coverage, which indicate that only a minority of employees are actually members of circles at any time. For example, in a longitudinal study of a carpet manufacturer in the Midlands, it was found that the proportion of workers in membership of quality circles never exceeded 10 per cent, and some groups (such as the highly unionized weavers) still refused to 'buy in' to the concept a decade after it had first been launched (Black and Ackers 1988: 13; Ackers *et al.* 1992: 64). Similarly low proportions of membership were reported by Hill (1991: 7–8).

Given the 'voluntary' nature of quality circles, this may not be surprising, but there are also examples where team briefing sessions or joint consultative committees fail to meet at regular and scheduled intervals. Perhaps they are held infrequently, or no longer meet, while in some cases they might never have met since the scheme was introduced, despite the belief of the senior manager who was its instigator and champion (Marchington *et al.* 1992). In other cases, schemes are launched in a blaze of publicity, only to fall foul of a range of operational difficulties: tight production or customer service schedules which make it problematic to arrange sessions at certain times of the week or year; shift-workers who are away from the workplace for several days at a time; employees on atypical contracts who are not scheduled to work at times when briefings are held; or a workforce which is dispersed throughout the community or the country (Marchington *et al.* 1989).

Competing initiatives and contradictory rationale

Even if EI schemes do cover the majority of employees in an organization, there are often problems in their introduction and implementation, as well as in their integration with existing mechanisms. In larger establishments, in particular, it would not be atypical for seven or eight different EI techniques to operate at the same time, covering the range of forms which were outlined earlier in this chapter. Some of these (such as joint consultative committees) may have been in existence for many years, whereas others (especially direct EI) will have been products of the last decade. On some occasions, these will have been introduced in a phased and planned manner, and attempts will have been made to ensure that there is at least some complementarity between these different techniques. In many other cases, however, recent initiatives owe rather more to fads and fashions, as well as moves by different departments to be seen as contributing to corporate success (Marchington *et al.* 1993). This multiplicity of EI arrangements can result in different techniques competing with each other, and in some instances flatly contradicting the aims and objectives of other initiatives, as for example between suggestions schemes whereby employees are paid for ideas, versus TQM initiatives in which employees are expected to search for continuous improvement as part of their normal duties.

The dynamics of EI can be graphically represented as a series of 'waves', as shown in Figure 11.1, with each line representing the ebb and flow of a particular technique over time and in comparison with each other at a large private service sector firm.

In addition, the fact that EI can be defined in such a way as to fall within the province of different departments also increases the likelihood of competing initiatives and quite contradictory rationales. These may even be introduced at the same time, with little or no coordination across the

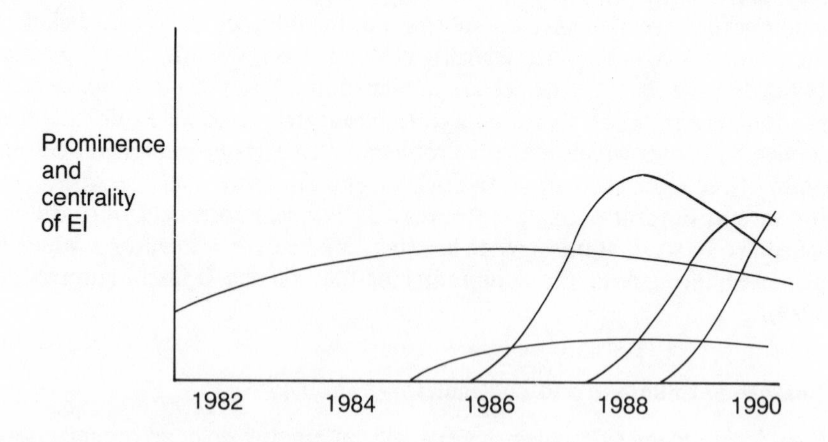

Figure 11.1 Waves of EI at a large private service sector firm

organization concerned. Plainly, this is more marked for different forms of EI, and it is possible that the motives which underpin and sustain representative participation are philosophically and practically at odds with those which lead to the implementation of TQM or customer care. However, the same sort of problem can arise with schemes which are similar in form, but which are driven by different departments; for example, a system for internal communications championed by a personnel department may have quite a different character to one which is promoted by a sales or public relations team. These notions of champions, 'impression management' and interdepartmental rivalries are developed in more detail in Marchington *et al*. (1993).

Of course, the conveyance of contradictory messages is not just confined to EI schemes, but can be seen more widely in relation to other management plans and policies. For example, a new initiative which is introduced, perhaps quite genuinely, with promises of empowerment and greater autonomy can soon founder if employees find other aspects of their work are more tightly controlled and overseen (Wilkinson *et al*. 1992). As Sewell and Wilkinson (1992) conclude, on the basis of a case study of TQM in a manufacturing company:

> on the one hand, the rhetoric of HRM preaches commitment based on trust, a culture based on equality and a unity of goals backed up by practical measures which try to minimise differences. . . . On the other

hand, they [the employees] are subjected to the closest scrutiny which is used to distinguish them from their peers on matters of the minutest detail.

(Ibid.: 112)

Lack of commitment by first-line managers

EI schemes often fail due to splits and discontinuities between different levels in the hierarchy, demonstrated by the reaction of supervisors to initiatives which they see as the brainchild of some young recruit on the promotion fast-track. It can be assumed, quite incorrectly, that first-line managers always identify with the organization for which they work and share managerial values about the desirability of EI. The language of team-working and empowerment, while potentially attractive to more senior managers, can appear highly threatening and problematic to their more junior colleagues whose authority has often been built on technical expertise and the restriction of information flows to the shop floor. Similarly, expectations that they should operate as 'coaches' as opposed to 'cops' can be seen by supervisors as being at odds with their own common-sense versions of what workers are 'really' like. In other words, rather than viewing EI as beneficial to the organization, instead it can be reinterpreted as 'soft' management and pandering to the workforce by long-haired idealists in corporate headquarters (Wilkinson *et al.* 1993) – in much the same way as the removal of clocking-on and -off systems is often seen as misguided. This is partly because supervisors see themselves as much closer to the people for whom they are responsible, rather than being a part of management, a feeling which may intensify as their job security is lessened and promotion opportunities are reduced (Partridge 1989: 213). To some extent, they are estranged from managerial goals and values (Scase and Goffee 1989: 28), and the highly mobile career paths of EI champions merely serve to convince them that their own contribution is not particularly valued by the organization.

Practical reasons for failure to implement EI

Even if supervisors do share the same values as their senior management colleagues, EI may still fail to be implemented fully in line with expectations for more practical reasons. First, supervisors and first-line managers already suffer from work overload in many organizations, and find it difficult to set aside time to brief or consult with their subordinates. This is particularly pronounced in situations where supervisors are not explicitly rewarded for developing EI, and their performance is judged against production or service criteria (e.g. number of items manufactured or queue lengths) which, on the surface at least, do not seem to be assisted by an EI programme. Although the mission statement, for example, may state that EI is a key objective of the organization, supervisors soon become aware that production or service considerations assume priority in the event of conflicting objectives. Second, given the desire by most organizations to implement new EI initiatives with a minimum of delay, supervisors often receive no more than a rudimentary level of training in how to operate the scheme. Little or no time is devoted to ensuring that they understand and accept the principles which underlie schemes, nor to training them in how to manage EI – such as how to brief a team effectively or seek suggestions from a quality circle (Marchington 1992a). Overall, the evidence indicates that major problems like these also occur in the USA at the supervisory interface (Klein 1984).

The evidence presented in this section clearly illustrates the problems which are encountered within management in operating EI, and converting it from policy into practice. Given, as suggested above, that managers are central to the effective functioning of EI and HRM, this must necessarily limit its potential impact on employee commitment and performance. Although a number of the problems which have been identified could well be alleviated by the provision of more effective training or other amendments to human resource practice, there remain more deep-seated concerns which cannot be addressed so easily, in particular relating to supervisory commitment and inter-functional rivalries within management.

THE IMPACT OF EI ON EMPLOYEE ATTITUDES AND PERFORMANCE

We have already noted that employees are a principal target of EI schemes, and it might therefore be concluded that EI would have an impact upon their attitudes and performance. Analysis of employee responses in the Marchington *et al.* (1992) survey suggested that EI has a mildly favourable impact on employee attitudes, or at least that the existence or promise of EI is associated with more positive attitudes. There are less data available on the links between attitudes and behaviour, however, or between EI and employees' commitment to work and their employing organization. The whole area is bedevilled with a range of methodological problems, as we see below. But, it is also suggested here that attitudes to work and to EI need to be placed firmly within the relevant organizational and commercial context, and that employee responses to EI may act as a conduit for more general feelings of support for their employer or anxiety about future job prospects.

There is a general consensus from the surveys (see, for example, Holter 1965; Hespe and Wall 1976; Ramsay 1976; Marchington 1980; Rathkey 1983; Dewe *et al.* 1988; Baddon *et al.* 1989; Allen *et al.* 1991) that employees are attracted to the general concept of involvement and participation;

indeed, it would be remarkable if they were not, given that the alternative is to argue for autocratic and non-communicative management styles! In principle, employees are keen to have more say within their establishments and to find out more about actions which are likely to impact upon their own jobs and activities at work. There are variations on the basis of certain personality and demographic characteristics according to the surveys, but nevertheless the common view is that employees are not satisfied with employers acting without some effort to keep them informed. For example, Gallie and White (1993) argue that their survey results suggest that

> participation is of fundamental importance for employees' attitudes to the organisations for which they work. It is strongly related to the way they respond to changes in work organisation and with their perception of the quality of the overall relationship between management and employees.
>
> (Ibid.: 44)

But there are limits to this desire for greater involvement, and certainly the attitude surveys suggest that employees are not searching for workers' control, or even for joint decision-making powers with management. Employees – in general – appear to be opposed to a style of leadership which merely informs them about decisions after the event, and appear to favour something in between a 'sells' style and a consultative approach; in other words, the implication is that employees like to have the opportunity to find out why (certain) decisions have been made, plus the potential to influence those which are felt to be within their own domain (Warr and Wall 1975). Of the forms of EI which have been analysed above, direct EI has been rated more highly than representative participation, and most employees appear to favour the option of profit-sharing ownership, if only because it may increase the size of their monetary rewards.

Employees appear keen to see schemes in their own place of work continue, whatever the specific technique in question. For example, nearly 90 per cent of respondents to the Marchington *et al.* (1992) survey indicated that they wished team briefing to continue at their place of work, while for quality circles the figure was 80 per cent, and for consultative committees and employee share ownership/profit sharing it was about 85 per cent of all those with experiences of these techniques (ibid.: 35–7). Proponents of EI should treat this figure with some caution, however, because some of the reasons for wanting particular schemes to continue suggest apathy and instrumentalism ('better than working', 'half an hour off work', 'a cash windfall') rather than high levels of commitment to the organization, and the questionnaires were administered at a time when economic prospects looked favourable. Wall and Clegg's (1979: 41) comment from many years ago is still apposite: 'in broad terms, the answer to the question, "Are workers demanding participation?'' is no; whilst the answer to the question, ''would workers like participation?'' is yes.'

We have already noted that team briefing is one of the most widespread of all EI techniques, with employees particularly keen on seeing this continue in workplaces where it is currently operated. Despite this, employees did not think that briefing made much impact upon employment relations or their attitudes to work. Although many more respondents felt that things had improved rather than worsened, the vast majority reckoned that there had been little or no change – following the introduction of team briefing – on their understanding of management decisions, the quality of upward communications and openness, or on their commitment to the organization. Indeed, in the case of commitment, over three-quarters of respondents indicated that there had been 'no change'. In a sense, such low figures may not be surprising, given that, for most employees, briefing constitutes such a small proportion of their working lives (about thirty minutes a month, typically). Even if the system worked well, therefore, its impact is only likely to be minor, compared with other aspects of the employment relationship, and we have seen already that in many cases problems within management render it markedly less effective. Cotton (1993: 87) makes a similar point in relation to quality circles most starkly: 'at most these [quality circle] programmes operate for one hour per week, with the remaining 39 hours unchanged. Why should changes in 2.5% of a person's job have a major impact?'

Despite this, some observers do claim that EI leads to higher levels of employee commitment to or identification with the organization, and higher levels of corporate performance. Many of these have their roots in the USA, where it is pioneered by management gurus who argue that American companies have fallen behind the Japanese because of a failure to 'involve' their staff. A highly influential article in *Newsweek* in 1981 indicated that a 'new industrial relations' was quietly being introduced into major US organizations, focused around 'worker involvement'. More recently, Peters (1988: 284–5) has suggested that employers should 'involve everyone in everything' with the result that 'productivity gains of several hundred percent can ensue'. Claims have also been made in relation to specific forms of EI, such as consultation (Cooke 1989), job redesign and teamworking (Walton 1985), and employee share ownership programmes (Rosen *et al.* 1985). In summarizing the American literature, Cotton (1993: 232) suggests that practices such as gain-sharing and self-directed work teams have a strong effect on employee attitudes, that job enrichment and quality of work life have an intermediate effect, while quality circles and representative participation have a weak effect on employees. At Japanese companies in Britain – where team briefing typically takes place daily – employees feel that it has impacted more strongly on their attitudes and commitment to the organization (see, for example, Marchington *et al.* 1994;

Wood and Mundy 1993). Gallie and White (1993: 39) go further, suggesting that quality circles 'are highly effective in giving employees a sense of participation over changes in work organisation', although great emphasis needs to be placed on the term 'sense of participation' in this quotation.

Other researchers are highly sceptical about the possible impact of EI on attitudes, and more especially on employee commitment and performance. Guest and Dewe (1991: 91) note from studies at three manufacturing plants that, for most employees, commitment to their employer (and union also) was calculative rather than deep-seated. Kelly and Kelly (1991: 43–4) conclude their review of research into new industrial relations practices in Britain by saying that, although employees may be induced to think positively about the schemes themselves, 'there is little or no evidence to suggest that these practices have altered workers' largely negative views of management in general and of union–management relations'. Guest (1992a: 131) also supports this line, arguing that there are problems in specifying precisely what is meant by commitment and how it is measured, which are not helped by the probability of multiple commitments (management, fellow workers, union, occupation, department, plant, or organization). Given the limited amount of time for which most employees are asked to be 'involved' by management, especially if it is 'bolted-on' to existing practices, it would be foolhardy to argue that EI is capable of changing attitudes and behaviour, without more fundamental adjustments across the whole of the employment relationship (Roberts and Wilkinson 1991: 410).

It is also apparent, though, that the impact of EI can vary significantly between organizations, even those with the same set of techniques. In a number of the case studies conducted by Marchington *et al.* (1992, 1994), employees were particularly positive about EI, feeling that it had been introduced by management for business-related reasons and to some extent to increase employee satisfaction. The predominant view among respondents was that EI had improved in recent years, and that benefits had flowed from specific techniques such as team briefing or profit-sharing. In each of these 'positive' cases, however, attitudes to the employer as a whole were also very positive, with nearly all respondents reporting that the company was 'a good one to work for'. In several other organizations, employees were particularly negative about EI and employee relations, viewing management with some hostility and displaying an overwhelmingly instrumental attachment to work. Management's reasons for introducing EI were often seen as little more than attempts at work intensification, and many more reported that EI had worsened over the last few years than suggested there had been improvements. Very few felt that specific EI techniques had led to any improvements in communications or their understanding of management decisions, nor had it led to any increase in their commitment to the organization.

These differences in views had little to do with the type or range of EI schemes practised at these organizations, nor with its history or development, but much could be explained by the way in which management responded to the competitive environment confronting the organization. In the cases where EI and management were seen in a predominantly negative light, there had been redundancies in recent times, and future prospects looked bleak to employees. Because most EI schemes are predicated upon a greater awareness of competitive pressures, it is hardly surprising that they should refer to this knowledge when evaluating EI schemes themselves. For example, regular bouts of 'bad news' conveyed through team briefing can result in employees having negative assessments of the briefing system itself. Similarly, a series of poor profit announcements may start to lead to conclusions that the employee share ownership scheme is not particularly good. Equally, a failure to take up ideas submitted through a quality circle programme, perhaps due to lack of money, can lead to criticisms of management and the circles themselves. In other words, negative evaluations of EI may be a barometer for more deep-seated anxieties about the future, while positive attitudes towards EI may be symptomatic of a 'feel good' factor about work and the employer.

Results from any employee attitude surveys must be treated with caution, however, for a number of methodological reasons. First, there is the problem of bench-marking and determining the best date at which to start making 'before and after' comparisons; in the case of the former, whether this should be at the time the new scheme was introduced, or at some time before preparations were commenced. Similarly, regarding the latter, attitudes can vary considerably over time, as well as in response to specific events (such as redundancy announcements or pay claims), which make comparisons problematic. Second, as we have seen above, it is extremely difficult in non-laboratory research to control for the influence of features other than EI on attitudes and behaviour, so as to isolate the relationship between just two variables. For example, claims that a new form of EI has led to reductions in labour turnover have to be assessed against the potentially greater influence of factors such as the rate of unemployment, the number of job vacancies locally, or the structure of pay differentials. Third, many organizations do not measure performance with sufficient precision to enable any correlations to be made, nor do they keep comprehensive and systematic data on absence or labour turnover. In most cases, therefore, analysts are reliant on management assessments of the perceived linkage between EI and behaviour at work, and the belief, as Lawler *et al.* (1992: 62) found, 'that EI is a viable way to increase organizational performance'. Finally, as suggested above, contrary to claims that EI can lead to cultural change and increased employee commitment to the organization, it could be argued that EI is as much affected by the prevailing organizational culture as it is a source of change; that is, the direction of causality of this relationship is opposite to that claimed by some of its proponents.

There is little doubt that employees like the idea of EI, and the vast majority certainly prefer the prospect of more participative styles of supervision, rather than more oppressive regimes of discipline and control. However, despite the appeal of EI in general terms, the evidence would suggest that it has only a limited impact upon employee attitudes and commitment, and even less on behaviour and performance. To some extent, this can be explained by the problems which managers face in effecting EI in the workplace, but it may also be unrealistic to expect 'partial involvement' – that is, schemes which are bolted on to existing frameworks of employee relations on an intermittent basis – to bring about a significant transformation in employee attitudes and behaviour.

EI AND WORKPLACE TRADE UNIONISM

EI is sometimes portrayed as a device which is designed expressly to limit the influence of workplace trade unionism or, where unions are not recognized, to prevent their development in the first place. Kelly (1988), for example, puts this quite succinctly when he suggests that

> by linking elements of workers' pay to company performance, providing information about company performance, and encouraging workers to contribute their own ideas for its improvement, the hope is that conflicts of interest can be weakened. Clearly, schemes of this kind, *if successful*, would pose a considerable threat to the role and possibly to the very existence of trade unions.
>
> (Ibid.: 265, my emphasis)

To be fair to Kelly, his link between EI and the future of trade unions is qualified and, given the discussion in the previous two sections, unions may have little to fear from recent developments in EI. Smith and Morton (1993: 102) are much less guarded, viewing direct employee involvement and joint consultation as part of a grand strategy to marginalize and weaken the unions further to the point where they are 'partially derecognized'. Moreover, some of the union pamphlets warn members of the potential dangers to union solidarity from EI; for example, the TGWU (1989: 2) is concerned about 'methods aimed at undermining collective bargaining and eroding trade union influence', while Parker and Slaughter (1988) argue that teamworking conflicts with worker solidarity so that members/employees have to 'choose sides' between union and employer.

Although there are some examples in Britain of EI being directly associated with a decline of trade union organization, this is by no means a widespread phenomenon. Indeed, there are also cases where unions have been able to limit the development of EI, or where parallel structures for collective bargaining and participation have remained in existence. In the remainder of this section, we examine these linkages more fully (see also

Marchington *et al.* 1992: 39–41; Storey 1992: 258–62; Guest 1992b: 5–8; Beaumont 1992: 121–5).

Where unions are currently recognized for bargaining purposes, and employers wish to undermine their role, managements can seek to upgrade joint consultative committees and direct EI so as to render bargaining and union membership less meaningful. The suggestion is that matters which previously were dealt with in the negotiating arena, where they could be subject to veto, are now communicated direct to all employees via team briefing and/or considered at JCCs where there is no formal opportunity to resist management plans and prevent their enactment. In other words, managements ensure that collective bargaining becomes progressively less central to the regulation of employment relations (what was termed the 'empty shell hypothesis' by Legge 1988), and is replaced by communications and consultation. The (re-)establishment of managerial influence over their staff is seen as a clear benefit by the major proponents of team briefing (Grummit 1983: 4–7); achievements such as the reinforcement of supervisors, the prevention of misunderstandings and control of the grapevine so as to prevent 'slanted' information reaching employees. Clearly, if team briefing is conducted according to plan, it may be more difficult for trade union representatives to counter management interpretations of events confronting the organization (Marchington and Parker 1990: 217–24). With regard to consultation, it is suggested that 'new style' JCCs have as their subject matter some of the key strategic decisions facing the organization, and shop stewards are 'involved' more closely in an understanding of management thinking and decision-making (Terry 1983: 56). For Chadwick (1983: 7), this represents 'a clear and well thought out strategy based upon the introduction of consultative arrangements to settle many of the issues previously determined by collective bargaining or custom and practice.'

There are examples of employers using communications to all employees instead of consultation, and using an upgraded version of the latter instead of negotiation (Marchington and Parker 1990: 222–3). Some of the conflicts and contradictions in this process are summed up well by Storey (1992) in his analysis of Austin Rover. He quotes one of the senior personnel managers who said 'the unions were invited to the party but they didn't seem to want to come. So, the party went ahead without them.' To which one of the stewards replied: 'The trouble is that [the party] had already started and in any case it was not the kind of party which we wanted to go to . . . basically they want more work out of fewer men' (ibid.: 250–1).

Even if employers are not implementing EI with the express purpose of undermining trade unionism and worker solidarity, some would argue that this is nevertheless a consequence of its operation. As with the previous argument, to be successful this requires management to conduct a well-orchestrated campaign in order to gain the supposed benefits from EI, and this can not be taken for granted. Nevertheless, in some organizations the general feeling (both among trade unionists and managers) is that the development of EI – as part of a more open approach to people-management – does lessen the role for workplace trade unionists. The more effectively that management communicates with staff and the greater the emphasis on quality issues and competitive advantage, the more likely it is that employees will see their futures tied in with the success of the company and trade unionism will decline in importance. In the case of a chemical firm studied over a number of years (Marchington and Parker 1990; Wilkinson *et al.* 1993), although the stewards continued to sit on JCCs and bargain with management, it was felt that direct forms of EI (especially the briefing and TQM systems) were de-emphasizing the role of the union and causing union members to identify more closely with management. But this weakened union influence also appears dependent on continued success in the product market and the maintenance of high wages and benefits.

In cases where unions are not recognized for collective bargaining purposes, there are suggestions that EI may take the place of trade unionism. In his description of leading non-union firms in the USA, Foulkes (1980) identifies a number of policies for communication and teamworking which were designed to ensure more cooperative employee–management relations. Equally, some of the well-known organizations in Britain which do not recognize unions for collective bargaining (for example, IBM, Marks and Spencer, J. Sainsbury) have well-developed mechanisms for communication, consultation and upward problem-solving. At the same time, it should be clarified that non-union firms *as a whole* are less likely than their unionized counterparts to operate HRM (Sisson 1993). Where EI is practised, team briefing and joint consultation can be used in attempts to ensure the systematic dissemination of standard information to all units (say, in a hotel group or a supermarket chain) and provide machinery for the resolution of wide-ranging grievances in a formal setting. Successful JCC structures can therefore come to be regarded as substitutes for union organization if staff feel that their anxieties are dealt with by management. In order for managements to maintain their position of primacy in these workplaces, however, they have to ensure that EI systems work according to plan and are not subject to the range of problems outlined in the previous two sections.

Other commentators are less convinced of this zero sum conception of the relationship between unions and EI – or between unions and HRM for that matter – and see the possibility that EI and workplace trade unionism can coexist and may even be integrated (Marchington and Parker 1990; Storey 1992). In the longer term, of course, parallel structures for EI and collective bargaining may involve dangers for the latter, or indeed well-developed negotiating processes may well be able to hinder the development of EI. A variety of outcomes seems possible, therefore, ranging from the cases of attempted 'union exclusion' which have been considered above, through to potential compatibility and synergy between EI and trade unionism, or even cases where unions are able to hinder and prevent the development of EI. Alternatively, the relationship may not be an issue at all to either party, with EI and trade union organization coexisting because they are perceived to have quite different 'zones' and to be quite independent of each other. Each of these scenarios can now be analysed.

Management–union complementarity

First, there are situations where a degree of complementarity exists between union organization and at least some parts of the EI mix; in our Employment Department study (Marchington *et al.* 1992), this was especially marked for the link between joint consultation and union organization. In several of these cases, management had sought to integrate EI and workplace trade unionism more fully. The most significant example of management support for unions was seen in another of the chemical firms where a representative of the shop stewards (chosen by the unions on a rotating basis) had been invited onto the management committee to consider options for a programme of organizational change. Part of the process of change included a wide-ranging involvement exercise, and most of the senior stewards (the craft workers were more ambivalent) actively contributed to these sessions. Senior managers were keen to preserve good relations between themselves and the senior stewards, and not to alienate them by introducing changes without union support. The senior stewards were aware of the potential dangers of being 'incorporated' into management, but saw their involvement in the change programme as essential for the future well-being of their members and the company. In addition, the stewards also participated in a JCC system and were happy to go along with team briefing at the plant. Moreover, this was an organization where employees reported very high levels of cooperation between management and workforce.

In those types of organization, where both managements and stewards feel that more can be gained by working with rather than against each other, this sort of outcome would not be unusual. Storey (1992: 247–8) records some moves to 'jointism' at Ford plants in the UK, while the personnel director is quoted as having said that 'We are engaged in a definite policy of "relationship building" with the unions. I am taking time out to meet informally with all the main national officers for this purpose.' However, it does rely on managements being prepared to open up to and consult with employee representatives, and not to pursue a blinkered policy of individualization which leaves the unions totally on the edge.

A dual approach

Secondly, EI (especially in its direct forms, such as briefing) and collective bargaining may run in parallel, with no obvious or overt relationship between them, in a 'dual' approach to the management of labour (Storey 1992: 258; Sisson 1993: 208). In these cases, union representatives may take an agnostic view of EI, regarding it as nothing to do with them and irrelevant to the processes of collective bargaining. Team briefing is often viewed in this way by union representatives, even though they are aware that (if done properly) it can reinforce management's ability to communicate their ideas to employees. Yet it is difficult for stewards to argue against forms of EI which are designed to improve communications, because failings in this area are regularly cited by them as a major problem for managers. In addition, stewards appear to accept that managements have the right to inform their staff on a regular and ongoing basis; in some of the companies studied by Marchington *et al.* (1992), union representatives actually pressed for new managerial initiatives to improve the flow of information to employees.

Trade union opposition to EI

Finally, we need to be aware of the fact that trade unions can also limit the development or prevent the implementation of EI, and there have been a number of cases reported over the years. This is only likely to occur in situations where employees are suspicious of management intentions in a climate of low-trust relations, where unions also retain the influence and ability to mobilize collective resistance. For example, trade unions opposed team briefing at West Yorkshire Passenger Transport Executive in the mid-1980s, persuading their members to 'attend without enthusiasm' – not difficult in some briefing sessions! In this case, union resistance hardened and became more entrenched once briefing had been implemented. At the Post Office, there was significant resistance to team briefing in its early days, largely because of the way in which it had been introduced and what were felt by union leaders to be attempts to subvert the communication process. Union instructions to boycott team briefing were only withdrawn (in 1988) after a High Court injunction had been won by management. Neither of these cases represents fertile ground on which to sow the seeds of high-level commitment or to persuade employees that management is keen to protect interests.

In the Employment Department study quoted previously (Marchington *et al.* 1992), in the docking case, there was evidence that management-initiated schemes had made little impact, compared with the existing patterns of local job control. Management was held in low esteem in a climate of low trust, as two quotes illustrate graphically: 'Management are not interested in involvement, it's a case of us and them, and it appears that management prefer it that way'; 'No information seems to filter down from management . . . they seem happier to inform the local media than their own staff.' EI also remained patchy in the transport company which was studied, and it was recognized by both parties that the process of change was likely to take a long time. Indeed, nationally, some of the unions had refused to participate in the programme of organizational change, and at local level support from the unions had been limited. Management at one of the sites regarded union hostility as the major obstacle to better EI, and union representatives felt that defending their current position was more important than getting embroiled in new management initiatives; this was understandable, given current doubts about the future of this particular site. It was in organizations such as these where the union continued to play a key role in internal communications, in contrast to most establishments where management was identified as the prime source of information.

The proposition that EI is capable of undermining trade unions (either by design or consequence) is a key component of many conceptions of HRM. This section has sought to demonstrate, however, that this is an unnecessarily simplistic view, based upon conspiratorial notions of management, and which is accurate in only a small proportion of workplaces. Even should managements wish to use EI to undermine trade unions – and there is evidence that, in most workplaces, this is not their principal objective – we have already illustrated that employers lack the cohesion, omnipotence and omniscience to effect this in any event. Once again, for the trade union–EI link, as with the sections in this chapter on management and employees, it is apparent that the reality of EI rarely corresponds with its rhetoric.

CONCLUSIONS

The 1990 Workplace Industrial Relations survey confirmed that EI had become more extensive across British employing organizations throughout the course of the late 1980s, and there is no reason to suppose that it has declined since that time (Gallie and White 1993). There is little doubt, therefore, that structures for EI have been created in many organizations over the last decade, and on this basis some extravagant claims have been made for its impact – in relation to commitment, acceptance of change, productivity, and labour turnover,

However, as this chapter has illustrated, the reality is often much more mundane. In many organizations, there has been a tendency to adopt a faddish approach to EI (as well as other features of organizational behaviour) which has resulted in conflicting and sometimes contradictory forms within the same organization; rarely has there been a well-planned and coordinated strategy for the development of EI as part of a broader

HRM strategy, which is itself firmly integrated into corporate objectives. Moreover, line managers have often lacked the enthusiasm and commitment which is expected of them in order to make EI work in practice, partly because the supposed benefits from wider involvement are not necessarily advantageous to managers themselves. In addition, however, in the rush to implement new initiatives, many employers have committed insufficient time and resources to training supervisors to deliver EI at the workplace. Given that some forms of EI are predicated upon the adoption of new styles of management ('from cops to coaches', for example), this omission can have severe consequences for the effectiveness of EI and HRM.

It is apparent that the impact of EI upon employees has been marginal, albeit slightly favourable in most cases, and rather more attractive than its authoritarian alternative. Such a cautious conclusion might well disappoint the proponents of EI, but perhaps little more could be expected, given the minor impact which EI has on most employees' lives. In terms of time alone, most employees who are 'involved' in team briefings, for example, find that this takes up less than thirty minutes per month – well under half of one per cent of their working time. For the most part, as well, their 'involvement' in this form of EI tends to be passive, and often it constitutes little more than listening to information, which is not seen to be of prime importance to their own task or department.

Finally, despite the dire warnings which have been issued by some academic commentators and trade union leaders, the impact of EI on the role of unions is far from clear, and in some cases EI has been integrated with existing union channels. In effect, although it is theoretically possible for EI to promote changes in employment relations, this is dependent upon a number of connections being made – especially by line managers. In the majority of cases, however, these connections are missed.

It is always difficult to predict future developments in any area of the social sciences, and given the political/legal context within which HRM is conducted, this is more hazardous than most. At a macro-level, much depends upon the degree to which European Community initiatives, via works councils for example, have any impact on employers in Britain. Foreign-owned establishments (especially those with units or a parent elsewhere in the EC) are likely to face additional pressures, regardless of which party holds office in Britain for the rest of the century. Indeed, a number of organizations entered into discussions about works councils early in the decade, such as Ford in 1993. At the same time, however, it is likely that employers will continue to experiment with new initiatives in direct EI, particularly if senior managers maintain their belief that this can be a major source of competitive advantage. Although a realist would caution against expecting too much from EI, such a person would also urge employers to devote more energy to increasing the amount of real 'involvement' in employing organizations and to ensuring that line managers are provided with a greater range of skills to make EI work on the shop floor or in the office. It could be argued that the haphazard, uneven and piecemeal way in which EI has been introduced into most employing organizations so far may not provide a fair indication of what it can achieve under a regime of 'soft' HRM.

REFERENCES

Ackers, P., Marchington, M. Wilkinson, A. and Goodman, J. (1992) 'The long and winding road; tracking employee involvement at Brown's Woven Carpets', *Employee Relations* 14(3): 56–70.

Allen, C., Cunningham, I. and McArdle, L. (1991) *Employee Participation and Involvement into the Nineties*, Stockton-on-Tees: Jim Conway Foundation.

Baddon, L., Hunter, L., Hyman, J., Leopold, J. and Ramsay, H. (1989) *People's Capitalism?*, London: Routledge.

Beaumont, P. (1992) 'Trade unions and human resource management', in B. Towers (ed.) *The Handbook of Human Resource Management*, Oxford: Blackwell.

Berggren, C. (1989) 'New production concepts in final assembly – the Swedish experience', in S. Wood (ed.) *The Transformation of Work?*, London: Unwin Hyman.

Black, J. and Ackers, P. (1988) 'The Japanisation of British industry; a case study of quality circles in the carpet industry', *Employee Relations* 10(6): 9–16.

Blumberg, P. (1968) *Industrial Democracy; the Sociology of Participation*, London: Constable.

Blyton, P. and Turnbull, P. (eds) (1992) *Reassessing Human Resource Management*, London: Sage.

Brannen, P. (1983) *Authority and Participation in Industry*, London: Batsford.

Brewster, C., Gill, C. and Richbell, S. (1983) 'Industrial relations policy; a framework for analysis', in K. Thurley and S. Wood (eds) *Industrial Relations and Management Strategy*, Cambridge: Cambridge University Press,

Buchanan, D. (1986) 'Management objectives in technical change', in D. Knights and H. Willmott (eds) *Managing the Labour Process*, Aldershot: Gower.

Chadwick, D. (1983) 'The recession and industrial relations; a factory approach', *Employee Relations* 5(5): 5–12.

Cooke, W. (1989) 'Improving productivity and quality through collaboration', *Industrial Relations* 28(2): 219–39.

Cotton, J. (1993) *Employee Involvement; Methods for Improving Performance and Work Attitudes*, Newbury Park, CA: Sage.

Daniel, W. and Millward, N. (1983) *Workplace Industrial Relations in Britain*, London: Heinemann.

Department of Employment (1989) *People and Companies: Employee Involvement in Britain*, London: HMSO.

Dewe, P., Dunn, S. and Richardson, R. (1988) 'Employee share option schemes; why workers are attracted to them', *British Journal of Industrial Relations* 26(1): 1–21.

Foulkes, F. (1980) *Personnel Policies in Large Non-Union Companies*, Englewood Cliffs, NJ: Prentice Hall.

Gallie, D. and White, M. (1993) *Employee Commitment and the Skills Revolution*, London: PSI Publishing.

Gold, M. and Hall, M. (1992) *European-level Information and Consultation in Multinational Companies; An Evaluation of Practice*, Dublin: European Foundation.
Grummitt, J. (1983) *Team Briefing*, London: Industrial Society.
Guest, D. (1990) 'Human resource management and the American dream', *Journal of Management Studies* 27(4): 377–97.
—— (1992a) 'Employee commitment and control', in J. Hartley and G. Stephenson (eds) *Employment Relations; the Psychology of Influence and Control at Work*, Oxford: Blackwell.
—— (1992b) 'Human resource management in the United Kingdom', in B. Towers (ed.) *The Handbook of Human Resource Management*, Oxford: Blackwell.
Guest, D. and Dewe, P. (1991) 'Company or trade union: which wins workers', allegiance? A study of commitment in the UK electronics industry', *British Journal of Industrial Relations* 29(1): 75–96.
Hall, M. (1992) 'Behind the European works councils directives; the European Commission's legislative strategy', *British Journal of Industrial Relations* 30(4): 547–66.
Hespe, G. and Wall, T. (1976) 'The demand for participation among employees', *Human Relations* 29(5): 471–505.
Hill, S. (1991) 'How do you manage a flexible firm? The total quality model', *Work, Employment and Society* 5(3): 397–415.
Holter, H. (1965) 'Attitudes towards employee participation in company decision making', *Human Relations* 28(5): 297–321.
Kelly, J. (1982) *Scientific Management, Job Redesign and Work Performance*, London: Academic Press.
—— (1988) *Trade Unions and Socialist Politics*, London: Verso.
Kelly, J. and Kelly, C. (1991) ' "Them and us": social psychology and the "New industrial relations" ', *British Journal of Industrial Relations* 29(1): 25–48.
Klein, J. (1984) 'Why supervisors resist employee involvement', *Harvard Business Review* September/October: 87–9.
Knights, D., Willmott, H. and Collinson, D. (eds) (1985) *Job Redesign*, Aldershot: Gower.
Lawler, E., Mohrman, S. and Ledford, G. (1992) *Employee Involvement and Total Quality Management*, San Francisco, CA: Jossey-Bass.
Legge, K. (1988) 'Personnel management in recession and recovery', *Personnel Review* 17(2): 2–70.
MacInnes, J. (1987) *Thatcherism at Work*, Milton Keynes: Open University Press.
Marchington, M. (1980) *Responses to Participation at Work*, Farnborough: Gower.
—— (1989) 'Employee participation', in B. Towers (ed.) *A Handbook of Industrial Relations Practice*, London: Kogan Page.
—— (1992a) *Managing The Team; A Guide to Employee Involvement in Practice*, Oxford: Blackwell.
—— (1992b) 'The growth of employee involvement in Australia', *Journal of Industrial Relations* 34(3): 472–81.
Marchington, M. and Parker, P. (1990) *Changing Patterns of Employee Relations*, Hemel Hempstead: Harvester Wheatsheaf.
Marchington, M., Parker, P. and Prestwich, A. (1989) 'Problems with team briefing in practice', *Employee Relations* 11(4): 21–30.
Marchington, M., Goodman, J., Wilkinson, A. and Ackers, P. (1992) *Recent Developments in Employee Involvement*, Employment Department Research Series No. 1, London: HMSO.
Marchington, M., Wilkinson, A., Ackers, P. and Goodman, J. (1993) 'The influence

of managerial relations on waves of employee involvement', *British Journal of Industrial Relations* 31(4): 553–76.

—— (1994) 'Understanding the meaning of participation: views from the workplace', *Human Relations* forthcoming.

Marginson, P., Edwards, P., Martin, R., Purcell, J. and Sisson, K. (1988) *Beyond the Workplace: Managing Industrial Relations in the Multi-Establishment Enterprise*, Oxford: Blackwell.

Millward, N. and Stevens, M. (1986) *British Workplace Industrial Relations, 1980–1984*, Aldershot: Gower.

Millward, N., Stevens, M. Smart, D. and Hawes, W. (1992) *Workplace Industrial Relations in Transition*, Aldershot: Dartmouth.

Oliver, N. and Wilkinson, B. (1992) *The Japanisation of British Industry: New Developments in the 1990s*, Oxford: Blackwell.

Parker, M. and Slaughter, J. (1988) *Choosing Sides: Unions and the Team Concept*, Boston, MA: South End Press.

Partridge, B. (1989) 'The problem of supervision', in K. Sisson (ed.) *Personnel Management in Britain*, Oxford: Blackwell.

Pateman, C. (1970) *Participation and Democratic Theory*, Cambridge: Cambridge University Press.

Pendleton, A. (1992) 'Employee share ownership schemes in the UK', *Human Resource Management Journal* 2(2): 83–8.

Peters, T. (1988) *Thriving on Chaos,* London: Macmillan.

Poole, M. (1986) *Towards a New Industrial Democracy; Workers' Participation in Industry*, London: Routledge & Kegan Paul.

—— (1989) *The Origins of Economic Democracy: Profit Sharing and Employee Shareholding Schemes*, London: Routledge.

Ramsay, H. (1976) 'Participation: the shop floor view', *British Journal of Industrial Relations* 14(2): 128–41.

Rathkey, P. (1983) *Participation and Industrial Democracy: The Shop Floor View*, Stockton-on-Tees: Jim Conway Foundation.

Roberts, I. and Wilkinson, A. (1991) 'Participation and purpose: boilermakers to bankers', *Critical Perspectives on Accounting* 2: 385–413.

Rosen, C., Klein, K. and Young, K. (1985) *Employee Ownership in America: The Equity Solution*, Lexington, KY: Heath.

Scase, R. and Goffee, R. (1989) *Reluctant Managers; Their Work and Lifestyles*, London: Unwin Hyman.

Schuler, R. and Jackson, S. (1987) 'Linking competitive strategies to HRM practices', *Academy of Management Executive* 1(3): 207–19.

Schuller, T. (1985) *Democracy at Work*, Oxford: Oxford University Press.

—— (1989) 'Financial participation', in J. Storey (ed.) *New Perspectives on Human Resource Management*, London: Routledge.

Sewell, G. and Wilkinson, B. (1992) 'Empowerment or emasculation? Shop floor surveillance in a total quality organisation', in P. Blyton and P. Turnbull (eds) *Reassessing Human Resource Management*, London: Sage.

Sisson, K. (1993) 'In search of HRM', *British Journal of Industrial Relations* 31(2): 201–10.

Smith, G. (1986) 'Profit sharing and employee share ownership in Britain', *Employment Gazette* September: 380–5.

Smith, P. and Morton, G. (1993) 'Union exclusion and the decollectivisation of industrial relations in contemporary Britain', *British Journal of Industrial Relations* 31(1): 97–114.

Storey, J. (ed.) (1989) *New Perspectives on Human Resource Management*, London: Routledge.
—— (1992) *Developments in the Management of Human Resources*, Oxford: Blackwell.
Terry, M. (1983) 'Shop stewards through expansion and recession', *Industrial Relations Journal* 14(3): 49–58.
Towers, B. (ed.) (1992) *The Handbook of Human Resource Management*, Oxford: Blackwell.
Transport and General Workers Union (1989) *Employee Involvement and Quality Circles? A TGWU Policy Booklet*, London: TGWU.
Wall, T. and Clegg, C. (1979) 'Who wants participation?', in D. Guest and K. Knight (eds) *Putting Participation into Practice*, Farnborough: Gower.
Walton, R. (1985) 'From control to commitment in the workplace', *Harvard Business Review* 63(2): 77–85.
Warr, P. and Wall, T. (1975) *Work and Well-Being*, Harmondsworth: Penguin.
Wilkinson, A., Marchington, M., Ackers, P. and Goodman, J. (1992) 'Total quality management and employee involvement', *Human Resource Management Journal* 3(2): 1–20.
—— (1993) 'Refashioning industrial relations: the experiences of a chemical company in the 1980s', *Personnel Review* 22(2): 22–38.
—— (1994) 'ESOPs fables – a tale of a machine tool company', *International Journal of Human Resource Management* 5(1): 121–43.
Wood, S. (1986) 'The cooperative labour strategy in the US auto industry', *Economic and Industrial Democracy* 7: 415–47.
Wood, S. and Mundy, J. (1993) 'Are human resource practices in Japanese transplants truly different?', paper presented at British Universities Industrial Relations Association Conference, York.

Part IV

International HRM

Chapter 12

HRM: the European dimension

Chris Brewster

INTRODUCTION

Some of the old cinemas, with what was then high-tech, wrap-around screens, used to show a sequence which started with a bird's-eye view of a small child. Then, through the use of telephoto lenses merging with satellite pictures, the camera slowly pulled back so that the child lost a little definition and became first one of a group of children and then gradually disappeared as the group became part of a street scene. The camera continued to pull back to reveal the street to be successively part of a suburb, a city, a conurbation, a country, a continent, and eventually an invisible dot on the planet Earth.

This chapter uses this extended focus-pulling as an analogy for examining human resource management (HRM) in Europe. The focus of much of the research and analysis of HRM, particularly in the UK, has been at workplace level. There is also a strong tradition comparing HRM in organizations of different size, sector or ownership within one country. At the other extreme, there are commentators who state, or imply, that their analysis is universal. This chapter adopts a mid-focus position, concentrating upon HRM in Europe.

It is unnecessary here to emphasize the growing economic integration of Europe. Most readers of this text will be well aware of developments in the region. One question that is worthy of attention, however, is whether the developing economic integration of Europe is being accompanied by a convergence of human resource management practices. How different are these countries, and does it make sense to speak of 'European' HRM? The chapter addresses this issue by focusing in quickly from the universality argument to identifying what distinguishes HRM in Europe from that in certain other regions of the world. A further turn of the focusing mechanism adds possible regional clusters within Europe. And a final turn brings into focus the different European countries. The chapter identifies common trends and variances between European countries on five topics in HRM that currently have a high profile in the literature, and which are exercising the European Union. These topics are: developments in pay and benefits; flexible working patterns; equality of opportunity; training; and employee relations.

The subjects, and much of the data presented here, are drawn from a major research project exploring HRM in employing organizations throughout Europe. Data were collected from the senior personnel executives of public and private sector organizations employing over 200 people in fourteen countries. In total, over 16,000 questionnaires were returned over a three-year period – full details are available in Brewster and Hegewisch (1994). Figures used in this chapter are for the most part taken from the twelve countries in the 1992 data: Table 12.1 indicates the countries, country abbreviations and base number of returns – other tables in the chapter are in percentages of this data base, and use the same country abbreviations.

Table 12.1 The research data base

Country	*No. of responses*	*Usable responses*
West Germany (D)	920	878
Denmark (DK)	470	329
Spain (E)	290	266
France (F)	766	661
Finland (Fin)	246	226
Greece (GR)*	122	90
Italy (I)**	203	188
Ireland (IRL)	269	130
Norway (N)	326	280
The Netherlands (NL)	230	127
Portugal (P)	100	93
Sweden (S)	369	322
Turkey (T)	142	123
United Kingdom (UK)	1343	1260

* 1993 data
** 1991 data

EUROPEAN HRM

There is, of course, one level at which HRM is universal. All organizations have to utilize, and hence to manage, human resources. Two of the classic texts identified four areas (employee influence, human resource flow, reward systems, work systems, in Beer *et al.* 1985) or a five-step cycle (selection, performance, appraisal, rewards and development, in Fombrun *et al.* 1984), which they imply can be used to analyse HRM in any organization anywhere in the world. However, HRM practices vary across the world. One question is whether there are common trends and whether, if such trends exist, they fit the concept of HRM as it was developed, originally, in the USA.

Is European HRM – our focus here – distinctive from that of, for example, Japan and the USA? The latter case is particularly important, given the power of the US version of human resource management. There are strong arguments that the US is an inappropriate model for Europe (see Cox and Cooper 1985; Thurley and Wirdenius 1991; Pieper 1990). The vision of HRM that has come to us in Europe from the USA is culture-bound (Trompenaars 1985; Adler and Jelinek 1986) and in particular a view of HRM as based on the largely unconstrained exercise of managerial autonomy has been attacked as being peculiarly American (Guest 1990; Brewster 1993). In Europe, organizations are not autonomous. They exist within a system which is constrained (or supported), first, at the national level, by culture and by extensive legal limitations on the nature of the contract of employment, and second, at the organizational level, by patterns of ownership (by the State, by the banking and finance system and by families) which are distinct from those in the USA. Additionally, at this level of HRM, there are constraints of trade union involvement and consultative arrangements.

Within Europe, selecting a slightly narrower focus, it is possible to distinguish distinct regional clusters. One analysis found evidence of 'three clusters: a Latin cluster [which includes Spain, Italy, France]; a central European cluster . . . and a Nordic cluster' (Filella 1991: 14). Possibly the central European cluster could be split, with Ireland and the UK on one side, and continental central Europe on the other. The Latin style of HRM is characterized, *inter alia*, by efforts to modernize HRM, a greater reliance on an oral culture and the presence of subtle 'political' structures which unconsciously nurture docile, dependent attitudes to authority. The Nordic approach to HRM would include the substantial, visible authority of the HR department, extensive written strategies, a widespread collective orientation to management, and extensive consultation. The continental central European model would involve lower authority for HR departments, extensive line management involvement in HR issues and legal support for collaboration with trade unions. Whether there is an 'offshore central European' model is open to question: it has been argued that in industrial relations, for example, the series of national-level agreements of the last few years has moved Ireland towards a continental pattern (Gunnigle *et al.* 1993). However, the UK model – with still-entrenched unions but no 'social partnership' approach, little legal intervention or support, and extensive decentralization of personnel issues, but little devolvement to line management (Brewster and Soderström 1994) – remains distinct. The UK is, more than geographically, somewhere between continental Europe and the USA.

In a particularly fascinating part of his analysis, Filella (1991) argues that the regional groupings may correspond to stages of socio-economic development. This would put the Latin countries at the lowest stage, the UK (and Ireland) at the next stage, continental central Europe at the penultimate stage and the Nordic countries at the top. There is a correlation between how seriously countries take people issues in the management of enterprises and their economic success (see Porter 1991; Brewster and Holt Larsen 1992).

Below the regional level, using the telephoto lens analogy for the last time, the distinctive nature of HRM in individual European countries is explored best by examining a number of issues in more detail.

Developments in pay

Pay is a central issue in human resource management. Trends in this area include, in particular, the increasing decentralization of pay determination and the growth of flexible pay systems.

The decentralization of bargaining structures has taken place both in countries with highly centralized systems of pay determination, such as Denmark and Sweden (although not without some alternating moves towards recentralization), and in countries with greater decentralization, such as the UK and France. In the latter two countries, only a minority of private sector organizations now negotiate over basic pay at national or industry level, for any staff groups, including manual workers. These trends have been encouraged by employers' federations in both countries; in some countries, and in some industries, they have withdrawn from industry negotiations, thus forcing company-level bargaining (Hegewisch 1991). National or industry-wide bargaining in some European countries is now mainly a public sector practice. In the UK, for example, only 22 per cent of private employers negotiate at industry level for manual workers, whereas 82 per cent of public sector employers implement national agreements.

Even in the UK, where there has been a concerted effort by government and employers' associations and by many employers to drive pay determination down to the company level, there are still 37 per cent of organizations where basic pay for manual workers is established in national industry bargaining. This is consistent with other evidence from the UK. The Marginson *et al.* (1988) research in the private sector and the WIRS surveys (Millward *et al.* 1993) both show a continuing degree of centralization in pay and other related HR issues, while reflecting moves towards decentralization. The Marginson *et al.* work also shows that, in a typically informal way, many multi-site UK businesses maintain a considerable involvement from head office in HR decision-making. These conclusions are not uncontroversial; in a summary of these surveys, and his own research on the topic, Kinnie (1989) concludes that, although there is some evidence of a move towards the decentralization of management and of bargaining structures in the UK, 'these changes do not necessarily lead to an increase in decision-making discretion for establishment managers' (ibid.: 33). Morris and Wood (1991), however, have argued that this may underestimate the extent of change.

The situation is of course fundamentally different in Denmark, Finland, Ireland, the Netherlands and Sweden, where over 60 per cent of employers still bargain at industry or national level (see Table 12.2). There has been a shift within multi-employer bargaining in Scandinavia from national to industry level, with agreements which leave greater scope for company implementation (Ahlen 1989; Hegewisch 1991; Scheuer 1992; Visser 1992). Nevertheless the commitment to multi-employer bargaining with trade unions remains high.

Least change can be discerned in Germany. Pay and conditions in Germany are regulated by collective agreements which are binding, through their membership of employers' associations, on 90 per cent of employers (Gaugler and Wiltz 1992). They allow, and even provide for, company-level bargaining over implementation in several areas. However, the relationship between industry-wide and company-level bargaining has been stable and there have been few signs of decentralization. The drastically new situation caused by reunification may put this system under some pressure.

Levels of pay determination are one issue: the substantive pay arrangements made at the various levels are another. Reward management has been the subject of much change and discussion over the last decade. The late 1970s and early 1980s were, in several European countries, a period of concern with high inflation, leading to increased government attempts to restrict wage agreements; in Italy and France at least there were also linked policy objectives of greater pay equality, expressed through flat-rate increases, or agreements to higher increases for employees on lower grades. During the second half of the 1980s and the early 1990s the pendulum swung the other way. Human resource management theories stress the need to make pay more performance-related, whether at individual or company level (despite the lack of evidence that PRP is correlated with organizational performance – see Chapter 10). Lower inflation has given companies greater scope for the introduction of performance rewards on top of cost of living increases; increasing competition and cash limits in the public sector have led more and more organizations to look for a direct link between rewards and contribution, and in some cases tight labour markets have increased the power of individual employees to negotiate particular deals. Variable pay, merit and performance-related pay have spread across Europe.

More than one-third of organizations in all countries surveyed (apart from Ireland) increased variable pay (Filella and Hegewisch 1994); the number of organizations decreasing variable pay is very small everywhere, nowhere reaching even 10 per cent. There has been a corresponding, though slightly lower, growth in the number of organizations offering increased non-money benefits (with the marked exception of France, where there is a cultural and traditional preference for money payments and comparatively little development of fringe benefits).

Table 12.2 The level at which basic pay is determined for manual staff

Country	*D*	*DK*	*E*	*F*	*FIN*	*GR*	*I*	*IRL*	*N*	*NL*	*P*	*S*	*T*	*UK*
National/industry-wide collective bargaining	NI	64	43	25	86	26	59	71	80	80	55	73	55	41
Regional collective bargaining	NI	18	20	7	7	38	2	8	25	NI	2	10	26	6
Company/division, etc.	NI	15	26	36	16	39	45	18	16	29	34	27	15	29
Establishment/site	NI	7	18	25	23	2	12	13	11	14	3	10	6	30
Individual	NI	13	3	11	13	6	9	6	17	9	15	18	7	7

Key: NI = not included.

Source: Brewster and Hegewisch (1994)

Table 12.3 Percentage of organizations offering certain incentives

Country	*D*	*DK*	*E*	*F*	*FIN*	*GR*	*I*	*IRL*	*N*	*NL*	*P*	*S*	*T*	*UK*
Employee share options	11	NI	11	12	13	7	15	28	14	18	8	10	1	37
Profit-sharing	60	6	17	70	14	13	6	15	5	38	29	18	11	26
Group bonus schemes	3	7	9	34	13	19	16	16	10	7	11	12	7	25
Individual bonus/commission	48	20	36	44	36	52	55	28	12	59	18	26	20	32
Merit/performance-related pay	21	54	56	70	31	37	84	51	14	21	60	12	52	65

Key: NI = not included.

Source: Brewster and Hegewisch (1994)

The research shows some correlation between those organizations which increased pay and benefits in response to recruitment difficulties and those which increased variable pay (Filella and Hegewisch 1994), thus encouraging the assumption that at least some of the increases were a response to market pressures, rather than a more fundamental shift in underlying payment philosophies. This impression is confirmed by organizations' use of merit or performance-related pay and other incentive payments. The practice of merit or performance-related pay is least common in the Scandinavian countries; even for managerial staff, Swedish, Norwegian and Finnish organizations report 12 per cent, 15 per cent and 31 per cent respectively using this form of incentive (Table 12.3). Merit pay is most widespread in the UK and Denmark, and in the southern countries (Spain, Portugal and Turkey). In Italy it has been estimated that the share of merit pay in white-collar wage packages between 1983 and 1988 grew from 13 per cent to 20 per cent (*IDS Focus* 1989: 10). The uptake in France has increased, encouraged partly by taxation policies. Marsden (1989) suggests that much of this increase in performance-related pay has been a reaction to pay policies at the beginning of the 1980s, which in both Italy and France led to a flattening of differentials. Overall, however, while there is an area of considerable cultural difference across Europe, undoubtedly the practice has become popular during the second half of the 1980s, with obvious consequences for both collective bargaining and the role of management.

There has been much less uptake of other forms of incentive pay, particularly those forms that link pay awards to company performance. Practices such as profit-sharing or employee share options in most countries are offered by only a minority of employers, even at managerial level. Employee share options have become popular in the UK, while in France over two-thirds of organizations offer profit-sharing to all levels of staff – a result largely of favourable tax incentives. In Germany, 60 per cent of organizations have profit-sharing schemes for managers (with much lower proportions for other staff groups).

The issue of incentive payments thus illustrates that, in spite of some common trends towards more variable pay and pay decentralization, national and cultural differences remain strong in remuneration policies across Europe. The trend towards pay flexibility should not hide the continuing importance of institutional pay bargaining systems and even legislation in the field of pay determination – a common feature of pay bargaining in Europe, where most countries have some form of national minimum wage (or a system of generalizing collective agreements across an industry). In most countries in Europe, legislation sets a framework for collective bargaining, by regulating the levels of bargaining, the status of agreements, the role and rights of bargaining partners as well as mechanisms of arbitration (Brewster *et al.* 1992; IDS/IPM 1992). While the 1980s might have seen a shift in the power of the negotiating partners, our data provide little evidence of a major threat to the overall systems of bargaining. It remains to be seen how far flexibility in payment structures and decentralization can survive the recession that hit most of Europe, and whether there will prove to have been a lasting shift towards a more performance-related pay culture or whether flexible pay was a reaction to good times and tight labour markets, which only works when it leads to increases in basic pay.

Flexible working practices

'Atypical' work patterns or contracts, such as temporary, casual, fixed-term, home-based and annual hours contracts, are continuing or are on the increase in every European country, despite differing legal, cultural and labour traditions (Brewster *et al.* 1993). Many of the highest increases (i.e. where more than half of all the organizations in the country have increased their use of a particular form of flexible working) have occurred in countries where there has traditionally been less use of such forms, indicating a levelling out and more widespread use of flexibility across Europe.

Flexible working patterns tend to be used as a response to the changing demographics within the labour market. The lack of a skilled labour force in some countries has forced a greater use of time flexibility. Schemes offering all or certain groups greater access to part-time work, job-sharing, term-time employment and career breaks have been seen as a means of retaining or enticing back into the labour market categories of staff who are unable to work full-time, particularly working mothers, carers or older workers.

However, recent years have seen a replacement of this demand-led rationale (especially in times of high unemployment) by a focus on organizational cost-effectiveness. People employed are the major operating cost for most organizations, so a focus on more efficient ways of working has led to a challenge to 'typical' employment contracts.

In the private sector, much of this challenge has arisen from increased international competition. The effect of this trend has been to put additional pressure on managements to increase productivity with reduced wage costs. In the public sector, reductions in public spending see organizations using flexible working practices as one contribution to maintaining services. The same practices have been used in both private and public sectors as a response to cost-saving measures which result in cuts in permanent posts or 'headcount'. The innovative use of working arrangements means that organizations can make better use of their capital equipment and resources by extending working hours to cope with increased demand. The increase in variable work patterns increases the cost effective use of labour by reducing employee costs and matching work provision more closely to work requirements.

Of course, the provision of labour on this basis does not always benefit the employees. Indeed, in many cases it operates directly against their interest, leaving many flexible workers with substantially reduced pay and with reduced protection in terms and conditions of work. The potential for exploitation of some workers on these forms of contract is causing increasing concern within the Commission of the European Community. The Social Charter includes a provision to extend workers' rights to individuals on atypical contracts, and the European Court of Justice has been making judgments under the equal opportunities legislation which are restricting the cost advantages of employing workers on these contracts.

The debate about these practices has been influenced by the 'flexible firm' model developed by Atkinson and associates at the Institute of Manpower Studies (Atkinson 1985). This argues that firms could be seen as developing a core of full-time permanent workers (who provide the competitive or central proponent of the organization's work, and are therefore treated as a key asset, with appropriate terms and conditions of employment, training and careers) and a periphery of 'atypical' workers (who are, in effect, dispensable).

The flexible firm model has been the source of considerable controversy (see e.g. Atkinson and Meager 1986; Pollert 1987, 1991; Rubery 1988; Casey 1991). Much of the debate turns around how 'strategic' the move to flexibility has been. It has to be said, however, that many of those who have looked for evidence of strategies here have taken a somewhat simplistic and naive view of what would constitute or indicate a strategy. Certainly there is evidence that organizations have responded to environmental pressure by increasing flexibility, and there is little evidence that this is related to any formalized policy documentation (Brewster *et al.* 1994).

One simple fact stands out: despite variations between countries, sectors, size of organization and types of flexibility, this is a continuing picture of growth (Table 12.4). Ten of the twelve countries in this survey showed their largest growth figures to be in the use of part-time, temporary or fixed-term contracts, rather than, for example, in shift working, overtime working or weekend working. Atypical contracts frequently apply to workers who enter the labour market for the first time, or who re-enter after they have had a break, for example to have children. Shift-working, overtime or weekend work (at least outside the retail sector) are much more often used for traditional workforces. However, other forms of 'atypical' contracts such as homeworking or annual hours, which were widely predicted to increase rapidly, continue to be used by only a small minority of organizations, across all countries surveyed. The lowest percentage of increase was in the use of homeworkers; where no country had more than 10 per cent of organizations increasing their use.

Only in Sweden, where a larger proportion of the working population have part-time employment than anywhere else in Europe, has there been a

Table 12.4 Organizations having increased or decreased the use of certain working arrangements over the last three years (percentage organizations)

Country	*D*	*DK*	*E*	*F*	*FIN*	*GR*	*I*	*IRL*	*N*	*NL*	*P*	*S*	*T*	*UK*
Part-time	**49**	**13**	**15**	**27**	**22**	**9**	**49**	**31**	**28**	**49**	**5**	**14**	**0**	**39**
work	6	34	5	5	6	6	6	4	10	2	7	24	2	8
Temporary/	**24**	**24**	**29**	**28**	**18**	**18**	**19**	**38**	**30**	**40**	**19**	**32**	**10**	**39**
casual	13	3	11	21	46	7	6	9	20	9	12	20	7	19
Fixed-term	**47**	**5**	**29**	**32**	**26**	**20**	**43**	**38**	**37**	**20**	**29**	**20**	**13**	**29**
contracts	12	2	8	19	44	3	5	4	13	20	27	4	7	6

(Bold figures represent increases: normal figures are decreases)

Source: Brewster *et al.* (1993)

significant decrease in part-time working. In that country, part-time work is being converted into full-time work. A quarter or more of all employers in Germany, Denmark, Spain, France, Finland, Ireland, Norway, Netherlands, Portugal, Sweden and the UK increased either temporary or fixed-term employment during the previous three years. (There is some trade-off between fixed-term contracts, where the date of the end of the contract is known from the outset, and more open temporary or casual contracts – this depends partly on local legal requirements. For an individual on a short fixed-term contract, however, the distinction may be of little importance.) A reduction in the use of these forms occurred in only a minority of organizations. However, in the large majority of organizations, the use of temporary or fixed-term employment, even with the high rates of increase, remains rather marginal (see Table 12.5). Employers who make substantial use of temporary work still represent significantly less than 20 per cent of organizations in most countries.

Analysis of the data indicates variations in the spread of certain forms of flexible work within countries. Public and private sector employers use flexible working in different proportions and in different ways, the contrast being particularly marked in the UK (Bruegel and Hegewisch 1993). While part-time work, for example, has grown particularly in the public sector, there are still stark differences between countries in the utilization of part-time workers, reflecting varying employment norms operating within public administration systems.

It has already been noted that while flexible employment contracts might benefit the individual employer, the same does not necessarily hold for the employee. Nor are such working practices costless for the economy as a whole, given that the State is likely to have to fund the bill for unemployment due to interrupted working patterns or training for workers whose lack of attachment to any one employer makes investment in their training unlikely. The European Commission has expressed its concern at the social consequences of flexible contracts and has put forward a number of proposals for greater protection of flexible workers.

Table 12.5 Percentage of organizations having more than 10 per cent of employees on forms of atypical contracts

	D	*DK*	*E*	*F*	*FIN*	*GR*	*I*	*IRL*	*N*	*NL*	*P*	*S*	*T*	*UK*
Part-time	23	37	6	2	6	2	6	12	37	20	–	51	4	26
Temporary/ casual	2	4	24	9	6	12	3	14	6	18	1	13	3	7
Fixed-term	7	7	26	12	14	18	10	13	9	92	35	1	37	5

Source: Brewster *et al.* (1993)

Disadvantages for managements of flexible working within the organization have been paid less attention in the past, but in certain areas are very real. Administratively, flexibility is more complicated, requiring greater complexity in such areas as recruitment, training and work organization. Recent research has shown that 'flexible workers' can be more expensive overall than 'standard workers' (Nollen 1992). Furthermore, the commitment of flexible workers may be less certain. By definition these workers have a lesser time commitment to an organization, and often a lesser psychological commitment too. This in turn raises issues of motivation, confidentiality and communication between managerial and non-managerial employees.

All of the results emerging from our survey suggest that organizations across Europe are moving towards greater flexibility, even if they are starting from different positions. The assumption is that the benefits of flexible working outweigh the disadvantages. At an organizational level, flexible patterns require a more definite focus on the actual work rather than the job, with costs providing a greater competitiveness and the practice also opens up opportunities for new sources of labour. In the clear majority of organizations across Europe the disadvantages are outweighed by the advantages. It seems likely that the total dominance of 'standard' working contracts has gone forever and that we can anticipate a continuing spread of atypical working.

Equality of opportunity

The equality of men and women in employment is one of the key tenets of European social policy, set out in the pay equality section of the Treaty of Rome in 1957 and expanded by several equal treatment directives in the 1970s. As a result, all EC member states have sex discrimination and equal pay legislation. Nevertheless, the area of equal opportunities, of practices and of support for working women, is one of the most divergent within Europe. In countries such as Denmark and France, and in the non-EC Scandinavian countries, childcare facilities are widespread; most women with children combine paid work with domestic responsibilities; in the Scandinavian countries, women's participation in paid work is now very nearly as high as that of men. At the other end of the spectrum are the more southern European countries, such as Greece or Spain, where women are only a third of the labour force and where public childcare and caring provisions are limited.

Whatever the proportion of women in the workforce, vertical and occupational segregation of women is a feature of all European countries, including the Scandinavian countries. Women work in female-dominated jobs, and they rarely reach positions of senior management. Another characteristic common to most European countries is women's predominance among part-time workers, although levels of part-time work vary substantially between countries (Bruegel and Hegewisch 1993).

Added to this, at least in countries such as Germany and the UK, there has, since the late 1970s, been increasing political and social pressures on companies to change employment practices and give a more prominent role to women. This has encouraged, for example, some of the larger banks in both Germany and Britain from the early 1980s to re-examine their graduate entry programmes and try to increase the number of women in senior positions. Even more active have been local authorities, which, from that time, have started to develop equal opportunities policies, positive action plans and to set targets for changes in the composition of their workforce. However, it has only been in the second half of the 1980s that such initiatives have been taken up by a broader number of organizations. Over one-third of organizations in Germany, Ireland, Norway, the Netherlands, Portugal, Sweden, Turkey and the UK monitor the share of women in recruitment and, even though the numbers are smaller in all countries, around a third of organizations also monitor the gender distribution of training and promotions. Such activities in the field of equal opportunities are markedly lower in France, Italy and Spain – significantly so for France, where although employers are legally bound to establish these statistics, there is little enforcement to ensure that the legislation is complied with.

Equal opportunities policies, of course, do not refer solely to gender inequality. In the English language the term is generally understood as including discrimination on the basis of race and ethnic background, as well as disability. Most European countries have some quota system for the employment of people with disabilities (although there is no general anti-discrimination legislation on the grounds of disability). Discrimination on the grounds of race or ethnic origin in employment is much less of a concern in most European countries, although there is strong evidence that because of discrimination, black and ethnic minority people are not utilized to their full potential. In Britain and the Netherlands, the issue of race discrimination in employment has been more prominent with employers during the last few years, although much less so than equal opportunities for women. The level of migrants, immigrants and black and ethnic minority people in the workforce in European countries varies from about 5 per cent in the UK and the Netherlands to 8 per cent in France and Germany and 25 per cent in Switzerland. But awareness and concern among employers about race discrimination in many countries remains low.

Training

The field of training provision in Europe is one of relatively great government intervention, but also one where levels of provision vary considerably between countries. In most countries the issue of training is seen as critical in the long-term strategy of organizations in terms of manpower planning, human resource allocation, fulfilling skills needs in the light of change, the development of management succession and career path planning, and as a means of aiding or substituting for recruitment (Holt Larsen 1994). Our data show a Europe-wide increase in investment in training at all levels, particularly for managerial and professional staff.

Whether training is treated as a cost or, as many organizations now claim it should be, as an investment (see Chapter 9), details of both expenditure and benefits are important. However, across Europe (with the exception of France, where the law requires organizations to spend at least 1.2 per cent of their pay bill on training: Bournois 1992), many organizations are unable to identify the actual percentage of wages and salaries spent on training.

Being unable to calculate these figures could be in part a consequence of the move to more decentralized training provision and the devolution of HR responsibilities as a whole. The increased responsibility of line management for training may result in a lack of centrally gathered information about the subject. This lack of information is not only found in European organizations. Grosseilliers (1986: 46) revealed that in the USA, '31 per cent of education directors at the largest corporations said they didn't know how much their companies spent on Training and Development'. This raises questions about how organizations actually evaluate the effectiveness of their training programme when this basic information is not available.

Of those organizations that do know how much they are spending, many are spending considerable amounts of money on training (2–4 per cent of wages and salaries bills on average; see Holt Larsen 1994). They are devoting substantial amounts of time to this purpose, as well. Table 12.6 uses manual workers, the group that receives least training, as an example. Even here, in eleven out of fourteen countries, more than 10 per cent of the organizations devote more than five days – out of a presumed working year of around 200 days – to training.

Table 12.6 Percentage of organizations (excluding 'don't knows') providing more than five days' training per year for manual workers

D	DK	E	F	FIN	GR	I	IRL	N	NL	P	S	T	UK
9	16	35	25	8	32	8	29	23	17	35	19	56	16

Source: Brewster and Hegewisch (1994)

To some extent, differential training provisions reflect the situation that employers are in with regard to the educational system from which they draw their employees. The high number of days employees spend on training in Spain, for example, is due to a level of state education which is insufficient for organizations' requirements – they have to supplement training internally. Similarly, the high quality of state provision in Germany explains the comparatively low level there.

Information on expenditure or on days spent on training is not enough: organizations also need to be able to assess the benefits – the need for training and the extent to which such needs are met. More than half of all organizations across Europe stated that they systematically analysed employee training needs. However, the methods most frequently used for this assessment tended to be the less formal ones, such as line management and employee requests.

A slightly smaller overall percentage of organizations go on to evaluate training, once given. Once again, where organizations do evaluate training it tends to be done in an informal manner. Evaluation is more likely to be conducted by informal feedback via line management or the trainees themselves, than by tests or formal evaluation. These informal methods of analysis and evaluation could be linked to growing line management responsibility in this area. A more cynical interpretation is that much training is still done as an act of faith, with no real expectation that the organization will be able to measure the resultant benefits.

Where is this training commitment most intensive? Managers in general receive more training than any other occupational group. Around one tenth of organizations provide management training of ten days or more. Further, the amount of money spent on management training over the last three years has increased in half or more organizations in every country except Finland (Holt Larsen 1994), even in a time of economic recession.

Trade unions

Compared to most other parts of the world, Europe is heavily unionized, and the trade unions are not 'going away'. Despite the view (fears or hopes?) of some commentators, relationships with trade unions are still a key issue for personnel departments in most European organizations. Union membership varies considerably of course – from nine out of ten employees in Norway, to no more than one in eight in France. However, individual membership is not a good indicator of trade union influence within organizations. Recognition levels are higher in the UK – for example, more than half of all establishments with more than twenty-five employees recognize trade unions (Millward *et al.* 1992): our survey shows that among organizations with more than 200 employees, more than seven out of ten organizations in Denmark, Spain, Italy, Ireland, Portugal, Turkey and the UK deal with unions. (The information was not collected in Germany and France, where negotiation is legally determined.) Trade unions are still an issue to be managed by European personnel professionals (Gunnigle *et al.* 1993).

In terms of the (usually American) theories of HRM, and even according to some European commentators, this may be something of a disappointment. In practice the picture is mixed: union influence is stable in most countries, sharply reduced in others (the UK, France, Italy) and, in some countries such as Germany more organizations report that union influence has increased than report it as having decreased. Overall, trade unions continue to play an important part in European personnel management. The reasons for this are complex: in part it is because of the trade union role in communication and consultation, which is legally determined in many European countries; and in part because of the attempts by some European governments and the European Community to emphasize the position of the 'social partners', as the EC calls them.

This last point is instructive. One of the main reasons that the trade unions continue to exert such an influence in Europe is that in most countries the unions are not seen, and do not see themselves, as 'adversaries'. Rather, they are seen as partners. They work with the organization for the success of the enterprise and those who work in it.

These issues of the trade union position are closely linked to the issue of communication with employees. This is a central strand in many theories of HRM, as well as being a live issue for trade unions, employers, governments and the European Community. Are employing organizations replacing representative channels with direct communication?

This is not a matter of organizational choice in many European countries.

Germany and the Netherlands have legislation which covers most organizations above a certain size, requiring them to establish works councils. These councils of employee representatives have considerable power to constrain managerial action. Similar, though less powerful, works councils operate in countries such as France – and some states such as Sweden give considerable legal codetermination powers to trade unions.

Some of our major findings on increases in the use of channels of communication are presented in Table 12.7. Decreases have been left out, as they are in nearly all cases negligible. The table shows a significant increase in all forms of communication: through representative bodies (trade unions or works councils), by direct verbal communication and by direct written communication. The latter two channels in particular have expanded considerably. To a degree, increases in direct communication to employees can be explained by the development of technology: word processors and mailmerge systems have opened up the possibility of sending 'individual' letters to all employees. However, possibility is one thing: the desire to take advantage of it is another. Clearly there is a widespread move across Europe to increase the amount of communication to employees.

Table 12.7 Channels of employee communication: percentage of organizations which have increased their use of selected methods

	D	*DK*	*E*	*F*	*FIN*	*GR*	*I*	*IRL*	*N*	*NL*	*P*	*S*	*T*	*UK*
Trade unions/ collective staff bodies	36	52	34	24	62	16	21	12	43	49	8	16	25	12
Verbally, direct to employees	47	65	43	58	66	44	51	58	47	43	45	63	33	63
Written, direct to employees	47	54	41	62	57	30	44	41	24	58	40	58	37	59

Source: Brewster and Hegewisch (1994)

The fact that this communication continues to utilize staff representative bodies, as well as going directly to employees, indicates that the objective is passing information. The assumption appears to be that passing a message through several channels increases its chances of being received. This inevitably reduces the importance of the union channel. The evidence here, however, suggests that employers in Europe are not using individual communication to replace trade union channels; rather, they are using both forms of communication.

In sum, the evidence on the trade unions is that they continue to be a significant feature of the European scene and that, whilst their influence may be declining currently in certain countries, there is little evidence of a concerted move against them by employers. However, national differences in extent, style and trends remain.

THE ROLE OF THE HR FUNCTION

Of course, developments in pay, flexibility, equality, training and union relationships are only part of a wide range of changes going on in Europe. What does this mean for the personnel department? Does the research show convergence in the way these departments operate? The answer, simply, is no. The research data (Brewster and Bournois 1991; Brewster and Holt Larsen 1992; Brewster 1993) show considerable stability over time, and considerable variation between countries. Spain and France, for example, consistently report seven or eight out of ten organizations having an HR director on the board (or equivalent), while in Italy and Germany only two or three out of ten organizations are in the same position. Most other European countries, including the UK, show a little less than half of the organizations with HR departments directly represented at the top decision-making level. The 1990 WIRS survey in the UK reports a similar finding (Millward *et al.* 1992). When it comes to a question – perhaps the key question – of HR influence on corporate strategy, there is more uniformity: in most countries the personnel departments are involved from the outset in strategy formulation in around half the organizations. Some of the reasons for the variations are clear. Germany tends to have more 'administrative' personnel departments, but with personnel issues being brought into corporate thinking through employee representation at the top level. Italy has personnel departments that are focused more on industrial relations issues (Cooper and Giacomelli 1992).

Issues concerning the decentralization of personnel management and the devolvement of personnel tasks to line management vary widely. Most larger organizations have policies on various aspects of HR determined mainly at the level of the national HQ (more so for pay and industrial relations; less so for recruitment and selection and health and safety). The UK tends to be at the more decentralized end of the personnel management spectrum – that is, the role of corporate HQs in personnel management policy is lower than in most other countries but, contrary to some assumptions, it is not the most decentralized – Denmark is. Even more of a surprise is its rating on sharing responsibility for personnel issues with line management. This has been more widely discussed in the UK than anywhere else in Europe. In fact, however, Britain is one of the countries where senior personnel specialists consistently report that primary responsibility for a range of personnel issues is *least* likely to be given to or shared with line managers. On a range of personnel issues it is the Italians who are most likely to lodge responsibility with the personnel department; the British

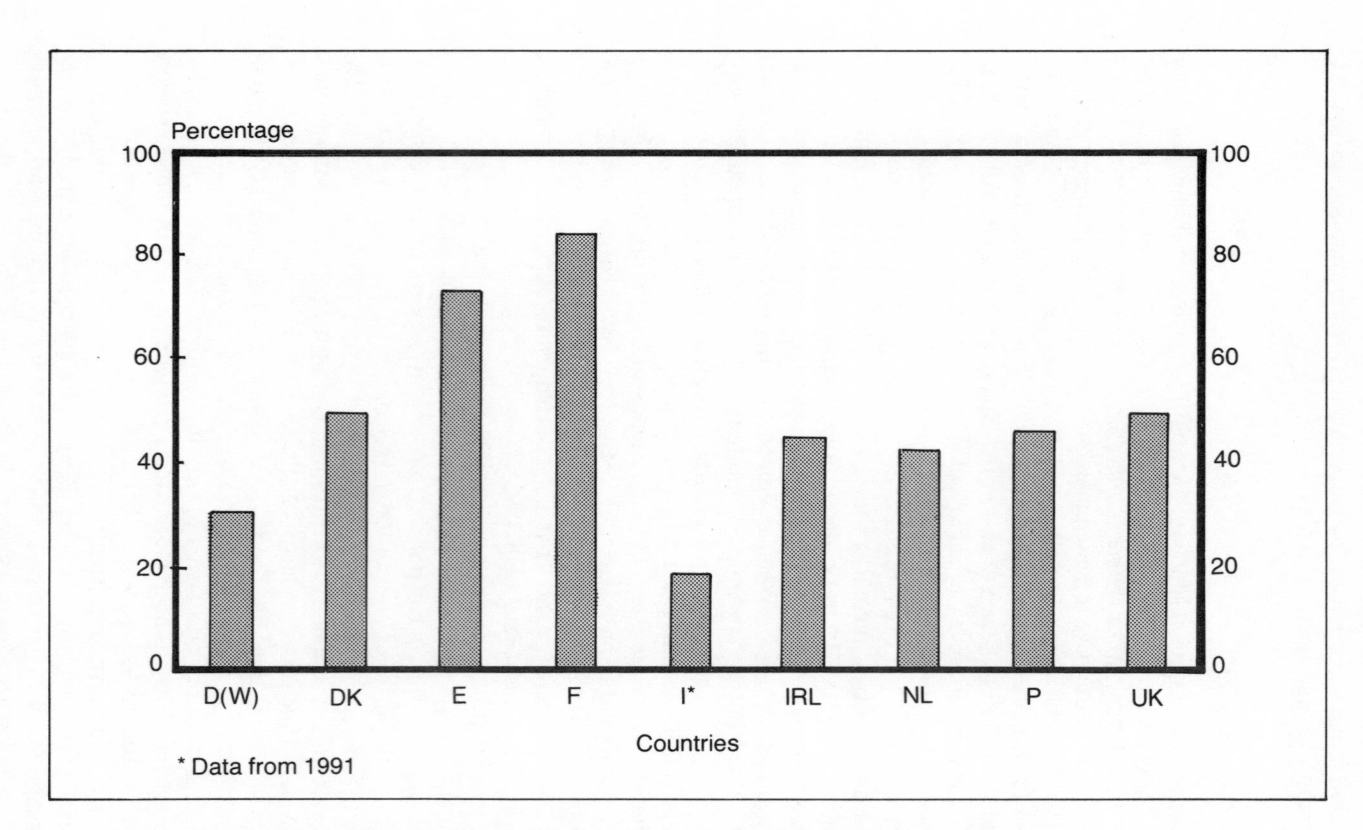

Figure 12.1 Percentage of heads of personnel/HR with a place on the board (EC countries only)
Source: Brewster and Hegewisch (1994)

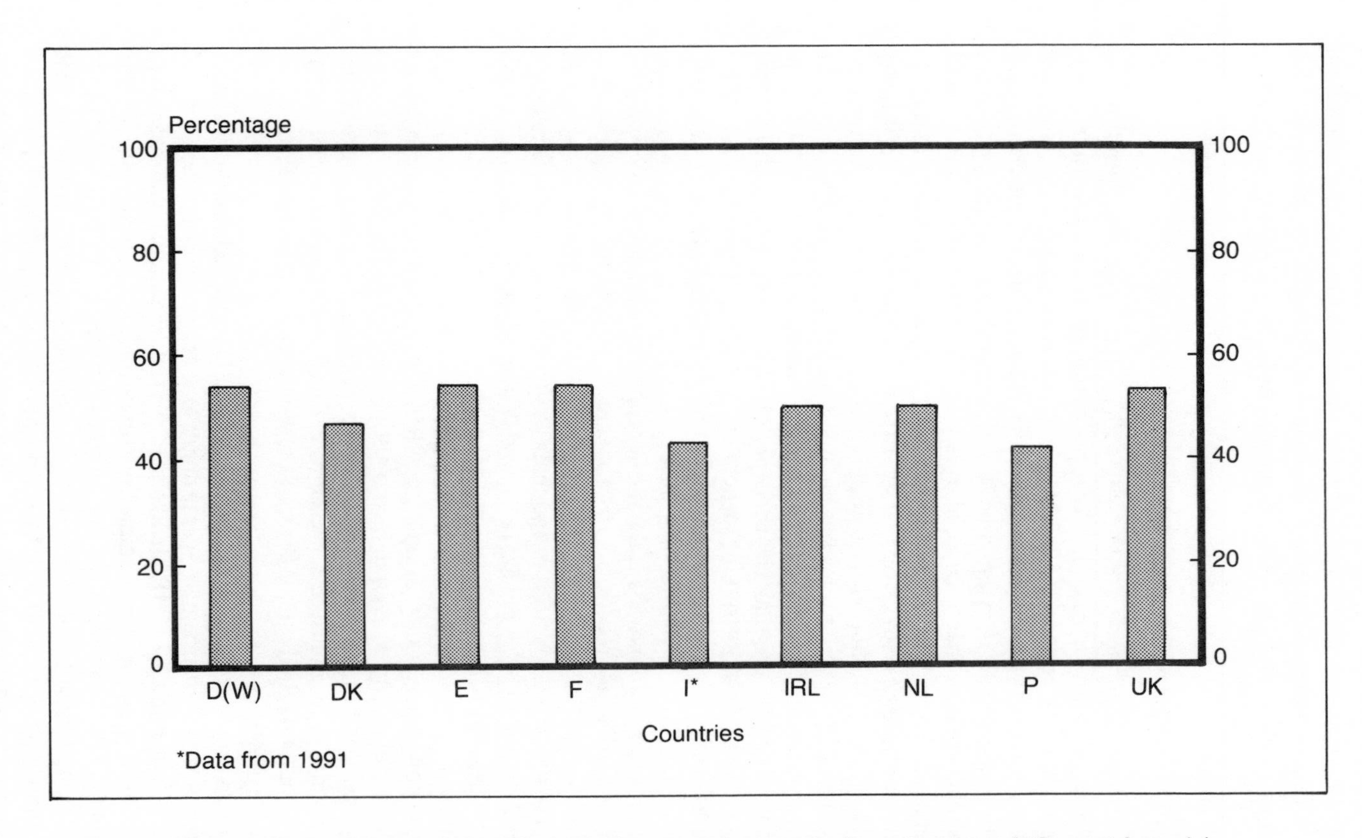

Figure 12.2 Percentage of HR departments involved in corporate strategy from the outset (EC countries only)
Source: Brewster and Hegewisch (1994)

come next. This stands in sharp contrast to the Danes, for example, who, on all issues, tend to give much greater responsibility to line managers. Furthermore, when asked about changes in responsibility, about half the European countries have been increasing line management responsibility faster than the UK.

THE 'EUROPEAN' MODEL OF HRM

It has been argued elsewhere (Brewster 1993) that a new 'European' model of HRM is required, one that takes account of State and trade union involvement – a concept of HRM which takes us back to the industrial relations system approach first outlined by Dunlop (1958). This changes the nature of the debate. Any attempt to deny the reality or the integrity of the HRM concept is probably doomed to failure. The terminology is too widely entrenched, in practitioner and in academic circles, for it to 'go away'. In these circumstances, suggestions that HRM is in some sense less 'legitimate' than, say, the discipline of industrial relations is a vain attempt to turn the clock back. However, to answer the question posed at the beginning, the evidence presented in this chapter is that current trends do not fit comfortably with the original US concepts of HRM. The trends show some areas (pay, flexibility, training) where the US approach works and others (such as trade union recognition and communications) where it does not. Rather than debate whether this means that HRM or personnel management or industrial relations is the more explanatory model, a more positive way forward is to redefine a 'European' approach to HRM; one that includes a significant role for the State and for trade unions. Thus, in this way, the industrial relations proponents can reclaim the area, insisting that, in Europe at least, it is crucial to view HRM as covering a wider field than just managerial behaviour.

Without some adaptation to take account of the European (and perhaps other?) non-American situations, the HRM concept will continue to attract fundamental critiques, even in its most sophisticated form, for its failure to accept different degrees of managerial independence, different approaches to working with employee representatives and governmental involvement and, most damagingly, its inability to link HRM to economic performance (Brewster 1993).

Building on the arguments in this chapter, it is suggested that these simple approaches are, in practice, increasingly less adequate as explanations of what is happening. The HR challenge to personnel management has arisen partly as a way of expounding, or propounding, a new role for the personnel/HR department, as the previous one is seen to be inappropriate to changing times. The evidence of data collected across Europe is that HR is not developing as a straightforward opposite, or negative, of personnel management. What is happening in Europe is that there is a move towards the HRM concept but one which, within a clearly established external environment, accepts the duality of people management. Thus objectives include both organizational requirements and a concern for people; the focus on both costs and benefits means fitting organizational policies to external cultures and constraints; union and non-union channels are utilized; the relationship with line managers at all levels is interactive, rather than driven by either specialists or the line.

In this context, the specialist department requires the ability to manage ambiguity and flexibility – issues which the management strategy gurus tell us are going to become ever more important: and perhaps issues where Europe has a lead.

This chapter has argued from European data and hence has restricted the analysis to Europe. It is believed that the 'European' approach projected here accords much better with the reality of current and developing practice than many of the more straightforward personnel management or HRM approaches elsewhere. And it may be that it is closer to reality in other continents and countries too.

REFERENCES

Adler, N.J. and Jelinek, M. (1986) 'Is "organisational culture" culture-bound?', *Human Resource Management* 25(1): 72–90.

Ahlen, K. (1989) 'Swedish collective bargaining under pressure: inter-union rivalry and incomes policies', *British Journal of Industrial Relations* 27: 330–46.

Atkinson, J. (1985) 'Flexibility, uncertainty and manpower management', *IMS Report* No. 89, Institute of Manpower Studies.

Atkinson, J. and Meager, N. (1986) 'Is flexibility just a flash in the pan?', *Personnel Management* 18(9): 26–9.

Beer, M., Lawrence, P.R., Mills, Q.N. and Walton, R.E. (1985) *Human Resource Management*, New York: Free Press.

Bournois, F. (1992) 'France', in C. Brewster, A. Hegewisch, L. Holden, and T. Lockhart (eds) *The European Human Resource Management Guide*, London: Academic Press.

Brewster, C. (1993) 'Developing a "European" model of human resource management', *International Journal of Human Resource Management* 4(4): 765–84.

Brewster, C. and Bournois, F. (1991) 'A European perspective on human resource management', *Personnel Review* 20(6): 4–13.

Brewster, C. and Hegewisch, A. (eds) (1994) *Policy and Practice in European Human Resource Management: the Evidence and Analysis from the Price Waterhouse Cranfield Survey*, London: Routledge.

Brewster, C. and Holt Larsen, H. (1992) 'Human resource management in European – evidence from ten countries', *International Human Resource Management Journal* 3(3): 409–34.

Brewster, C. and Soderström, M. (1994) 'Human resources and line management', in C. Brewster and A. Hegewisch (eds) *Policy and Practice in European Human Resource Management: the Evidence and Analysis from the Price Waterhouse Cranfield Survey*, London: Routledge.

Brewster, C., Hegewisch, A. and Mayne, L. (1994) 'Flexible working practices: the controversy and the evidence' in C. Brewster and A. Hegewisch (eds) *Policy and Practice in European Human Resource Management: the Evidence and Analysis from the Price Waterhouse Cranfield Survey*, London: Routledge.

Brewster, C., Hegewisch, A., Holden, L. and Lockhart, T. (eds) (1992) *The European Human Resource Management Guide*, London: Academic Press.

Brewster, C., Hegewisch, A., Lockhart, T. and Mayne, L. (1993) *Flexible Working Practices in Europe*, London: IPM.

Bruegel, I. and Hegewisch, A. (1993) 'Flexibilisation and part-time work in Europe', in R. Brown and R. Crompton (eds) *The New Europe: Economic Restructuring and Social Exclusion*, London: UCL Press.

Casey, B. (1991) 'Survey evidence on trends in "non-standard" employment', in A. Pollert (ed.) *Farewell to Flexibility?*, Oxford: Basil Blackwell.

Cooper, J. and Giacomelli, G. (1992) 'Italy' in Brewster *et al.* (eds) *The European Human Resource Management Guide*, London: Academic Press.

Cox, J. and Cooper, L. (1985) 'The irrelevance of American organisational sciences to the UK and Europe', *Journal of General Management* 11(2): 27–34.

Dunlop, J. (1958) *Industrial Relations Systems*, New York: Henry Holt & Co.

Filella, J. (1991) 'Is there a Latin model in the management of human resources?', *Personnel Review* 20(6): 15–24.

Filella, J. and Hegewisch, A. (1994) 'European experiments with pay and benefits policies', in C. Brewster and A. Hegewisch (eds) *Policy and Practice in European Human Resource Management: the Evidence and Analysis*, London: Routledge.

Fombrun, C.J., Tichy, N.M. and Devanna, M.A. (1984) *Strategic Human Resource Management*, New York: John Wiley.

Gaugler, E. and Wiltz, S. (1992) 'Germany' in Brewster *et al.* (eds) *The European Human Resource Management Guide*, London: Academic Press.

Grosseillier, L. (1986) 'What companies do to evaluate the effectiveness of training programs', in H.B. Bernhard and C.A. Inglois, 'Six lessons for the corporate classroom', *Harvard Business Review* 66(5): 40–8.

Guest, D. (1990) 'Human resource management and the American dream', *Journal of Management Studies* 27(4): 377–97.

Gunnigle, P., Brewster, C. and Morley, M. (1993) 'Changing patterns in industrial relations: evidence from the Price Waterhouse Cranfield Project', *Journal of the European Foundation for the Improvement of Working and Living Conditions* 7.

Hegewisch, A. (1991) 'The decentralisation of pay bargaining: European comparisons', *Personnel Review* 20(6): 28–35.

Holt Larsen, H. (1994) 'Key issues in training and development', in C. Brewster and A. Hegewisch (eds) *Policy and Practice in European Human Resource Management: the Evidence and Analysis*, London: Routledge.

IDS/IPM (1992) *Pay and Benefits: European Management Guides*, London: IPM.

Kinnie, N. (1989) 'The decentralisation of industrial relations? – recent research considered', *Personnel Review* 19(3): 28–34.

Marginson, P., Sisson, K., Martin, R. and Edwards, P. (1988) *Beyond the Workplace: the Management of Industrial Relations in Large Enterprises*, Oxford: Blackwell.

Marsden, D. (1989) 'Developments of pay level patterns and flexibility in Western Europe', paper to the Eighth World Congress of the International Industrial Relations Conference, Brussels.

Millward, N., Stevens, M., Smart, D. and Hawes, W.R. (1992) *Workplace Industrial Relations in Transition*, Aldershot: Dartmouth.

Morris, T. and Wood, S. (1991) 'Testing the survey method: continuity and change in British industrial relations', *Work, Employment and Society* 5(2): 259–82.

Nollen, S.D. (1992) 'The cost effectiveness of contingent labor', *Proceedings 9th*

World Congress, Vol. 6 (Communication Abstracts), Geneva: International Industrial Relations Association.

Pieper, R. (ed.) (1990) *Human Resource Management: An International Comparison*, Berlin: Walter de Gruyter.

Pollert, A. (1987) 'The flexible firm: a model in search of reality (or a policy in search of a practice)?', *Warwick Papers in Industrial Relations*, no. 19.

—— (ed.) (1991) *Farewell to Flexibility?*, Oxford: Basil Blackwell.

Porter, M. (1991) *The Competitive Advantage of Nations*, New York: Free Press.

Rubery, J. (1988) *Women in Recession*, London: Routledge.

Scheuer, S. (1992) 'Denmark: return to decentralisation' in A. Ferner and R. Hyman, *Industrial Relations in the New Europe*, Oxford: Blackwell.

Thurley, K. and Wirdenius, H. (1991) 'Will management become "European"? Strategic choices for organisations', *European Management Journal* 9(2): 127–34.

Trompenaars, A. (1985) 'Organisation of meaning and the meaning of organisation: a comparative study on the conception of organisational structure in different cultures', unpublished PhD thesis, University of Pennsylvania.

Visser, J. (1992) 'The Netherlands: the end of an era and the end of a system', in A. Ferner and R. Hyman (eds) *Industrial Relations in the New Europe*, Oxford: Blackwell.

Chapter 13

HRM: an American View

Thomas Kochan and Lee Dyer

HUMAN RESOURCE MANAGEMENT AND NATIONAL COMPETITIVENESS

Can the United States maintain its traditional position of economic leadership and one of the world's highest standards of living in the face of increasing global competition? Concerned observers cite the following negative trends: lagging rates of productivity growth, non-competitive product quality in key industries, structural inflexibilities, and declining real wage levels and flat family earnings (Carnavale 1991). Further, they offer a plethora of proposed solutions, covering both broad public policies and practices.

The latter often call upon organizations to do a better job of developing and utilizing their human resources (Cyert and Mowery 1986; Marshall 1987; Walton 1987; Dertouzos *et al.* 1989). Newly industrializing economies such as Mexico, Brazil, and some of the Asian countries compete in world markets with wages that range from 10 to 30 per cent of those paid in more advanced countries such as Japan, Germany, and the US. For companies in the more advanced countries to compete in world markets without lowering wages and living standards requires not only ever-increasing levels of productivity, but also finding other sources of competitive advantage, such as high product quality, product differentiation, innovation, and speed to market.

However, competing on these grounds often requires major organizational transformations in human resource policies and practices. This is especially the case for US firms, that have grown up under the legacy of scientific management and industrial engineering principles that emphasize the separation of decision-making from doing and narrow divisions of labour and functional specialization. It is also true for unionized firms that have long done business under the 'New Deal' model of labour relations, which emphasizes job control, unionism and the separation of managerial prerogatives from worker and union rights.

The past decade has witnesses an explosion of interest in human resource

The past decade has witnessed an explosion of interest in human resource management and the growth of new academic journals, professional societies, and industry–university research and educational partnerships. All of these share the view that human resource issues should and, given the increased awareness of their importance, shall be elevated to new levels of influence within corporate decision-making and national policy-making. In the US, these expectations and arguments have been voiced before, in some cases way before (Slichter 1919; Douglas 1919). Nonetheless, even today we find that the human resource function within many American corporations remains weak and relatively low in influence, relative to other managerial functions such as finance, marketing and manufacturing (Kochan and Osterman 1991). Moreover, despite the outpouring of academic writing on 'strategic human resource management', little progress has been made in developing systematic theory or empirical evidence on the conditions under which human resources are elevated to a position where the firm sees and treats these issues as a source of competitive advantage. Nor is there much research that actually tests the effects of different strategies on the competitive position of the firm.

Countless national competitiveness commissions and at least three national commissions sponsored by current or former US Secretaries of Labour have documented the need for the country, as well as individual firms, to invest more in human resources and encourage the development of workplace innovations to fully utilize employee talents once developed. But, so far, these clarion calls have often fallen on either deaf or hostile ears. Corporate managements, for reasons we will document below, have not been particularly enthusiastic, and responses from labour leaders have been mixed. Many of the recommended practices have been pioneered in non-union firms and some union leaders see them as inherently anti-union in nature. Yet the economic pressures of the 1980s led to a certain amount of joint union–management experimentation, and these experiences have produced a cadre of local and, to a lesser extent, national union leaders who are advocates. As yet, however, no clear vision or strategy on these issues has been articulated by the labour movement. And, finally, there has been virtually no action on the part of national policy-makers to create either the environment or the substantive policies needed to encourage or require either firms or unions to act more forcefully in this regard.

Why does the rhetoric so far outstrip the reality? One (although certainly not the only) answer is that theorists and researchers have cast their models of human resource management and related policy issues too narrowly. Specifically, they have relied too heavily on top management and human resource managers within corporations to drive the necessary transformation. Too little consideration has been given to the organizational and institutional contexts in which firms formulate and implement their human resource strategies and policies. Moreover, the literature has tended to treat each firm as an independent actor whereas, as we argue below, it is now clear that the practices of individual firms are influenced not only by their own business strategies, technologies, and structures, but also by the practices of other firms in their product and labour markets, as well as by the activities of their suppliers and customers, of trade unions, and of public policy-makers (Dyer and Holder 1988). Thus, we see the need to bring labour and government back into our theories and models of human resource management policy and practice. To do this we need to integrate recent works from human resource management with research from industrial relations, political economy, and internal labour markets. In this chapter we turn to that task.

GENERIC PRINCIPLES OF MUTUAL COMMITMENT FIRMS

Many terms have been used to describe firms that seek to treat human resources as a source of competitive advantage and to do so in a manner that preserves high standards of living: 'high involvment' (Walton 1985), 'excellent' (Peters and Waterman 1982), 'best practice' (Dertouzos *et al.* 1989), 'transformed' (Kochan *et al.* 1986), and 'high involvement' (Lawler 1986). We will use the term 'mutual commitment' (Walton 1985). We prefer this term since, as will be evident below, we believe that achieving and sustaining this approach requires the strong support of multiple stakeholders in an organization and in the broader economy and society in which the organization is embedded.

Figure 13.1 summarizes a set of generic principles that characterize the 'mutual commitment' approach. It is important to realize that these are broad principles which are operationalized in quite different forms across countries and firms. Therefore, they do not translate into a universal set of 'best practices', but rather stand as broad guidelines to be implemented in ways that conform to particular cultural or organizational realities. Further, much work remains to be done to test the validity of these principles, to describe and analyse the different practices used to meet these principles, and to assess the interrelationships among the principles, practices and important societal, organizational and individual outcomes in different settings.

Figure 13.1 organizes the principles according to the three-tiered institutional framework presented in Kochan *et al.* (1986). At the highest level of the firm, first, it is essential that business strategies should not be built around low costs, and especially not around low wages, salaries, and benefit levels, but rather around such sources of competitive advantage as affordable quality, innovation, flexibility, speed, and customer service (Carnavale 1991). Second, key decision-makers must be guided by a set of values and traditions – often referred to as organizational culture – that views

Strategic Level

Supportive Business Strategies
Top Management Value Commitment
Effective Voice For HR In
Strategy Making And Governance

Functional (Human Resource Policy) Level

Staffing Based On Employment Stabilization
Investment in Training And Development
Contingent Compensation That Reinforces
Cooperation, Participation, And Contribution

Workplace Level

Selection Based On High Standards
Broad Task Design And Teamwork
Employee Involvement In Problem-Solving
Climate Of Cooperation And Trust

Figure 13.1 Principles guiding mutual commitment firms

employees as valued stakeholders in the organization, not as mere cogs in the machine. Within any given business strategy and strategic context, top managers have significant discretion in human resource matters; values and traditions often dictate how, and how wisely, this discretion is used. Finally, at the strategy and policy-making level it is necessary that there be one or more mechanisms for giving voice to employee and human resource interests in strategy formulation and organizational governance processes. One possibility is the use of planning mechanisms to ensure that human resource issues receive their just due in the formulation of business strategies (Dyer 1983; Schuler and Jackson 1987). In other contexts, informal labour–management information-sharing and consultation might be used. In still others it might be more formal forms of worker representation in corporate governance structures (e.g., labour leaders on the board of directors, works councils).

Moving down to the human resource policy level, we suggest three additional principles that are important for achieving comparative advantage from human resources. First, staffing policies must be designed and managed in such a way that they reinforce the principle of employment security and thus promote the commitment, flexibility, and loyalty of employees. This does not imply guarantees of lifetime employment, but it does imply that the first instinct in good times and bad should be to build and protect the firm's investment in human resources, rather than to indiscriminately add and cut people in knee-jerk responses to short-term fluctuations in business conditions (Dyer *et al.* 1985). Closely related is the matter of training and development. Clearly, firms that seek competitive advantage through human resources must make the necessary investment to ensure that their workforces have the appropriate skills and training, not only to meet short-term job requirements, but also to anticipate changing job requirements over time. That is, they – and their employees – must be prepared to adopt the concept of lifelong learning.

The third critical principle at the human resource policy level concerns compensation. Basic compensation levels must be adequate to attract and retain a committed, cooperative and involved workforce, and the compensation structure must be seen as being internally equitable by employees at various levels in different functions. Over and above competitive basic compensation levels and structures would be variable, or contingent, compensation schemes (e.g., bonus plans) designed to reinforce desired forms of quality, flexibility and the like, as well as to provide the firm with a means of controlling its labour costs in tough times without reverting to lay-offs.

Finally, we move to the level of day-to-day interactions of employees with their environment, supervision, and jobs. Here we see several principles as critical. Clearly, in selection, high standards must be set regarding the level of skill, training and educational preparation required of new recruits. The ability to learn and the willingness to continue to learn over the course of one's career becomes an extremely important personal attribute for employees in mutual commitment firms. Second, the education and skills preparation of employees must be fully utilized on the job. This requires job and career structures that eschew narrow, Tayloristic job assignments in favour of flexible work organization that features expanded jobs and the free-flowing movement of employees across tasks and functional boundaries.

A third principle at the workplace level deals with opportunities for employees and/or their representatives to engage in problem-solving and decision-making in matters which involve their jobs and the conditions surrounding their jobs – what Lawler (1988) refers to as job involvement. The fourth and final workplace principle relates to the quality of relationships between employees, their representatives, and managers. A high-conflict/low-trust relationship (Fox 1974) is seen as incompatible with the task of building and maintaining mutual commitment. This does not mean that all conflicts between employees and employers wither away. Indeed we continue to assume that conflicting interests are a natural part of the employment relationship, but that these conflicts cannot be so all-encompassing that they push out the potential for effective problem-solving and negotiations. Instead they must be resolved efficiently and in a fashion that maintains the parties' commitment and capacities for pursuing joint gains.

Obviously the above set of principles constitutes a caricature of actual organizations. No organization is expected to meet all of these principles perfectly or through the same set of practices. Nonetheless, in the broadest sense it is postulated that when these principles are properly operationalized they will come together in the form of an integrated system that, other things being equal, will produce globally competitive business results as well as globally competitive standards of living for employees.

The preceding principles have been presented as if firms have total discretion over the choice of their human resource strategies, and as if each firm's choice is independent of the strategies followed by other firms. But neither of these premises is the case. External factors, particularly the role of the trade unions, the State (government policy) and, in some countries, industry associations all influence and/or constrain the range of choices open to decision-makers. Moreover, individual firms are heavily influenced by the strategies followed by others in their product and labour markets, supplier and customer networks, and industries. Thus, a critical factor is the rate and depth at which the concepts underlying these principles are diffused across different institutions and institutional decision-makers, as well as across various firms and industries.

EXTENT OF DIFFUSION OF MUTUAL COMMITMENT PRINCIPLES

Unfortunately no single data base currently exists that allows us to estimate precisely how widespread the principles reviewed above are in US organizations today. It is probably fair to say that very few organizations have yet embraced the full set of principles in a coherent fashion. Clearly, however, the past decade has been a time of great experimentation with various of these principles, to the point that it is probably fair to say that most large and perhaps even a majority of relatively small firms have experimented with one or more of them at one time or another.

Supportive competitive strategies

We believe that one of the most powerful determinants and reinforcing forces for a mutual commitment human resources strategy lies in the nature of competitive business strategies. Clearly, many US firms recognize this as well. In some ways, however, large US firms suffer from the legacies of their prior successes in taking advantage of the vast size of the US markets.

For this reason, they have experienced more difficulty adapting to export markets and the flexible production and differentiated competitive strategies needed to support mutual commitment human resource strategies (Carnavale 1991; Piore and Sabel 1984).

In the clothing industry, for example, despite the obvious difficulty of competing with imports from low-wage countries, American manufacturers and unions have made only limited progress in abandoning their traditional individual piecework and related mass production strategies in favour of practices that would give them advantages in time to market and quick response to changing customer preferences (National Clothing Industry Labor Management Committee 1991). As a result, imports are taking a greater share of the market both at the low-price points where mass production continues to dominate, and at the high-price points where styling, fashion, and variability in tastes matter most.

In the US airline industry, the low-cost strategies of Continental and Eastern Airlines served to limit the success of the high-growth and service differentiation strategies of firms such as American and Delta Airlines, in the first decade following industry deregulation (Kochan and McKersie 1991). Thus, while low-cost strategies are difficult to sustain over the long run, especially when faced with competition from abroad, a significant number of American firms continue to give priority to this strategy and thereby slow the pace of innovations in human resource practices.

Managerial values and organizational culture

As noted earlier, we continue to see top executive and line management support as a necessary condition for introducing and sustaining the types of human resource strategies described in Figure 13.1. Yet there is little in the history of American management, or in the behaviour of American management currently, to suggest that management alone, left to its own devices, will produce the transformations in organizational practice needed to sustain and diffuse the delineated human resource principles. While some, perhaps even many, top executives share supportive values, they are buffeted by equally strong countervailing pressures that call for quick action taken to bolster the short-term interests of major shareholders.

Consider, for example, the following description of the dominant managerial strategies of the 1980s, offered by the top human resource executive at General Electric, one of the firms often cited as symbolizing exemplary practices:

> Economic power in the Eighties – the power to launch and sustain the dynamic processes of restructuring and globalization – has been concentrated especially in the hands of the larger companies, along with the financiers and raiders who alternatively [*sic*] support or attack them. If

> the Eighties was a new Age of the Entrepreneur – and small business did in fact account for most of the new job creation in the United States – it was Corporate America that accounted for most of the economic disruption and competitive improvement; it took out people, layers and costs while rearranging portfolios and switching industries. . . . Across the decade in the US alone, there was over a trillion dollars of merger and acquisition activity. Ten million manufacturing jobs were eliminated or shifted to the growing service sector. Deals were cut and alliances forged around America and around the world.
>
> From where the shots were called was well-known. Restructuring and globalization did not emerge from employee suggestion boxes; they erupted from executive suites. . . .
>
> So competitive rigor – imposed by companies in their employer roles and demonstrated by their restructuring and globalizing moves – was widely accepted because its rationale was widely understood. Given this climate – along with a political environment of relative deregulation – companies in the Eighties could focus more on portfolios than on people; fire more than hire; invest more in machines than in skills.
>
> The obvious reality of tough competitive facts inspired fear in employees and gave employers the power to act. Shuttered factories and fired neighbors is restructuring without subtlety: people could see the damage and feel the pain.
>
> (Doyle 1989: 1–2)

This, then, is perhaps the dominant political environment of corporate decision-making and governance that must be taken into account in building theoretical and action models in the human resource management arena.

Human resources in business strategy formulation

Clearly, very few if any inroads have been made into top-level business strategy formulation by either informal or formal forms of employee representation; the European experience remains distinctively European (Kochan *et al.* 1986). Some progress has been made in bringing human resource considerations into business strategy sessions through the integration of formal planning processes – exactly how much progress, however, it is difficult to say. Recent surveys suggest that at least some level of integration has been achieved by between 20 per cent and 45 per cent of medium-sized and large firms (Burack 1986; Nkomo 1986). More intensive case studies support these figures, but call into question the depth of the integration in many cases (Buller 1988; Craft 1988). Functionally, some progressive human resource departments are striving to adopt a so-called business partner role, which puts them in a position to interject human resource considerations in ongoing business decision-making (Dyer and Holder 1988). But, again, while the trend is in the right direction, at this juncture the development is probably neither very widespread nor particularly deep.

Employment security

Diffusion of the practices needed to demonstrate a commitment to employment continuity is particularly limited in the US (Dyer *et al.* 1985). Massive lay-offs became commonplace during the 1980s, affecting not only blue-collar and clerical employees, but also traditionally immune professional and managerial employees as well.

During this time, even firms that had garnered reputations over the years for eschewing lay-offs – Eastman Kodak and Digital Equipment Corporation, for example – gave up the practice (Foulkes and Whitman 1985). Many of these firms strove to handle their employment reductions in ways that smoothed the effects on both employees and survivors – by providing severance pay and outplacement services, for example. In general, however, employee cutbacks have been so severe and handled so badly that there appears to be widespread agreement among employers and employees that there has to be a better way. Whether these attitudes will eventually translate into a more systematic management of staffing levels and processes, however, remains to be seen.

Training and development

US firms spend huge sums on training and development (some estimates put the number at $30–40 billion per year). Still, in per capita terms the amount spent pales in comparison with the amounts spent by the US's most formidable international competitors (Kochan and Osterman 1991). For example, MacDuffie and Kochan (1991) found that US car-makers do less training than their Japanese and European counterparts, in part because US work systems demand fewer skills and in part because the US lacks national policies and infrastructures that support or require such firm-level investment.

Compensation

Current rhetoric clearly supports the use of variable, or contingent, compensation schemes at all levels of employment (such practices are already reasonably widespread among executives and upper-level managers). Arguments supporting these schemes, however, are as often couched in labour cost terms as in motivational terms which, of course, exposes employees, even relatively low-paid ones, to a downside risk on their earnings, a perspective that is hardly consistent with the philosophy of mutual commitment. At any rate, variable, or contingent, compensation is still another area where rhetoric seems to have outstripped reality by a fairly wide margin. Surveys show that such pay plans, including profit-sharing, gain-sharing, and group incentives, tend to be in effect in no more than one-fifth of medium-sized and large firms (Conference Board 1990; O'Dell 1987). Further, many of these plans are experimental, having been instituted only within the last five years, and they often affect only relatively small numbers of employees.

Selection standards and flexible work organizations

Some argue that selection standards in US firms are rising in response to technological and work design trends that are upskilling jobs. Others argue (or complain bitterly) that they are lowering, in response to shortages of qualified employees. In fact, there probably is some of both going on. Certainly, the desirability of moving to more flexible, and hence more demanding, forms of work organization is a shibboleth among many management writers in the US. In practice, however, the legacy of Taylorism and job control unionism (narrow job classifications, tightly circumscribed seniority and wage rules, and carefully guarded managerial and supervisory prerogatives) serves as a severe constraint on diffusion. Not surprisingly, the most highly visible and widespread use of work teams and other flexible forms of work organization has been found in new or 'greenfield' plants that are relatively free from these historical traditions (Walton 1980). In existing settings, some corporations have used the incentive of capital investments in new products or technology, and thus in job retention, to encourage (or require) local plant managers and, where present, union leaders, to reform their work systems. Chrysler, for example, took this approach in negotiating 'Modern Operating Agreements' (MOAs) in six of its facilities in the late 1980s (Lovell *et al.* 1991). Yet even the Chrysler experience repeats that which Walton (1985) and others have well documented, namely that such experiments seem to have some staying power, but that they generally fail to spread to other units within the firm. As such, they become experimental islands in a sea of traditional practices. Interestingly, the use of flexible work systems seems to be gaining faster acceptance among plant managers, local union leaders, and employees than among higher-level managers and national union leaders, whose support will clearly be required for diffusion to take hold.

To cite one example, Digital Equipment Corporation recently announced that it planned to close the two plants in its organization that had, by its own account, gone further than any others in committing to and implementing flexible, team-based work systems. One of these was a greenfield site specifically designed as an experimental plant from which others were expected to learn, and the other was an existing facility that invested heavily in the changeover and which won a number of awards from Digital management for its 'manufacturing excellence'. Both fell victim to top management decisions to move production to other facilities in a corporate downsizing move. We dwell on this case not to single out Digital, since in many ways this company has gone further than most others down the path of mutual commitment (Kochan *et al.* 1986). Rather, we use the case simply to illustrate the dependence of many workplace innovations on higher-level corporate decision-making. Ultimately, those within the management structure advocating manufacturing innovations lost the political debate to finance specialists who could demonstrate the logistical savings that would accrue from moving the products produced in these facilities to other locations.

Employee participation

There has probably been more experimentation with employee participation, or involvement, in workplace problem-solving and decision-making than with any other of the mutual commitment principles. A survey conducted in the mid-1980s showed that more than half of firms with 1,000 or more employees had implemented some version of quality circles or other employee participation programmes (Alper *et al.* 1985). More recent reports, although less well documented, suggest that the pace of experimentation may have quickened since that time. Even friendly observers, however, have noted that many of these participatory efforts encounter the same sorts of difficulties as do workplace innovations (with which they are, in fact, often linked), thus making them difficult to sustain, let alone diffuse (Lawler and Mohrman 1985; Drago 1988).

Low-conflict, high-trust environment

Measures of conflict in the workplace are difficult, if not impossible, to come by. Surveys of employee attitudes, however, including trust levels, are commonplace. While isolated companies continue privately to report stable (or in some cases even improving) employee attitudes, the overall pattern suggests a general erosion among virtually all employee groups. The decline is particularly sharp in measures of employee trust in management and in their companies generally (Fisher 1991; Gordon 1990; Hay Group 1991; Kanter and Mirvis 1989). Here there is diffusion; alas, the direction is directly counter to the principles of mutual commitment.

AN ALTERNATIVE CHANGE MODEL AND SOME PROPOSITIONS

Formal models of organizational change are not well developed with respect to human resource management issues. Implicit in the US literature on strategic human resource management, however, are two general propositions. First, that human resource policies and practices need to be matched to firms' competitive business strategies. And second, that change occurs when top executives and/or key line managers take sufficient interest in human resource issues to give them, and their professional human resource staffs, positions of high priority. These propositions reflect a fundamental weakness of human resource management theories: a myopic viewpoint which fails to look beyond the boundary of the individual firm.

Some years ago we (Kochan and Dyer 1976) noted the limitations of this view when applied to joint efforts to introduce and manage change in union–management relations. At that time we argued for a change model that recognized the diversity of stakeholder interests and the role of structural bases of power that affect such change efforts. In a similar vein, Kochan and Cappelli (1984), Jacoby (1985) and Baron *et al.* (1986) have emphasized the importance of external forces – union growth, government policy interventions, tight labour markets and/or crises such as the two World Wars – as predictors of innovation in human resource management practice.

Others have emphasized the importance of the politics of corporate decision-making (Pettigrew and Whipp 1991; Thomas 1992). Support for investment in or consideration of human resource policies is generally sought within broader contests for financial and other resources. The outcomes of these political contests depend heavily on the extent to which advocates can couch their arguments in the prevailing rationales or decision routines used in capital budgeting (e.g. payback periods, rates of return, cost savings, and headcount reductions). This political view can be extended to incorporate broader issues of corporate governance. Doyle's previously quoted description of the US approach to corporate restructuring notes that the speed of adjustment is often a function of the relative power and pressures exerted by shareholders or of takeover threats. In this view, support for human resource initiatives involves a contest not only among functional units within the firm (e.g., human resources and finance), but also among the interests of employees, shareholders, and other stakeholders.

In the precursor to this volume (Storey 1989), Purcell noted that the trend toward divisional or profit centre ('M-form') organizational structures also serves as a constraint on the elevation of human resources to levels of strategic importance. In these structures human resource decisions tend to be decentralized to the divisional level. This reduces the likely effects of overall corporate value systems and policies, and increases the probability that decision horizons will be short-term.

Two recent international studies reinforce the importance of developing models that extend beyond the boundaries of individual firms. Both Walton (1987) and Cole (1989) stress the importance of national and industry-level infrastructures for supporting the diffusion of innovations in human resource practices across national economies; both cite the lack of such infrastructures as a reason why the US lags in this respect.

Thus, a stronger model of change that considers internal political and external institutional and policy variables is required if we are to understand and effectively promote the diffusion of human resource innovations across the American economy. While we do not pretend to have a well-developed and tested model in hand at this point, the following key propositions for testing can be offered in the interest of developing such a model:

> *Proposition 1* The capacity of any individual firm to initiate and sustain human resource innovations is constrained by the extent to which these innovations are similarly adopted by other firms in its product and labour markets and customer and supplier networks.

The nub of this proposition is that no firm can transform its human resource practices alone. Human resource innovations are likely to suffer from what is called a 'market failures' problem (Levine and Tyson 1990). That is, while all firms and the macroeconomy would be better off if they all invested in human resource innovations, any particular firm will fail to capture the benefits of such investments if others fail to follow suit. This is most clearly seen in the area of investments in training. Leading firms, such as Motorola, IBM, Ford, and General Motors, that invest a great deal in training and development run the risk of losing these investments because their employees can attract a wage premium from firms that prefer to skim the labour market. This, in turn, reduces their incentives to invest to below the level that would prevail if all firms were developing their own internal labour markets.

The importance of suppliers and customers participating in human resource innovations can clearly be seen in the context of total quality management efforts. Final assemblers can realize the full pay-off of such efforts only if their suppliers meet corresponding quality standards. Thus, it is not surprising that such companies, and particularly Japanese plants operating in the US, have demanded that their suppliers develop parallel quality improvement programmes in order to become or to remain preferred suppliers. Obviously, the reverse logic applies to customers. In one study of car suppliers, for example, Gillett (1992) found that the extent of innovations in internal management systems varied directly with the expectations of the firms' customers. Change was quickest in coming and most far-reaching among those supplying Japanese customers, who not only demanded them, but also facilitated their implementation. It was slowest and least extensive among those supplying divisions of American firms that were themselves less committed to similar innovations.

While a number of leading firms are now demanding higher quality from their suppliers, or are being required to provide it to their customers, so far their reach has been rather limited and narrowly focused. The general weakness of industry associations in the US, along with the reluctance of firms to invervene in the human resource and labour-management relations affairs of their suppliers and customers, suggests that this avenue of change will have an important but limited impact. This, however, is a promising avenue for empirical research. It will be interesting to see, for example, if the pressures on suppliers, and of customers, produces a sustained and broad commitment to total quality, and whether this will carry over into areas of human resource management that face less direct, market-driven, across-firm pressure.

> *Proposition 2* Top and line management commitment is a desirable, but unlikely and generally insufficient condition for transforming human resource practices.

Virtually every article written on human resource innovations contains the obligatory final paragraph asserting the necessity for top management support for successful implementation. Yet, as previously noted, these managers are under many competing pressures from inside and outside the firm, and there is no reason to believe that employee and human resource considerations will tend to prevail in their strategic decision-making and day-to-day actions. While some chief executives, particularly the founders of such major companies as Polaroid, IBM, Digital Equipment, and Hewlett Packard, are well known for values that have long supported human resource innovations, such is not the case in most US firms, where less visionary CEOs have risen through the ranks of finance, marketing, manufacturing, or law, with little or no formal exposure to the human resource function or need to demonstrate human resource management skills.

US firms tend to promote and transfer managers rapidly, which also limits the power of managerial values as a driver of human resource innovations. Such rapid movement provides little incentive or opportunity for managers to develop the personal trust and commitment necessary to support such innovations. Under such circumstances, managers are likely to view investment in human resources as short-term costs that will at best produce pay-offs for their successors. A study of innovations at a number of Chrysler plants found that the average tenure of a plant manager was under two years, and that each time the manager turned over, the process of change was noticeably slowed (Lovell *et al.* 1991).

The vast majority of top American executives believe that unions are unnecessary and undesirable in their firms (but perhaps not in the broader society). This evaluation is often translated into a high priority for union avoidance and/or containment. This, of course, limits the options for human resource professionals within such firms, since they must be careful to try to achieve desired innovations without the active involvement of union officials or, if a firm is non-unionized, to introduce innovations in ways that avoid creating the collective equivalent of a union.

In brief, the values of top executives and line managers are an important source of support that needs to be garnered. But reliance on a strategy of expecting these values to develop naturally is likely to continue to create islands of innovation that do not diffuse or that are not sustained. Thus, legal, structural, or personal bases of power that elevate the influence of employee and human resource policy interests will need to supplement and reinforce the values and commitment of top executives and line managers.

Proposition 3 Human resource innovations require a coalitional, multiple stakeholder change model.

If human resource professionals are in a relatively weak position in managerial hierarchies, and their more powerful line managers and top executives are only sporadic allies in the innovation process, a broader base of support and power will be needed to sustain innovations. The lessons of the historical models cited above suggest that these broader stakeholders include government regulatory agencies, employee and/or trade union representatives, and industry and/or professional associations. Historically, most democratic societies have relied on the pressure of unions to discipline and motivate management to upgrade human resource standards and practices. Continued decline in trade union membership in the US not only weakens this potential source of pressure, it creates a cycle of mistrust and adversarial tensions that limits the capacity of union leaders to work cooperatively with management on innovative programmes. Union leaders instead come to feel threatened and, in turn, define their primary challenge as a fight for survival and legitimacy. Thus, a cycle of low trust and high conflict gets perpetuated in a way that drives out opportunities for jointly sponsored innovative activities. Reversing this cycle would go a long way toward the diffusion of the mutual commitment principles noted above.

Similarly, to subvert the 'market failures' effect noted above, government policy-makers will also need to be enlisted as part of a coalition supporting human resource innovations. This, in turn, requires a significant shift in the behaviour, and perhaps the mindset, of human resource management professionals who generally endorse voluntary industry efforts over government policies that would require or mandate innovative practices. This commitment to voluntarism is rooted both in an ideological predisposition to protect the prerogatives and autonomy of individual firms, and a recognition of the enormous diversity of the American economy. Yet herein lies a paradox. As long as these values and considerations dominate the politics of human resource management professionals, the diffusion, sustainability, and impact of the very principles they espouse are likely to remain quite limited.

Proposition 4 Human resource professionals need to be open to learning from international sources. Transferring innovations across national borders and organizational boundaries offers the best opportunities for achieving broad, non-incremental change in human resource practices.

One important lesson brought home forcefully by Japanese direct investment in the US is that American managers perhaps have more to learn about human resource management from foreign competitors than they have to offer. The US car industry is perhaps the most visible example of this. Since the mid-1980s the most productive and highest quality car manufacturing plants in the US have been those that are Japanese-owned and -managed (Krafcik 1988). The New United Motors Manufacturing Inc (NUMMI) facility, jointly owned by General Motors and Toyota, but managed by the latter, has received the most attention because it achieved bench-mark levels of productivity and quality with an American workforce and union and with less technological investment than exists in most American-owned and -managed plants in the US. The dominant lesson from this case is that there is much value in a holistic approach to human resource management that is integrated with the dominant production system and which emphasizes the mutual commitment principles previously noted (Shimada and MacDuffie 1986).

Indeed, the human resource approaches introduced in NUMMI and other Japanese firms represent fundamental changes that cut across all three levels of the framework introduced in Figure 13.1. In some instances, US car companies are attempting to achieve similar systemic changes in their facilities and in new organizations such as GM's Saturn Division. Thus, the visible presence and high level of performance achieved with a human resource management system fundamentally different to that of comparable American facilities has been an extremely powerful spur to transforming practices across this industry.

The lessons offered to the US by other countries are not limited to Japan. Recently, policy-makers and academics (and an increasing number of union leaders) have become interested in the German apprenticeship and training system, as well as German-style works councils. Because these institutions require greater government and joint labour–business–government interaction and consensus, however, they have received only limited attention and support to date from the general business community and human resource managers and professionals.

Proposition 5 Documenting the effects of human resource policies on economic outcomes of interest to managers and employees is critical to sustaining support for these innovations. Learning networks that involve all the diverse stakeholders with an interest in these innovations can then speed the transfer, acceptance, and use of this knowledge in other settings.

NUMMI came to serve as an important spur to innovation in the automobile industry because word of its economic performance levels spread so quickly. More recently, MacDuffie and Krafcik (1989) have shown that the positive performance effects of the NUMMI approach generalizes to other facilities as well. As a result, the virtues of this approach are becoming even more widely accepted throughout the world car industry. Unfortunately, this is all too rare an example. Few human resource practices or interrelated systems of practices are evaluated in as systematic and convincing a fashion as has been the case in the car industry.

This approach was possible because the industry's major stakeholders accepted standard performance bench-marks (hours per car for productivity and number of defects per car and/or number of customer complaints per car for quality) and then cooperated with university researchers to collect, analyse, and publish the results of across-plant and across-firm comparisons (without revealing the identity of individual plants or firms). This type of learning network stands as a model of what is needed to accelerate the process of knowledge generation and innovation diffusion.

SUMMARY AND CONCLUSION

In summary, we believe that the type of change model that is necessary to support diffusion of human resource innovations has four main elements. First, it starts with a clear model of the generic principles or requirements that must be met. Second, it casts its vision internationally to discover world-class bench-marks. Third, it engages a broad coalition of human resource and labour advocates within and outside the firm in a network that works together to promote and diffuse innovations. Fourth, it then provides the analytic data required to evaluate and disseminate the economic effects of the innovations. With the strength of this broad base of support and harder evidence for the effects of the innovations, informed government representatives can then contribute by providing the national or macro-level infrastructure and policies needed to go from micro-firm specific islands of innovation to changes of sufficient scope and magnitude to make a difference in national competitiveness and standards of living. If this is done, the field of human resource management will have achieved its own transformation from the traditional image of personnel administration to a truly strategic orientation and contribution. If, on the other hand, events fail to move in these directions, the voices of human resource managers and professionals in many firms are destined to remain buried deep within the managerial hierarchy pleading for, but only sporadically receiving, the support and commitment of their more powerful managerial brethren.

Obviously, this view requires a substantial investment in high-quality research to identify promising human resource innovations and to evaluate their effects on organizational and individual outcomes of interest to multiple stakeholders. Presupposed is a broadened perspective of the relevant stakeholders to include not only top managers (and maybe stockholders), but also various types of employees, labour leaders and purveyors of public policies. Also presupposed is a multi-national – or global – view, as well as a corresponding willingness to learn from the lessons of other countries. All this may represent a particularly radical departure for US scholars.

There is no assumption here that prevailing sentiments extolling the virtues of various forms of human resource innovations and the new-found influence of today's human resource managers represent either reality or inevitability. To achieve global competitiveness and satisfactory standards of living will require broadened perspectives of human resource systems, the development of more realistic models of organizational change, and a mountain of convincing evidence. Absent these, and the prevailing rhetoric cannot help but fall on deaf ears.

REFERENCES

Alper, W.S., Pfau, B. and Sirota, D. (1985) 'The 1985 national survey of employee attitudes executive report', sponsored by *Business Week* and Sirota and Alper Associates, September.

Baron, J.N., Dobbin, F.R. and Jennings, P.D. (1986) 'War and peace: the evolution of modern personnel administration in US industry', *American Journal of Sociology* 92: 350–84.

Buller, P.F. (1988) 'Successful partnerships: HR and strategic planning at eight top firms', *Organizational Dynamics* autumn: 27–43.

Burack, E. (1986) 'Corporate business and human resource planning practices: strategic issues and concerns', *Organizational Dynamics* summer: 73–86.

Carnavale, A.P. (1991) *America and the New Economy*, Washington, DC: The American Society for Training and Development.

Cole, R.E. (1989) *Strategies for Learning*, Berkeley, CA: University of California Press.

Conference Board (The) (1990) 'Variable pay: new performance rewards', *Bulletin* No. 246.

Craft, J.A. (1988) 'Human resource planning and strategy', in L. Dyer (ed.) *Human Resource Management: Evolving Roles and Responsibilities*, Washington: Bureau of National Affairs.

Cyert, R.M. and Mowery, D.C. (eds) (1986) *Technology and Employment*, Washington, DC: National Academy Press.

Dertouzos, M., Solow, R. and Lester, R. (1989) *Made in America*, Cambridge, MA: MIT Press.

Douglas, P. (1919) 'Plant administration of labour', *Journal of Political Economy* 27, July: 544–60.

Doyle, F.P. (1989) 'The global human resource challenge for the nineties', paper delivered to the World Management Congress, New York, September 23.

Drago, R. (1988) 'Quality circle survival: an explanatory analysis', *Industrial Relations* 27(3).

Dyer, L. (1983) 'Bringing human resources into the strategy formulation process', *Human Resource Management* 22(3): 257–71.
Dyer, L. and Holder, G. (1988) 'A strategic perspective on human resource management', in L. Dyer (ed.) *Human Resource Management: Evolving Roles and Responsibilities*, Washington, DC: Bureau of National Affairs Books.
Dyer, L., Foltman, F. and Milkovich, G. (1985) 'Contemporary employment stabilization practices', in T.A. Kochan and T.A. Barocci (eds) *Human Resource Management and Industrial Relations*, Boston, MA: Little Brown.
Fisher, A.B. (1991) 'Morale crisis', *Fortune* November 18: 70–82.
Foulkes, F. and Whitman, A. (1985) 'Market strategies to maintain full employment', *Harvard Business Review* July–August: 4–7.
Fox, A. (1974) *Beyond Contract: Trust and Authority Relations in Industry*, London: Macmillan.
Gillet, F. (1992) 'Supplier–customer relationships: case studies in the auto parts industry', MS thesis, MIT.
Gordon, J. (1990) 'Who killed corporate loyalty?', *Training* March: 25–32.
Hay Group (The) (1991) *1991–92 Hay Employee Attitudes Study*, Hay.
Jacoby, S. (1985) *Employing Bureaucracies*, New York: Columbia University Press.
Kanter, D. and Mirvis, P. (1989) *The Cynical Americans: Living and Working in an Age of Discontent and Disillusion*, San Franciso, CA: Jossey Bass.
Kochan, T.A. and Cappelli, P. (1983) 'The transformation of the industrial relations and personnel function', in P. Osterman (ed.) *Internal Labor Markets*, Cambridge, MA: MIT Press.
Kochan, T.A. and Dyer, L. (1976) 'A model of organizational change in the context of union–management relations', *Journal of Applied Behavioral Science* 12: 58–78.
Kochan, T.A. and McKersie, R.B. (1991) 'Human resources, organizational governance, and public policy: lessons from a decade of experimentation', in T.A. Kochan and M. Useem (eds) *Transforming Organizations*, New York: Oxford University Press.
Kochan, T.A. and Osterman, P. (1991) 'Human resource development and utilization: is there too little in the US?', paper prepared for the Time Horizons Project of the Council on Competitiveness, MIT.
Kochan, T.A., Katz, H.C. and McKersie, R. (1986) *The Transformation of American Industrial Relations*, New York: Basic Books.
Kochan, T.A., Osterman, P. and MacDuffie, J.P. (1988) 'Employment security at DEC: sustaining values amid environmental change', *Human Resource Management Journal* Fall.
Krafcik, J.F. (1988) 'World class manufacturing: an international comparison of automobile assembly plant performance', *Sloan Management Review* 30: 41–52.
Lawler, E.E. III (1988) 'Choosing an involvement strategy', *The Academy of Management Executive* 2(3): 197–204.
—— (1986) *High Involvement Management*, San Francisco, CA: Jossey Bass.
Lawler, E.E. III and Mohrman, S.A. (1985) 'Quality circles after the fad', *Harvard Business Week* 63: 65–71.
Levine, D.I. and Tyson, L.D'A. (1990) 'Participation, productivity, and the firm's environment', in A.S. Blinder (ed.) *Paying for Productivity*, Washington, DC: The Brookings Institution.
Lovell, M. *et al.* (1991) *Chrysler and the UAW: Modern Operating Agreements*, report to the US Department of Labor Bureau of Labor Management Relations and Cooperative Programs, Washington, DC.
MacDuffie, J.P. and Kochan, T.A. (1991) 'Determinants of training: a cross

national comparison in the auto industry', paper presented at the 1991 meetings of the Academy of Management, August.

MacDuffie, J.P. and Krafcik, J.F. (1989) 'Flexible production systems and manufacturing performance: the role of human resources and technology', paper delivered at Annual Meeting of the Academy of Management, Washington, DC, August 16.

Marshall, R. (1987) *Unheard Voices*, New York: Basic Books.

National Clothing Industry Labor Management Committee (1991) *A Strategy for Innovation*, New York: National Clothing Industry Labor Management Committee.

Nkomo, S. (1986) 'The theory and practice of HR planning: the gap still remains', *Personnel Administrator* August: 71–84.

O'Dell, C. (1987) 'People, performance, and pay', American Productivity Center.

Peters, T. and Waterman, Jr., R.H. (1982) *In Search of Excellence*, New York: Harper & Row.

Pettigrew, A. and Whipp, R. (1991) *Managing Change for Strategic Success*, Oxford: Blackwell.

Piore, M. and Sabel, C. (1984) *The Second Industrial Divide*, New York: Basic Books.

Purcell, J. (1989) 'The impact of corporate strategy on human resource management', in J. Storey (ed.) *New Perspectives on Human Resource Management*, London: Routledge.

Schuler, R.S. and Jackson, S.E. (1987) 'Linking competitive strategies and human resource management practices', *Academy of Management Executive* August: 207–19.

Shimada, H. and MacDuffie, J.P. (1986) 'Industrial relations and "humanware": Japanese investments in automobile manufacturing in the United States', working paper, Sloan School of Management, MIT.

Slichter, S. (1919) 'The management of labor', *Journal of Political Economy* 27: 813–39.

Storey, J. (ed.) (1989) *New Perspectives on Human Resource Management*, London: Routledge.

Thomas, R.J. (1992) *What Machines Can't Do: Organizational Politics and Technological Change*, Berkeley, CA: University of California Press.

Walton, R.E. (1980) 'Establishing and maintaining high commitment work systems', in Kimberley, J.R. and Miles, M. (eds) *The Organizational Life Cycle*, San Francisco, CA: Jossey-Bass.

—— (1985) 'Toward a strategy of eliciting employee commitment based on policies of mutuality', in R.E. Walton and P.R. Lawrence (eds) *HRM Trends and Challenges*, Boston, MA: Harvard Business School Press.

—— (1987) *Innovating to Compete*, San Francisco, CA: Jossey-Bass.

Chapter 14

International human resource management

Hugh Scullion

INTRODUCTION TO INTERNATIONAL HUMAN RESOURCE MANAGEMENT

The aim of this chapter is to explore the field of 'international HRM'. This may be defined as the human resource management issues and problems arising from the internationalizaton of business, and the human resource management strategies, policies and practices which firms pursue in response to the internationalization process. Dowling's summary of the literature (1988) on the differences between domestic and international HRM suggests that international HRM is more complex than domestic HRM. Morgan (1986) suggests that the complexities of operating in different countries and employing different national categories of workers are the main factors which differentiate domestic and international HRM, rather than any major differences between the HRM functions performed.

An understanding of international HRM is of growing importance at the present time, for a number of reasons:

1 Recent years have seen rapid increases in global activity and global competition (Young and Hamill 1992). As the multi-national corporations (MNCs) increase in number and influence, so the role of international HRM in those MNCs grows in significance (Dowling *et al.* 1994).
2 The effective management of human resources internationally is increasingly being recognized as a major determinant of success or failure in international business. In international business, the quality of management seems to be even more critical than in domestic operations (Dowling and Schuler 1990: 6–11; Tung 1984: 129).
3 Shortages of international managers are becoming an increasing problem for international firms. A survey of 440 European firms suggested that a shortage of international managers was the single most important factor constraining corporate efforts to expand abroad. Almost one-third of the executives surveyed had experienced difficulties in finding managers with the necessary international experience and orientation (*International Management* 1986). A more recent study of forty-five British and Irish

international firms revealed that two-thirds of the companies had experienced shortages of international managers and over 70 per cent indicated that future shortages were anticipated (Scullion 1992b). These findings suggest that the successful implementation of global strategies depends, to a large extent, on the existence of an adequate supply of internationally experienced managers.

4 The human and financial costs of failure in the international business arena are frequently more severe than in domestic business (Dowling and Schuler 1990: 10). In particular, indirect costs such as loss of market share and damage to overseas customer relationships may be considerable (Zeira and Banai 1984).

5 The advent of the Single European Market (SEM) and the rapid growth of British direct investment abroad (Hamill 1992) mean that international HRM issues are increasingly important concerns in a far wider range of organizations than the traditional giant multi-nationals. International human resource management problems are becoming ever more important for a growing number of smaller and medium-sized companies which have significantly internationalized their operations in recent years (Scullion 1992b).

6 There is evidence that many companies underestimate the complex nature of HRM problems involved in international operations. There is also some evidence to suggest that business failures in the international arena may often be linked to poor management of human resources (Tung 1984; Desatnick and Bennett 1978). The international literature indicates that expatriate failure continues to be a significant problem for many international firms (Dowling *et al.* 1994).

The evidence suggests that the 1990s will be an era of greater turbulence and complexity in international markets (Barham 1991). The international business environment will be characterized by new economic alignments, new sources of competition, globalization and fragmentation of markets and new forms of international alliances which involve competitive collaboration. In this context, effective international human resource management will become even more important in the future; yet in practice, many organizations are still coming to terms with the human resource issues associated with international operations (Dowling 1986). The field of international human resource management is only slowly developing as a field of academic study, and has been described by one authority as being in the infancy stage (Laurent 1986: 91). While there has been an increased interest in international HRM teaching/research over the past five years, there is still relatively little empirical research which documents the international HRM strategies and practices of international firms – particularly firms which have their headquarters outside North America.

There are five sets of issues which are normally encompassed by the term 'international HRM'. This chapter considers each in turn. The first briefly explores the links between strategy and international HRM in international business firms. The second is international staffing, the area which has to date enjoyed the bulk of research on international HRM. The third is expatriate performance and assessment. The fourth focuses on international HRM policies and pays particular attention to international management development. The fifth area of concern relates to the newer international organizational arrangements, including joint ventures and strategic alliances.

STRATEGY AND INTERNATIONAL HRM

Although the literature on international HRM tends to focus on the management of expatriates, there is increasing interest in its relationship with strategy and organizational structure (Kobrin 1992: 1). As Tichy *et al.* (1982) argue, the fundamental strategic management problem is to keep the strategy, structure and human resource dimensions of the organization in direct alignment. The central issue is not to identify the best international HRM policy *per se*, but rather to find the best fit between the firm's international environment, its overall strategy, its HRM policy and implementation (Adler and Ghadar 1991).

In the international firm, pressures to integrate across national borders (to standardize products and rationalize manufacturing) and to centralize and/or coordinate research and development have increased dramatically in the last decade (Kobrin 1992). These pressures for the global integration of markets arise from the scale and complexity of research and development efforts needed to remain technologically competitive and, in some industries, the high fixed costs of efficient production. Yet there are some products and services that demand accommodation to local customers, tasks, habits and regulations. Thus for many multi-nationals, the likelihood of operating in diverse environments has never been greater, while at the same time, multi-national firms also face pressures to fragment strategy to respond to local and national differences. It has been argued that the core strategic problem of top managers in international firms is balancing the economic need for integration with the social, cultural and political pressures for local responsiveness (Porter 1986; Bartlett and Ghoshal 1989; Prahalad and Doz 1987).

There has been increasing awareness of the strategic importance of HRM, and an increasing understanding that a firm's strategic choice imposes limits on the range of HRM practices (Schuler and Johnson 1989; Snell 1992). This argument has been extended to the multi-national context. The argument is that there should be distinct differences in international HRM policy and practice in multi-domestic and globally integrated firms (Kobrin 1992; Schuler *et al.* 1993). Edstrom and Lorange (1984) relate HRM practice to strategy through case studies of four Swedish firms, finding that global firms use more expatriates and fewer local nationals in key roles. They conclude that strategic differences are clearly reflected in HRM policy. Other researchers suggest linkages between product life cycle stage/international strategy and HRM policy and practice (Adler and Ghadar 1991; Milliman *et al.* 1991). They argue, for example, that international firms serving multi-domestic markets use expatriates to achieve integration and control, while multi-nationals pursuing a price strategy use international positions to develop an integrated global organization.

The problems of control in any diversified, multi-divisional firm are exacerbated in the multi-national where operations are dispersed over considerable geographic and cultural distances and the environment is complex and heterogeneous (Baliga and Jaeger 1984). Edstrom and Galbraith (1977) suggest three modes of control in the MNE:

1 Personal or direct control.
2 Bureaucratic control, which relies on recording and reporting.
3 Control by socialization, where the 'functional behaviours and rules for determining them were learned and internalized by individuals thereby obviating the need for procedures, hierarchical communication and surveillance'.

Edstrom and Galbraith argue that control through centralization is impossible in the large organization. In the multi-national context, bureaucratic control involves transferring home country nationals and expatriates who remain 'the agent of the centre in the periphery' (Kobrin 1992).

Dowling and Schuler (1990) suggest a twofold taxonomy: output control, which involves monitoring through data, and cultural control, which tends to be behavioural and subjective: 'social interaction, personnel transfers, and the socialization of employees to direct and control subsidiary performance'. It has been argued, however, that control modes may change as the firm's strategy evolves over time. During the early ethnocentric stage of a firm's international involvement, home country expatriates exercise tight control. As strategy becomes polycentric, there is a marked decline in the number of expatriates abroad and their function shifts to communication and coordination of strategic objectives. Finally, with globalization and evolution of a geocentric strategy, there is a need for a broad range of executives with international experience (Adler and Bartholomew 1992).

The conclusion of a recent review of multi-national strategy and international HRM is clear: global strategy is a significant determinant of IHRM policy and practice. However, it is important to note that in this study, *causality is bi-directional*. International human resources are a strategic resource which affect, or should affect, the formulation of strategy as well as its implementation (Kobrin 1992).

Strategic international human resource management?

Schuler *et al.* (1993) cite several reasons for the emergence of the concept of strategic international HRM, including the growing recognition:

- that HRM at any level is important to strategy implementation
- that major strategic components of multi-national enterprises have a major influence on international management issues, functions, policies and practices
- that many of these characteristics of strategic international human resource management (SIHRM) can influence the attainment of the concerns and goals of MNCs
- that there are a wide variety of factors that make the relationship between MNCs and SIHRM complex, thereby making the study of SIHRM challenging as well as important.

Schuler *et al.* define strategic international human resource management as: 'human resource management issues, functions and policies and practices that result from the strategic activities of multinational enterprises and that impact the international concerns and goals of those enterprises' (ibid.: 720). Their model suggests that there are two major strategic components of MNEs that give rise to and influence strategic international human resource management: inter-unit linkages and internal operations. Regarding the former, international firms are concerned with how effectively to manage their various operating units in different countries. In particular, they are interested in how these units are to be differentiated and how they are to be integrated (Ghoshal 1987). For strategic international resource management (SIHRM), however, it has been suggested that the issues associated with differentiating and integrating the units of an MNE represent a major influence on SIHRM issues, functions, policies and practices. With respect to the latter, MNEs are also concerned that each unit has to be operated as effectively as possible relative to the competitive strategy of the MNE and the unit itself (Schuler *et al.* 1993). Thus, for MNEs, these concerns regarding the internal operations of the units are also strategic (Prahalad and Doz 1987). They can influence the level of effectiveness of the MNE and strategic international human resource management in significant ways. How these internal operations and the inter-unit linkages of MNEs more precisely influence SIHRM is discussed elsewhere (Schuler *et al.* 1993).

The implication of this analysis is that the field of HRM has become more linked to the needs of the business, which in turn have become more international and strategic. Hence the emergence of the field of strategic international HRM and the growing recognition that the success of global business depends most importantly on the quality of the MNE's human resources and how effectively the enterprise's human resources are managed and developed (Bartlett and Ghoshal 1992).

INTERNATIONAL STAFFING

To date, the bulk of research on international human resource management has been in the area of staffing (Butler *et al.* 1991). Much of this research stems from concern among practitioners about the high costs of making poor staffing decisions and suggests there are two main implications of international staffing errors: first the financial and emotional costs of an expatriate's early return from an international assignment, and second, the possible 'invisible' damage to local relations (e.g. local staff members, customers, host government officials). These implications may be difficult to identify and assess but are relatively common, and frequently go unrecognized. The main topics in international staffing research have focused on nationality of subsidiary managers, selection criteria for managers, and more recently on models to use in the staffing process (ibid.).

Nationality

International firms face three alternatives with respect to the staffing of management positions abroad: the employment of parent country nationals, host country nationals, or third country nationals. The nationality question centres on human resource concerns, strategic concerns related to the firm's flexibility in making strategic shifts, and on maintaining a global perspective versus local needs. The research on international staffing reflects both the human resources and the more strategic orientations. The research on executive nationality policies indicates that a multinational company can choose from five options: ethnocentric, polycentric, geocentric, mixed, and *ad hoc* (Heenan and Perlmutter 1979; Dowling and Welch 1988).

An ethnocentric approach to staffing results in all key positions in a multi-national company being filled by parent country nationals (PCNs). This practice is common in the early stages of internationalization. Other reasons for pursuing an ethnocentric staffing policy are the perceived lack of qualified host country nationals (HCNs) and the perceived greater ability of the PCNs to coordinate subsidiary–parent relations and to transfer know-how from the parent to the subsidiary (Edstrom and Galbraith 1977). Researchers have, however, identified a number of major problems with an ethnocentric approach (Zeira 1976; Dowling and Schuler 1990):

- The effective adaptation of PCNs to a host country may take a long time.
- This approach to staffing limits the promotion opportunities of local managers (HCNs), which may lead to low morale and increased turnover.
- PCNs are not always sensitive to the needs and expectations of their host country subordinates.

- Frequently, difficult equity issues arise when PCN and HCN compensation packages are compared.

A polycentric staffing policy is one where HCNs are recruited to manage subsidiaries in their own country and PCNs occupy positions in corporate headquarters. There are a number of advantages to this approach (Dowling and Schuler 1990):

- It eliminates language barriers and the adjustment problems of expatriates and their families.
- Employing HCNs allows the possibility of a lower profile in the host country.
- A polycentric approach allows continuity of management within the host country.
- The employment of HCNs is generally less expensive.
- Finally, this approach enhances the morale and career opportunities of local staff.

Notwithstanding that a number of these advantages address some of the shortcomings of an ethnocentric policy, the literature identifies a number of disadvantages which may be associated with a polycentric policy (e.g. Dowling and Welch 1988). The major difficulty is that of bridging the gap between the host country managers at subsidiary level and the parent country managers at corporate headquarters level, which may arise due to a combination of language barriers, conflicting national loyalties and cultural differences (Kobrin 1992; Dowling and Welch 1988). A major disadvantage of a polycentric approach is that a multi-national firm could become a loose 'federation' of independent national units with weak links to corporate headquarters. A second major problem with this approach concerns the career paths of HCN and PCN managers. HCN managers have limited opportunities to gain experience outside of their own country. PCN managers also have limited opportunities to gain experience abroad. As top management positions at headquarters are only held by PCNs, the senior corporate management group may have little international experience to draw on. It has been argued that this lack of experience is a liability in an increasingly competitive international environment (Dowling and Welch 1988).

In the geocentric approach, the best people are sought for key jobs throughout the organization, regardless of nationality. This approach has two main advantages: first, it enables a multi-national firm to develop a pool of senior international managers and, second, it reduced the tendency of national identification of managers with subsidiary units of the organization. There are, however, three main problems in implementing a geocentric staffing approach. First, it is increasingly the case that many host countries use their immigration laws to require the employment of local nationals

(HCNs) where possible. Second, a geocentric policy can be difficult to implement because of increased training, compensation and relocation costs. Third, longer lead times and more centralized control of the staffing process are required to implement successfully a geocentric staffing policy. This necessarily reduces the independence of subsidiary management, and this loss of autonomy may be resisted (Dowling and Welch 1988; Dowling and Schuler 1990).

The fourth approach to international staffing is a regional policy with regard to executive nationality. Heenan and Perlmutter define a regiocentric policy as functional rationalization on a more-than-one country basis. The specific mix will vary with the nature of a firm's business and product strategy. Robock and Simmonds (1983) give three examples of how the nature of a business or product strategy influences staffing policies. First, if regional or area expertise is important (e.g consumer goods and/or limited product lines), then the need for PCNs will be low relative to the need for experienced HCNs and TCNs (third country nationals). Second, when product expertise is particularly important, PCNs tend to be used more frequently because of the need for quick access to parent country sources of supply and technical information. Third, service industries such as banking tend to use a relatively large number of PCNs, particularly where a firm is serving parent-country multi-national clients in foreign locations (ibid.).

The literature taking a more strategic approach on the issue of nationality of subsidiary managers has emphasized the need for some multi-nationals to have a global strategy with the flexibility to shift resources among units. A global strategy which requires that staffing decisions be centralized at corporate headquarters means trade-offs for the MNC. First, there is less flexibility in adapting to local markets. Second, when a firm pursues a global strategy, it frequently emphasizes the organizational culture worldwide, trying to supersede local culture. This may lead to conflict between national culture and corporate culture (Schneider 1986). In many cases, local culture is stronger than corporate culture and limits consistency in international human resource management within the firm (Laurent 1986).

Comparative international staffing practices

Recent empirical research on trends in international staffing policies and practices reveals a sharp contrast between European and US firms, and suggests other reasons for maintaining a flexible staffing policy. The findings of a recent study on staffing practices in UK and Irish multinationals showed that a majority of companies continued to rely heavily on expatriates to run their foreign operations. In this study, while almost 50 per cent of companies had formal policies which favoured using host country managers to run their foreign operations, in practice just over one-third operated with HCNs in senior positions abroad. In other words, two-thirds of the companies relied primarily on expatriates to run their foreign operations. Furthermore, the trend has moved in the direction of greater use of expatriates, with half the companies in the sample (twenty-two out of forty-five) reporting an increase in the use of expatriates over the previous decade and only 20 per cent reporting a reduction in the use of expatriates (Scullion 1991).

The above study also identified a number of reasons for employing expatriates in British MNCs. The first was the lack of availability of management and technical skills in some countries. The second major reason cited for using expatriates was the objective of control of local operations, a finding which was consistent with previous research (Torbiorn 1985; Brewster 1991). A further reason for using senior expatriates was to maintain trust in key foreign businesses following large international acquisitions. This finding is particularly interesting because previous research has suggested that the employment of expatriates will be lower in acquired companies than will be the case in greenfield sites (Hamill 1989). The emergence of trust as a major factor in relation to very senior expatriates is related to the rapid growth in the number and scale of foreign acquisitions by British companies in the 1980s (Scullion 1991). One interesting finding was that using expatriates for management development purposes was increasing in significance for British multi-nationals. This practice was in sharp contrast with US MNCs, where management development concerns were less significant in international staffing (Dowling and Schuler 1990) and reflects the tendency of British companies to see expatriation as part of the career development process (Hamill 1989).

The performance of foreign subsidiaries has frequently emerged as a significant factor influencing the use of expatriates, and the literature has often reported that crises accentuate headquarter's control (ibid.). Another factor influencing the approach adopted by companies was a strong expectation on the part of major foreign customers (and sometimes senior foreign government officials) that the top managers in the host country should be parent country nationals. Public relations and marketing were usually the key roles, in this context. Previous research has largely ignored this factor because it has concentrated on the very largest multi-nationals and has tended to neglect the service sector (Brewster 1991: 33). Finally, almost half of the companies in this study identified weaknesses in their training and development of HCN and TCN managers as an important reason to explain their continued use of expatriates beyond the early stages of internationalization. These findings raise serious questions about the ability and commitment of some British multi-nationals to identify and develop host country managers in their foreign operations (Hailey 1992). Indeed, it has been argued that the failure of the localization process to create new generations of skilled local staff to take over key positions may in part reflect the self-fulfilling nature of ethnocentrism (Banai 1992). It is suggested that while MNCs are quick to assign expatriate managers at the right points in the MNC life-cycle, they are also slow to assign HCNs when desired. The argument is that where ethnocentric attitudes are self-perpetuated, this will limit the corporate headquarters ability to adjust HRM policy to their strategic approach (ibid.).

The findings of the study on UK MCNs (Scullion 1991) reveals sharp differences between UK and American experience. In recent years there has been a tendency among American MNCs to assign more HCNs to key positions in foreign subsidiaries (Harris and Moran 1987; Kobrin 1988). Indeed, Kobrin suggested that the tendency of US multi-nationals to reduce the number of expatriates had gone too far. Kobrin (1988) argued that US firms have tended to use HCNs to replace expatriates primarily in response to the difficulties US managers have experienced in adjusting to other cultural environments. He suggests that expatriate reduction may result in US multi-nationals facing reduced identification with the global organization and its objectives, difficulties in exercising control, and a lack of opportunities for American managers to gain international experience abroad. The principal concern is that American multi-nationals could face major strategic management control problems where managers identified with local units, rather than with global corporate objectives (ibid.: 68–73).

The sharp differences in approach to international staffing by US and UK multi-nationals provide support for the view that we need a more European approach to international HRM (Brewster and Burnois 1991). Mayrhoffer (1992) identifies a number of reasons why an ethnocentric approach to staffing will be particularly appropriate to the European context over the next decade. First, control over foreign operations through personal control mechanisms will be important for many of the companies entering the European business scene and for companies in their first stages of internationalization. Similarly, it has been argued that the disadvantages of ethnocentrism will be less significant in the European context – for example, new flexible staffing solutions are emerging which reduce the impact on the private lives of managers and their families (Mayrhoffer 1992).

By examining what significance an ethnocentric staffing strategy has in the specific European context, the assumptions which underly the mainly North American literature on international staffing can be critically assessed. Mayrhoffer's study concludes that the basic assumptions connected with international staffing only partly apply to Europe (ibid.). This provides further support for those expressing caution regarding an uncritical and unmodified adaptation of concepts derived in the North American context (Brewster and Burnois 1991).

Much of the early research on international staffing was largely descriptive and lacking in analytical rigour. This research was mainly prescriptive in nature and primarily concerned with advising firms on how to select expatriate managers. More recently, however, research has shifted towards considering staffing questions in a more strategic context. In an effort to consider the range of possible headquarters–subsidiary relationships, researchers are suggesting more 'variety' (Doz and Prahalad 1986) in approaches to staffing and other IHRM activities (Boyacigiller 1990; Kobrin 1988). In certain subsidiaries, for example, an ethnocentric approach may be appropriate; in others, a polycentric approach may work better. Rather than adhering to a particular policy, researchers are urging MNCs to consider global strategy as well as local conditions in determining appropriate staffing approaches (Butler *et al.* 1991; Hamill 1989).

EXPATRIATE PERFORMANCE

Expatriate failure rates

An important issue in the international staffing literature is that of expatriate failure, which is usually defined as the premature return of an expatriate manager (Dowling and Welch 1988). The costs of expatriate failure are both direct (salary, training costs, travel and relocation expenses) and indirect (damaged relations with host country organizations and customers, loss of market share and requests that PCNs be replaced with HCNs. Zeira and Banai (1984) argue that MNCs should consider these factors as the real costs of the failure of international managers, rather than the direct costs cited above. The literature suggests that expatriate failure remains a significant problem, particularly for US MNCs, where failure rates remain relatively high – Henry (1965) reported a figure of 30 per cent, and similar figures have been used since (Dowling *et al.* 1994). Brewster (1991), however, comments that in most cases, it is unclear where the figures originate. Mendenhall and Oddou (1985) report that the estimated expatriate failure rate in US MNCs from 1965 to 1985 fluctuated between 25 and 40 per cent; Desatnick and Bennett (1978) claim that this figure rises to 70 per cent in developing countries.

However, in general, reported expatriate failure rates are considerably lower in the more solidly research-based studies (Brewster 1991). In Tung's (1981) study of eighty US MNCs, 24 per cent of companies reported a failure rate of less than 10 per cent; 69 per cent of companies reported a 10–20 per cent failure rate, and only 7 per cent of companies reported a higher figure. Tung's study on comparative expatriate failure rates in US, European and Japanese multi-nationals showed US companies as having both higher expatriate failure rates and a higher percentage of companies reporting recall rates of 10 per cent or more than European or Japanese companies (Tung 1982). Tung also asked her sample of multi-national managers to indicate reasons for expatriate failure in their companies; her findings are summarized in Table 14.1. Findings on British MNCs are also included in the table.

Table 14.1 Reasons for expatriate failure (in descending order of importance)

American	*Japanese*	*United Kingdom*
1. The inability of spouse to adjust	1. Inability to cope with larger overseas responsibility	1. The inability of the spouse to adjust
2. Manager's inability to adjust	2. Difficulties with new environment	2. Other family problems
3. Other family problems	3. Personal or emotional problems	3. Concerns over re-entry
4. Manager's personal or emotional maturity	4. Lack of technical skills	
5. Inability to cope with larger overseas responsibility	5. Inability of spouse to adjust	

Sources: American and Japanese: adapted from Tung (1982: 55–71), cited in Dowling and Welch (1988); United Kingdom: Scullion (1993)

A major finding from a recent empirical study of forty-five British and Irish multi-nationals was that 90 per cent of companies were generally satisfied with the overall performance of their expatriate managers. Under 10 per cent of companies reported expatriate failure rates higher than 5 per cent, and only two companies reported a failure rate of 20 per cent or above (Scullion 1991). One interesting finding of this study was that the two companies with the highest expatriate failure rate had undergone the internationalization process in the recent past. A major conclusion of the study was that the expatriate failure rate in British and Irish multi-nationals is considerably lower than in US companies. British expatriate failure rates were similar to Australian (Dowling and Welch 1988) and Scandinavian rates (Bjorkman and Gertsen 1990).

This finding is consistent with the conclusion of previous research which suggests that European MNCs experience lower expatriate failure rates than US companies (Tung 1982; Brewster 1988; Scullion 1991). Three major reasons were given to explain the low British expatriate failure rate:

1 British companies felt they had more effective HRM policies covering international transfers. In particular, it was felt that closer attention was paid to the selection of expatriates, and that higher calibre managers went abroad.
2 International experience was more highly valued, and expatriate assignments were frequently regarded as being a key part of the overall management development process.

3 There was the widely held view that British managers were more international in their orientation and outlook than US managers (Hamill 1989; Scullion 1991).

A further and potentially controversial reason which should not be overlooked is the possibility that British multi-nationals experience lower failure rates because they are prepared to accept lower standards of performance (Hamill 1989) – expatriates who are under-performing may not be recalled for a number of reasons, including the difficulty of finding a replacement and the loss of face involved.

The low British expatriate failure rate did not mean, however, that companies were not concerned with the performance of expatriates. From the company perspective, a definition of failure based on the premature return from an international assignment almost certainly under-estimates the problem (Scullion 1991). Brewster (1991) makes the point that expatriate under-performance is a more frequent problem than failure of the type that requires repatriation. This suggests that the expatriate return rate is a far from perfect measure of success or failure, and raises questions about the usefulness of defining expatriate failure so narrowly.

Family-related problems, particularly the inability of the spouse to adapt to the new culture, emerged as the major reason for poor performance in international assignments in a recent study of British MNCs (Scullion 1991). This finding is consistent with previous research on US and European multinationals (Tung 1982;Brewster 1991). Recent European research highlights the importance of considering the 'family' factor in the selection and training practices of multi-nationals; yet, while most UK companies in a recent study claimed that they recognized the importance of this factor to successful performance in an international assignment, in practice only a minority reported that they actually took it into consideration in their selection decisions (Scullion 1991). Australian research, however, suggests that early recalls were attributed as much to a lack of technical skills as to the failure of the spouse to adjust (Dowling and Welch 1988). Interestingly, concern over re-entry was cited as a significant reason affecting expatriate performance in UK MNCs (Scullion 1993), reflecting the growing significance of repatriation problems for UK MNCs (Johnston 1991).

In Tung's study there were considerable national differences in the reasons cited for expatriate failure. In Japanese MNCs, for example, the inability of the spouse to adjust was not regarded as a significant factor affecting expatriate performance. This was related to the role and status of the spouse in Japan (Tung 1984). However, Dowling *et al.* (1994) suggest that other social factors may contribute to this finding. They argue that, because of the competitive nature of the Japanese education system, the spouse commonly opts to remain in Japan with the children. Tung also suggests that the longer-term orientation of the Japanese companies towards expatriation allows the Jananese expatriate more time to adjust to the foreign situation (Tung 1984). One weakness of the above literature is the relative failure to consider the effects of poor performance from the perspective of the expatriates themselves. Poor performance in the international assignment, or early recall, may lead to loss of self-esteem, self-confidence and prestige among peers. In addition, the expatriate's family relationship may be threatened (Dowling *et al.* 1994). This suggests that future research should take a broader perspective and should focus more on the expatriate perspective.

In an important review of the expatriate acculturation literature, Mendenhall and Oddou (1985) identified a major problem area in expatriate selection as being the ingrained practice to operate with the 'domestic equals overseas performance' equation. Technical expertise and domestic track record are by far the two dominant selection criteria. Mendenhall and Oddou conclude that the field of expatriate selection and training suffers from two interdependent problems: first, there is an inadequate understanding of the relevant variables of expatriate acculturation, which leads to a second problem, the use of inappropriate selection and training methods.

The overall purpose of Mendenhall and Oddou's review was to determine the key dimensions involved in the expatriate adjustment process and to examine the implications of these dimensions for the selection and training of expatriates. They concluded that there are four key dimensions in the expatriate adjustment process:

1 the self-oriented dimension
2 the others dimension
3 the perceptual dimension
4 the cultural toughness dimension.

Mendenhall and Oddou also make a number of recommendations concerning the selection and training of expatriates. First, selection procedures of MNCs should be changed from their present one-dimensional focus on technical competence as the primary criterion, to a multi-dimensional focus based on criteria relating to the factors identified in their review. Second, the toughness of the culture to which a future expatriate will be assigned should be assessed by comparing the host country's political, legal, socio-economic and business systems to those in the parent country. In practice, however, research suggests only a small minority of companies formally assessed a candidate's relational ability (Tung 1981; Scullion 1993). Given the research available (e.g. Hays 1974; Dowling *et al.* 1994) which links relational abilities to expatriate success, this suggests a significant weakness in the expatriate selection procedures of the majority of MNCs in the above studies.

A recent study by Ronen (1989) brings together the dimensions of expatriate success identified by Tung and by Mendenhall and Oddou. In Ronen's model there are five categories of attributes of success: job factors, relational dimensions, motivational state, family situation and language skills. Ronen concludes, however, that the relative importance of each category is difficult to establish due to the problems in assessing expatriate and managers' evaluations and because of the lack of systematic evaluation of such data.

EXPATRIATE PERFORMANCE ASSESSMENT

The whole question of performance measurement and management in multi-national companies involves a complex range of issues (Schuler, Fulkerson and Dowling 1991) and research to date suggests that rigorous performance appraisal systems for expatriates are far from universal (Brewster 1991; Schuler *et al.* 1991). This is perhaps surprising, given the high costs of expatriate failure and the growing tendency to see expatriates as key human assets (Adler and Bartholomew 1992). The assessment of expatriate performance demands an understanding of the variables that influence an expatriate's success or failure in a foreign assignment. It has been argued that the three major variables include the environment (culture), job requirements, and personality characteristics of the individual (Schuler *et al.* 1991). Problems in cultural adjustment which may impact on the manager's work performance should be considered when assessing an expatriate's performance in a new job (Mendenhall and Oddou 1988).

The literature also identifies a number of principal constraints on strategic performance measurement and management in MNCs. These include the possible conflict between global and subsidiary objectives, the problem of non-comparable data between subsidiaries, the volatility of the international market, and variable levels of market maturity. These factors make objective appraisal of subsidiary (and expatriate) performance more complex. Further, it is important to reconcile the tension between the need for universal appraisal standards with specific objectives in local units, and to recognize that more time may be needed to achieve results in markets which enjoy little supporting infrastructure from the parent company (Schuler *et al.* 1991).

The criteria used for the performance appraisal of international managers in practice has received relatively little attention in the literature (Brewster 1991). It has been suggested that these criteria generally are a function of the nature of the assignment, the stages of international business development and the international HRM philosophy or approach of the MNC (Schuler *et al.* 1991). There would appear to be growing interest, however, in evaluating managers on the basis of subsidiary performance using achievement of long-range goals rather than short-term measures, such as profit or return on equity. In conclusion, it would seem that there are many factors which impact the performance of expatriate managers and that, because of this complexity, it can be difficult to make fair evaluations and comparisons of managerial contributions (ibid.).

INTERNATIONAL MANAGEMENT TRAINING AND DEVELOPMENT

Expatriate training and development

The primary reason for international companies undertaking training and development programmes for expatriates continues to be the cost of expatriate failure (Dowling and Welch 1988). As Robock and Simmonds (1983) have noted,

> however imperfect training may be as a substitute for actual foreign living experience, it is valuable if it can reduce the often painful and agonizing experience of transferring into another culture and avoid the great damage that culture shock and cultural misunderstanding can do a firm's operating relationship.
>
> (Ibid.: 562)

The need for expatriate training becomes clear if we understand the complexity of the role of the parent country national manager (Dowling and Welch 1988). The role of the PCN manager has been described as one of 'realising the expectation of a psychologically close, yet physically distant stakeholder in an environment containing other role senders who are psychologically distant, but physically close' (Torbiorn 1985: 59).

Two additional problem areas make training and development for international assignments more complex than that for domestic assignments. First, since the stress associated with a foreign assignment falls on all family members (Harris and Moran 1979; Harvey 1985), the issue of training programmes for the spouse and family needs to be addressed. Second, the growing significance of repatriation problems for many MNCs (Johnston 1991; Scullion 1992b) highlights the failure by international firms to develop training programmes to facilitate re-entry of expatriate executives into the domestic organization.

A comparative study of MNC training practices found that US MNCs tend to use pre-departure training programmes less frequently than European and Japanese firms (32 per cent, compared with 69 per cent and 57 per cent respectively) (Tung 1982). Dowling and Welch (1988) comment that the high expatriate failures among US executives are hardly surprising, in view of this relatively low level of training.

Cross-cultural training has long been advocated as a means of facilitating effective cross-cultural interactions (Brislin 1986), yet in practice most firms do not use cross-cultural training. Recent studies suggest that only around

30 per cent of US managers destined for international assignments receive cross-cultural training (Black 1988; Black and Mendenhall 1990). The main reason for the low use of cross-cultural training appears to be that top management just does not believe the training is either necessary or effective (Mendenhall and Oddou 1985; Dowling and Schuler 1990). The research evidence on the training of expatriates for international assignments in European MNCs suggests that European firms undertake more training (Torbiorn 1982; Tung 1982; Brewster 1991). A study of European MNCs highlighted that informal briefings were used by two-thirds of MNCs as standard policy and that formal training courses were used by nearly half. A more recent study of forty-five UK MNCs reported that over 60 per cent of firms undertook preparatory training for some expatriate assignments, although interestingly, this study reported that only 5 per cent of companies provided training for international transfers to other European countries (Scullion 1993). Some European MNCs use 'look-see' visits for their expatriate managers, and some companies arranged shadowing opportunities in which employees take responsibility for a business unit abroad before moving to the foreign country (Brewster 1991; Scullion 1994).

Several models of training and development for expatriate managers have been developed over the last decade. Some contingency models consider the task, the individual and the environment before deciding the depth of training required (Tung 1981). Rahim's model (1983) makes a clear recognition of both internal and external influences on the training and development process. Mendenhall and Oddou (1986) have developed a 'cross-cultural training approach', consisting of three levels:

1 information-giving approaches (e.g. factual briefing and awareness training)
2 affective approaches (e.g. culture assimilation training, critical incidents and role plays)
3 immersion approaches (e.g. assessment centres, field experience, and simulations).

One advantage of this model over the previous contingency models is that it provides more specific guidelines. According to the model, the depth of training provided should depend on the length of stay, the degree required to ensure integration into the host culture and the cultural 'difference' of the host country from the home country (Mendenhall and Oddou 1986; Mendenhall, Dunbar and Oddou 1990).

International training and development for host country nationals and third country nationals

The shortage of 'international managers' is becoming an increasing problem for international firms (*International Management* 1986; Scullion

1992a). While the faster pace of internationalization was cited in a recent study as the primary reason for shortages by the majority of firms, half the firms cited failures to recruit effectively, retain and develop host country managers as a key reason to explain shortages (Scullion 1994). A number of factors make the recruitment of HCN managers more difficult and costly compared to recruiting in the home country. These include the following: lack of knowledge of local labour markets, ignorance of the local education system and the status of qualifications, language and cultural problems at interviews, and trying to transfer recruitment methods which work well at home to foreign countries (Scullion 1992a; Dowling and Schuler 1990).

Many international firms have tended to neglect the training and development needs of their host country managers and focus virtually all of their management development efforts on their parent country national managers (Schaeffer 1989). The literature highlights three important lessons for international firms which are seeking to provide management training and development for HCNs and TCNs. First is the need to avoid the mistake of simply exporting parent-country training and development programmes to other countries (Dowling and Schuler 1990). Second, the management development programmes for host country and third country nationals need to be linked to the strategic situation in each country, as well as to the overall strategy of the firm (Scullion 1992b). Third is the need to utilize much further the practice of developing host country managers through developmental transfers to corporate headquarters. It has been argued that this type of international transfer exposes HCNs and TCNs to the headquarters' corporate culture and facilitates their developing a corporate perspective (Oddou and Kerr 1993). It has also been argued that this approach to development can be very effective in helping to develop global management teams, and is a necessary part of successfully operating a truly global firm (Edstrom and Galbraith 1977).

Oddou and Kerr's (1993) study of European MNCs' strategies for internationalizing managers identifies the need for a closer study of the barriers to bringing foreign nationals to head office. For example, relocating dual-career couples is becoming nearly a world-wide issue for many multinational firms (Dowling and Schuler 1990). Also, some cultures are less mobile and less willing to move. The type of incentive and compensation packages for those 'hard-to-move' high-potential managers will also be an important dimension in a company's ability to bring people to the corporate office (Oddou and Kerr 1993).

Strategies for internationalizing managers

A recent study of UK MNCs identified five main strategies by firms to respond to the shortages of international managers (Scullion 1992b):

1 More than one-third of the companies in this study reported that they were sending young high-potential managers on international assignments, partly for developmental purposes. This was in sharp contrast to the previous practice, when many MNCs relied on developing a cadre of career expatriates who moved from one international position to the next (Brewster 1991).
2 There was a more general trend to give international experience to a wider range of managers, and not just to a relatively small group of expatriates. Increasing numbers of international firms were also using short-term developmental assignments in order to develop larger pools of employees with international experience.
3 There was a rapid growth in the importance of external recruitment to fill management positions abroad. Over 25 per cent of companies had introduced external recruitment in the past five years, whereas traditionally the majority of British MNCs had relied almost exclusively on internal recruitment for expatriate positions, as internal candidates had established track records and their loyalty to the company was proven.
4 One-third of the companies reported that they were attempting to sell themselves more effectively to graduates through various types of marketing designed to highlight the international nature of their activities. Less than 20 per cent of companies, however, had broadened their source of graduate recruitment to include some continental European countries.
5 There was growing recognition of the importance of developing effective international management programmes to help secure an adequate supply of international managers. The majority of firms reported that they were allocating more resources to international management education and training for senior managers. In the light of the acute shortages of international managers with language skills the introduction of language training for senior and middle managers was seen as an important development (Scullion 1991).

There were two areas, however, where the companies in the above study were clearly failing to take effective action to ease the acute shortage of international managers. First, there was no evidence that British multinationals were taking serious steps to increase the proportion of women in international management. International management has long been a masculine preserve in Europe and the United States: Adler's study estimated that under 3 per cent of North American expatriates are female (Adler 1984). In the study of British MNCs, no company claimed to have more than 3 per cent of female expatriates. Indeed, the evidence suggests that women in British MNCs are not making as much progress in international management as women in US multinationals (Adler 1984; Scullion 1992). The lack of willingness to recruit and develop women as international managers is worrying, as recent research suggests that in many ways women are well suited to international team management (Barham and Devine 1991; Adler 1987; Jelinek and Adler 1988).

The second area which impacts on the supply of internationalists is the failure by the majority of companies to address adequately repatriation problems. The repatriation of managers has been identified as a major problem for multi-national companies in the UK and North America (Harvey 1989; Johnston 1991; Scullion 1993). For many UK MNCs, this problem had become more acute in recent years because expansion of foreign operations had taken place at the same time as the rationalization of UK operations. A key problem for the majority of companies was finding suitable posts for repatriates. From the repatriate perspective other problems associated with reintegrating into the UK are loss of status, loss of autonomy, loss of career direction and a feeling that international experience is undervalued by the company (Johnston 1991).

There is growing recognition that where companies are seen to deal unsympathetically with the problems faced by expatriates on re-entry, managers will be more reluctant to accept the offer of international assignments (Scullion 1994). Research in North America indicates that 20 per cent of all managers who complete foreign assignments wish to leave their company on return (Adler 1986); this was also a growing problem for British MNCs, particularly when many companies are willing to pay a premium to attract the experienced international manager. Yet, while it is widely accepted that the costs of expatriate turnover are considerable (Dowling and Schuler 1990), very few British firms had formal repatriation programmes to assist managers and their families with repatriation difficulties. Similarly, very few companies had introduced mentor systems designed to assist the career progression of the expatriate manager. Many expatriate managers were concerned about losing out on opportunities at home, and in some companies this was a constraint on their willingness to go abroad. The clear implication is that UK companies need to give a higher priority to the issue of repatriation in order to encourage international mobility and to help secure an adequate future supply of international managers (Scullion 1992b).

Barriers to international mobility

Research suggests that the problem of ensuring an adequate supply of international managers is further exacerbated by growing resistance to international mobility. In a recent study, more than half the firms (twenty-six out of forty-five) suggested that individuals were becoming less internationally mobile, just at the time when there was a growing need for international managers because of expansion abroad. The reduction in international mobility was attributed to several factors, including continued rationalization in the UK, which created uncertainties regarding re-entry; the growing unwillingness to disrupt the education of children, the growing importance of quality of life considerations, and finally, continued uncertainty regarding international terrorism and political unrest (Scullion 1992b).

At the present time, concerns about dual-career problems and disruption to children's education are seen as major barriers to future international mobility by many companies (Harvey 1985; Coyle 1988). In the past, working spouses were less common, generally female, and were prepared to follow their partner's career transfers. More frequently now, however, spouses must also leave a job or career in order to follow their partner to a foreign country (Hall and Richter 1988; Hall and Hall 1987). The growing significance of the dual-career problem can be illustrated by two developments. First, more and more women have or seek careers, not just jobs. For many, it would be impossible to continue their careers in a foreign country (Devanna 1987). Increasingly international mobility is limited by the dual-career factor, which also poses restrictions on the career development plans of multi-nationals. Second, there is some evidence to suggest that families are less willing to disrupt their personal and social lives than was the case in the past (Barham 1991; Brewster 1991; Coyle 1988). This discussion suggests that restrictions on international mobility appear to be growing just at the time when the need for international mobility is becoming vital for the internationalization of UK businesses, and that the problem of international mobility could emerge as a key factor in determining the international capability of a firm (Scullion 1992b).

The Single European Market – the HRM challenge

In the late 1980s there was much talk of the need to create 'Euro-managers' in time for 1992. Storey (1992) highlights that experienced 'international managers' were, however, inclined to refer to the 'myth' of the Euro-managers. While the notion of the Euro-managers may not quite be a myth, it has been argued that recruiting and retaining international managers involves the broad span of HRM motivation, recruitment, rewards – and welfare. Making managers is closely linked to the whole question of managing the management 'stock' (ibid.).

This argument finds support from an empirical study which asked forty-five UK companies to identify the main HRM challenges they faced arising from the advent of the Single European Market. Eighty per cent of firms felt that the main challenge was to secure an adequate supply of international managers, and over 70 per cent of companies identified recruitment as a priority area. A majority of firms said they needed to upgrade management skills and competences in order to compete effectively in the new Europe (Scullion 1994), and there was particular concern over the managerial skills and competences needed to deal with the complex HRM issues and problems associated with the growth of international joint ventures and strategic alliances (Burnois 1992; Burnois and Chauchat 1990). These issues will be briefly examined in the final section.

The above discussion suggests that the most formidable task facing UK companies wishing to operate abroad is the recruitment and development of a broad cadre of managers and executives who understand and can operate effectively in the international market. Further, the main conclusion from most current reviews is that companies need to take a strategic approach to management development (Storey 1992). In practice, the impact of the Single European Market on HRM strategy varies according to the stage of internationalization and the overall strategy of the firm (Scullion 1992b). Most multi-national firms traditionally pass through various stages of internationalization, during their evolution from a domestic to a truly global organization (Negandhi 1987). For some well-established international firms and transnationals, the impact of the Single European Market on HR strategy was marginal rather than central. By contrast, for 'new' international firms, which had internationalized in the recent past with a European focus, the Single Market represented a major HR challenge.

NEW INTERNATIONAL BUSINESS ARRANGEMENTS AND HRM

The 1980s were characterized by a proliferation of new forms of international business activity. These new forms were primarily non-equity arrangements such as joint ventures, collaborative arrangements, strategic alliances, licensing agreements, management contracts and subcontracting (Young and Hamill 1992; Enderwick and Barber 1992). This section will briefly examine some of the HRM issues associated with international joint ventures (IJVs) and strategic alliances, as it has been argued that the effective management of human resources is a critical factor determining the success or failure of these arrangements (Shenkar and Zeira 1987).

A variety of reasons (motivations) are cited in the literature for firms entering into IJVs. The most important reasons which are summarized by Schuler *et al.* (1991) are:

- to gain rapid market entry
- to increase economies of scale
- to gain local knowledge
- to gain market image
- host government pressure
- to obtain vital raw materials
- to improve competitive advantage in the face of global competition

- to develop cost effective and efficient responses to the globalization of markets.

For many firms, several of these reasons apply at the same time (ibid.).

Despite the rapid growth of IJVs over recent years, many companies still actively avoid joint ventures, preferring 100 per cent ownership to the drawbacks of loss of control and profit that can accompany shared ownership (Gomes-Casseres 1989). In addition, research has indicated relatively high 'failure' rates of IJVs – figures of 30–50 per cent are typically cited (Killing 1983; Dutton 1988). Failure rates are difficult to measure, however. Joint ventures can be deemed successful in spite of poor financial performance; conversely, they can be considered unsuccessful in spite of good financial performance (Schuler 1991). The rapid increase in international partnerships among competitors does not, however, necessarily imply the dawn of a new cooperative era in the global economy (Ohmae 1985). Pucik (1988: 244) argues that the change from competitive to collaborative strategies is often a tactical adjustment aimed at specific market conditions. The potential competitive relationship between partners distinguishes strategic alliances that involve *competitive collaboration* from more traditional complementary ventures.

HRM and international joint ventures

Lorange (1986) suggested there will be several HRM policy issues associated with managing international joint ventures:

- assignment of executives
- evaluation and promotion of managers
- the type of control system used
- the loyalty of managers to the joint venture or to their respective parents
- the expected time for managers to spend on strategic versus operational issues.

The issue of manager loyalty has emerged in several studies (e.g. Kanter 1989). From the parent company perspective, control of the joint venture can be sought by appointing managers who are loyal to the parent company. Loyalty to the parent company, however, cannot be guaranteed: 'The ability to appoint the joint venture general manager increases the chances that the parents' interests will be observed, but it is no guarantee that the joint venture general manager will always accommodate that parent's preferences' (Schaan 1988: 14). The global versus local balance issue has been addressed in terms of MNC control systems by Doz and Prahalad (1986). They recognize the difficulties of managers being sensitive to local conditions and loyal to the parent company, arguing for 'strategic control variety', which involves adapting control systems to fit three dimensions in MNCs:

1 the type of business
2 the type of subsidiary
3 the ownership of the venture.

It is suggested that there will be differences in HRM activities and local/global perspectives depending on the type of venture (ibid.).

Shenkar and Zeira's review of the literature (1987) identifies a number of potential HRM problem areas in IJVs (similar to the issues highlighted by Lorange). These are staffing, promotion, loyalty, delegation, decision-making, communications and compensation. Their review also highlights the limitations of the literature. In particular, it indicates that the conclusions of these studies are narrowly based on research conducted at a limited number of IJVs in a few countries. Three further points can be made on the review. First, these findings were not the result of research primarily concerned with human resource management issues in international joint ventures. Second, they were largely based on research conducted in US–Japanese joint ventures, which may not be typical of IJVs. And third, they have very much a 'problems' or 'difficulties' orientation, and rather neglect the broader set of HRM issues associated with international joint ventures (Beaumont 1991).

More recently, it has been argued that collaboration may provide an opportunity for one partner to internalize the skills of the other (Hamel 1991). It is suggested that the strategic agenda for the HRM function in firms involved in international alliances should be centred around the process of learning. In the context of competitive collaboration, the competitive advantage of the firm can only be protected through the organization's ability to accumulate invisible assets through international learning. Given the importance of knowledge acquisition and skill-building within international alliances it has been argued that the transformation of the HR system to support the process of organizational learning is the key strategic task currently facing the HR function in many multi-nationals (Pucik 1988).

To conclude this brief review of international joint ventures and HRM, we can suggest that the growth of new forms of international business operations has significantly increased the demand for senior managers with international experience (Enderwick and Barber 1992). At the same time, these new business forms demand additional abilities, placing a premium on cultural empathy, negotiating skills, awareness of the difficulties of managing from a minority position, and a broader understanding of the people side of the business (Lane and Beamish 1990). It has been argued that IJVs should ideally be staffed with managers who are flexible in terms of different management styles and philosophies (Lei and Slocum 1991). The major conclusion of this review of human resource management practices in international joint ventures is that practice is running well ahead of research in this subject area, and that further research is essential to help close this gap (Beaumont 1991).

CONCLUSIONS

This chapter has reviewed recent research on the human resource management issues and questions arising from the internationalization of business. The research has been uneven in the areas covered and to date, the majority of international HRM research has focused on two related areas. The first is international staffing, which primarily deals with the problems of selecting and managing expatriate managers. The second is international management development. Two areas which have been little covered in the literature and which need to be addressed by researchers are international career management and the influence of human resource planning on international staffing.

It has been argued that much of the international HRM literature is still open to the criticisms of Schollhammer (1975), as being:

1 descriptive and lacking in analytical rigour
2 *ad hoc* and expedient in research design and planning
3 self-centred, in the sense that the existing research literature is frequently ignored
4 lacking a sustained research effort to develop case material

In addition, it is still the case that the bulk of international HRM research has been conducted by American researchers, has primarily been concerned with American expatriates, and continues to be written from an American rather than an international perspective (Boyacigiller and Adler 1991).

While it is recognized that the international HRM issues which have been researched are of practical importance to personnel managers, this work has been recently criticized by Kochan *et al.* (1992) as focusing too narrowly on functional activities and as lacking appropriate theoretical structures. Indeed, they suggest that much of the international human resource management literature suffers from the same conceptual and normative limitations of much of the traditional domestic personnel research, and that the work is largely an extension of the field of personnel management designed to meet the needs of international companies.

In summary, the essence of the critique of Kochan *et al.* is that the current literature in international HRM defines the field too narrowly. In addition to their concern that the research is influenced by a discussion of concepts and issues, with little backing in systematic research, they argue that a new field of international human resource studies should be built round a broader set of questions, which should consider the lessons and outcomes for *all* stakeholders not just multi-national firms and their managers.

A further criticism of the international HRM literature is the failure to deal adequately with the management of managers as employees. Edwards *et al.* (1993) point out that problems of control and autonomy affect managers as much as other groups of workers, and argue that the industrial relations approach provides an analytical perspective which is capable of treating managers as employees. It is also suggested that this approach enables researchers to be more sensitive to and better able to understand the dynamics of the management process in MNCs (Edwards *et al.* 1993).

Despite the criticisms of international HRM research set out above, it can be argued that considerable progress has been made, given the relatively recent emergence of the discipline. There has been a growing awareness of the importance of HRM in the global arena and a greater understanding of the international dimensions of HRM (Dowling *et al.* 1994). The trend over recent years has been to extend the linkage of HRM with business strategy into the international arena. This chapter has suggested that international human resource management, like human resource management strategy generally, must be linked to the strategic evolution of the firm. This applies equally to small and medium-sized firms, as well as to emerging transnationals. It has highlighted some of the HRM issues and challenges which firms face as they undergo the internationalization process. It also suggests that, for UK multi-nationals, the recruitment and development of 'international managers' will be the key challenge of the 1990s.

REFERENCES

Adler, N.J. (1984) 'Women in international management: where are they?', *California Management Review* 26(4): 78–89.

—— (1986) *International Dimensions of Organizational Behaviour*, Boston, MA: PWS-Kent Publishing Company.

—— (1987) 'Women as androgynous managers: a conceptualization of the potential for American women in international management', *International Journal of Intercultural Relations* 407–36.

Adler, N.J. and Bartholomew, S. (1992) 'Managing globally competent people', *Academy of Management Executive* 6: 52–64.

Adler, N. and Ghadar, F. (1991) 'Strategic human resource management: a global perspective', Fourth Conference on Comparative Management, Koahsiung, Taiwan, June. Cited in S.J. Kobrin (1992) 'Multinational strategy and international human resource management policy', unpublished paper, The Wharton School, University of Pennsylvania.

Baker, J. and Ivancevich, J. (1971) 'The assignment of American executives abroad: systematic, haphazard or chaotic?', *California Management Review* spring 13(3).

Baliga, B.R. and Jaeger, A.M. (1984) 'Multinational corporations: control systems and delegation issues', *Journal of International Business Studies* XV(2): 25–40.

Banai, M. (1992) 'The ethnocentric staffing policy in multinational corporations: a self-fulfilling prophecy', *The International Journal of Human Resource Management* 3. 451–72.

Barham, K. (1991) 'Developing the international manager', in P. Reid (ed.) *Global Management: Culture, Context, Competence*, Ashbridge Management College.

Barham, K. and Devine, M. (1991) *The Quest for the International Manager: A Survey of Global Human Resource Strategies*, London: The Economist Intelligence Unit.
Bartlett, C. and Ghoshal, C. (1989) *Managing Across Borders: The Transnational Solution*, Boston, MA: Harvard Business School Press.
—— (1992) 'What is a global manager?' *Harvard Business Review* September/October: 124–32.
Beaumont, P. (1991) 'Human resource management and international joint ventures: some evidence from Britain', *Human Resource Management Journal* 1(4): 90–101.
Björkman, I. and Gertsen, M. (1990) 'Corporate expatriation: an analysis of firms and country-specific differences in Scandinavian, unpublished paper cited in Brewster, C. (1991) *The Management of Expatriates*, London: Kogan Page.
Black, J.S. (1988) 'Work role transitions: a study of American expatriate managers in Japan', *Journal of International Business Studies* 30(2): 119–34.
Black, J.S. and Mendenhall, M. (1990) 'Cross cultural training effectiveness: a review and a theoretical framework for future research', *Academy of Management Review* 15(1): 113–36.
Boyacigiller, N. (1990) 'The role of expatriates in the management of interdependence, complexity and risk in multinational corporations', *Journal of International Business Studies* 21(3): 357–81.
Boyacigiller, N. and Adler, N. (1991) 'The parochial dinosaur: organizational science in a global context', *Academy of Management Review* 16(2): 262–90.
Brewster, C. (1988) *The Management of Expatriates*, Human Resource Research Centre Monograph 2, Cranfield: Cranfield Institute of Technology.
—— (1991) *The Management of Expatriates*, London: Kogan Page.
Brewster, C. and Burnois, F. (1991) 'A European perspective on human resource management', *Personnel Review* 20(6): 4–13.
Brislin, R.W. (1986) 'A culture general assimilator: preparation for various types of sojourns', *International Journal of Intercultural Relations* 10: 215–34.
Burnois, F. (1992) 'The impact of 1993 on management development in Europe', *International Studies of Management and Organisation* 22, spring: 7–29.
Burnois, F. and Chauchat, J.H. (1990) 'Managing managers in Europe', *European Management Journal* 6(1), March: 3–18.
Butler, J.E., Ferris, G.R. and Napier, N.K. (1991) *Strategy and Human Resources Management*, Cincinatti, OH: South-Western.
Cascio, W.F. and Serapio, M.G. (1991) 'Human resource systems in an international alliance: the undoing of a done deal?', *Organizational Dynamics* winter: 63–74.
Coyle, W. (1988) *On the Move: Minimising the Stress and Maximising the Benefit of Relocation*, Sydney: Hampden Press.
Desatnick, R.L. and Bennett, M.L. (1978) *Human Resource Management in the Multinational Company*, New York: Nichols.
Devanna, M.A. (1987) 'Women in management: progress and promise', *Human Resource Management* 26(4): 469–81.
Dowling, P.J. (1986) 'Human resource issues in international business', *Syracuse Journal of International Law and Commerce* 13(2): 255–71.
—— (1988) 'International and domestic personnel/human resource management: similarities and differences', in R.S. Schuler *et al.* (eds) *Readings in Personnel and Human Resource Management* (3rd edn), St Paul, MN: West Publishing Co.
Dowling, P.J. and Schuler, R.S. (1990) *International Dimensions of Human Resource Management*, Boston, MA: PWS Kent.
Dowling, P.J. and Welch, D. (1988) 'International human resource management: an Australian perspective', *Asia-Pacific Journal of Management* 6(1): 39–65.

Dowling, P.J., Schuler, R.S. and Welch, D. (1994) *International Dimensions of Human Resource Management* (2nd edn), Belmont, CA: Wadsworth.
Doz, Y. and Prahalad, C.K. (1986) 'Controlled variety: a challenge for human resource management in the MNC', *Human Resource Management* 25(1): 55–71.
Dutton, D.K. (1988) 'International joint ventures: a framework for analysis', *Journal of General Management* 14(23), winter: 83–91.
Edstrom, A. and Galbraith, J. (1977) 'Transfer of managers as a coordination and control strategy in multinational organizations', *Administrative Science Quarterly* 22: 248–63.
Edstrom, A. and Lorange, P. (1984) 'Matching strategy and human resources in multinational corporations', *Journal of International Business Studies* XV(2): 125–38.
Edwards, P.K., Ferner, A. and Sisson, K. (1993) 'People and the process of management in the multinational company: a review and some illustrations', *Warwick Papers in Industrial Relation*, No. 43, July, University of Warwick.
Enderwick, P. and Barber, K. (1992) 'International human resource management in the 1990s', in S. Young and J. Hamill (eds) *Europe and the Multinationals*, Aldershot: Edward Elgar.
Ghoshal, S. (1987) 'Global strategy: an organizing framework', *Strategic Manage- Journal* 8: 425–40.
Gomes-Casseres, B. (1989) 'Joint ventures in the face of global competition', *Sloan Management Review* spring: 17–25.
Hailey, J. (1992) 'Localization and expatriation: the continuing role of expatriates in developing countries', EISAM Workshop, Cranfield, September.
Hall, D.T. and Richter, J. (1988) 'Balancing work and home life: what can organizations do to help?', *Academy of Management Executive* 2(3): 213–23.
Hall, F.S. and Hall, D.T. (1987) 'Dual careers – how do couples and companies cope with the problems?', *Organisational Dynamics* spring: 57–77.
Hamel, G. (1991) 'Competition for competence and interpartner learning within international strategic alliances', *Strategic Management Journal* 12: 83–103.
Hamill, J. (1989) 'Expatriate policies in British multinationals', *Journal of General Management* 14(4): 18–33.
—— (1992) 'Cross-border mergers, acquisitions and alliances in Europe', in S. Young and J. Hamill (eds) *Europe and the Multinationals*, Aldershot: Edward Elgar.
Harris, P.R. and Moran, R.T. (1987) *Managing Cultural Differences* (2nd edn), Houston, TX: Gulf.
Harvey, M.G. (1985) 'The executive family: an overlooked variable in international assignments', *Columbia Journal of World Business* spring: 84–92.
—— (1989) 'Repatriation of corporate executives: an empirical study', *Journal of International Business Studies* spring: 131–44.
Hays, R.D. (1974) 'Expatriate selection: insuring success and avoiding failure', *Journal of International Business Studies* 5: 25–37.
Heenan, D.A. and Perlmutter, H.V. (1979) *Multinational Organization Development*, Reading, MA: Addison-Wesley.
Henry, E.R. (1965) 'What business can learn from peace corps selection and training', *Personnel* 41, July–August.
International Management (1986) 'Expansion abroad: the new direction for European firms', 41(11): 21–5.
Jelinek, M. and Adler, N.J. (1988) 'Women: world-class managers for global competition', *Academy of Management Executive* 2(1): 11–19.
Johnston, J. (1991) 'An empirical study of repatriation of managers in UK multinationals', *Human Resource Management Journal* 1(4): 102–8.

Kanter, M.R. (1989) 'Becoming PALS: pooling, allying and linking across companies', *Academy of Management Executive* 3(3), August: 183–93.

Killing, J.P. (1983) *Strategies of Joint Venture Success*, London: Croom Helm.

Kobrin, S.J. (1988) 'Expatriate reduction and strategic control in American multinational corporations', *Human Resource Management* 27(1): 63–75.

—— (1992) 'Multinational strategy and international human resource management policy', unpublished paper, The Wharton School, University of Pennsylvania.

Kochan, T., Batt, R. and Dyer, L. (1992) 'International human resource studies: a framework for future research', in D. Lewin *et al.* (ed.) *Research Frontiers in Industrial Relations and Human Resources*, Madison, WI: Industrial Relations Research Association.

Lane, H.W. and Beamish, P.W. (1990) 'Cross-cultural co-operative behaviour in joint ventures in LDCs', *Management International Review*, Special Issue: 87–102.

Laurent, A. (1986) 'The cross-cultural puzzle of international human resource management', *Human Resource Management* 25: 91–102.

Lei, D. and Slocum, J.W. (1991) 'Global strategic alliances: payoffs and pitfalls', *Organizational Dynamics* winter: 44–62.

Lorange, P. (1986) 'Human resource management in multinational cooperative ventures', *Human Resource Management* 25(1): 133–48.

Martinez, J.I. and Jarillo, J.C. (1991) 'The evolution of research on co-ordination mechanisms in multinational corporations', *Journal of International Business Studies* 20(3): 489–514.

Mayrhoffer, W. (1992) 'Ethnocentrism revisited. In defence of an "outdated" staffing approach in the European context', Cranfield: workshop on international and expatriate management, 21–2 September.

Mendenhall, M. and Oddou, G. (1985) 'The dimensions of expatriate accumulation: a review', *Academy of Management Review* 10: 39–47.

—— (1986) 'Acculturation profiles of expatriate managers: implications for cross-cultural training programs', *Columbia Journal of World Business*, 73–9.

—— (1987) 'Expatriate selection, training and career pathing: a review and critique', *Human Resource Management*, Fall.

—— (1988) 'The overseas assignment: A practical look', *Business Horizons* 78–84.

Milliman, J., Von Glinow, M., Nathan, B. (1991) 'Organizational life cycles and strategic international human resource management in multinational companies: implications for congruence theory', *Academy of Management Review* 16: 318–39.

Morgan, P.V. (1986) 'International human resource management: fact or fiction', *Personnel Administrator* 31(9): 43–7.

Negandhi, A.R. (1987) *International Management*, Newton, MA: Allyn and Bacon.

Negandhi, A.R. and Welge, M. (1984) *Beyond Theory Z: Global Rationalization Strategies of American, German and Japanese Multinational Companies*, Greenwich, CT: JAI Press.

Oddou, G. and Kerr, C.B. (1993) 'European MNC strategies for internationalising managers: current and future trends', in P.S. Kilbride and B. Shaw (eds) *Proceedings of the Third Conference on International Personnel and Human Resource Management*, Vol. 1.

Ohmae, K. (1985) *Triad Power: The Coming Shape of Global Competition*, New York: Free Press.

Porter, M. (1986) *Competition in Global Industries*, Boston, MA: Harvard Business School Press.

Prahalad, C.K. and Doz, Y. (1987) *The Multinational Mission*, New York: The Free Press.

Pucick, V. (1988) 'Strategic alliances, organizational learning, and competitive advantage: The HRM agenda', *Human Resource Management*, spring 27(1): 77–93.

Rahim, A. (1983) 'A model for developing key expatriate executives', *Personnel Journal* 62(4): 312–17.

Robock, S.H. and Simmonds, K. (1983) *International Business and Multinational Enterprises*, Homewood, IL: Irwin.

Ronen, S. (1989) 'Training the international assignee', in I. Goldstein (ed.) *Training and Career Development*, San Francisco, CA: Jossey-Bass.

Schaan, J.L. (1988) 'How to control a joint venture even as a minority partner', *Journal of General Management* 14(1): 4–16.

Schaeffer, R. (1989) 'Managing international business growth and international management development', *Human Resource Planning* March: 29–36.

Schneider, S. (1986) 'National vs corporate culture: implications for human resource management', *Human Resource Management* 27: 133–48.

Schollhammer, H. (1975) 'Current research in international and comparative management issues', *Management International Review* 15(2–3): 29–40.

Schuler, R. and Jackson, S. (1989) 'Determinants of human resource management priorities and implications for industrial relations', *Journal of Management* 15(1): 89–99.

Schuler, R., Dowling, P.J., De Cieri, H. (1993) 'An integrative framework of strategic international human resource management', *International Journal of Human Resource Management* 4(4).

Schuler, R.S., Fulkerson, J.R. and Dowling, P.J. (1991) 'Strategic performance measurement and management in multi-national corporations', *Human Resource Management* 30: 365–92.

Schuler, R.S., Jackson, S.F., Dowling, P.J., Welch, D.E. and de Cieri, H. (1991) 'Formation of an international joint venture: Davidson instrument panel', *Human Resources Planning* 14(1): 51–60.

Scullion, H. (1991) 'Why companies prefer to use expatriates', *Personnel Management* November.

—— (1992a) 'Attracting management globetrotters', *Personnel Management* January.

—— (1992b) 'Strategic recruitment and development of the "International manager": some European considerations', *Human Resource Management Journal* 3(1): 57–69.

—— (1993) 'Creating international managers: recruitment and development issues', in P. Kirkbride (ed.) *Human Resource Management in Europe*, London: Routledge.

—— (1994a) 'Expatriate selection, training and performance in UK multinationals', University of Newcastle upon Tyne, School of Business Management, working papers.

—— (1994b) 'Staffing policies and strategic control in multinationals', *International Studies of Management and Organisation*, in press.

Shenkar, O. and Zeira, Y. (1987) 'Human resources management in international joint ventures: directions for research', *Academy of Management Review* 12(3), July: 546–57.

Snell, S.A. (1992) 'Control theory in strategic human resource management: the mediating effect of administrative information', *Academy of Management Journal* 35: 292–327.

Storey, J. (1992) 'Making European managers: an overview', *Human Resource Management Journal* 3(1), autumn.

Tichy, N., Fombrun, C. and Devanna, M.A. (1982) 'Strategic human resource management', *Sloan Management Review* winter: 47–61.

Torbiorn, I. (1982) *Living Abroad: Personal Adjustment and Personnel Policy in the Overseas Setting*, New York: Wiley.

—— (1985) 'The structure of managerial roles in cross-cultural settings', *International Studies of Management and Organization* 15(1): 52–74.

Tung, R.L. (1981) 'Selection and training of personnel for overseas assignments', *Columbia Journal of World Business* 16(1): 68–78.

—— (1982) 'Selection and training procedures of US European and Japanese multinationals', *California Management Review* 25(1): 57–71.

—— (1984) 'Strategic management of human resources in the multinational enterprise', *Human Resource Management* 23(2): 129–43.

Young, S. and Hamill, J. (eds) (1992) *Europe and the Multinationals*, Aldershot: Edward Elgar.

Zeira, Y. (1976) 'Management development in ethnocentric multinational corporations', *California Management Review* 18(4): 34–42.

Zeira, Y. and Banai, M. (1984) 'Present and desired methods of selecting expatriate managers for international assignments', *Personnel Review* 13(3): 29–35.

Chapter 15

Future prospects

John Storey

The chapters in this book have described and evaluated the nature and significance of the key developments in human resource management. The meanings, attributes, advantages and disadvantages of innovations in this field have been fully explored. But what of the future? What does it hold for the HRM phenomenon?

There are conflicting tendencies.

On the one hand, as noted at the very beginning of the book, there are many signs that HRM has carved a secure foothold. There are also important intellectual and practical developments in the cognate fields of corporate strategy, industrial economics and organizational change which lend powerful underpinnings to the central tenets of HRM. The idea of resource-based competitiveness, intangible resources, core competencies, the learning organization, the intelligent enterprise and capabilities for success (Barney 1991; Hall 1992; Prahalad and Hamel 1990; Quinn 1992), can all be seen to add fuel to the HRM trajectory. The idea of people as the key to success has arguably never been quite so centrally and strategically placed.

But, on the other hand, there is also a tidal ebb running in a very different direction. There is increasing evidence of the cost-minimization, low-skill, low-pay, corner-cutting approach. Sisson (in Chapter 4) has pointed out that much of the recent evidence of employment practices among small and medium-sized employing organizations indicates a situation more akin to *Bleak House* than HRM. And, in Chapter 5, Guest similarly draws attention to the 'black hole' employment category where both HRM and traditional industrial relations are sacrificed in favour of derecognition and a least-cost strategy. Perhaps more importantly, behind these specific practices there are wider movements which are fundamentally inimical to HRM. Most notable here are the increasing vehemence of contemporary attacks on personnel management; the concentration of attention on the concept of 'value-added'; zero-budgeting; the renewed popularity of the idea of out-sourcing and the core–periphery model; and, driving most of the above, business process re-engineering.

At the time of writing there would appear to be an assault, unprecedented in its ferocity, being mounted against personnel management of all varieties. The business columnist of one British broadsheet newspaper expresses this well: 'Many of us have long held the view that personnel management, or human resource management as companies sometimes insist on calling it, is a uniquely irrelevant function fulfilling no obvious purpose other than to stifle initiative, flair and creativity' (*Independent*, 12 May 1994). This commentator was in fact drawing upon a research paper by Fernie, Metcalf and Woodland of the Centre for Economic Performance at the LSE (Fernie *et al.* 1994). The LSE paper resulted from further statistical analysis of the third workplace industrial relations survey (Millward *et al.* 1992). It explored the association between six sets of personnel characteristics and a measure of the 'climate' of management–employee relations. The main overall finding was that there was little evidence that 'climate' was influenced by features such as single status, boardroom representation for a personnel specialist, formal procedures (for discipline, grievances and bargaining) or profit-related pay. Employee involvement which entails two-way communication did, however, seem to make a difference. As is perhaps evident, many of the six characteristics are as much associated with traditional personnel management as with HRM *per se*. No matter: this type of finding is being seized upon to enhance the assault on all forms of personnel/HR as a specialist function.

A popular current line at management conferences addressed (and often organized) by management consultants, many of whom have themselves vacated important personnel directorships, is a critique of the whole gamut of traditional personnel activities – and, to a considerable extent, a critique of any notion of a separate personnel function. The argument is based on the concept of 'value added' and the philosophy of business process re-engineering (Hammer and Champy 1993). Any activity not justifiable in terms of meeting customers' 'real requirements' becomes a candidate for elimination. By implication, the whole suite of traditional personnel management activities, and indeed the function itself, is increasingly being thrown open to question. Insofar as line managers are expected to 'own' the vital remaining people management activities it might be thought that the internal re-allocation of responsibilities is a matter of no great consequence. But, in a context where devolved business units are subject to stringent short-term targets, the outlook for strategic HRM should perhaps be considered as unpropitious.

A half-way house that is nowadays sometimes touted is the idea of 'zero-based budgeting'. This leaves potential scope for the personnel function but removes the security of an allocated budget. Under this regime, line managers (or, more aptly, team leaders of key processes in a re-engineered organization) are free to purchase (or not) the various services put on offer by the HR or personnel function. What are the likely outcomes of this sort of arrangement? The pessimistic view is that it again casts doubt on the viability of far-sighted human resource management. Unit managers, it is claimed, would be unlikely to have the necessary insight into the range of possibilities. Accordingly, it is suggested, they would be most likely to opt for the least-cost set of alternatives (again, as measured by short-term considerations). A more optimistic perspective envisages re-engineered organizations operating zero-based budgeting with top management and process teams sufficiently re-educated in market awareness and process needs to be able to draw upon a re-engineered human resource function for critical services. The focus will be upon core processes. Unnecessary, cumbersome and bureaucratic procedures and rules which have accreted in consequence of personnel's well-intentioned but mistaken pursuit of 'best practice' will be cut away.

Not only will this free the organization from elaborate paper-based appraisal and job-evaluation schemes; in addition, it is claimed, people in re-engineered organizations will be able to forget about trying to pursue team-working, empowerment and the other buzz words. These are seen as abstractions which cannot be directly achieved. But, after taking a process perspective, team-working and empowerment are likely to result. If one has faith in this optimistic scenario then the central tenets of HRM will not only be preserved but will be re-discovered as the vital components of the new competitive organizations of the future.

REFERENCES

Barney, J. (1991) 'Firm resources and competitive advantage', *Journal of Management* 17: 99–120.

Fernie, S., Metcalf, D. and Woodlands, S. (1994) 'Does HRM boost employee management relations?', *Working Paper Number 548*, Centre for Economic Performance, London School of Economics.

Hall, R. (1992) 'The strategic analysis of intangible resources', *Strategic Management Journal* 13: 135–44.

Hammer, M. and Champy, J. (1993) *Re-engineering the Corporation*, New York: HarperCollins.

Millward, N., Stevens, M., Smart, D. and Hawes, W.R. (1992) *Workplace Industrial Relations in Transition*, Aldershot: Dartmouth.

Prahalad, C.K. and Hamel, G. (1990) 'The core competence of the organisation', *Harvard Business Review*, May–June.

Quinn, J.B. (1992) *Intelligent Enterprise: A Knowledge and Service-based Paradigm for Industry*, New York: Free Press.

Index